BATTLEGROUND
THE MEDIA

BATTLEGROUND

THE MEDIA

VOLUME 1 (A–N)

Edited by Robin Andersen and Jonathan Gray

GREENWOOD PRESS
Westport, Connecticut • London

Library of Congress Cataloging-in-Publication Data

Battleground: the media / edited by Robin Andersen and Jonathan Gray.
   p. cm. — (Battleground)
  Includes bibliographical references and index.
  ISBN 978–0–313–34167–0 (alk. paper)
  1. Mass media—Political aspects.   I. Andersen, Robin.   II. Gray, Jonathan (Jonathan Alan).
P95.8.B38 2008
302.23—dc22   2007032454

British Library Cataloguing in Publication Data is available.

Library of Congress Catalog Card Number: 2007032454
ISBN: 978–0–313–34167–0 (set)
     978–0–313–34168–79 (vol. 1)
     978–0–313–34169–4 (vol. 2)

First published in 2008

Greenwood Press, 88 Post Road West, Westport, CT 06881
An imprint of Greenwood Publishing Group, Inc.
www.greenwood.com

Printed in the United States of America

∞

The paper used in this book complies with the
Permanent Paper Standard issued by the National
Information Standards Organization (Z39.48–1984).

10 9 8 7 6 5 4 3 2 1

CONTENTS

GUIDE TO RELATED TOPICS

Journalists in Peril
Nationalism and the Media
Parachute Journalism: International News Reporting
Piracy and Intellectual Property
Runaway Productions and the Globalization of Hollywood
Tourism and the Selling of Cultures
World Cinema

JOURNALISM AND REPORTING
Advertising and Persuasion
Al-Jazeera
Alternative Media in the United States
Anonymous Sources, Leaks, and National Security
Bias and Objectivity
Blogosphere: Politics and Internet Journalism
Conglomeration and Media Monopolies
Disabilities and the Media
Embedding Journalists: How Close Is Too Close?
Global Community Media
Government Censorship and Freedom of Speech
Hypercommercialism
Islam and the Media
Journalists in Peril
Media and Citizenship
Media and the Crisis of Values
Media and Electoral Campaigns
Media Watch Groups
Minority Media Ownership
News Satire: Comedy Central and Beyond
Paparazzi and Photographic Ethics
Parachute Journalism: International News Reporting
Presidential Stagecraft and Militainment
Propaganda Model
Public Opinion: Are Polls Democratic?
Public Sphere
Representations of Class
Representations of Race
Representations of Women
Sensationalism, Fear Mongering, and Tabloid Media
User-Created Content and Audience Participation
Video News Releases: A Hidden Epidemic of Fake TV News
Youth and Media Use

FILM AND CINEMA
Body Image
Bollywood and the Indian Diaspora
Celebrity Worship and Fandom

INTRODUCTION

Few institutions are as powerful or as thoroughly suffused into every aspect of our daily lives as are the media. From computers to television, film to music, cell phones to newspapers, most of us spend much of our waking hours using, consuming, or creating media. From entertainment fare to nonfiction programming and from videogames to theme parks, media corporations are highly conglomerated, profit-seeking entities, and also the couriers, purveyors, creators, and editors of the messages, texts, and images that comprise the information age. It is, therefore, no surprise that the media have become a hub of controversy and a battleground for issues as disparate as election campaigns and the critical satire of Comedy Central, to depictions of race, gender, and sexuality. With its power to regulate such a powerful industry, government has become a battleground site as independent media producers and public interest groups struggle over the policies that shape the landscape of media—from current public access television to the future of the Internet. Many of these controversies extend well into cultural and social realms because they focus debate around the values expressed in media messages and the effects they have on children, teens, our knowledge of the world, members of other religions or groups, and even of our own bodies and social identities. As entries on the Digital Divide and Representations of Class illustrate, media issues also provide a lens into social and economic inequities. The ways in which we define ourselves and our communities are reflected and shaped by such formats as the so-called reality shows and by citizens themselves as they create media content and find their voices as bloggers on the Internet.

In this ever evolving geography of symbolic techniques, media and marketing strategies, new and traditional genres, and new media technology, the task of editing a collection of entries on controversies has proven challenging, illuminating and remarkably difficult, as each new day and news cycle brings yet more issues worthy of coverage. Nevertheless, in these two volumes, we have assembled some of media studies' smartest critics, experts, and researchers to discuss the more pressing concerns and "battlegrounds" in contemporary media. Some entries focus on age-old topics that precede our modern era and others chart more recent trends. However, rather than become distracted by the superficial details and names of 2007, these entries focus on underlying issues and concepts. In addition to comprehensive definitions and dominant themes, we have tried to present key influences that set the parameters for the arguments brought to bear in media debates by scholars, public interest groups, industry professionals, and readers and audiences alike. True to the nature of media studies—an interdiscipline sitting at the crossroads of more traditional fields such as sociology, political economy, art, rhetoric, anthropology and political science (just to name a few)—we offer here a broad range of entries concentrating not only on humanistic themes but also from social scientific perspectives. Undoubtedly all readers will imagine entries that could have been written, more controversies that could have been explored, and favorite arguments downplayed, but we hope these volumes illuminate core principles and provide a set of guideposts able to direct the inquisitive reader in continued exploration of the themes, issues and perspectives of their choice. We offer ways of beginning discussion, thought, and deliberation, not, as is often the case with encyclopedias, to close off discussion. The production of these two volumes has proven to be a dynamic process, and we hope Battleground readers engage with these volumes with equal enthusiasm.

By way of defining "the media," we have frequently concentrated on mass media, and this emphasis has in turn resulted in thorough coverage of television. New media theorists often argue that the day of a computer-centered media diet will soon be upon us, but in 2007 television remains the preeminent mass medium in the United States, with near-total coverage across the population, and frequently central to popular culture. Even those who do not watch television are often aware of its key figures and programs. Television is often the central cog in many media empires' machinery, it is cause for more alarm and concern than are most media, and it networks many other media, telling us, for instance, of movies to come and of magazine heroes and villains. Much of the commercial content and traffic on the Internet is directed from more traditional forms of media, including television, and their formats, themes, economics, and regulatory histories help shape the landscape of new media. This increasingly wide range of new technologies, varying formats, and symbolic practices are interconnected through economies and technologies; with this in mind, we include in this collection a variety of entries on film, magazines, newspapers, music, new media, and mobile media.

The need for some entries will appear patently obvious to many readers, while other entries focus on "buried" issues—ones that achieve less popular presence often precisely because corporate-owned media either willfully neglect discussion of such issues, or at the least, find it beneficial to their business practice to allow issues to go unnoticed, thereby avoiding needed public debate. The Video News Release, for example, may not be a household phrase, but we argue that it should be; similarly, other entries examine noncorporate media. Since the media industry enjoys such a considerable monopoly on many citizens' attention, everyday discussions are often informed and framed by the news and entertainment content brought to their attention by media companies. In this collection, we hope not only to examine the agendas set by mainstream media, but also to unearth hot-button issues that corporate media do not discuss with enough frequency. In addition, considering the aesthetic influences, motivations, and struggles of alternative media and independent cultural productions, allows us to see the dominant media in new and revealing ways. As Marshall McLuhan noted, just as fishes do not notice the existence of water till out of it, the media flows all around each one of us, our habitat and our lived environment, and thus this collection will at times focus on media issues that have become as invisible to us as water is to fish.

While it is common to talk of "the media" as if it were a monolithic entity, and while corporate collusion sometimes makes it appear uniform and singular, of course there is no such entity called "the media." Instead, the media is a collection of programs, films, songs, stars, and games from varying sources, which are consumed by varying citizens and consumers, often in varying ways. Media are regulated differently and are produced differently. Thus, "the media" is a huge amalgam of variation and difference, rendering it hard if not impossible to generalize about "the media" as a whole. We intend the entries in these two volumes to tackle different zones of the media universe, thereby not only presenting disagreements and controversies within any given entry, but also producing disagreement between different entries. With audiences, programs, producers, regulators, citizens, artists, and institutions all active agents in the production of "the media," one will find a different picture of the media universe depending upon which agent(s) one focuses on, as will be evident across the many entries in these two volumes.

Each entry includes an opening that explains a key controversy or battleground topic, the entry proper, and a list of further readings. The latter, in conjunction with the general bibliography at the end of Volume 2, should help readers find more discussion of the issue at hand. We also encourage readers to follow the cross-references throughout, as inevitably many issues build on the shoulders of others, and some entries are illuminated further by yet other entries. The cross-references should offer readers an Ariadne's thread through the collection.

Finally, as editors, we must offer thanks to the many individuals who have helped us put this collection together, namely our fantastic contributors and Daniel Harmon at Greenwood Press. We would also like to thank Guy Robinson and Monica Grant for assistance and support: juggling so many entries taxes the brain, and we thank them for helping us to keep our gray matter in order.

Robin Andersen and Jonathan Gray, August 2007

À LA CARTE CABLE PRICING

In 2004, a coalition of public interest advocates concerned about rising cable television bills and cultural conservatives offended by sexuality explicit TV programs joined forces in support of so-called à la carte cable, which would allow subscribers to pay for only the channels they want to watch rather than pay set fees for packaged channels. Cable viewers may have long wondered why they should pay for a plethora of channels when they might only watch a few with any regularity, but community organizations representing historically underrepresented groups have opposed à la carte pricing with concern for how this might negatively impact program diversity.

THE COALITION FORMS

The à la carte coalition developed after the notorious 2004 Super Bowl halftime reveal where Justin Timberlake tore off a piece of Janet Jackson's costume, exposing her right breast. Soon after, Nathan Deal, the Republican congressman from Georgia, authored an amendment to a bill that would allow cable and satellite providers to offer subscribers the choice to pay for individual channels. The consumer advocacy groups Consumers Union and Consumer Federation of America joined the cultural conservatives from Concerned Women for America and Parent Television Council (PTC) in a letter of support for the amendment. The influential PTC has made "cable choice" a central component of its campaign to rid cable television of indecency. Other strategies to enforce indecency standards for cable operators have faced legal hurdles because cable operators have maintained First Amendment protections against such content regulations (see http://www.parentstv.org/PTC/cable/main.asp). Consumers Union, meanwhile, has advocated for ownership restrictions to curtail the power of media conglomerates from using their leverage to charge cable operators large fees for programming. They have also called for reinstating cable-rate regulations given that cable rates had risen 2.5 times faster than inflation since Congress eliminated rate regulations in 1999. But regulators have resisted these efforts. Thus, Consumers Union focused on à la carte pricing as a strategy to lower costs, increase quality, and allow viewers to not pay for channels they do not want to watch.

Most cable providers strongly opposed these efforts to tamper with their profitable, vertically integrated business models and editorial powers to bundle programs and set subscription rates. Other media conglomerates that did not own cable systems, such as Disney, also opposed à la carte because they made huge profits by using broadcast retransmission consent rules (Disney owns ABC and major-market TV stations) to demand large fees and prime channel positions for their cable networks (such as ESPN, ESPN2, and the Disney Channel, in the case of Disney). But cable networks focused on African American- and Latino-themed programming also vocally opposed the amendment supporting à la carte, fearing that their channels with more targeted audiences would perish under such a scheme. In April 2004, Alfred Liggins, chairman of TV One, the cable network targeting African American adults, wrote an op-ed in the *Washington Times* arguing against à la carte. A month later, Debra Lee of BET, Jeff Valdez of Sí TV, Kent Rice of the International Channel, Mike Hong at Imaginasian TV, and Rudy Ibarra from Outstanding Latin Entertainment wrote letters to the House Committee on Energy and Commerce stating that under à la carte their networks would never have launched without the guaranteed access to viewers needed to attract start-up capital. The Congressional Black Caucus also joined these programmers in opposing à la carte (for a narrative of these early developments see http://www.publicintegrity.org/telecom/report.aspx?aid=395).

SÍ TV

Sí TV, an English-language cable/satellite channel focused on the diverse Latino cultures in the United States, has been a vocal opponent of à la carte pricing. Founded as a production company in 1997, producing programs such as *The Brothers Garcia* for Nickelodeon, Sí TV launched as a network in February 2004 with financial backing from the satellite TV distributor EchoStar and cable operator Time Warner. Original series include *LatiNation*, a weekly magazine about Latino culture in the United States; *The Rub*, a nightly show about sex, love, and relationships; *The Drop*, a weekly music and variety show; *Circumcised Cinema*, a series that reedits Mexican B movies; and *Not-So-Foreign Filmmakers Showcase*, about the multicultural independent film scene. Other series directly engage with political issues, such as *Breakfast, Lunch, and Dinner*, a mealtime discussion show on topics such as prisoner rights, racial discrimination, and gay marriage; and *Urban Jungle*, a reality series that places privileged suburban kids in South Central Los Angeles to live like immigrants.

In 2007 Sí TV and TV One, the African American–targeted network, created the Alliance for Diversity in Programming to promote diverse television programming and oppose à la carte pricing. However, the Center for Digital Democracy, an organization committed to diversity in the Internet broadband era, has implied that with Time Warner as a major investor, Sí TV's opposition to à la carte supports their corporate sponsor rather than television diversity. But the broad support for the Alliance from Latino organizations including the Hispanic Federation, the Labor Council for Latin American Advancement, and the National Council of La Raza indicates that opposition to à la carte pricing is not simply pro–cable industry.

In reaction to this opposition, the House Committee abandoned the amendment and asked the Federal Communications Commission (FCC) to study the potential impact of à la carte. In the spring and summer of 2004, civil rights organizations representing communities of color implored the FCC to dismiss the idea that they argued, in the words of the Leadership Conference on Civil Rights, "could diminish what little diversity is currently on cable and put minority and women programmers at risk." Other civil rights organizations opposing à la carte included the League of United Latin American Citizens, the NALEO Education Fund, Allianza Dominicana, the National Hispanic Policy Institute, the Hispanic Federation, the NAACP, the National Urban League, the National Conference of Black Mayors, the National Coalition of Black Civil Participation, the National Congress of Black Women, the Minority Media and Telecommunications Council, and the National Asian Pacific American Legal Consortium. Women's organizations also united in opposition, including the Sexuality Information and Education Council, the Global Fund for Women, the Feminist Majority, American Women in Radio and Television Inc., and the National Council of Women's Organizations. Geraldine Laybourne, co-founder of Oxygen, strongly opposed the measure, arguing that her channel targeting young women viewers would never have launched under à la carte pricing.

Also in opposition were fiscally conservative organizations such as Citizens for a Sound Economy, the Cato Institute, and the Heritage Foundation. Unlike their social conservative counterparts who supported à la carte as a means to insulate families from television sex and violence, these conservatives categorically opposed any government regulations. As the Cato Institute put it in its FCC filing, "This debate really comes down to the question of whether government should preempt an industry's preferred (and quite successful) business model" (for a list of comments from à la carte opponents see http://www.media.espn.com/MediaZone/PressKits/NCTA/quotes.htm).

THE FCC'S RESPONSE

In July 2004, Booz Allen Hamilton released a report commissioned by the National Cable & Telecommunications Association supporting these groups' assertions that mandated à la carte and themed groupings of channels, such as a family-friendly tier, would reduce program diversity and raise subscription rates for those who purchased nine or more channels (see http://www.ncta.com/pdf_files/Booz_Allen_a_la_Carte_Report.pdf). Under the direction of then FCC Chairman Michael Powell, who supported free-market principles, the FCC accepted the report's findings to not mandate pricing. The report's conclusions were also partially supported by the U.S. General Accounting Office's October 2003 study (see http://www.gao.gov/new.items/d048.pdf).

However, the social conservatives in the House Committee, and the vocal à la carte supporter Senator John McCain, chair of the Senate Committee on Commerce, Science, and Transportation, strongly encouraged the FCC to continue studying the issue. Lending momentum for further study was Powell's announcement in January 2005 that he would resign, and three months later President Bush's appointment of Kevin Martin, an FCC commissioner who had made opposition to indecency a cornerstone of his television policy, to the chairmanship. So the FCC's media bureau went to work on the issue, but instead of conducting additional research it merely revisited portions of the Booz Allen study and identified "problematic assumptions" and "biased analysis." For example, the bureau argued that the Booz Allen report mistakenly assumed that under à la carte, viewers would watch less TV and that diversity would not necessarily decrease because advertisers would likely find niche channels with paying subscribers more valuable.

But the bureau's report is most enthusiastic about saving money for "mainstream" audiences and increasing ratings for the most popular channels. In supply-side economic language that refers to "market efficiencies" and optimizing aggregate "consumer value," the report embraced the likelihood that à la carte would create more choices for "mainstream consumers" but less "niche programming that appeals to a small set of subscribers." What this says to the civil rights organizations and "niche" channels such as Sí TV and TV One, which are mostly produced and watched by historically underrepresented groups, is that a properly efficient marketplace, restored by à la carte pricing, would rightly weed out these "over-valued" niche networks (see http://hraunfoss.fcc.gov/edocs_public/attachmatch/DOC-263740A1.pdf).

As Patricia Williams has demonstrated, in conceiving the general viewing public as segregated into "mainstream" and "niche" audiences, we suppress the interests of historically marginalized communities under the guise of a "neutral 'mass' entertainment." Rather than define a mainstream culture that is oblivious to its dominant status across class, gender, and race, against a ghettoized cultural "other," as Williams argues, we should develop "a view of a market in which there are not merely isolated interest groups, of which the 'mass market' may be one, but in which 'mass' accurately reflects the complicated variety of many peoples and connotes 'interactive' and 'accommodative' rather than 'dominant' or even just 'majoritarian.'" Thus, allowing viewers to channel surf across a variety of channels, even ones they do not watch regularly, creates a more diverse representation of our mass culture that is available to all.

FROM CONSUMER CHOICE TO CULTURAL DIFFERENCE

Though cable operators have maintained opposition to à la carte, several large systems have offered "family-friendly" bundles, such as Time Warner's "Family Choice Tier," which was made available in March 2006. But waiting for cable giants like Comcast (which owns TV One) and Time Warner (which owns Sí TV) to decide what constitutes diversity and how much we should pay for bundled programming does not solve the structural issues of vertical integration, media conglomeration, and the unequal distribution of advertising dollars for programs that include the perspectives of communities of color. When the progressive Consumers Union and the Free Press support à la carte in opposition to a broad spectrum of communities of color, and they do so by framing the issues using the classical economic language of individual consumer choice (the title of a Consumers Union report supporting à la carte is "Let the Market Decide"), we risk reproducing the abstracted, universalistic discourses of consumer choice and neutral markets that have reinforced current neoliberal free-market structural arrangements rather than invoking the cultural rights of historically disempowered groups and the necessity that we all interact broadly with cultural difference instead of walling off our television viewing through personalized channel subscriptions.

Rather than narrowing viewership of culturally diverse networks such as Sí TV through à la carte pricing, perhaps the industry needs prompting to make these diverse networks more widely available. Placed on limited digital tiers, Sí TV reached less than 14 million subscribers as of 2007, while close to 80 million households had access to "mainstream" cable/satellite networks. In this case, the cable marketplace, as a space for the general public to participate in the diversity of Latino culture in the United States, falls far short of creating a common space for engaging with cultural difference.

See also Cable Carriage Disputes; Conglomeration and Media Monopolies; Government Censorship and Freedom of Speech; Media Reform; Minority Media Ownership; Obscenity and Indecency; Regulating the Airwaves; Representations of Race; Representations of Women.

Note

An earlier version of this article was published in *Flow*, an online journal of television and media: see "À la carte Culture," *Flow* 4, No. 3 (April 2006) at www.flowtv.org.

Further Reading: Gripsrud, Jostein, ed. *Television and Common Knowledge.* New York: Routledge, 1999; Lewis, Justin, and Toby Miller, eds. *Cultural Policy Studies: A Reader.* Oxford: Blackwell Publishing, 2002; Secrest, Lawrence W., and Richard E. Wiley. "Recent Developments in Program Content Regulation." *Federal Communications Law Journal* 57, no. 2 (March 2005): 235–42; Williams, Patricia J. "*Metro Broadcasting, Inc. v. FCC:* Regrouping in Singular Times." In *Critical Race Theory: The Key Writings That Formed the Movement,* ed., Kimberle Crenshaw, Neil Gotanda, Gary Pelle, and Kendall Thomas, 191–200. New York: The New Press, 1995.

John McMurria

ADVERTISING AND PERSUASION

Advertising is the driving force behind American business and the largest industrial economy the world has ever known. It is the mediator between the consumer and the vast array of products available from manufacturers across the global. As a mode of communication, it employs powerful persuasive strategies designed to convince viewers, readers, and audiences of all media that purchasing products will make them popular, relieve their anxiety, and gratify almost any need. As an aesthetic form, it has been called the art of capitalism, and because of the emotional techniques it often employs, it has been condemned as manipulative and psychologically harmful. Advertising continues to penetrate public space and find new distribution sources with each new, popular media format, and the debate over advertising's influence on society and culture is continually renewed.

With economies of scale, for over a century industrial capitalism has been able to manufacture and deliver commodities to world markets on an unprecedented scale, with Americans comprising the largest market for world goods. The availability of such a quantity of products demands rapid distribution in retail outlets, from high-end department stores to the expanding box stores that now pock the county's landscape. Products must be sold to consumers whose spending consistently outstrips their income, and desire to purchase more products must be continually stimulated. Advertising brings together media and marketing research, extraordinary creative talent and vast audiovisual resources including new computer-based digital technologies, all with the purposes of selling the commodities capitalism has to offer.

STRATEGIES OF PERSUASION

Often the material differences that distinguish one product from its competitor are slight, and marketers understand that relying simply on product information is not an effective way to instill desire for products. In today's advertisements, the psychological and emotional strategies of persuasion are referred to as the "soft" sell, and they vary greatly from one commercial campaign to another, but many are familiar as recognizable standards.

Celebrity Endorsements and Brand Identity

The celebrity pitch is ever popular because audiences admire the glamour and often trust those they have come to know through popular media. Products endorsed or used by the familiar faces on TV and in magazines are effective ways of compelling consumers to buy more things. If Michael Jordan likes Nike, and sports fans like Michael Jordan, then those fans will be more inclined to want the products he uses. Behind simple admiration is also the implied promise that sports gear of a particular brand will increase the consumer's chances of better performance. "Liking sports" also becomes a consumer identity, and wearing certain sports gear distinguishes the consumer as a sports fan. Brands associated with particular players and teams further refine these cultural signifiers of identity. In this way, sports clothing of all sorts becomes equally important as a cultural communicator and not just an item of apparel. As a form of symbolic communication, sports gear is worn as much for style as for athletic activity. As products move further away from materiality, and exist as cultural symbols, "style over substance" becomes a quality of consumer culture.

Models of Perfection

For the female consumer of beauty, fashion, and glamour products, celebrity endorsement is also essential. Far more effective than extolling the ingredients or quality of any particular brand of make-up, perfume, or shampoo is the promise that those products are the very ones used by the beautiful models and celebrities that populate the landscape of popular culture. In what is called "latent content," the message implies that the beautiful, perfect models have been transformed by the products into the stunning visions seen in the advertisements; as one cosmetics company teases, "Maybe she's born with it. Maybe it's Maybelline." But consumers are rarely aware that pictures of models have almost always been "touched up" to present perfect images. Graphic digital technology is also used to create larger-than-life advertising images that seem perfect, and along the way cultural standards of beauty become impossible for average consumers to emulate. When women are constantly told they can and should look like the glamorous models in advertisements, it is no wonder that the majority of American women are dissatisfied with their own body image. Underlying many advertising appeals to join the world of beautiful people and fantasy wish fulfillment is the anxiety of not fitting in or living up to the cultural standard.

Anxiety

Some strategies of persuasion play on personal anxieties, especially those for hygiene products. The word halitosis entered the cultural lexicon in early Listerine advertisements, and since then, dandruff, bad breath, and hair loss have all been portrayed as impediments to social acceptance, mobility, and fulfilling

---

MINORITY REPORT: FUTURISTIC VISIONS OF CONSUMER CULTURE

In preparation for the film Minority Report, Tom Cruise and the film's creators reportedly consulted with marketing and advertising professionals in order to more accurately portray what the world of consumer culture might look like in the year 2050. In Minority Report, the body becomes branded and the market penetrates every aspect of life and body. In the film Cruise is seen walking though a Gap store as sensors automatically "read" the individual human code identified in his irises. An automated voice reminds him of his last purchase in an attempt to interest him in another. Some of the most chilling scenes in the movie revolve around the idea that marketing information is inscribed within the human body, specifically within the eyeball. The eye-reading technology exists within a total information society, and that information has a dual purpose. It is also used for state control. In one of the most gruesome sequences, the film presents a distopian future in which the commercial information is shared with a repressive governing regime with severe consequences to individual liberty. As he struggles to maintain his freedom, Cruise's character is forced to have his eyes brutally removed. The film is fiction and it depicts an extreme case, but it serves as a warning of the dangers of accumulating, cross-referencing, and centralizing huge amounts of personal data on individual citizens and making it available to those who would use it for political purposes.

---

interpersonal relationships. Products are offered as the solutions to these personal and social problems. Mothers who wash their children's clothes in certain brands of detergent are assured happy, healthy kids who will continue to love them while wearing their clean, white, stain-free garments. Such promises are often made through compelling scenarios depicted visually on television and in magazines. A variety of ads that play on guilt are directed toward parents. From the OnStar automotive assistance system to airbags and tires, these ads make the point that if you love your children you will use these products. Children sometimes featured sitting in the backseat talk about how happy they are that their Dad bought a particular car.

Language of Association

Images are key to the persuasive strategies of advertising. Visual messages can make associations and create implied meanings without advertisers ever having to make direct promises about the quality of their products. Taking a picture of gold nuggets placed next to coffee beans and adding the caption, "The Gold Standard in Coffee," allows the consumer to associate the value of gold with that of coffee. The photograph and caption transfer the cultural value of gold onto the brand of coffee being advertised. But even a casual "decoding" or "textual analysis" of the ad can reveal the false nature of the communication. Under logical and visual analysis, it becomes clear that the quality of a mined metal has little to do with the flavorful taste of an agricultural product, and that gold and coffee have little real connection. Yet visual and verbal associations allow advertisers to make claims about products without having to verify them or state them directly. In this way, consumers often accept obvious exaggerations without critically evaluating them. Media literacy has become an important educational curriculum designed to help the public, especially children, understand the ways in which persuasion carries implied meanings that do not hold up under scrutiny.

The Promise of Belonging through Consumption

With the slogan "Pepsi, The Choice of a New Generation," Madison Avenue launched the lifestyle ads of the 1970s. Such ads often promised satisfaction through group consumption. A picture of a group of friends all wearing the same Dockers khakis, or all drinking the same soda, is an image of belonging. Products confer a sense of group identity and a way to recognize other members of the same peer group, now defined as a consumption subgroup. The ad's promise of fulfilling interpersonal relationships is made visually. Because of the documentary nature of the photograph, it is indisputable that the consumption subgroup is content being together. However, if these implied messages were stated directly, "Wear these jeans and you will have the friends you want," or "The people who drink Coke have more friends," the assertion would be much less credible and therefore much less effective as persuasion. In this way, marketing strategies and aesthetic design work together to create more powerful modes of persuasive communication, both visual and verbal.

Marketing Segmentation

Lifestyle ads were designed to appeal to consumption subgroups, and since then the consuming public has been increasingly differentiated into smaller groups of people that share similar demographics, such as age, gender, race, education, and income. Market researchers look for other consumption indicators as well, and "psychographics" add values, beliefs, opinions, and behavioral practices to the mix. Carving up what was once a huge, ill-defined mass public into smaller groups has allowed the advertising industry to target consumers with messages specifically designed to more clearly defined tastes. Selling products by associating them with the values and sensibilities of various subgroups is referred to as "marketing stratification" and remains dominant within the industry. Agencies and their clients are willing to pay higher ad rates for messages they can be confident will reach the people most likely to be persuaded by the targeted message. With each new marketing campaign, a once-broad public continues to be refined into specific market segments.

Such marketing practices work hand-in-hand with media and have influenced the economics and program design of not only broadcast and cable media, but radio, magazines, and Internet content as well. With its multiple channels, cable television originated as a "narrowcasting" medium, in which programming directed at specific audiences dovetailed with the advertising created to appeal to those same tastes and sensibilities. In this way viewers were defined as consumers and targeted as markets for specific products. As numbers of viewers are sold to advertisers through rating, and with higher rates for audiences "primed" with compatible programming, television, radio, and other media are increasingly defined as marketing mediums as well as entertainment or information sources. These marketing practices and the merger of media content with advertising campaigns paved the way for the insertion of advertising into programs themselves, and product placement became a dominant commercial practice during the last two decades of the twentieth century.

Commercializing the Media

The deregulation of broadcasting, beginning in the early 1980s, lifted restrictions on the amount of advertising that could be aired on television. This resulted in the further commercialization of programming and the development of program-length commercials, which characterize many shows that feature products from beginning to end. Infomercials—long-form advertisements that mimic the formats of other shows, especially news and information programming—became popular on late-night television and cable services alike. Public interest groups are critical of these developments and have appealed to the Federal Communications Commission for regulations that would force these shows to be identified as commercially designed programs. Media watch groups have also criticized new hybrids of commercial media such as advertisements produced in public relations firms disguised as information segments that now frequently air on local news programs.

ADBUSTERS AND "CULTURE JAMMING"

Founded in 1989 by Kalle Lasn and Bill Schmalz in Vancouver, Canada, Adbusters is an anti-consumerist organization that has mixed education, research, activism, and art to complain about advertising's many excesses. Adbusters is particularly well known for its parodic advertisements that mock the bravado, false promises, and absurd logic of ads. Thus, for instance, taking aim at Camel cigarettes' animated character Joe Camel, a series of Adbusters ads follow "Joe Chemo," showing him hospitalized by his addiction. Another parodic ad for Calvin Klein's Obsession depicts, in classic black-and-white photography style, a young woman bent over a toilet bowl, offering the suggestion of a more sinister "obsession" with thinness fueled by Calvin Klein ads. Adbusters publishes a reader-supported magazine, and has also been instrumental in launching the annual Buy Nothing Day and TV Turnoff Week.

Adbusters and its fellow culture-jammers aim to rob advertising signs, symbols, and logos of their power, and to implore citizens to read ads critically. But in a sign of how invested media corporations are in pursuing advertising by making their messages ad-friendly, commercial broadcasters in both the United States and Canada have refused to play Adbusters's anti-ads. Thus, other culture-jamming groups have taken to "repurposing" outdoor advertising and to reclaiming public space, using pranks, anti-ads, and media events to "jam" advertising. One long-standing group, the San Francisco Billboard Liberation Front, adds critical commentary, often amusing and witty, to billboards. For example, a McDonald's ad depicting a breakfast sandwich with the tag line, "Suddenly you're a morning person," in the Downtown Berkeley BART stop was changed to read "Suddenly you're a nothing person."

STEALTH STRATEGIES

As the fast-moving, highly competitive world of advertising seeks new media formats and persuasive strategies to promote product brands, corporate image, and commercial icons, a variety of edgy advertising practices under an assortment of titles have emerged in recent years. From brand buzz, to seeding, stealth, undercover, guerilla and renegade, these practices are designed to enter into the consumer's consciousness just under the critical radar that recognizes advertising as persuasive communication. These undercover formats have an important shared characteristic; their promotional aspect is not revealed and they lack recognizable "sponsorship." To the hip new marketers, sponsorship has become a dirty word. Unlike product placement and other hybrids of commercial media, these persuasions are often interpersonal and take place in both public and private places. For example, a man on the street asks a passerby to take his picture. As the interaction proceeds, opportunity to promote the camera arises. The passerby would be surprised to find that the man has actually been hired to sell the camera. In another example, a person may sit down at a bar and order a drink within earshot of others, then strike up a conversation.

He or she is selling a particular brand of alcohol. And some companies pay college students to "buzz" the latest CD from a musical group to their friends at parties.

Other unconventional sales promotions take place in retail stores and at the point of purchase. In some boutique clothing stores, employees are now paid to be "peer trend setters." These people casually offer comments about what products and styles are hip and fashionable to shoppers who are looking for clothes and sampling products. "Seeding" a new product can be done by leaving empty bottles or cans on tables at locales where targeted consumers will see them and assume they are popular with other members of their consumption group.

Humans have long engaged in market relationships, trading and bargaining for goods and services, but drawing out the differences between earlier forms of market interactions and present business strategies reveals that bargaining entails the application of individual skills, a type of personal theater of pretext, pretend, persuasion, and resistance. But with stealth marketing the interaction assumes a false premise. By concealing its purpose, the "mark" does not have the chance to display skill or offer resistance. The playing field is not level. At its worst, some forms violate trust and may create a cultural atmosphere that spoils the public sense of mutual respect and honesty. For these reasons, some marketers have made strong statements against these practices.

MARKETING DISCRIMINATION

As advertisers' data regarding consumer purchasing behavior has increased in recent years, so too has marketing discrimination, whereby certain real or potential customers are given better treatment, while other real or potential customers are ignored. Hence, for instance, since statistics suggest that the elderly do not consume as highly as do younger shoppers, and that they are more likely to have developed brand loyalties that will not easily be swayed, many advertisers ignore this market completely, meaning that advertising-driven media forms such as television and magazines are often overwhelmingly youth-focused.

Moreover, as database marketing has become a hot trend, advertisers and retailers are now able to personalize their advertising, no longer just relying on broad demographic trends. Thus, many retailers and other businesses are mailing coupons and special notices only to "good" customers, or to those deemed *likely* to be good customers. When mixed with television viewing data recorded by cable boxes, DVRs, and TiVo, and with developments in digital television delivery being made, this trend could easily result in differentiated programming or personalization for different audience members. Some citizens welcome the prospect of personalized marketing, but personalized marketing means not simply that each person will receive different ads, programming, and services, but that some may receive no or poor programming or service, hence further threatening the democratic potential of broadcasting and other supposedly "mass" media.

ADVERTISING AND POLITICS

If we look at social-cause marketing from this point of view, we might say that every aspect of our lives, even political ideas, becomes fertile ground for marketing products. Some popular commercial campaigns now revolve around political ideas, many promising social change and a more peaceful world through the purchase of products. In fact, a prominent critic of consumer culture, Thomas Frank, argues that one of the only spheres where protest and criticism are currently acceptable in our culture is adverting. Online messages for Diesel clothing tell consumers that to achieve "successful living" they must "take action," fight, shout, and wake up "the rebel inside you." With visual references to baby-boom hippies, a young woman in a headband makes the peace sign and compels us to "reject the established mints" and eat Mentos. Another Mentos ad references "flower power," a countercultural slogan from the 1960s, with a daisy and the words "peace, love and happy mints." Playtex promises a new "women's movement" by which the company means "freedom from seams and stitches" with the Only You bra. Like many "postmodern" commercial messages, these ads are presented with a sense of irony, making claims, yet making fun of themselves at the same time for making such silly claims. Nevertheless, they successfully tie political impulses for peace, social change, and women's liberation to consumer identities and purchasing products.

Social-causal marketing, both serious and comedic, has been criticized for making arbitrary claims that mislead consumers and negatively effect political participation. Critics argue that advertising in general, and "socially conscious" commercials in particular, lead to a passive, uninformed public. Such advertisements appeal to the political desires for freedom and equality, yet offer no real strategies to achieve social change. Purchasing products does little to move the world in the direction depicted in the ads. Buying Mentos will not lead to world peace; wearing Diesel clothing will not change the world; and women cannot achieve equal status, respect, and independence by wearing a particular bra. When political sentiments are directed toward consumption, the public is compelled to consume, not actually participate in politics in ways that might achieve social and political goals.

This leads us to understand the commercialization of politics in a complicated light. Advertising's effect on American politics has been felt more directly through election campaigns that have become a type of commercial politics, in which highly targeted political messages are designed through the use of focus groups and directed toward voting subgroups, each of which is watching or listening to its favorite program. In a process that mirrors the selling of products, an image of a political leader is also sold to the public, turned audience and then consumer. As politicians devise persuasive messages they must "stay on message," and authentic discourse becomes harder to find in the political arena. It reaches greater levels of distortion with negative political advertising that often plays on fear, anxiety, and disgust. "Going negative" is also known to "turn off" the voting public, causing political analysts to charge that commercially driven election campaigns create a cynical, politically disengaged citizenry. For these reasons, and because of the high cost of airtime, campaign reformers advocate that corporate media outlets should provide "free time" for political candidates to better serve the public interest and to disentangle the candidates from the special interests, which are often the ultimate funding sources for expensive ad campaigns.

SWEATSHOPS AND THE ENVIRONMENT

It is frequently asserted that we live in a postindustrial society with an economy driven by information systems and symbolic culture. Advertising is certainly part of that symbolic culture, but commercial messages are, most of the time, selling goods, the products of industrial production, even though such commodities are often produced in other, less developed countries. Americans for the most part are not exposed to the factory conditions and the exploitation of workers who toil under extreme conditions in underpaid jobs. Nike has long been criticized for refusing to pay a fair wage in countries such as Indonesia, Vietnam, Mexico, and China, even though its advertising campaigns feature powerfully humanistic visions of individual liberation. Writers such as Naomi Klein have documented the exploitation of cheap labor markets by American companies and popular brand labels. It can be said that advertising creates a symbolic world that surrounds everything from trainers to sports gear, from dolls to toys, in a fantasy of consumer culture, which removes products from the unpleasant realities of their production. Left uninformed about corporate global practices, the consumer is more susceptible to commercial persuasions. Public interest advocates, human rights organizations, and labor groups such as the Workers Rights Consortium have pressed for external monitoring of factory conditions in countries around the world, and these proposals, together with environmental concerns, have been brought to bear on international trade organizations and the major economic summits of the developed world.

At the beginning of the twentieth century, industrial capitalism seemed to hold the promise of well-being and economic security to a Western world eager to achieve a standard of living unparalleled in human history. Indeed, early advertisers were often visionary utopians who advocated for personal growth and spiritual attainment. By the twenty-first century, the promise of industrial production heaves under the weight of an environmental crisis, including air and water pollution, toxic by-products, and the destruction of human environments as well animal habitats. The unanticipated and unwanted side effects of industrial production are now widely understood, such as the extravagant depletion of global resources, and global warming, the consequence of greenhouse gases discharged into the atmosphere due to an unsustainable level of energy use. Thus far, with only a few exceptions, advertising has not been able to come to terms with the need for conservation and more ecologically sound, environmentally friendly corporate practices. Instead, ads have used the beauty of the natural world in images of nature as just one more "selling hook." The extraordinary imagery of pristine landscapes used to sell SUVs illustrates this point. These vehicles have become, for critics, the symbol of conspicuous consumption of unrenewable fossil fuels and one of the worst offenders for releasing harmful levels of emissions into the atmosphere.

Advertising influences society and culture on many levels. It compels us to define who we are and what will make us happy. In a very real way, advertising propels our consumption lifestyle and is intimately tied to a set of market relationships that drives the global economy. Only by understanding the broader role advertisements play in culture, the environment, and the globe will we be better able to make choices about what to buy and how we want to live.

See also Body Image; Branding the Globe; Hypercommercialism; Media and Electoral Campaigns; Media Literacy; Pharmaceutical Advertising; Political Entertainment; Product Placement; Ratings; Representations of Women; Television in Schools; Video News Releases; Youth and Media Use; Women's Magazines.

Further Reading: Andersen, Robin. *Consumer Culture and TV Programming.* Boulder, CO: Westview Press, 1995; Andersen, Robin, and Lance Strate. *Critical Studies in Media Commercialism.* London: Oxford University Press, 2000; Berger, John. *Ways of Seeing.* New York: Penguin Books, 1974; Ewen, Stuart. *Captains of Consciousness: Advertising and the Social Roots of the Consumer Culture.* New York: Basic Books, 2001; Frank, Thomas. *The Conquest of Cool: Business Culture, Counterculture and the Rise of Hip Consumerism.* Chicago: University of Chicago Press, 1997; Frith, Katherine Toland, ed. *Undressing the Ad: Reading Culture in Advertising.* New York: Peter Lang, 1998; Goldman, Robert, and Stephen Papson. *Sign Wars: The Cluttered Landscape of Advertising.* New York: Guilford Press, 1996; Jacobson, Michael F., and Laurie Ann Mazur, *Marketing Madness: A Survival Guide for a Consumer Society.* Boulder, CO: Westview Press, 1995; Jhally, Sut. *The Codes of Advertising: Fetishism and the Political Economy of the Consumer Society.* New York: Routledge, 1990; Marchand, Roland. *Advertising the American Dream: Making Way for Modernity 1920–1940.* Berkeley: University of California Press, 1985; McAllister, Matthew P. *The Commercialization of American Culture: New Advertising, Control and Democracy.* Thousand Oaks, CA: Sage, 1995; Quart, Alissa. *Branded: The Buying and Selling of Teenagers.* Cambridge, MA: Perseus Publishing, 2003; Turow, Joseph. *Niche Envy: Marketing Discrimination in the Digital Age.* Cambridge, MA: MIT Press, 2006; Williamson, Judith. *Decoding Advertisements.* London: Marion Boyars, 1978.

Robin Andersen

AL-JAZEERA

The Qatari-based Al-Jazeera satellite channel, the first 24-hour all-news network in the Arab world, has been surrounded by much controversy since its inception. Its uninhibited critique of authoritarian governments has infuriated many Arab officials, who have not been used to seeing a broadcast network that is not appeasing their policies. Its exclusive broadcast of tapes by Osama bin Laden and his lieutenants and its unvarnished reporting on the wars in Afghanistan and Iraq and the most recent war in Lebanon have catapulted it into the international media spotlight. It has been heralded by its admirers as a beacon for freedom of expression, and accused by its critics of sensationalism and biased reporting. Indeed, some U.S. officials charged the station with anti-American bias for its coverage of the "war on terror."

Al-Jazeera is an anomaly that has defied all odds. It came out in a region that has not been known for its free and open media environment; it was launched by Qatar, a small peninsular country in the Persian Gulf that hardly had any impact on the Arab media scene before Al-Jazeera; it challenged the Western news networks' monopoly over the global news flow; and it gave the Arab people a platform through which they can express their opinions without red lines, listen to different points of view, and engage in lively and bold political debates about issues that used to be buried under the carpet of government censorship before the advent of Al-Jazeera. When covering the wars in Afghanistan and Iraq, the station includes a wide spectrum of international opinion, but has been criticized in some official U.S. circles for including graphic images of the U.S. bombing in the Middle East. Its daring coverage has made it the news station of choice for more than 40 million Arab viewers worldwide.

AL-JAZEERA TIMELINE

November 1, 1996—Al-Jazeera launches with a start-up grant of $140 million from the Qatari emir.

January 1, 1999—Expands from 6 hours a day to 24 hours a day.

October 7, 2001—Broadcasts a statement by Osama bin Laden two hours after the U.S.-led coalition begins military strikes against Afghanistan.

October 30, 2001—When asked by a correspondent from Al-Jazeera's Washington bureau about the authenticity of pictures showing Afghani children as war casualties, U.S. Secretary of Defense Donald Rumsfeld accuses the network of propounding Taliban propaganda.

November 13, 2001—The United States launches a missile attack on Al-Jazeera's office in Kabul, Afghanistan. Although no Al-Jazeera staff are hurt in the attack, the building is destroyed and some employees' homes are damaged. In a letter to Al-Jazeera dated December 6, 2001, U.S. Assistant Secretary of Defense Victoria Clarke states, "The building we struck was a known al Qaeda facility in central Kabul."

March 4, 2003—The New York Stock Exchange bans Al-Jazeera (as well as several other news organizations) from its trading floor indefinitely, citing "security concerns" as the official reason. A few months later the ban was rescinded, according to a New York Stock Exchange spokesperson.

April 8, 2003—U.S. bombs hit Al-Jazeera's office in Baghdad, killing reporter Tareq Ayyoub. At a briefing in Doha, Qatar, the network's managing director says the Pentagon was informed of the network's location in Baghdad several months before the war started. Brigadier General Vincent K. Brooks says of the Al-Jazeera attack, "This coalition does not target journalists. We don't know every place journalists are operating on the battlefield. It's a dangerous place, indeed."

September 23, 2003—Iraqi interim government suspends Al-Jazeera (and Al-Arabiya, an Arab news channel based in Dubai, United Arab Emirates) from reporting on official government activities for two weeks for what it says was support of recent attacks on government members and U.S. forces.

August 7, 2004—The Iraqi interim government shuts down the Baghdad office of Al-Jazeera for one month, citing national security concerns. Later, the shutdown is extended indefinitely, and the offices sealed. Al-Jazeera continues to report from Iraq through a network of stringers.

June 2005—Rumsfeld accuses Al-Jazeera of encouraging Islamic military groups by airing beheadings of American troops in Iraq. In response, the network says in a statement that "Al-Jazeera . . . has never at any time transmitted pictures of killings or beheadings and . . . any talk about this is absolutely unfounded."

November 15, 2006—Al-Jazeera International is launched with four bureaus in Washington, DC; London; Kuala Lumpur, Malaysia; and Doha, Qatar.

Adapted from the Project for Journalism Excellence: http://www.journalism.org/node/1530.

A BRIEF BACKGROUND

Al-Jazeera, which means "the island" in Arabic, was launched by Qatar's progressive emir (the Arabic equivalent of a prince) Sheikh Hamad bin Khalifa Al-Thani in November 1996 as part of his move to introduce democratization to his tiny state in the Persian Gulf. The British-educated emir, who overthrew his father after a nonviolent coup in 1995, planned for Al-Jazeera to be an independent and nonpartisan satellite TV network free from government scrutiny and manipulation.

The launching of Al-Jazeera followed the termination of a contract in April 1996 between Rome-based, Saudi-owned Orbit Radio and Television Service and the Arabic TV division of the BBC News Service. After the failure of that venture, the majority of the BBC's Arabic TV service editorial staff members were recruited by Al-Jazeera, which also inherited the BBC network's editorial spirit, freedom, and style. This core group of newly recruited staff members received their training in a Western journalistic environment, and they were familiar with the Arab political environment, with all its nuances and intricacies—qualifications that made them the final ingredient in the recipe for Al-Jazeera's eventual success (see el-Nawawy and Iskandar 2003).

The Qatari emir offered an initial pledge of around $140 million to help launch and subsidize Al-Jazeera over a five-year period through November 2001, after which the network was to become a financially independent commercial enterprise in much the same form as CNN. Al-Jazeera, however, has failed to raise enough money through other means and is still receiving financial support from the Qatari government, which owns some of the network's shares.

Al-Jazeera's popularity had been limited to the Arab world until the 9/11 attacks on New York and Washington, DC. Since then, Al-Jazeera, which had exclusive videotapes of Al-Qaeda training camps in Afghanistan and footage from the wars in Afghanistan and Iraq, has become a global news source. Today,

AL-JAZEERA INTERNATIONAL

As part of its plans for international expansion and global reach, Al-Jazeera launched its English-language network, called Al-Jazeera International (AJI), on November 15, 2006. The new network, which was launched after prolonged delays and months of preparation because of technical and political problems, has offices in Washington, DC; London; Kuala Lumpur, Malaysia; and Doha, Qatar.

The new network, which is also funded by the Qatari emir, appeals to the Western audience as well as the non-Arabic-speaking Muslim populations in countries such as Indonesia and Bangladesh. It has employed several high-profile Western journalists, including British talk host and interviewer David Frost, former "Nightline" correspondent Dave Marash, and Josh Rushing, the ex-Marine best known for his lead role in the critically acclaimed 2004 documentary about Al-Jazeera called *Control Room*.

A pressing question regarding Al-Jazeera International is: What kind of identity and market niche will the new network establish for itself? "From its onset, [AJI has tried to] act as a counterbalance to the Western-centric reporting of the established [Western] channels" by marketing itself as "the voice of the South." AJI "opened with an in-depth review of the humanitarian crisis in Gaza, followed by another on Darfur. Reports on Iran and Zimbabwe followed with African and Arab issues dominating the agenda" (Nkrumah 2006).

Al-Jazeera houses a staff of more than 400 journalists and 50 foreign correspondents working in 31 countries. More importantly, Al-Jazeera has created a niche for itself by identifying a market demand for serious and independent journalism, with content mostly dedicated to political matters that are of key concern to the Arab people.

AL-JAZEERA PROGRAMS: A BREATH OF FRESH AIR IN A POLITICALLY RESTRICTIVE ENVIRONMENT

Al-Jazeera has revolutionized the Arab media scene by airing what no other Arab news organization dared to: the hard, often harsh truth of Arab life, culture, and politics. It has posed the first serious challenge to the censorial culture of political and media restraint in the Arab world. The network's shockingly open and passionate political talk shows tackle sensitive issues that have always been considered "taboo" by Arab standards, like sex, polygamy, apostasy in Islam, banned political groups, torture, and corruption of Arab officials. Many of these shows take a news approach that allows for presenting "clashing perspectives" of political opponents. Such an approach "was not only an innovation on Arab television but was also unfamiliar in a region where the voice of authority is rarely challenged openly, whether at school or university, within families or at work" (Sakr 2004, p. 157).

Al-Jazeera's talk shows, such as *More than One Opinion*, *Open Dialogue*, and *Without Borders*, open the floor for free and open debates and heated discussions that are aired live, with no room for editing on the part of Al-Jazeera staff.

These programs feature academics, experts, politicians, and activists who represent different sides of the same issue. In this free marketplace of ideas, the audience members have a platform to call in and express their opinions on what the guests have to say. In fact, Al-Jazeera has a talk show titled *Al-Jazeera Pulpit*, which is devoted exclusively to taking live phone calls from ordinary people to know their opinions and their stances on various political issues.

Al-Jazeera viewers, who were initially shocked by the approach and editorial style of its talk shows, became used to controversial confrontations, contentious views, and loud debates "with Islamists and anti-Islamists pitted against each other, as well as people of all political persuasions and dissidents from Morocco to Egypt and Palestine to Bahrain" (Sakr 2001, p. 58). For those viewers who have been yearning for an Arab news network through which they can express their views without inhibitions, Al-Jazeera is a breath of fresh air in a heavily censored environment. In his comment on the impact of Al-Jazeera talk shows on Arab audiences, Faisal Al-Kasim, the host of *The Opposite Direction*, the flagship talk show on Al-Jazeera, argues that while Arab television networks have become used to reporting the trivia and the news that glorifies the rulers, Al-Jazeera talk shows "have damaged this decaying media and whetted the appetite of the Arab people for more talking" (Al-Kasim 2005, p. 104).

It was no surprise that Al-Jazeera's talk shows would anger most Arab government officials, who were not used to seeing an Arab television station challenge their policies or take a line that is contradictory to their agendas. Countries' outrage with Al-Jazeera took different forms: many countries sent official complaints to Qatar. In fact, more than 450 complaints were received by Qatari diplomats from various Arab states during the first few years following the start of Al-Jazeera. Some countries temporarily closed down Al-Jazeera bureaus; others withdrew their ambassadors from the Qatari capital, Doha; still others, faced with the impossibility of jamming the Al-Jazeera signal, went as far as shutting down power to several major cities to prevent their people from watching Al-Jazeera programs.

AL-JAZEERA AND "CONTEXTUAL OBJECTIVITY"

The term objectivity itself, when used within a journalistic context, signifies the adoption of a position of detachment, and it suggests the absence of subjectivity, personalized involvement, and judgment. This ideal or mirage is one that is particular to journalists and the institutions in which they operate.

It would be unrealistic to expect Al-Jazeera, or any other media outlet for that matter, to be absolutely objective. Even if absolute objectivity were possible, there is no absolute truth or reality to be absolutely objective about. A more accurate and more realistic term to apply to Al-Jazeera is "contextual objectivity," which demonstrates the hybrid struggle between attaining objectivity in news coverage by covering all sides of the story while appealing to network audiences through contextualization. Contextualization demonstrates a situational perspective, allowing for sensitivity to the environment in which the network is broadcasting. Contextualizing a certain event is governed by the realization that objectivity is in the eye of the beholder—the audience seeking the "truth."

Contextual objectivity can be witnessed in virtually every media outlet today. All media have inherent biases, and all news is manufactured to appeal to a certain audience. That is why people prefer one network over another. But the question is: how do networks strike the balance that provides audiences with a true representation of real events while still appealing to public sensibilities? While most news networks engage in contextual objectivity, consciously or otherwise, in their day-to-day coverage, Al-Jazeera is perhaps the first network to articulate this approach as a network philosophy. The channel's motto, "The Opinion and the Other Opinion," repeated frequently during program intermissions, is an indication that the channel aspires to cover all sides to a particular story, and that it has instituted a pluralistic media discourse. Al-Jazeera believes that public discourse can only be equitable and effective if all possible opinions and views are expressed and demonstrated equally, whether they are Israeli, Palestinian, American, or Turk. Al-Jazeera's philosophy suggests that "truth" is the culmination of multiple conglomerated subjectivities (see el-Nawawy and Iskandar 2002).

But in the process of trying to live up to its motto, Al-Jazeera has also tried to appeal to the values and beliefs of its Arab audiences. This seemingly paradoxical dilemma is for some a form of contextual objectivity. Al-Jazeera has been telling the American side of the story in Iraq, even as it sympathizes with the plight of the Iraqi people for independence. Its sympathy with the Palestinian cause does not deter it from interviewing Israeli journalists and politicians.

CONTEXTUAL OBJECTIVITY IN AL-JAZEERA'S COVERAGE OF AMERICA'S "WAR ON TERROR"

Contextual objectivity on Al-Jazeera is best explained in the framework of the network's coverage of America's "war on terror," or as Al-Jazeera refers to it, the "so-called war on terror." This war, which has been launched by the U.S. administration in the aftermath of the September 11 events of 2001, has sparked major debates over the definition of terror, its social and political implications, and the extent of the news media's adherence to the journalistic principles of balance, truth, and objectivity, especially during times of political strife.

The world media systems have not agreed upon a universal definition of terror. In fact, the concept of terrorism is "contested, value-laden and open to multiple meanings located within broader cultural frames, so that, to some extent, terrorism is in the eye of the beholder" (Norris et al. 2003, p. 6). Each media system may perceive a terrorist event differently. For some, it may be a suicide; for others it may be a martyrdom. That is why one man's terrorist is another man's freedom fighter. Al-Jazeera, in its portrayal of practitioners of violence as either "terrorists" or "freedom fighters," reflects its political culture, its value system, and ideological and commercial interests that tend to drive media anywhere. "This raises the very question of whether and to what extent [Al-Jazeera] can be truly objective when reporting from the Arab world about issues that matter to Arabs the most." Or yet another question: "Can an Arab channel reporting on Arab issues remove itself from its Arab perspective?" (Zayani 2005, p. 18).

Addressing these questions in the context of America's "war on terror" is especially important given the way U.S. president George W. Bush described the parties involved in this war as "either with us or against us." Bush's pronouncement has placed media outlets like Al-Jazeera in a cultural split of "us" and "them." The implied cultural assumption for the American broadcast networks, which are products of the American culture, was that they were the platform for the "us" in the war against "them." However, Al-Jazeera, which is a product of the Arab culture, found it difficult to join the "us" side (i.e., the American side) when most of its viewers were obviously non-Americans who had some reservations about the way the war was conducted. That is why, whenever Al-Jazeera presented news from an Arab perspective in America's "war against terror," it was automatically perceived by U.S. officials as anti-American (see Zaharna 2005).

In fact, several senior U.S. officials repeatedly criticized Al-Jazeera, accusing it of fueling anti-American sentiment and giving terrorists a podium because of its airing of tapes from Osama bin Laden and other Al-Qaeda lieutenants. Al-Jazeera defended its position by saying that bin Laden is one side of the story that had to be presented, and that the airings of his tapes on the network were followed by panels including American and Arab analysts to dissect his messages.

CONCLUSION

Al-Jazeera's editorial policy relies on balancing different perspectives against each other while trying to present a context that suits the Arab cultural and political environment. That has earned it legitimacy, credibility, and popularity on a regional and international level. It has also encouraged other networks in the Arab world to emulate its style and integrate its editorial policy in their programming.

Unfortunately, though, the United States perceives a strong element of bias in Al-Jazeera's overall coverage. In the U.S. official circles, Al-Jazeera's seeming exercise of contextual objectivity is equated to being at least "anti-American." However, in the Arab world, where the majority considers Al-Jazeera to be a symbol of democracy and free speech, a few critics still accuse the channel of being "pro-American." This is evidence that the channel must be doing something right, and an inadvertent reaffirmation of the network's success at employing, implementing, and engaging in contextual objectivity.

See also Bias and Objectivity; Global Community Media; Islam and the Media; Paparazzi and Photographic Ethics; Parachute Journalism; Political Documentary; Presidential Stagecraft and Militainment; Sensationalism, Fear Mongering, and Tabloid Media.

Further Reading: Al-Kasim, Faisal. "'The Opposite Direction': A Program Which Changed the Face of Arab Television." In *The Al-Jazeera Phenomenon: Critical Perspectives on New Arab Media,* ed. Mohamed Zayani, 93–105. Boulder, CO: Paradigm, 2005; el-Nawawy, Mohammed, and Adel Iskandar. *Al-Jazeera: The Story of the Network that is Rattling Governments and Redefining Modern Journalism.* Boulder: Westview, 2003; el-Nawawy, Mohammed, and Adel Iskandar. "The Minotaur of 'Contextual Objectivity': War Coverage and the Pursuit of Accuracy with Appeal." *Transnational Broadcasting*

Studies Journal 9 (2002). http://www.tbsjournal.com/Archives/Fall02/Iskandar.html; Miladi, Noureddine. "Mapping the Al-Jazeera Phenomenon." In *War and the Media: Reporting Conflict 24/7,* ed. Daya Kishan Thussu and Des Freedman, 149–60. London: Sage, 2003; Miles, Hugh. *Al-Jazeera: How Arab TV News Challenged the World.* London: Abacus, 2005; Nkrumah, Gamal. "Voice of the South." *Al-Ahram Weekly* 821, November 23–29, 2006; Norris, Pippa, Montague Kern, and Marion Just. "Framing Terrorism." In *Framing Terrorism: The News Media, the Government and the Public,* ed. Pippa Norris, Montague Kern, and Marion Just, 3–26. New York: Routledge, 2003; Sakr, Naomi. "Al-Jazeera Satellite Channel: Global Newscasting in Arabic." In *International News in the 21st Century,* ed. Chris Paterson and Annabelle Sreberny, 147–68. Luton: University of Luton Press, 2004; Sakr, Naomi. *Satellite Realms: Transnational Television, Globalization and the Middle East.* London: I. B. Tauris, 2001; Zaharna, R. S. "Al-Jazeera and American Public Diplomacy: A Dance of Intercultural (Mis-) Communication." In *The Al-Jazeera Phenomenon: Critical Perspectives on New Arab Media,* ed. Mohamed Zayani, 183–204. Boulder, CO: Paradigm, 2005; Zayani, Mohamed. "Al-Jazeera and the Vicissitudes of the New Arab Mediascape." In *The Al-Jazeera Phenomenon: Critical Perspectives on New Arab Media,* ed. Mohamed Zayani, 1–46. Boulder, CO: Paradigm, 2005.

Mohammed el-Nawawy

ALTERNATIVE MEDIA IN THE UNITED STATES

Democracy demands broad and inclusive public discourse and freedom of expression. Over the years, mainstream media have been criticized for walling off public debate on important issues, and in the age of corporate conglomeration, critics continue to challenge the loss of diverse voices across the media spectrum. An authentic democracy needs dialogue, and alternative media have long provided the space for a multiplicity of viewpoints excluded from much of public debate. The alternative press has a long and important history in the United States, and in recent years new technologies have been designed and employed by independent and community producers that have provided access to channels, equipment, and communities not served by corporate media outlets. Alternative media are a site of controversy for a range of issues from professionalism to regulation, and debates within organizations continue as new production styles raise issues about innovation, formatting, and audience expectations.

OTHER VOICES

The British colonies in North America became a nation through the mobilizing efforts of small publishers. Thomas Paine and Benjamin Franklin were just the most prominent of the leaders whose fingers pulled proofs off rebel presses. Democracy has been synonymous with free speech since the early American rebellion against corrupt state power and the lack of political representation. The country's founders fought for freedom of expression, and those rights and liberties have been codified, challenged, and renewed throughout the history of the republic. At the turn of the twentieth century, President Theodore Roosevelt coined the term "muckraker" for the audacious exposés that challenged entrenched wealth and corruption, both public and private. Those journalistic traditions remain an essential aspect of American media culture and continue to influence alternative and freelance journalists.

Alternative media, sometimes referred to as community media, are often tied to social movements for change and racial and economic justice. In the 1960s "underground" newspapers flourished with antiwar voices and iconoclastic comic artists such as R. Crumb. These papers grew out of the civil rights movement, in which newspapers by the Black Panthers and others were key tools, educating and mobilizing like-minded supporters for often militant actions that challenged racism. Earlier in the century, antiwar voices had been published in a magazine called *The Masses*, which included art by the "Ashcan School" of painting—including William Glackens and John Sloan—and writers John Reed and Max Eastman, among others. During WWI an entire press run of this magazine was seized by the U.S. Postal Service. The government accused the magazine of undermining the war effort.

The legacy of these traditions can be found in the long-form investigative reporting in much of the alternative press, in magazines and publications such as *Mother Jones, CounterPunch, The Progressive, Harper's,* and *The Nation*, among others. These alternative sources of information stand outside a media world dominated by corporate giants who have been charged with restricting information unfavorable to the business sector. Corporate media counters that the alternative press is not popular, and the critiques it offers are outside of mainstream concerns and issues. Defenders argue that slick styles and sensational formats attract readers and audiences to material that distracts the public from important democratic debates.

BROADCASTING AND CABLE CHANNELS

Although electronic transmission in the United States had a lively start with thousands of amateur radio broadcasters, the trend for decades after the Radio Act of 1927 tended toward greater and greater consolidation of corporate use of the airwaves. VHF and UHF television channels took a similar pattern. In the 1970s cable distribution advanced and more channels came on line, offering a full channel of news (Cable News Network [CNN]), 24-hour sports channels such as ESPN, and full-time entertainment channels, such as HBO, Showtime, and A&E, the arts and entertainment network. However, these new channels soon became commercially driven as part of the larger holdings of corporate media empires.

NONCOMMERCIAL MEDIA

Not all broadcast stations are commercial. There is electromagnetic spectrum space allocated for noncommercial and educational uses. Originally, many of these channels were run by colleges and universities, although most of them are now nonprofit entities that make up the key stations of PBS (Public

Broadcasting Service) and NPR (National Public Radio), both funded by the Corporation for Public Broadcasting (CPB), which receives money from Congress. Although structured purposefully to be shielded from direct political influence, over the course of its history funding for public broadcasting has been subject to political pressures, with congressional members, predominantly from the Republican party, periodically calling for an end to financial support. Because of the lobbying power to promote the commercial media sector in the United States, overall funding for public networks is much less than that allocated in other industrialized countries. The fact that the funding does not cover production and ongoing expenses has meant that these networks must rely on donations from public and corporate donors. Critics of the programming content of public broadcasting argue that corporate donors have undue influence over programming decisions. They charge that they have all but eliminated the experimental and diverse programming originally envisioned for PBS. Others argue that the lack of relevant programming should be attributed to the faulty visions of those within the public broadcasting system. Because of such problems, independent producers and unions have had to march, petition, and sue to get their voices, shows, and programming agendas heard on public broadcasting.

ARTICULATING THE NEED FOR ALTERNATIVES

Advocates for developing an alternative media system that is more inclusive and able to accommodate a diverse set of opinions and voices also point to the regulatory rollbacks of laws that once required commercial media outlets to fulfill their public interest mandate. The authority by which all channels operate requires that they broadcast "in the public interest, convenience and necessity." Many argue that that goal, codified into law in 1934, was made irrelevant when broadcasters claimed that such cartoon fare as *The Flintstones* and *The Jetsons* was "educational." Community and activist groups who form a major constituency for alternative media point out that even commercial time, driven ostensibly by a "free market," is often closed to alternative viewpoints, even for those willing to pay commercial rates. Peace activists and unions have had to take networks to court to be able to buy standard commercial time for 30-second spots. The "Fairness Doctrine," which was ushered in after WWII in an effort to combat potential dominance of public airwaves by particular parties, has been eliminated. Public interest groups have argued that these changes led to the present media landscape, and they contend that commercial media do not represent the broader public. They point to the inordinate amount of public space for the strident pronouncements of ultraconservatives such as Rush Limbaugh and Bill O'Reilly, among others, and the lack of alternative space for counter agendas and independent voices. In earlier times the Fairness Doctrine would have required that "the other side" of an important issue be included, a demand the public can no longer make. Cable talk show hosts and producers point to the diversity of their guest lists, but detractors argue that conservative hosts set the agendas and enjoy a discursive advantage.

PACIFICA NETWORK

After WWII, media producers looking for distribution sources outside of the mainstream media were able to create radio venues for alternative voices. Pacifica Network, founded in the 1950s by Louis Hill, acquired five stations in major cities: Los Angeles; San Francisco; New York; Washington, DC; and Houston. Because this community radio network is able to sustain itself through listener contributions, the stations were not subject to the pressures of NPR and the need for corporate sponsors. However, while this network has served communities for years and developed innovative programs that draw on the strength of activist groups, individual talent, and academic producers, among others, the network has been beleaguered by budget shortfalls and internal disputes over competing visions for alternative media.

PEG ACCESS

In the early 1980s, when cable technology dramatically increased the number of channels and services available, public and alternative media entered an era of expansion and innovation. Channels for public, educational, and government (PEG) access were mandated through cable franchises in thousands of cities and towns across the country. PEG access channels provide live coverage of town meetings, high school basketball games, and space for community organizations and individuals to have ongoing programming. In many cities, these channels have become important locations for community dialogue. The local franchises often provide a percentage of the cable revenue for funding media centers to program these channels. This funding is based on the fact that the cable lines utilize a public resource: the local rights-of-way. In order to build the cable system, access to local streets and manholes is needed. In exchange for this, local franchise authorities have negotiated for channels, equipment, staff, and housing for local media centers. Tucson, Arizona; Burlington, Vermont; and Grand Rapids, Michigan are just a few of the places where PEG access resources have brought a good measure of democratic expression to local issues. However, the channel space has increasingly become a desirable asset, and the cable corporations and companies have been fighting hard to try to undercut access use and free up more channels for commercial programming.

PAPER TIGER TELEVISION

Paper Tiger Television started as a public access program in New York City. Artists and activists worked with cultural critics to produce educational and informational programs that aired over two access cable channels. From the beginning, many of the shows focused on media themes, offering critiques of programs, newspapers, and regulatory and ownership issues, controversies that continue to surround the corporate media. The Paper Tiger collective has lasted 27 years, producing over 400 programs. Paper Tiger expanded from cable and continues to distribute its programs to schools, colleges, community groups, and overseas venues.

Instead of trying to mimic the expensive, slick production style of mainstream mass media and what marketing consultants call the "packaging" of news programming, Paper Tiger created a "public access aesthetic" that included innovative and inexpensive set designs, handmade graphics, and alternative location settings. Dedicated to the inclusion of original and creative artistic expression, the collective developed a working analysis that argued that alternative formats were as important as content. The style and look of the Paper Tiger video aesthetic was contentious, with some critics charging that audiences would not take seriously shows that diverged from the high production qualities recognizable on network TV and even in some documentary formats. Yet Paper Tiger continued its unconventional and inexpensive style, and such innovations predated the now popular look of many independent videos, especially those shared on online venues such as YouTube and others.

DEEP DISH TELEVISION

Deep Dish Television can be understood as the logical outgrowth of the public access structure, providing a distribution network for public access video and independently produced programming. Initiated in 1986, its goal was to collect programming from community stations and video artists from across the country and provide a national distribution source for that programming. Programs are uplinked to a satellite feed that can be received at local community media centers, where they can be rebroadcast on community, public, and access stations. As a "grassroots" network, Deep Dish has produced its own programs with the help of individual donors and foundation support. Programs and even series that address specific topics from an in-depth perspective exemplify a very different type of reporting of historical and cultural events, political scandals and corruption, and war. After 20 years, assessing these often groundbreaking series allow media analysts and the public alike to fully appreciate the role of and need for alternative media (see sidebar, "Shocking and Awful: Deep Dish Television Responds to War"). The most successful of the Deep Dish uplinks has been the daily news program *Democracy Now!* with award-winning journalist Amy Goodman. This ongoing international news program began as a radio show on the Pacifica network and became a television series through the Deep Dish network of local stations.

SHOCKING AND AWFUL: DEEP DISH TELEVISION RESPONDS TO WAR

In the days before the invasion of Iraq, as the U.S. military planned a massive aerial bombing campaign of Baghdad, the Pentagon phrase "Shock and Awe" was repeated with enthusiasm on mainstream television. At the same time, Deep Dish TV was setting in motion a plan to record, illuminate, document and bear witness to what would be left out of the commercial media war-coverage frame. They would title the 13-part series of 28-minute programs *Shocking and Awful*, and the group of independent artists and media producers would tell the story of the Iraq war in a way completely unlike that of commercial media.

In March 2003 when the bombing started, Americans were invited to look through the elevated eyes of the warriors in control of the exciting high-tech weapons. The digital imaging of weapons is a graphic style recognizable now across the media spectrum from TV news to films and video games. Its prominence confers a kind of video-game sensibility to war, one antithetical to concerns for the victims on the ground and such digital thrills are easily dissociated from the killing of real people. The Deep Dish series brought those people to life.

An overpowering impression begins to take hold as viewers are shown how people, art treasures, antiquities, and important archeological sites have been destroyed—none of it makes any sense.

But before the bombing it seemed to make sense on American television as former generals and news celebrities alike spoke of strategies and battle plans, and made use of Pentagon-supplied graphic illustrations. The producers of Deep Dish also used graphics, but they were used to illustrate other perspectives of war. Editors visually superimposed the faces of children inside the target structures as cable-news generals illustrated aerial weapons on news shows. Exciting images of advanced weapons systems are far less convincing when noncombatant victims are pictured on the receiving end. The technique shatters the meaning and sensibility made of war on U.S. media.

Recognition of the compelling quality of the series, and the public need for a twenty-first-century creative merger between critical art and politics, was conferred by the Whitney Museum of American Art in New York City, which aired the tapes continuously at its 2006 Biennial from March 2 to May 28.

As telecom corporations such as AT&T and Verizon move to provide video programming, pressure builds to minimize the public interest requirements for PEG access and to eliminate local franchise regulations. Media activists are working to ensure that PEG access will stay in cable and serve as a model for other platforms.

PUBLIC INTEREST SET-ASIDE

Direct Satellite Broadcasting (DBS) is one arena to have developed a "public interest" set-aside. DBS can provide the sort of channel choice that cable provides via satellite. It is the only programming available in many rural areas where cable lines are not cost-effective. In the late 1990s, when DBS systems were being marketed around the country, organizations such as the Consumer Federation and the Instructional Telecommunications Foundation lobbied to make sure that some sort of public "payback" would be required from these systems. After several years of lobbying and activism, 4 percent of DBS channels were required to be educational and nonprofit. This has enabled the University of California and University of Washington as well as several consortia of colleges to have national programming via satellite. It has also enabled two "alternative" channels: Link TV and Free Speech TV, which provide national space for, among others, antiwar activists and environmental advocates. Free Speech TV airs *Democracy Now!*, the television version of the popular Pacific Radio news program first distributed by Deep Dish TV, and has garnered a huge audience and an active constituency of alternative media advocates.

LOW-POWER RADIO

Another venue for alternative voices is low-power radio. Much of the radio spectrum in the United States is unused and in the 1990s, with the availability of low-cost electronic equipment, creative young people began pirate stations to play music that wasn't allowed on commercial media, and to provide space for environmental and community discussions. In the past the argument against this sort of anarchic broadcasting had used the fear of interference, but the antennae of low-power transmitters can be set so that they do not interfere with commercial channels. With the availability of low-cost transmission equipment, so many of these stations had developed by the late 1990s that a movement began to grow to legalize low-power broadcasting. Prometheus Radio is a Philadelphia organization that grew out of a pirate broadcast to become an organizing hub and station-building center. The FCC (Federal Communications Commission) has allowed several hundred low-power stations, which now provide information and cultural programming to diverse groups including farm workers, crab fishermen, and immigrants.

INDYMEDIA

In 1999, while preparing for the meetings of the World Trade Organization (WTO) in Seattle, alternative media makers from around the country formed the "Independent Media Center" and created a Web site: www.indymedia.org. Long before YouTube and other commercial Web video, this site became a global node for activism, providing easy posting of audio and video, still photographs, and graphics, greatly expanding activist news and information. PDF files were posted so that local groups could print out a daily newspaper. The excitement of this project spread to many countries, and Indymedia has been an important locus for alternative news especially during crises, such as the economic collapse of Argentina in 2001.

AIR AMERICA

Air America was initiated in 2003 to be an alternative to conservative talk networks. It enabled progressive voices, such as feminist Laura Flanders, to be available on the AM dial. Although it generated impressive audience ratings, the lack of commercial sponsorship forced it into bankruptcy in 2006. However, it still continues as a programming source in several cities.

CONCLUSION

The growth of the Internet has lead some to discount the importance of regulated broadcast spaces. Nevertheless, the overwhelming majority of people still depend on the car radio and the TV set for information and entertainment. Broadcast media in the public interest remain a goal that the Internet does not supplant. Indeed, all of the above-mentioned pressures and struggles apply to the Internet as well. It, too, is being forced to become more commercial; and media reformers and activists are now fighting a battle similar to those waged in the past, to secure the Internet's neutrality so that service providers not be allowed to privilege one source over another. Like broadcast and cable media, the Internet needs to be held accountable to the public interest.

See also Blogosphere; Conglomeration and Media Monopolies; Embedding Journalists; Global Community Media; Government Censorship and Freedom of Speech; Media Reform; Media Watch Groups; National Public Radio; Net Neutrality; Pirate Radio; Political Documentary; Public Access Television; Public Broadcasting Service; Regulating the Airwaves; Sensationalism, Fear Mongering, and Tabloid Media.

Further Reading: Atton, Chris. *Alternative Media*. Thousand Oaks, CA: Sage, 2002; Boyle, Dierdre. *Subject to Change: Guerilla Television Revisited*. New York: Oxford University Press, 1997; Chester, Jeff. *Digital Destiny: New Media and the Future of Democracy*. New York: The New Press, 2007; Cooper, Mark, ed. *The Case against Media Consolidation: Evidence on Concentration, Localism and Diversity*. Philadelphia: Temple University Press, 2007; Couldry, Nick, and James Curran, eds. *Contesting Media Power: Alternative Media in a Networked World*. New York: Rowman and Littlefield, 2003; Downing, John D. H. *Radical Media: Rebellious Communication and Social Movements*. Thousand Oaks, CA: Sage, 2000; Halleck, DeeDee. *Hand Held Visions: The Impossible Possibilities of Community Media*. New York: Fordham University Press, 2002; Klinenberg, Eric. *The Battle to Control America's Media*. New York: Henry Holt, 2007; Starr, Jerry. *Air Wars: The Fight to Reclaim Public Broadcasting*. Boston: Beacon Press, 2000.

DeeDee Halleck

ANONYMOUS SOURCES, LEAKS, AND NATIONAL SECURITY

Free flow of news is the oxygen of a democracy, and without confidential sources, a truly free press could not exist. If the press is to perform its watchdog function, it is essential for a news organization to use information from those not in a position to identify themselves. But many critics feel that the press misuses confidential sources, particularly in stories where national security issues are at stake.

This country was founded on the principle that the press be free and fearless. The First Amendment to the constitution provides for a press that acts as a fourth branch of government, endowed with the ability to question those in any of the three other branches of government—the executive, the legislative, and the judicial.

When the First Amendment was adopted at the end of the eighteenth century, journalism was very different from what it is today. There was no television, no radio, no photography, no Internet, and no large media companies. Instead, in the broadsheets of that day, there were lots of opinions, and lots of mundane bulletin board material, like lists of when commercial ships were to set sail. But from the start, reporters played their assigned role: they were skeptical of what the government told them, and they questioned official pronouncements.

The framers were insistent that the press be independent, that it provide a check on official action. The press was not supposed to be a cheerleader for actions of government. Many years later, this view was neatly captured by Finley Peter Dunne, who wrote wildly popular, satirical "Mr. Dooley" columns in the early twentieth century that were nationally syndicated. The fictional Dooley was an opinionated, first-generation, Irish American bar owner who criticized the nation and its most powerful people. It was Dooley who thought the duty of a newspaper was to "afflict the comfortable and comfort the afflicted." This comment has been attributed by some writers to Henry Louis Mencken. Thomas Griffith asserts in *The Waist-High Culture* (1959), though, that the phrasing was Dooley's first.

The practice of anonymously leaking information to the press is as old as the country. George Washington often was angered because word-for-word accounts of his Cabinet meetings were published in newspapers of the day. Washington thought his political rival, Thomas Jefferson, was intent on embarrassing him and therefore probably leaked this information. In the nineteenth century, journalists were known to bribe clerks to turn over government documents. The clerks remained anonymous.

Contemporary journalists have a finer sense of propriety; they ordinarily do not bribe anyone. But confidential sources remain the lifeblood of this country's journalism, particularly in Washington, where reporters keenly feel they have an obligation to provide the public with necessary information. If use of confidential sources was prohibited, readers would be cut off from a great deal of information. On the other hand, attributing information to confidential sources is not fully satisfactory, arousing genuine issues about the credibility of the information. It is not possible to gauge the reliability of information if readers do not know its sources. When modern journalists must resort to anonymity, they need to tell readers and viewers as much as possible about their sources, but they often fall short of this goal.

"RELIABLE SOURCES"

For much of the last half of the twentieth century, journalists would almost routinely attribute nonpublic information to "reliable sources." But this formulation was not very helpful. Of course, the source was "reliable." Why else would it be used? This particular locution—"reliable sources"—appears much less frequently these days.

Dangers abound in using—or overusing—anonymous sources: reporters may subject themselves to being manipulated by someone who passes on information for personal gain. Readers may suspect that the anonymous sources just do not exist, and thus undercut the credibility of the press.

The country's best reporters, including those who regularly write about national security issues, almost always rely on well-placed sources who reporters promise not to identify under any circumstances. Sometimes, these sources are whistleblowers, who feel strongly that the public should know about a governmental abuse and would lose their jobs if their identity were disclosed. Reporters, in turn, are generally respectful of genuine national security issues. They do not knowingly publish stories that would endanger lives or affect the security of this country.

Sources rarely are totally altruistic. They usually have their own motives for talking to reporters and for wanting the public to know certain information. In the end, it is probably impossible for journalists to understand these motives and to make judgments based on what these motives are. "My own view is that the law can't and shouldn't distinguish, and I would say journalists can't and shouldn't distinguish between good sources and bad, virtuous sources and unvirtuous ones," says Floyd Abrams, probably the leading First Amendment lawyer in the country. "If a journalist grants confidentiality, I think the journalist has to keep her word."

Probably the most famous anonymous source, W. Mark Felt, was an FBI official who finally disclosed his identity in 2005. Until then, he was known as "Deep Throat," the source who provided invaluable guidance to the *Washington Post*'s Bob Woodward in his reporting on the Watergate scandal with Carl Bernstein. Even though decades had passed, once Felt made his disclosure, some fellow agents thought Felt had committed an outrage in telling government secrets to reporters. Other people felt he was a hero. Felt's motives were complicated. He viewed himself as a patriot. He was also angry that President Richard Nixon had not given him the top job at the FBI. Whatever his motives, his information was invaluable in helping to unseat President Nixon.

The use of anonymous sources—so successful in the *Washington Post*'s reporting on Watergate—had a decided downside. In 1981, Bob Woodward, then an editor, oversaw an article by Janet Cooke, a young reporter who wrote a powerful story about an eight-year-old boy named Jimmy, who was a heroin addict. Neither Woodward nor the other editors insisted on knowing Cooke's source. She had told the editors that the drug supplier would kill the boy if she squealed to her editors. They did not press. Months later, Cooke won a Pulitzer Prize, journalism's highest honor, but her story quickly unraveled. Questions

---

WASHINGTON RULES

In Washington, journalists and sources communicate in their own peculiar, often convoluted way, with their own special terms of art. "On the record" is straightforward and means you can be quoted by name and title. After that, things get murky. In "on background" conversations, officials describe facts and policy in an informal way and are not to be quoted. Materials can be attributed to "senior administration officials." "Deep background" material can be printed only if it is not specifically attributed to anyone. (The story can be couched in terms of "it has been learned that"). Finally, in "off the record" conversations, the information cannot be published, but journalists can only use what they are told to guide their research. They can confirm the information elsewhere.

This system is far from perfect. It can confuse even the most savvy participants. At the I. Lewis "Scooter" Libby trial in 2007, for instance, Libby's press aide, Cathie Martin, testified that he often spoke "off the record" when he really meant "deep background."

---

were raised about false entries on her résumé, and soon after she confessed that "Jimmy" was a fabrication.

That episode led to soul-searching in journalism and the reexamination of how anonymous sources were used. Some news outlets curtailed the use of anonymous sources, but the major news organizations continued to rely on anonymous sources, particularly in national security matters.

CASE STUDY: THE PLAME CASE

For years, the government in power—whether Democrat or Republican—investigated unauthorized leaks of information, usually focusing on the people who leaked the information, not the reporters. Leakers were almost never found. What has changed in recent years is that the government has begun in earnest to look at reporters as well, not necessarily to prosecute them but to have the reporters lead them to the source who gave up classified information.

From 2003 to 2007, two issues, leaks and national security, held center stage in Washington. The dispute began with President Bush's 2003 State of the Union address, in which he claimed that Saddam Hussein had sought to obtain uranium in Africa as part of a campaign to build up weapons of mass destruction. In July 2003, Joseph C. Wilson IV, who had served as acting ambassador to Iraq at the time of the Persian Gulf War in the early 1990s, wrote a pivotal op-ed article for the *New York Times* in which he contradicted what Bush had said in his State of the Union address. Wilson related how the CIA had sent him to Niger in 2002 to figure out whether Iraq had, in fact, sought to purchase uranium ore. Wilson's investigation concluded that there was no credible evidence that Saddam Hussein had made any such effort, and he charged that senior Bush administration officials had distorted intelligence about Iraq's effort to obtain uranium to buttress the case for going to war.

Later that month, Robert Novak, a veteran conservative syndicated columnist, cited two unnamed senior administration sources who told him the selection of Mr. Wilson to conduct this investigation had been pushed by his wife, Valerie Plame, a CIA "operative on weapons of mass destruction." (Years later, Plame appeared before a Congressional committee and sharply disputed that she had any meaningful role in the decision to send her husband to Niger.) Quite possibly, it was felt, a public official had anonymously disclosed the information about Ms. Plame's job in an effort to smear her husband.

President Bush was very public in condemning the leak and he promised to fire anyone involved in the leak. An aggressive special counsel, Patrick J. Fitzgerald, was named to find out which Bush administration officials leaked the identity of Ms. Plame, which might have been a federal crime. In the end, no one was fired.

Karl Rove, Bush's powerful deputy chief of staff, confirmed Ms. Plame's identity to two reporters, but continued in his job.

Ultimately, nobody was criminally charged with knowingly leaking the name of an undercover CIA officer. But I. Lewis "Scooter" Libby, Vice President Dick Cheney's former chief of staff, was convicted of perjury, obstruction of justice and lying to the FBI. He was found guilty of lying about his role in a White House campaign to discredit Wilson, a vocal critic of the Iraq war. Stripped of the complex legal language, Libby's crime was that he had not given a grand jury an accurate version of his conversations with reporters. Libby could have reasonably anticipated that reporters would keep his confidences, as is their custom. But they were pressured by a vigorous prosecutor, and they buckled. At the trial, the chief witnesses against Libby turned out to be reporters who had once used him as a source.

In the course of the investigation of Libby, Judith Miller, then of the *New York Times* and one of the reporters who had used Libby as a source, was subpoenaed. She had indeed discussed the Wilson investigation with Libby, as he had with other reporters, but Miller never wrote a story. In her confidential conversation, she had promised Libby not to disclose who he was. And Libby provided information on the understanding that it could be used so long as he was not named directly. When the prosecutor demanded she discuss that conversation, Miller balked. Upholding the important principle that reporters must protect the identity of confidential sources, she went to jail to protect Libby's identity. Then after 85 days, she was released from jail once Libby explicitly gave her permission to testify—first at the grand jury, then at trial. And eventually that testimony helped to convict Libby of federal charges.

To complicate matters, Miller was a very controversial reporter with a political cloud over her head. She had been singled out by certain critics on the left as someone who had written stories about weapons of mass destruction that were uncritically favorable to the administration in the run up to the invasion of Iraq. However, at the time she was writing, many people, including Saddam's own generals, felt that the Iraqi leader had weapons of mass destruction.

Months after she was released, in a television interview, Miller said: "Going to jail for me was not a career move, not a career enhancement move. Going to jail was something I felt I had to do. I didn't want to do it. I hadn't sought a confrontation with the government. I'd never written anything. It was a question of principle and conscience. And whatever anyone else said, in a way, was irrelevant to me. It was painful. It was extremely painful for my friends and family. But I knew why I was in jail. And I knew that I was in jail for a cause that I thought was essential to our profession. So I was very comfortable with the decision. But was it painful? Yes. Was it disappointing? Yes. Was it infuriating? Yes. It's journalism."

As principled as Miller thought her cause, she was unable to explain to the broader public why her resistance to the government served a noble purpose. What Miller's travails showed was that if journalism, particularly in Washington, must be an insider's game, journalists then need to explain their role more convincingly.

See also Bias and Objectivity; Government Censorship and Freedom of Speech; Journalists in Peril; Media and Electoral Campaigns; Media Watch Groups; Presidential Stagecraft and Militainment.

Further Reading: Griffith, Thomas. *The Waist-High Culture.* New York: Harper and Brothers, 1959; Kovach, Bill, and Tom Rosenstiel. *The Elements of Journalism.* New York: Crown Publishers, 2001; Lippmann, Walter. *Public Opinion.* New York: Free Press Paperbacks, 1997; Manoff, Robert Karl, and Michael Schudson, eds. *Reading the News.* New York: Pantheon, 1986; Starr, Paul. *The Creation of the Media: Political Origins of Modern Communications.* New York: Basic Books, 2004; Wilson, Joseph. *The Politics of Truth: A Diplomat's Memoir: Inside the Lies that Led to War and Betrayed My Wife's CIA Identity.* New York: Carroll and Graf, 2004.

Tom Goldstein

AUDIENCE POWER TO RESIST

Educators, policy makers, and parents worry about the negative effects of the media. Blaming the media for eating disorders, violence, sexuality, profanity, war, sexism, racism, homophobia, hedonistic consumerism, and seemingly all other imaginable ills is a common occurrence. But to what degree can we as audience members resist the messages that bombard us daily? Surely, not all who watch a sexist television program, for instance, walk away sexist. In this battleground issue, many believe the opposite, that audience members are not so easily influenced and have the power to resist violent, antisocial messages, and unhealthy persuasion. Is attacking the media a way of avoiding, as some say, engaging with lack of social and economic equality, and other problems equally as responsible for the social ills that are too easily blamed on the media?

MEDIA EFFECTS

Media messages hold remarkable power to normalize certain behavior, to render other behavior "deviant" or abnormal, and to lead us toward or away from certain beliefs and frames of mind with their emotive, narrative, and/or informational allure. Given its scope of coverage, the mass media have unrivalled abilities to project images and ideas to a vast number of citizens, a talent or curse that has been praised and feared since the advent of mass media.

At the same time, however, all too often the media become a scapegoat when deeper social problems afflict a society or individual: thus, for instance, blaming school shootings and other violent crimes on gory horror films, violent video games, and countercultural music is much easier than inquiring into the complex social realities that lead to a youth going on a killing rampage. As such, the allegation of media responsibility can sometimes erase the apparent need for personal and societal responsibility, with the abstract "media" serving as a catch-all for societal problems, and a red herring for causational analysis.

Similarly, allegations of media effects risk posing the notion of an unthinking, easily influenced mass of media consumers. Media effects discourse has often been criticized for underestimating the mental capacities of youth and children in particular, but also for a patriarchal elitism that frequently posits women and the "uneducated" working classes as easily influenced, with images of screaming teenage pop music fans, obsessed soap opera fans, and high school dropouts who believe anything the television says, working to assure the rest of us that we are a sage, enlightened group. Many allegations of media effects therefore mask culturally based attacks on taste, whereby it is *others'* media that worry us, not our own.

The fact is, though, that many media messages are far less persuasive. If media messages were more successful, and if media audiences were as gullible as some critics contend, complaints from the advertising industry of the difficulty of persuading consumers would be nonexistent. Instead, after any television ad break, all viewers would feel the need to buy everything advertised and we would similarly feel the need to wear everything we see stars wearing, and to behave exactly as our favorite film and television characters behave. The absence of "total effects," and the complex nature of media effects is further illustrated when millions of high schoolers who watch gory horror films, play violent video games, and listen to countercultural music, for instance, exhibit no need or desire to engage in mass murder. Many audience members resist thousands of media messages weekly.

THE "ACTIVE AUDIENCE"

Belief in the freedom of audiences to read against the grain of media messages came to a head with the work of media theorist John Fiske. Fiske posed that audiences are "active," by which he meant that we *actively* make sense of all that we consume, thinking through what the messages mean, choosing what to accept and what to reject, rather than watching *passively*, mindlessly accepting everything that comes our way, as if the media injected their messages into us with a virtual hypodermic needle. Whereas a belief in media effects looks at the construction of a message, and then its journey to the consumer via a process that oftentimes suggests that the consumer is a mere receptacle, a belief in active audiences looks at the consumer first, as an individual who approaches a media message with certain desires and needs, thus suggesting that individuals have control over media messages, not vice versa.

The process of media consumption can also be seen as communal and social, not just individual. Thus, instead of seeing both media message and consumer as isolated in a vacuum together, we should realize that many messages are discussed afterwards (or beforehand), thereby subjecting them to scrutiny. Many studies of media effects find that effects are strongest immediately following consumption, meaning that when audience members stop to talk or think about media messages, the effects often diminish. Media effects studies are also often conducted in artificial environments, hence overlooking the corrective effects of familial or friend discussion and debriefing. Media literacy helps us to see the strategies and patterns behind media messages, and with so much everyday talk being about the media, we often share our media literacy with others, ensuring a greater level of media savvy overall. Precisely because so many individuals fear media effects, therefore, warnings of the media surround us, encouraging us to be wary in general, but also offering specific strategies for reading against the grain in particular. Some of these warnings are offered by the media themselves, as good parody and satire. Some in particular operate as media literacy primers on media genres, as does *The Daily Show with Jon Stewart* with the news, or *The Simpsons* with the family sitcom.

Also, as consumers, we are capable of enjoying a media message without wholly agreeing with it. Some television programs, for instance, have intriguing characters, are filmed in attractive and artistic ways, and/or examine places of considerable interest. But we can like one part of a program and dislike another, loving the "look" of a show, say, but dismissing its politics, or loving one character yet despising another. All of us no doubt have had the experience of falling in love with a song whose lyrics elude us, an experience that illustrates how easily media messages can be parsed and divided. Even fans, then—those consumers who seem most obviously passive—are often active, thoughtful, and/or discriminating readers, viewers, and listeners.

AN EXAMPLE: CULTURAL IMPERIALISM

A particular example of the debate over media consumption and audience power can be found with regards to the suggestion that American media are a "cultural imperialist," Americanizing the planet and socializing the youth of the world to yearn for all things American. American media have a foreign presence like no other national media, their music, films, and television dominating many foreign markets. But some argue that non-Americans are free to resist the messages of American ideology embedded in so many of these global media messages, and that to argue otherwise is to belittle the intelligence of foreign

---

TELEVISION WITHOUT PITY (www.televisionwithoutpity.com)

Considerable evidence of active audience behavior can be found at the Web site Television Without Pity. The site offers hundreds of discussion boards on new and old television series, and postings from site moderators and from the site's thousands of posters frequently approach the programs from a satiric, critical angle. Thus, amidst the many professions of idolatry of other shows, one finds *Are You Hot?* described as having "telegraphed more like a slave auction than something sexy and fun to watch" and *Just Legal* is said to have been "a wreck from the first fifteen seconds of the pilot, and it only got worse from there." Even posters who follow a program closely, clearly enjoying it, prove ready, willing, and able to share frustrations with gender or race depictions, overt and gaudy consumerism, and with its politics, or simply to mock unrealistic events and characterization, or transparent attempts by a show's writers to create emotion and pathos. Television Without Pity serves as a running dialogue between viewers and television, one that illustrates the many complex interactions between consumer and media.

---

consumers. Researchers Elihu Katz and Tamar Liebes, for instance, found that Arab viewers of *Dallas* enjoyed the television program, yet rejected outright its glorification of American capitalism, seeing the program instead as an illustration of all that is wrong with American capitalism, and seeing its characters as immoral. Sometimes, then, messages can "boomerang," swinging back on themselves. The ultrapatriotic film *Independence Day* remains one of the global box office's all-time champions, but viewers from Vancouver to Hong Kong reported audiences cheering the scene in which aliens destroy the White House, suggesting the degree to which audiences can empathize with various figures in a media narrative, and can actively read against the narrative's interests.

LIMITATIONS OF THE ACTIVE AUDIENCE APPROACH

However, the example of American media overseas also highlights the limitations of active audience theory. First of all, while international viewers may have rejected *Dallas* and *Independence Day*, they were still stuck with the shows. We might be able to read against a media message, but that gives us no power in and of itself to create a new or better message. Thus, we should never romanticize reading against the grain as an "answer" to problematic messages. Nationally chauvinist, racist, sexist, or other detrimental messages are best challenged by messages that are not detrimental, and as powerful an act as the deflection of detrimental messages can be, such an act does not create better messages. With the news, for instance, we might sense that coverage is biased, but in the absence of alternative coverage, we are left with only the biased account.

Second, reading against the grain can prove tiring. Many of us turn on the television or our CD player, go to a movie, or buy a book or magazine in order to relax. In such situations, it is often *easier* to read with the grain. While all of us are capable of "active" viewing, and while all of us *are* active viewers at some point, the experience of being a *passive* viewer is often sought out and relished. At certain times, we might "forget" to be active, or might go along with a media message merely because we are not in the mood to fight it.

Ultimately, it is helpful to view media effects as akin to the sowing of seeds. Seeds—or messages—are scattered liberally on the ground—or audience. Many seeds will fail to grow, but others will flourish. What makes the media powerful is not that they regularly convince all viewers to follow their messages, for this is rarely if ever the case. Rather, the media are powerful because occasional seeds do grow. To become confused and believe that all seeds grow is foolish, but we would be equally foolish to assume that simply because many seeds die on the ground, therefore *all* seeds perish. For example, many listeners may dismiss a racist song as vile, but its power lies with the few listeners who take it to heart.

AUDIENCE REBELLION

Beyond simply fighting a media message in the act of consumption, audiences can also mobilize themselves in ways that speak back to media creators. Peggy Charren's successful initiative to start a parents advocacy group, Action for Children's Television, ended in pushing Congress to introduce legislation that limited advertising in children's television programming; Christian groups have boycotted films or television programs into financial death; and Bill Maher's *Politically Incorrect* was forced off the air in 2002 after his controversial comments concerning the 9/11 terrorist attacks led to a threatened boycott of his show's advertisers. On one hand, media producers have often proven remarkably indifferent to their everyday consumers' requests, but on the other hand, many media corporations live in constant fear of offending highly mobilized consumer groups (as with the Christian Right through such groups as Focus on the Family), and thus self-censor in order to avoid audience rebellion.

To some, the most obvious and effective form of audience rebellion would entail turning off the television, radio, CD player, and so forth. However, avoiding the media proves increasingly hard in a mediated world, and with all the information and entertainment that we receive from the media, to mix metaphors, a "cold turkey" approach risks throwing out the baby with the bathwater. Moreover, going cold turkey still leaves the messages there for other consumers. As such, the continuing challenge for consumers will be to navigate through the media in ways that expose them to their better messages, yet with viewing strategies, awareness, and media literacy to avoid and/or see through the detrimental ones.

In the meantime, any discussion of media effects must remember that media consumption never happens in a blank setting: rather, we approach any act of consumption in a certain place, with a certain mindset, perhaps with a certain group, and all of these variables change the nature of our interaction with the media. Media effects are never just about messages and about the media: they are also about the complex history of the audience, and all study of media effects therefore requires close study of the audience.

See also Celebrity Worship and Fandom; Children and Effects; Communication Rights in a Global Context; Cultural Appropriation; Cultural Imperialism and Hybridity; Media Literacy; Media Reform; User-Created Content and Audience Participation; Violence and Media; Women's Magazines; Youth and Media Use.

Further Reading: Bird, S. Elizabeth. *The Audience in Everyday Life: Living in a Media World.* New York: Routledge, 2003; Brooker, Will, and Deborah Jermyn, eds. *The Audience Studies Reader.* New York: Routledge, 2002; Condit, Celeste. "The Rhetorical Limits of Polysemy." In *Television: The Critical View,* 5th ed., ed. Horace Newcomb. New York: Oxford University Press, 1994; Fiske, John. *Television Culture.* New York: Routledge, 1987; Fiske, John. *Understanding Popular Culture.* New York: Routledge, 1989; Gillespie, Marie. *Media Audiences.* Milton Keynes, UK: Open University Press, 2006; Jenkins, Henry. *Textual Poachers: Television Fans and Participating Culture.* New York: Routledge, 1992; Katz, Elihu, and Tamar Liebes. *The Export of Meaning: Cross-Cultural Readings of Dallas.* Cambridge: Polity, 1994; Morley, David. *Television, Audiences and Cultural Studies.* New York: Routledge, 1992; Ross, Karen, and Virginia Nightingale. *Media and Audiences: New Perspectives.* Milton Keynes, UK: Open University Press, 2003.

Jonathan Gray

B

BIAS AND OBJECTIVITY

Citizens who live in a democracy depend on the news media to help them stay informed about the world and the important issues that affect their lives. Reliable information goes to the core of the democratic process. Citizens make decisions, vote, and take actions based on the information they receive from the press. Journalism articulates a set of standards and practices that establish a professional commitment to neutrality and balance in relation to the people and events reported in the media. The idea of objectivity is a central ethos of journalism, acknowledging reporters' commitment to disseminating unbiased news and information. At the same time, by articulating professional canons and declaring the goals of objectivity, legitimacy and credibility are conferred upon the profession. The role of the press is central to Western enlightenment values, and the journalistic standard of objectivity is acquiring new global significance as reporters seek different roles and institutional supports within formerly Communist and authoritarian regimes. Whether objectivity can be realized in practice, however, or whether it is a useful concept for attaining the information goals of a democracy, remain debatable questions.

WHAT IS OBJECTIVITY IN REPORTING?

News reporting in the pursuit of truth without fear or favor is undoubtedly a positive value. Few reporters would want to be considered unable or unwilling to produce accurate, unbiased news accounts for citizens of democracies who need to make informed judgments about public affairs. But in an age when journalism, with increasing frequency, is criticized for biased and unfair reporting, it appears that the matter of objectivity is not so clear cut. Under scrutiny, the concept of objectivity has been found to lack a clear definition. In fact, it seems to have many meanings and is often interpreted differently by journalists themselves. One research team, Wolfgang Donsbach and Bettina Klett, found at least four different ways that working journalists defined objectivity. In some cases, it is seen as the negation of subjectivity; the proscription that journalists keep their own ideas, interpretations and opinions out of a story. In another definition, an objective story is one that includes fair representations of each side in a controversy. Another way journalists identify the practice, is the need to adopt an attitude of balanced skepticism towards all sides in a dispute. Some journalists think of objectivity as the inclusion of facts to contextualize an issue.

While seeking an authoritative definition that illuminates the practice and concept, it becomes clear that objectivity is actually multifaceted and should be defined as an interrelated complex of ideas and practices. Objectivity seems to provide journalists and the public alike with a general model for conceiving of and evaluating news stories and reports. It also describes news institutions and their newsgathering and disseminating strategies. For an inclusive definition, it is important to understand that objectivity is no one thing, but a socially constructed concept that delineates complex professional practices. Robert Hackett and Yuezhi Zhao suggest that such an "objectivity regime" must be identified on several levels or dimensions. First, objectivity comprises the goals that journalists and their editors strive for. Referring to the work of Denis McQuail, these can be divided into values concerning journalism's ability to impart information about the world. Such information must separate fact from opinion, and it must be accurate and complete. It also describes a set of values concerning the stance reporters should take towards the value-laden meanings of news. These values are identified as detachment, neutrality, impartiality and independence, avoiding partisanship, personal biases, ulterior motives, or outside interests.

In addition to values and responsibilities, journalism professor W. Lance Bennett has noted that the concept of objectivity also embodies a set of newsgathering and presentational techniques, such as "documentary reporting practices." The separation of hard news from commentary allows news reporters to transmit only "facts" that they can observe or that "credible" sources have confirmed. These practices are graphically illustrated in the pages of newspapers when they separate factual reporting from the opinion pieces in the editorial section.

Objectivity is also part of the embedded institutional framework of complex news organizations with legal protections. The media, particularly the news media, function under legal guarantees of free speech designed to insure independence from the state. Such protections have come to assume a degree of professionalism with regard to conduct and appropriate skills. In addition, though most news organizations are part of larger profit-seeking corporate conglomerates, the concept of objective journalism within this institutional framework assumes the separation of editorial and marketing functions within news divisions.

Finally, objectivity is an active ingredient in public discourse. It provides the language for everyday assessments of journalistic performance. This language includes synonyms, such as "fairness" and "balance," which some people see as more flexible and achievable substitutes for objectivity. Objectivity is often counterposed to "bias," most frequently partisan or political bias; arguments have also been advanced that media representations embody technological, gender or cultural biases.

HISTORICAL ROOTS OF OBJECTIVITY

Just as trying to define objectivity is complicated, tracing its historical trajectory is equally complex, and at times the subject of debate, especially with regard to its emergence in American journalism. As an ideal, objectivity is neither universal nor timeless, and has emerged in specific historical, political and cultural contexts.

Geopolitically, adherence to objectivity is more typical of journalism in the United States, Britain, and Canada than in continental Europe, with its stronger tradition of partisanship in the press, or in theocratic or authoritarian regimes, where journalism is mandated to serve the state and/or an official ideology. In the Middle East, Al-Jazeera, broadcasting out of Qatar, challenge traditional reporting from authoritarian regimes, but evoked the ire of the United States with alternative representations of the war on terror. Even where it is most entrenched, the objectivity regime is more characteristic of some news media (such as the "quality" press, public service broadcasting, news reports) than others (such as tabloid newspapers, entertainment-oriented television, opinion columns).

Historically, objectivity as a paradigm in Anglo-American journalism displaced explicit partisanship during the nineteenth and early twentieth centuries. Media scholar, Dan Schiller sees the roots of objectivity in the democratic discourse of universal natural rights in the nineteenth-century labor press. A more conventional view links objectivity's origins to the emergence of technology (photography, the telegraph) and associated organizational forms (news wire services, the "inverted pyramid" form of reporting) that appeared to capture reality. The emergence of advertising for mass markets contributed greatly to the decline of the partisan press; nonpartisan "objective" journalism enabled newspapers to pursue the broadest possible readership, and thus advertising revenue.

Cultural currents and historical events also contributed to the formulation of objectivity as a value. Mitchell Stephens traces the roots of objectivity to "reverence for facts," and the development of the scientific method in the late nineteenth century. A significant turning point for journalism occurred after the First World War. Modern war propaganda influenced public support for war, and the carnage left in its wake compelled scholars, commentators, and social scientists alike to reevaluate the role and practices of the press. The rise of the new public relations industry, Freudian psychology, historically unprecedented totalitarian regimes in Europe, and the Great Depression, all contributed by the 1930s to a culture's loss of confidence in the reliability of the press, the rationality of citizens, and the viability of liberal-democratic capitalism. Objectivity in North American journalism became more narrowly and technically defined as certain types of "factual" statements, rather than a universalizing discourse of truth in the public interest.

Over the next few decades other reporting approaches, such as interpretive reporting, adversarial/critical journalism, and enterprise reporting have been developed that sometimes questioned the values of objectivity. Those alternative models and competing styles that once seemed to directly challenge the objectivity regime, however, have generally been contained or marginalized by the regime.

DEBATES OVER OBJECTIVITY: EPISTEMOLOGICAL AND POLITICAL CRITIQUES

Underlying various critiques and defenses of journalism objectivity are contending epistemologies, or different models for understanding the relationship between the texts of news reports, and the reality they seek to describe. *Positivism,* once a dominant position in Western thought, was firmly based in the European Enlightenment's confidence in scientific method, rationality and progress. It asserts the possibility of accurate descriptions of the world-as-it-is, through the careful observation of events, perceivable through the senses. Positivism underlies the commonsense criticism of news that it should be objective and accurate, but often is not, due to various factors that introduce "bias" in reporting. Often, conservative critics cite the presumed "left-liberal" political views of journalists, an interpretation of news bias common in the United States, but less so in other Western liberal democracies; it is a view that has in turn been criticized for intellectual inconsistency and for its assumption that journalists themselves are primarily responsible for news agendas. Others argue that a variety of organizational and institutional factors, such as the demand for ratings-boosting stories shape the news. Herman and Chomsky have countered the liberal bias model with a contrary view that sees news as failing to obtain objectivity due to the "conservatizing" pressure of powerful elites, such as media owners, advertisers, governments, and/or official sources. This view has also been criticized as paying insufficient attention to the institutional autonomy of journalism and the full range of external influences operating on the news. Many point to the increasing influence of the public relations industry that promotes stories for both private and commercial interests.

If these critiques rest on the epistemological assumptions of positivism, a contrary epistemological position is evident in recent social theory, in trends that emphasize the importance of language or "discourse" in shaping human understanding of reality. *Conventionalism* holds that human perception of the world is always mediated by our mental categories and our procedures of knowledge production. In this view, news reporting is as much a construction of the social world, as a reflection of it; objective journalism cannot live up to its ideal, because knowledge of the world independent from the standpoint of the observer is impossible. Claims to achieving objectivity in the news, then, must be regarded as assertions of the power to define reality, rather than legitimate claims to have accurate knowledge of it. In the view of its critics, however, this epistemological position tends towards a self-contradictory relativism, which sees no independent way to assess the truth-value of competing news accounts or discourses. Some analysts argue that this position leaves journalists with no mandate or motivation to attempt to distinguish between truth and propaganda.

A third epistemology, *critical realism,* avoids both positivism's l faith in superficial facts, and conventionalism's dead-end relativism. Knowledge of the real is possible, it asserts, but only through engaging in the work of theorizing, and exploring the structures and processes that underlie individual events. From this standpoint, news reporting may be criticized not because objectivity is impossible in principle, or because individual journalists or news reports have departed from the (otherwise desirable and achievable) standards of objectivity but because the structures and procedures of actually existing journalism constitute a deficient *form* of objectivity. This standpoint offers some sophisticated critiques of the objectivity regime as generating, paradoxically, *ideological* accounts of the world, accounts that are partial and one-sided, or that reinforce existing relations of power. One line of critique suggests that objectivity serves to disguise the value assumptions and commitments that unavoidably influence the selection and presentation, the framing, of news reports. Reports may quote "both sides" in a controversy, thus appearing to be balanced and impartial while at the same time confining the definition of what is at issue, and marginalizing other perspectives. Thus, U.S. television reports of the Iraq war policy often feature Democratic and Republican party leaders criticizing each other, while leaving unexamined their shared assumption that what is at stake is how to achieve victory or reduce American casualties, rather than, for example, reducing Iraqi suffering or strengthening international law.

RECENT CHALLENGES AND CONTEXTS

Arguably, objectivity has remained a dominant norm in North American journalism during much of the past century because it has served a variety of functions and interests. Because objectivity allows press reporting to appear as if it does not favor one opinion over another, it is able to amass broad audiences. The proclamation of professional standards provides political legitimacy for the monopoly press, and by simply presenting the voices of different politicians, the claim to objectivity helps define and manage the relationship between reporters and their political sources. Journalism scholar Gaye Tuchman's seminal work detailed how objectivity enhances journalists' claim to professionalism, and constitutes a "strategic ritual" that protect them from such hazards as lawsuits and editors' reprimands.

Yet current developments in the political economy of news media are potentially undermining the objectivity regime. The internet facilitates the diffusion of opinion and personal experience, blurs the distinction between producers and audiences, and bypasses journalists as professional gatekeepers. The deregulation of broadcasting and the relative decline of public service broadcasting have intensified commercial pressures since the 1980s. Channel proliferation has fragmented audiences, and more and more conventional media are owned by conglomerates seeking high and immediate profits. Consequences arguably include the erosion of the universalizing stance of objectivity, and the decline of public affairs information in the conventional news media, and conversely, the rise of opinionated pundits, politically partisan media, such as Fox News in the United States, and infotainment.

Contrary to the objectivity norm, recent reform movements within journalism have called for the explicit pursuit of specified goals. In the United States, civic journalism challenges reporters to abandon the stance of detachment in favor of reinvigorating public political life. Internationally, and particularly in strife-torn countries such as Indonesia, the Philippines and Rwanda, practitioners and educators critique conventional news reportage of conflicts as tantamount to "war journalism" that too often exacerbates violence. For scholars Jake Lynch and Annabel McGoldrick, who articulate an alternative notions of peace journalism, far from being neutral observers, journalists are caught in a feedback loop with political players; and the ethos of objectivity, with its emphasis on official sources, two-sided conflict, and events rather than processes, impedes a morally and professionally justifiable incentivization of peaceful outcomes. Critics such as Thomas Hanitzsch however, dismiss peace journalism as another form of advocacy, usurping what should be the role of public relations.

In the Anglo-American heartland, faith in objective reporting may be eroding, but no single norm or regime has emerged to supplant it. Meanwhile, in many non-Western "transition societies," objectivity may be gaining a new lease on life under the impact of media globalization, and as an alternative to the state-oriented authoritarianism of the past.

See also Al-Jazeera; Alternative Media in the United States; Anonymous Sources, Leaks, and National Security; Blogosphere; Conglomerates and Media Monopolies; Disabilities and the Media; Embedding Journalists; Hypercommercialism; Journalists in Peril; Media and Citizenship; Narrative Power and Media Influence; National Public Radio; Paparazzi and Photographic Ethics; Parachute Journalism; Presidential Stagecraft and Militainment; Public Broadcasting Service; Public Sphere; Sensationalism, Fear Mongering and Tabloid Media; Representations of Women; Video News Releases.

Further Reading: Bennett, W. Lance. *News: The Politics of Illusion.* 6th ed. New York: Pearson, 2005; Donsbach, Wolfgang, and Klett, Bettina. "Subjective Objectivity: How Journalists in Four Countries Define a Key Term of Their Profession." *Gazette,* 51, (1993): 53–83; Hackett, Robert A., and Zhao, Yuezhi. *Sustaining Democracy? Journalism and the Politics Objectivity.* Toronto: Garamond, 1998; Hallin, Daniel. *The 'Uncensored War': The Media and Vietnam.* Berkeley: University of California Press, 1989; Hanitzsch, Thomas. "Journalists as Peacekeeping Force? Peace Journalism and Mass Communication Theory." *Journalism Studies,* 5 (2004): 483–95; Herman, Edward, and Noam Chomsky. *Manufacturing Consent: The Political Economy of the Mass Media.* New York: Pantheon, 1988; Lichtenberg, Judith. "In Defence of Objectivity Revisited." In *Mass Media and Society,* 3rd ed., ed. James Curran and Michael Gurevitch, 238–254. London: Arnold,

2000; Lovell, Terry. *Pictures of Reality: Aesthetics, Politics and Pleasure*. London: British Film Institute, 1980; Lynch, Jake, and McGoldrick, Annabel. *Peace Journalism*. Stroud, United Kingdom: Hawthorn, 2005; McChesney, Robert. *The Problem of the Media*. New York: Monthly Review Press, 2004; McQuail, Denis. *Media Performance: Mass Communication and the Public Interest*. London: Sage, 1992; Norris, Christopher. *Uncritical Theory: Postmodernism, Intellectuals and the Gulf War*. London: Lawrence and Wishart, 1992; Schiller, Dan. *Objectivity and the News*. Philadelphia: University of Pennsylvania Press, 1981; Schudson, Michael. *Discovering the News: A Social History of American Newspapers*. New York: Basic Books, 1978; Stephens, Mitchell. *A History of News: From the Drum to the Satellite*. New York: Penguin, 1988; Tuchman, Gaye. "Objectivity as Strategic Ritual: An Examination of Newsmen's Notions of Objectivity." *American Journal of Sociology*, 77 (1972): 660–79.

Robert A. Hackett

BLOGOSPHERE: POLITICS AND INTERNET JOURNALISM

Today's blogs reflect a style of politics and the press that was a major force in American society almost to the time of the Civil War. At the same time, they are showing how quickly and effectively new technologies can be used to affect contemporary affairs. Certainly, since the start of the 2004 presidential campaign, the blogs have become an increasingly important part of the American political landscape.

BACKGROUND

Over the last quarter of the twentieth century, both news media and political organizations in America became more and more centralized, the former to the point where they were associated almost exclusively with New York City, the latter with Washington, DC. Technological innovations, particularly in the area of communications, made it more financially attractive to consolidate ownership of news media operations and allowed political leaders to remain in close touch with supporters a long distance away. Though more efficient, these changes also led to increased alienation from both news media and politics on the part of the average American.

At the same time, the debates of the nation began to be used by the news media for ratings. No longer were they as interested in the quest for solution. Both politicians and the news media participated in this, the politicians to stake out a definable public image and the news media defining the debates as entertainment, looking for continued conflict (and, therefore, continued viewership) instead of progress toward resolution. Much of this left the public decidedly cold.

When the blogs appeared, they provided a link back to another era of American politics and journalism, a time of direct popular participation in both, but one that began to disappear as the Civil War approached. In the early years of the American republic, newspaper editors were directly involved in the political process. In fact, their newspapers were the networks that allowed for the creation of political parties. At that time, journalism, as the distinct profession known today, did not exist; certainly, there were no guidelines for ethical behavior on the part of the press. So, the articles that appeared ranged from scurrilous attacks all the way to the most considered reflection—and sometimes by the same author.

The political press of that early era died out as newspapers became commercial products that needed to distance themselves from politics in order to assure the widest possible circulation, and as journalists began to see theirs as a special mission framed by the First Amendment's "freedom of the press" guarantee, something that had earlier been considered only as a protection of open political expression, but that had evolved into a right for the new and distinct "fourth estate."

The desire to be directly involved in the debates in the press, however, did not disappear even as it became increasingly difficult for individuals to find voice

---

"FREQUENTLY ASKED QUESTIONS" AT DAILY KOS

Who posts here?

The quick answer is "anyone who wants to." There are a wide variety of people writing diaries and comments on dkos. They include elected politicians, candidates hoping to become elected politicians, experts in a range of fields, and active bloggers from around the net. The vast majority of writers, however, are ordinary citizens interested in talking about and participating in the political process. The majority of people posting here fall on the liberal side of the US political spectrum, however people of conservative views are welcome to come and debate. If you are polite, you will be treated politely. Unfortunately, there are some people who post comments or diaries with the sole purpose of provoking others. These people are called trolls. Some tips and techniques for dealing with trolls are described below. . . .

Diaries

Most of the action takes place inside of diaries. These are written by users, and then read and commented on by other users. . . . Most diaries appear in the Recent Diary list on the right-hand side of the screen. By default, this shows the last 20 diaries that have been posted; this can be reset as high as 50 diaries using the field at the bottom of the list. People reading diaries can recommend them (see below). If a diary receives enough recommendations, it will automatically be promoted to the Recommended Diary list, which sits above the Recent Diary list. Recommended diaries tend to attract a wider audience and more comments than most diaries. The length of time that a diary spends on the Recommended list depends on how many users recommend it; it can vary from a few minutes to more than one full day. Diaries moving to the Recommended list is a democratic process; the diaries on the list are the ones that received the most "votes" to be there.

From Daily Kos, http://www.dkosopedia.com/wiki/DailyKos_FAQ, one of the premier political group blogs.

---

in newspapers. Just so, the craving to participate in political debates remained intact, though the debates were removed to distant locations. Not surprisingly, then, when the blogs appeared, they provided an outlet for pent-up energies and emotions—expanding, as a result, with a vigor that surprised almost everyone, but particularly those politicians and members of the press who had become increasingly distant from the American population.

WHAT IS A BLOG?

A blog (from "Web log") is an interactive Web page that allows an individual to post entries that are immediately available for viewing (and, sometimes, for comment) on the World Wide Web. Blogs evolved from online bulletin boards where people could participate in "conversations" through posts and responses. One main difference from the "bulletin boards" is that anyone can create their own blog, and for free (unless they want a fancier one), controlling both look and access. Another is that the blogs tend to be more flexible and responsive to the individual than earlier forums for Internet discussion.

People blog on all sorts of topics, but the best-known blogs tend to be those concerned with political issues. The most popular of all are the group political blogs, where anyone can join, presenting their own diaries and commenting on the diaries of others. In general, these tend to attract the like-minded—one of the greatest criticisms of them is that they tend to stifle debate within them by hounding out those (often called "trolls") whose viewpoints are different from the mainstream of the particular blog. Because of their real similarities, political blogs, whether right wing or left, were soon referred to in the commercial news media as "the blogs" rather than simply as blogs, giving them a sense of being a single, coherent force which, in fact, they never have been.

FREE REPUBLIC

Who reads FR?

Over 200,000 people have registered for posting privileges on Free Republic since inception in 1996 and our forum is read daily by tens of thousands of concerned citizens and patriots from all around the country and all around the world. Oh, we're big stuff all right....

Who runs Free Republic?

Free Republic, LLC is a non-commercial, limited liability company founded and operated by Jim Robinson, a private citizen of Fresno California.

Free Republic is not a for profit commercial enterprise in the sense of a traditional business selling a product or service at a profit for its shareholders. We sell no product or service. We have no clients, customers or employees. We do not accept paid advertising. Free Republic is not affiliated with any political party, group, news source, government agency or anyone else.

Supporters of the Blogs

Many political bloggers see their movement as a "netroots" or grassroots movement that is trying to wrest political control from the "inside the beltway" politicians of Washington,

DC and as a "citizen journalist" movement to connect the press back to the general population. They consider theirs an anti-elitist movement in a long tradition of American populism. They point to declining voter turnout and a general dissatisfaction with the news media as the results of increasing centralization in both the political and journalistic arenas and claim that the blogs are a central tool for turning these trends around.

Of importance to the blog movement is the concept of "amateurism." Though there are media and political professionals who blog, much of the success of blogging comes from the amateurs, people whose passions, and not their careers, have brought them into this new arena. They feel that the careerist agendas of the professionals keep them from responding to the real needs and desires of the population and eventually separate them off, creating a modern elite that has very little understanding of the American people.

The defenders of the blogs see them as a means of revitalizing a nearly moribund American political system, one that includes the political parties and the news media that cover them. They feel that the blogs will bring more and more people into political activity and will create a new cadre of "citizen journalists," people who care enough about a particular issue to investigate it carefully and then present their findings on their blogs. They feel they are reclaiming politics and the news media from forces that moved them away from their traditional American base within the general public.

From the home page of Free Republic, http://www.freerepublic.com/home.htm.

DOUBTERS OF THE BLOGS

In the more established quarters of political and news media power, many see the blogs as an intrusion by the unlearned and unskilled. In addition, in the eyes of many journalists, the very fact of writing for an audience demands adherence to certain ethical standards—one is not able to say whatever one wants in a public journalistic arena if one wants to be considered an ethical journalist. Instead, one must strive for "balance," walking a line between any two sides of an issue and treating all opinions with respect. In addition, according to these journalists, one must leave one's politics at the door, reporting with candor and "objectivity."

The belief in these kind of journalistic ethics has been growing and evolving since the time of the "penny press" before the Civil War, when newspaper editors started to distance themselves from the politics they covered. It was expressed most forcefully several generations later by Adolph S. Ochs on taking control of the *New York Times* in 1894. On August 18, 1896, he wrote, "It will be my earnest aim that the *New York Times* give the news, all the news, in concise and attractive form, in language that is parliamentary in good society, and...to give the news impartially, without fear or favor, regardless of party, sect, or interests involved." Belief in such an attitude was solidified in electronic media through the influence of Edward R. Murrow of CBS News in the 1940s and 1950s.

To someone attempting to follow in the footsteps of Ochs and Murrow, the blogs, with their overtly partisan and sometimes quite vituperative attacks and commentaries, seem an affront to good journalism, debasing an entire profession simply by their proximity. Buried in an avalanche of blogs, these people fear, audiences may no longer recognize "good" journalism when they see it. Therefore, they either attack the blogs as a whole or try to find a way of channeling them into a more traditional framework.

Another criticism of the blogs is that they are available to only one side of the digital divide. That is, because they require the use of technology both for participation and for reading, they are open only to those with access generally associated with a certain degree of wealth. Liberal bloggers came under criticism in September 2006 when a meeting was arranged between a group of them and former President Bill Clinton in his offices in Harlem, an historically African American neighborhood in New York City. The bloggers who attended were all white and middle class, pointing out the fact that the blogs have become a forum for few from minority communities and even fewer from amongst the poor.

A BLOGGING SUCCESS

One of the most significant aspects of the blogs is their ability to keep alive (or even bring alive) a story that the commercial news media have overlooked. The first of these to have a significant political result was sparked by the comments of Trent Lott at a celebration of the 100th birthday of former "Dixicrat" Strom Thurmond. Lott's comments were seen by many bloggers as having distinct racist overtones—and they refused to let the matter die, though it remained unreported by most of the news media.

Because of other connections between Lott and questionable organizations and stances concerning race, many of them brought to light and mentioned repeatedly by bloggers, the commercial news media did eventually begin to cover the story. No matter how much Lott tried to quell it, the controversy continued to grow, to the point where President Bush felt he needed to comment on it, chastising Lott. Soon thereafter, Lott resigned his position in the Republican leadership as Senate majority leader and the outrage died down.

A BLOG TIMELINE

February 1978—The first Bulletin Board System (BBS) is established: the Computerized Bulletin Board System of Chicago.

1978—CompuServe begins first real-time chat.

1985—The WELL, one of the first significant dial-up BBSs, goes online.

1994—First Web logs appear.

April 1999—Peter Merholz coins the word "blog."

May 2002—Daily Kos, the largest political blog, is founded.

December 2002—Mississippi Senator Trent Lott's possibly racist comments on retiring Senator Strom Thurmond are publicized by bloggers, forcing his eventual resignation as Senate Majority Leader.

Summer 2004—Bloggers invited as credentialed journalists to both Republican and Democratic National Conventions.

September 2004—"Rathergate." Bloggers raise questions about the authenticity of documents used in a *60 Minutes 2* story, leading to the retirement of CBS anchorman Dan Rather.

January 2005—"The Gannon Affair." A supposed journalist is exposed by bloggers as a political operative and former male escort after asking a question in which he derided two senators during a presidential press conference.

April 2006—Stephen Colbert at the White House Correspondents Dinner. With the president in attendance, comedian Colbert delivers barbs pointed at both Bush and the press corps but is ignored by the major commercial media until bloggers force them to take notice.

August 2006—Lamont beats Lieberman with blogger support. Challenger Ned Lamont upsets Connecticut Senator (and former vice-presidential candidate) Joe Lieberman in a heated primary battle. Both sides point to bloggers as significant contributors to the race.

CITIZEN JOURNALISM

Two strands of amateur journalism have begun to coalesce through the blogs, both known as "citizen journalism." One of these is concerned with local reporting and community building; the other concentrates on investigative reporting. An example of the former is iBrattleboro, a site dedicated to the coverage of Brattleboro, Vermont. An example of the latter is ePluribus Media, which focuses on taking amateur research to the highest level possible.

iBrattleboro (http://www.ibrattleboro.com) is determinedly local. At the top of the site, one reads, "Welcome to Brattleboro's original, locally-owned citizen journalism site. Read and write your own news, interviews, and more. Pick a local Brattleboro story and cover it yourself or with friends." Sites like this one have sometimes been disparaged as "church bulletins," but they are providing an active avenue for community involvement in the dissemination and discussion of local news. Community pressure, through feedback comments on particular stories, keeps iBrattleboro focused on its primary brief.

ePluribus Media, on the other hand, is geographically quite diverse, its community coming only through its Web site for its journal (http://www.epluri busmedia.org) and through its community Web site, its blog (http://scoop. epluribusmedia.org/). Like iBrattleboro, in addition to being determinedly amateur, ePluribus Media offers book reviews, opinion pieces, interviews, and a wide variety of other sorts of articles. Its focus, however, is on research into a variety of politically related issues and on fact checking all information before it is placed on the journal site (as a blog, the community site is not held to quite the same high standard). Among journal articles, one may find work on voting rights, posttraumatic stress disorder, the effects of Hurricane Katrina, and much more.

Like the other citizen journalism sites, the energy behind both of these comes from passionate amateurs, people who care about their communities and the issues facing them. They see themselves as distinct from professional journalists simply because they can indulge themselves, researching and writing on whatever they want, rather than on what is assigned through a news-media hierarchy. For the most part, they hold themselves to the same high standards as professional journalists.

CONCLUSION

Though they have been in existence barely a decade, the blogs reflect a desire for individual expression that is even older than the American republic. In the tradition of Benjamin Franklin, who had to use a pseudonym to first get his work in print, the bloggers push against media barriers, attempting to wrest control from the powers that they see as constricting personal rights to say what one will. Because of their libertarian bent, the blogs range from vitriol to vanity, enmity to elegance. This bothers many in the older commercial news media, who want to see more regularity in both presentation and response to the news. This also means that no one can predict what the blogs will be in a few years. Not even the bloggers know that.

See also Alternative Media in the United States; Bias and Objectivity; Digital Divide; Global Community Media; Google Book Search; Internet and Its Radical Potential; Media and Citizenship; Media and Electoral Campaigns; Net Neutrality; Online Publishing; Political Documentary; Public Sphere; User-Created Content and Audience Participation.

Further Reading: Burden, Matthew. *The Blog of War: Front-line Dispatches from Soldiers in Iraq and Afghanistan.* New York: Simon and Schuster, 2006; Davis, Richard. *Politics Online: Blogs, Chatrooms, and Discussion Groups in American Democracy.* New York: Routledge, 2005; Hall, R. Scott. *The Blog Ahead: How Citizen-Generated Media Is Radically Tilting the Communications Balance.* Garden City, NY: Morgan James Publishing, 2006; Kline, David, and Dan Burstein. *Blog! How the Newest Media Revolution Is Changing Politics, Business, and Culture.* New York: CDS Books, 2005; Kuhns, Peter, and Adrienne Crew. *Blogosphere: Best of Blogs.* Indianapolis, IN: Que, 2006; Mapes, Mary. *Truth and Duty: The Press, the President, and the Privilege of Power.* New York: St. Martin's, 2005; Meyer, Philip. *The Vanishing Newspaper: Saving Journalism in the Information Age.* Columbia: The University of Missouri Press, 2004; Moulitsas, Markos, and Jerome Armstrong. *Crashing the Gates: Netroots, Grassroots, and the Rise of People-Powered Politics.* White River Junction, VT: Chelsea Green, 2007; Starr, Paul. *The Creation of the Media: Political Origins of Modern Communications.* New York: Basic Books, 2004.

Aaron Barlow

BODY IMAGE

Ideas of beauty vary, but since the turn of the twentieth century, the "thin ideal" has dominated conceptions of female beauty in America. Beginning in the 1970s, researchers began testing whether dissatisfaction with one's body image encouraged women to develop eating disorders (especially anorexia and bulimia) in an effort to attain the "thin ideal." More recently, researchers have been concerned with a seemingly opposite problem: a rise in overweight and obesity in the United States. Both problems appear to have strong roots in media images, whether of dangerously unhealthy "ideals" for women in particular, or of the pleasures offered by yet another sugary treat.

Body image is a person's perception of his or her own body size, shape, and attractiveness. It is our mental image of our physical self, and it is not necessarily accurate or consistent. Our body image is "elastic," changing in response to different moods or to external stimuli. Many researchers have examined the ways in which body image may be influenced by exposure to images of others, such as models in fashion magazines or advertising, or television and movie stars. Because American media have presented the "thin ideal" almost exclusively as the most desirable body type for women, researchers have tried to discover how repeated exposure to such images affects women's self-perception and satisfaction with their own bodies.

Most high-fashion models are severely underweight, as measured by the Body Mass Index (BMI). The average model is 5'9" and weighs 110 pounds, which translates into a BMI of 17. (A BMI of 19–23 is considered normal weight.) Although ultrathin, waif-like models were banned from the catwalk in Madrid's September 2006 fashion show, the industry still demands very thin models (with a desired figure of 34"-24"-34") who can wear clothing in size 2 or 4. This is the body type found almost exclusively in fashion magazines in the United States. Many film and television stars, singers, and other celebrities also struggle to match the "thin ideal," and popular magazines are filled with photos and news stories tracking their weight gains and losses. The images of women found in American film, television, and advertising reinforce the desirability of the "thin ideal" with very little exception.

Most of the research conducted on body image has employed empirical or quantitative methods. These have included asking women to complete self-report surveys or to use psychological assessment scales such as the Stunkard Body Figure Rating Scale or the Body Cathexis Scale to indicate their body image and body satisfaction. These assessment scales consist of a series of body outlines or silhouettes that range from very thin to obese. Subjects are usually asked to identify the silhouette they think looks most like them and to indicate the figure they find most attractive. Most research has found that women tend to overestimate the size of their own bodies. Additionally, a majority of women perceive themselves as larger than their "ideal" size and surveys have shown that between 55 and 75 percent of women in North America feel dissatisfied with their bodies. These tendencies seem to be even stronger shortly after women read fashion magazines featuring models who match the "thin ideal."

These feelings of body dissatisfaction have been shown to encourage some girls and women to engage in unhealthy eating practices, including eating disorders such as anorexia nervosa (a severe reduction in calorie intake) or bulimia nervosa (binge eating followed by purging). Eating disorders, defined by

BODY SIZE AND SHAPE

	Height	Weight	Dress Size	Measurements
Average woman	5'4"	145	11–14	36"-30"-41"
Fashion model	5'9"	110	2–4	34"-24"-34"
Store mannequin	6'0"	N/A	6	34"-23"-34"
Barbie	6'0"	101	4	39"-19"-33"

Source: Adapted from ANRED (Anorexia Nervosa and Related Eating Disorders), http://www.anred.com/stats.html.

the National Institute of Mental Health (NIMH) as "serious disturbances in eating behavior" that are often paired with "feelings of distress or extreme concern about body shape or weight," typically begin when girls are between ages 11 and 13. One recent University of Minnesota study found that teenage girls who frequently read magazine articles about dieting were more likely in later years to practice extreme weight-loss measures, such as vomiting, than girls who never read such articles. Men can also develop these same eating disorders, and an estimated 5 to 15 percent of people with anorexia or bulimia are male. According to the National Institute for Mental Health, between 0.5 and 3.7 percent of females suffer from anorexia at some point during their lives, while between 1.1 to 4.2 percent of women suffer from bulimia. (About half of the individuals who have been anorexic later develop bulimia.) Deaths attributed to anorexia and bulimia, especially among fashion models and other celebrities, have raised a great deal of concern about the health effects of extreme dieting in pursuit of the "thin ideal."

COMPLICATIONS OF RACE, CLASS, AND AGE

Research on body image has sometimes been criticized as focusing too much on the experiences of young white girls and women in the United States at the cost of ignoring differing expectations and experiences for women and girls of color or for older individuals. Some have argued that the "thin ideal" constitutes a standard of beauty among whites, but that African Americans and Latinas in particular grow up with different cultural ideals of beauty and attractiveness. In response, scholars contend that while there may be some cultural differences in what is considered desirable or attractive, all girls are exposed to the same narrow range of media images of beauty found in magazines, television, film, and advertising. Girls of all races or ethnicities are barraged by messages about their bodies, skin, hair, and faces, and although these messages may at times be contradictory, increasingly one of the few common experiences for girls in the United States has been the pressure to diet in order to fit into mainstream American culture. Some studies focusing on women of color have found that as an individual's socioeconomic status increases, so does the pressure to attain the "thin ideal." Becky Thompson, for example, has argued that a desire to be thin—or to want one's daughters to be thin—may be a result of economic, racial, ethnic, and religious discrimination that parents experienced. Because other physical features (skin or eye color, hair texture, height, etc.) are not easily (if at all) alterable, more emphasis may be directed towards weight. Recent studies, then, have concluded that girls, whether African American, Latina, Asian, or white, grow up learning that being thin is valued. These arguments are strengthened by evidence that eating disorders are increasing among women of color.

Because eating disorders typically begin when girls enter puberty, most research on body image has focused on adolescent girls and women in their early 20s, although some studies have discovered very young girls (age 6) and women in their 70s with eating disorders. A few studies have examined body image among older women. Their findings suggest that women's dissatisfaction with their body shape and size persists across their life span, and that even in later life women tend to be more dissatisfied with their bodies than men. Older women may not feel this dissatisfaction as strongly as younger women, however, and their "ideal" body size has been found to be larger than that of younger women.

HISTORICAL AND CULTURAL APPROACHES

Rather than using empirical methods like surveys, assessment scales, or laboratory experiments to investigate body image, some scholars have explored this topic within a historical framework, arguing that such research can offer a better understanding of the role of culture in shaping an individual's attitudes and practices in relationship to food, diet, and body image. Scholars such as Susan Bordo and Kim Chernin have noted that body norms and ideals have changed over time, often in conjunction with changes in a nation's overall wealth. Initially in Western cultures, a rotund figure was the visible sign of economic success. During the Victorian era, as food became more readily available to members of the middle class and not just the rich, the aristocracy began to adopt the "thin ideal" as a different way to make class distinctions apparent. A thin body began to represent wealth and status, power and control. By the late nineteenth century, the middle class adopted a concern with body image and began dieting to attain an idealized weight or shape. A rounded body was no longer seen as a sign of success, but of moral failing or a lack of control, while a healthy and fit body was equated with self-control, self-denial, and willpower.

Primarily, though, women serve as the representatives of class distinctions; a slender and attractive wife can represent a husband's success. Though the "thin ideal" emerged in the Victorian era, it was a thin waist in particular (along with an ample bosom and hips) that was prized. Corsets helped women achieve this look, though at the cost of fainting or suffering serious physical ailments from having their waists constantly cinched to extremely thin (and dangerous) dimensions. The changing shape of women's bodies has in many ways served to reflect larger cultural values. In periods when women were striving to demonstrate their equality (especially in the 1920s and again in the 1960s and 1970s), a thin, straight figure was prized. In times when gender differences seemed more important (as in the 1950s and again in the 1980s), women with somewhat fuller figures (especially in terms of large breasts) were perceived as more desirable and attractive. The "tyranny of slenderness" (in Kim Chernin's phrase) that began at the turn of the twentieth century has been amplified in recent decades with chemical diets and surgery in an ever-escalating pursuit of the "perfect body."

Men's bodies, too, are subject to cultural demands and expectations. Men are often expected to demonstrate their self-discipline and control by their size and shape also, but in the form of increased bulk and muscle rather than by adherence to a "thin ideal." Rather than starving or purging themselves to attain a body ideal, men may be more likely to engage in demanding exercise regimes to develop muscle mass. The feeling that one's body is never big or strong enough can lead to a condition known as "muscle dysmorphia." Getting bigger can also be achieved by overeating or binge eating. According to the NIMH, between 2 and 5 percent of Americans struggle with binge eating, an eating disorder that also affects more women than men.

OVERWEIGHT AND OBESITY

According to recent studies, more than 65 percent of adult Americans (men and women age 20 and older) are overweight, with about 30 percent of this group being classified as obese (at least 20 percent above normal weight as measured by the BMI). Although some individuals consider the "obesity epidemic" to be exaggerated, arguing that BMI measures can be inaccurate and that excess weight alone is not necessarily a health problem, medical studies have linked overweight and obesity to increased risk of type 2 diabetes, heart disease, high blood pressure, and stroke. While more men (67 percent) than women (62 percent) are overweight, women are more likely to be obese. Overweight and obesity are found among every population group, but these conditions are more prevalent among people of color (Hispanics, African Americans, American Indians/Alaska Natives, and Pacific Islanders) and among low-income individuals. Additionally, according to the Centers for Disease Control and Prevention (CDC), almost 9 million children ages 6 to 19 (about 15 percent of children in the United States) are obese. Because obesity rates are increasing faster than genetics alone can account for, most researchers studying this phenomenon look to eating disorders (especially binge eating) as well as changes in the foods we eat as the chief culprits.

The food industry in the United States is a trillion-dollar business, with over 7 billion spent on advertising each year. Typically, the foods most heavily advertised in the United States are the cheapest as well as the most calorie-dense: processed foods filled with sweeteners and fats (soft drinks, candy, and snack foods) that are generally lacking in nutritive value. With thousands of new food products introduced into grocery stores each year, the food industry must work hard to persuade consumers to eat more. Appeals used in food advertising rarely concern the taste, nutritive value, or ingredients of foods. Instead, food is linked to much stronger emotional appeals. Bordo and Kilbourne both analyze the ways in which food advertising heightens women's anxieties about weight (often describing foods in quasireligious terms such as "temptation," "sin," and "guilt"), while simultaneously linking food (and even binge eating) to fantasies of pleasure and indulgence. Food in advertising is often eroticized and linked to sexuality and love. It is also linked to many other values, such as one's ability to be a good mother, to display status, to be cool or hip, or to be well liked and admired.

Ironically, both an anorexic girl and an obese woman may in fact be starving themselves to death, one by reducing nearly all calories, but the other by reducing those calories that supply the nutrients the body needs to be healthy. Media images and advertising often profit from and are complicit in both acts.

See also Advertising and Persuasion; Dating Shows; Gay, Lesbian, Bisexual, Transgendered, and Queer Representations on TV; Media and the Crisis of Values; Representations of Class; Representations of Masculinity; Representations of Race; Representations of Women; Sensationalism, Fear Mongering, and Tabloid Media; Women's Magazines.

Further Reading: Beardsworth, Alan, and Teresa Keil. *Sociology on the Menu: An Invitation to the Study of Food and Society.* London: Routledge, 1997; Bordo, Susan. *Unbearable Weight: Feminism, Western Culture, and the Body.* Berkeley: University of California Press, 1995; Bordo, Susan. *The Male Body.* New York: Farrar, Straus and Giroux, 1999; Centers for Disease Control and Prevention, National Center for Health Statistics, National Health and Nutrition Examination Survey, Health, United States, 2002. http://www.cdc.gov/nccdphp/dnpa/obesity/; Chernin, Kim. *The Hungry Self: Women, Eating and Identity.* New York: Times Books, 1985; Chernin, Kim. *The Obsession: Reflections on the Tyranny of Slenderness,* 1st ed. New York: Harper and Row, 1981; Counihan, Carole M., and Steven L. Kaplan, eds. *Food and Gender: Identity and Power.* Amsterdam: Harwood Academic, 1998; Critzer, Greg. *Fat Land: How Americans Became the Fattest People in the World.* Boston: Houghton Mifflin, 2003; Kilbourne, Jean. *Can't Buy My Love: How Advertising Changes the Way We Think and Feel.* New York: Simon and Schuster, 1999; Kilbourne, Jean. *Slim Hopes.* Dir. Sut Jhally. Media Education Foundation, National Institute of Mental Health. "Eating Disorders: Facts about Eating Disorders and the Search for Solutions," 2001. http://www.nimh.nih.gov/publicat/eatingdisorders.cfm; Nestle, Marion. *Food Politics: How the Food Industry Influences Nutrition and Health.* Berkeley: University of California Press, 2002; Thompson, Becky W. *A Hunger So Wide and So Deep: American Women Speak Out on Eating Problems.* Minneapolis: University of Minnesota Press, 1994; Wolf, Naomi. *The Beauty Myth.* New York: Chatto and Windus, 1990.

Jean Retzinger

BOLLYWOOD AND THE INDIAN DIASPORA

With approximately 20 million South Asians, more than 30 million Chinese, 13 million Jews, and 300 million people of African descent living as migrant populations, it has become difficult to sustain the idea that cultural identities are tied to a particular place in the world. Multiple connections are developed as immigrants forge and sustain social relations that link together their societies of origin and settlement. Their embeddedness in more than one society, enabled by communications technologies, not only highlights how social relations have changed but also raises an important question: how do migrants reconstruct a sense of belonging in new places, far removed from their homeland? Often, the most available resources are media products, but does a notion of citizenship that is based on consumption serve only the interests of the cultural industries? What do migrants stand to gain or lose in defining citizenship through media consumption?

While globalization is observable at many levels, and indeed, pervades many aspects of daily life, defining what the term means has remained difficult partly because it involves many different dimensions. However, it is possible to highlight two interrelated features of globalization for they are central to understanding how relationships among culture, place, and identity have changed over the past two decades. These are migration, and technologies of communication.

Rapid mobility of people across local and national borders, and new technological developments that ensure the flow of information and images across these borders, have transformed social relations. There is nothing "local" about where we live now, for every realm of our lives—work, finance, entertainment, health, and so on—is now connected to other places and people around the world. Easier and cheaper access to telephones, cable and satellite television, and the Internet have opened up newer routes for us to visit faraway locations and "go places," all from the comfort and familiarity of our homes and local settings.

Our experience of the world has also been changed by another kind of flow that lies at the heart of globalization—migration. How do migrants craft a sense of community and cultural identity? What cultural resources are available and how are these resources mobilized towards fashioning a sense of cultural identity that avoids the two extremes of cultural ghettoism and complete assimilation into the host society?

MEDIA AND DIASPORIC IDENTITY

If understood as a problem of reconstructing a sense of "home" away from "home," we can recognize the important role that imagination plays in everyday life in migrant settings. Driven in part by memory and nostalgia, diasporic communities are involved in a constant dialogue between their past and a new present, with the homeland embodying tradition and authenticity. In this setting, music, films, and television shows from "home" have not just enabled large numbers of people to maintain relations across great distances, strengthening transnational kinship, religious, economic, and political ties. Transnational media function as repositories for content and images that help *reimagine* culture that was formerly tied to a specific locality. In other words, media are not mere artifacts evocative of a "home" left behind—in shaping *how* the "home" is remembered, they reconfigure memory and nostalgia in important ways. With few other cultural institutions in place for immigrants to tap into, media have assumed a central role in diasporic communities' maintaining and reinventing sociocultural linkages and identities.

The value of media, among a mix of other influences such as family visits, pilgrimages, travel to the home country, local ethnic organizations, and places for religious worship, lies in their ability to permeate various social rituals. Studying the circulation and consumption of bhangra music and dance among Asians in Britain, Gayatri Gopinath points out that popular culture forms are more than just entertainment. In a diasporic setting, popular cultural forms become strategic tools for keeping alive certain traditions, and most crucially, serve as a bridge between generations. In the United States, performances of song-and-dance sequences from Bollywood films as part of "India Night" cultural shows on college campuses are another instance of media becoming a key resource for immigrant youth to define cultural identity in relation to other racial and ethnic groups and for their parents to participate in this process. As scholars like Henry Jenkins and Sunaina Maira have observed, mixing classical dance with contemporary club moves and remixing bhangra music with hip-hop rhythms, such performances reflect the creative and surprising juxtapositions that happen in a migrant setting as people construct the "home" as both a world away and right in one's own backyard.

KABHI KHUSHI KABHIE GHAM...(HAPPINESS AND TEARS, 2001, DIR. KARAN JOHAR)

Kabhi Khushi Kabhie Gham...(K3G) is a story of an affluent Indian family: Yashvardhan, Nandini, and their two sons—Rahul and Rohan. The family is split apart when Rahul marries Anjali, a girl from a lower-class neighborhood in Delhi, instead of the girl his father has chosen. Yashvardhan disowns Rahul, and Rahul and Anjali move to the United Kingdom accompanied by Anjali's younger sister Pooja and Rahul's nanny. When Rohan learns about these incidents, he vows to reunite the family. Rohan moves to London and makes his way into Rahul's family under an assumed name and reconciles the family.

K3G is one of the biggest hits of Bollywood. Major stars, catchy songs, and elaborately choreographed dances all contributed to the film's success. But the importance of *K3G* lies in its departure from earlier Bollywood narratives in recognizing and representing nonresident Indians (NRIs). Over nearly three decades, Bollywood films have tended to position the diaspora as impure and India as the crucible of virtues. Furthermore, in these films, claims about the diaspora's impurity are made by resorting to stereotypes of diasporic women as "Westernized" and "immoral."

K3G is no different from such films in its portrayal of gender norms, but does mark a significant shift. *K3G* renders the diaspora less impure and more as an acceptable variant within a transnational "Indian" family. While one can point to several scenes in the film, the key moment is when Anjali and Rahul's son (Krish), born and raised in England, sings the Indian national anthem at a school function in London. Instead of singing "Do Re Mi," Krish surprises everyone by singing the Indian national anthem. Such sequences function both as reassurance for Indian immigrants that they can live abroad, yet claim cultural citizenship in India, and as an acknowledgment of India embracing the NRI as one of its own. The diaspora is no longer different and threatening.

Cultural citizenship, then, can be understood as imagining one's membership in relation to a national culture even if one is not a citizen of that nation in strictly legal or political terms. In other words, being Indian American is as much a matter of consuming Bollywood films, participating in a Bollywood fan community, or remixing bhangra music as it is about owning two passports and being a dual citizen.

While acknowledging that definitions of cultural identity in diasporic settings can challenge rigid ideas of what it means to be "Indian" or "American," some scholars point out that these seemingly flexible modes of defining one's identity are only available at the cost of being commodified and sold as marketable demographics to advertisers. Critics also point out that governments also play a role in these processes and work to circumscribe what it means to belong in a particular nation. In other words, there are some very real limits to "cultural citizenship." To understand this complex dynamic—of opportunity and risk—let us turn our attention to the case of Bollywood in diasporic communities.

CASE STUDY: BOLLYWOOD AND THE INDIAN AMERICAN DIASPORA

Films from India have always traveled to different parts of the world, and have been an important form of cultural exchange between India and the Middle East, several countries in Africa, and Eastern Europe. In the United States, Bollywood films were brought in by Indian families who moved there when the U.S. government changed its migration policy in 1965 to allow people from non-European nations to live and work in the United States. In several cities across the United States, Indian families met during the weekend to watch a Hindi-language film. Screenings were usually held in university halls rented for a few hours during the weekend, with films screened off 16-mm, and later, 35-mm reels. These weekend screenings, with an intermission that lasted 30 to 45 minutes, were an occasion, apart from religious festivals, for people to wear traditional clothes, speak in Hindi or other Indian languages, and participate in a ritual that was reminiscent of "home." These screenings were marked as an exclusively *Indian* space, away from mainstream society, where families could meet and participate in a ritual of sharing personal and collective memories of life in India and introduce their children to different aspects of "India" and "Indianness."

While this mode of viewing has changed with the availability of videocassettes and DVDs through Indian grocery stores and through online outlets such as Netflix, Bollywood films continue to play a key role in community events such as the "India Night" cultural shows on college campuses where second-generation Indian Americans perform song-and-dance sequences from popular Bollywood films. Further, while advances in communications have facilitated contact with India, over a period of time, work and other social engagements in the diaspora result in most migrants gradually losing touch with day-to-day developments in India. Thus, by defining various social rituals and shaping interactions that these rituals have created, Bollywood films have helped sustain expatriate Indians' desire to perform their "Indianness" and define their belonging in "India."

MTV DESI: MISREADING DESI YOUTH CULTURE

People of South Asian origin use the term "desi" to refer to each other—it means "from the homeland," but also positions one as South Asian outside the geographic area of South Asia. Identifying "desis" as a niche market, MTV Networks launched an on-demand channel called MTV Desi in July 2005 with content that was a mix of Bollywood music, Indi-pop (popular music produced both within the Indian subcontinent and in the diaspora), and shows sourced from MTV India.

Eighteen months later, MTV Networks pulled the plug on MTV Desi, admitting that the "premium distribution model for MTV Desi proved more challenging than anticipated." However, given the image of South Asians as affluent minorities, and the logics of the television marketplace in the United States, where niche marketing to racial and ethnic minorities is seen as sound business strategy, it would seem that MTV Desi did nothing wrong in identifying its market. It seems MTV Desi failed to strike a chord among viewers because it had misread desi youth culture.

There are two important lessons that emerge from the MTV Desi experiment that highlight the complex and hybrid nature of diaspora cultures. First, MTV Desi failed to recognize that desi identity has been shaped as much by mainstream American popular culture as by "Indian" influences. While Bollywood and bhangra music may serve as a resource for desi youth to define their identity in relation to ethnic and racial categories in the United States, they are not all-encompassing. Second, MTV Desi did not realize that there is no nostalgia for the homeland among desi youth who grew up in the United States. MTV Desi, at the end of the day, may have appealed more to expatriate Indians who grew up with MTV India than to second-generation desis.

In fact, in an MTV Desi video clip that circulated widely, a 20-something desi said as much: "You are not an Indian…you are desi. You are *of* South Asia, not *from* South Asia…you don't speak Hindi or Gujarati or Urdu…you don't know the backstreets of Karachi or Bombay." Desi tastes and needs, as MTV Desi realized, are formed at the intersection of several different flows of popular culture and these cannot always be mapped neatly in national terms.

Further, in recent years, Bollywood's convergence with the Internet has made overseas audiences an integral part of the film industry. In addition to watching films, they are able to access content and participate in a national culture in a more direct and immediate fashion than was previously possible. In other words, new media have further reduced the time-lag between India and the diaspora where Bollywood is concerned. Non-Resident Indians (NRIs) are now part of the same cultural space as Indians within India. The question is, are all NRIs part of this global cultural space that is being defined by Bollywood? What are the exclusions built into this notion of cultural citizenship?

THE LIMITS OF CULTURAL CITIZENSHIP

First, it is important to recognize that Bollywood is only one of several film industries in India. While Bollywood is certainly the most well known outside

India, and can claim the status of a "national" cinema because the films are made in Hindi (India's national language), several regional-language film industries (Tamil, Telugu, Malayalam, and Bengali) are just as prolific and successful. Furthermore, given that the Indian diaspora in countries such as the United States is highly diverse in terms of language and region, it is important to qualify claims of Bollywood's influence in the diaspora by pointing out that families from the states of Tamilnadu or Andhra Pradesh are more likely to watch Tamil and Telugu language films rather than Hindi-language Bollywood films.

Second, we need to note that not all Bollywood films are successful in the diaspora. Even a cursory glance at box office figures indicates that only a certain kind of big-budget, family-oriented film does well among NRIs. In these family-centric Bollywood films, class, regional, linguistic, and religious differences are consistently erased in favor of an "Indian" family that is highly educated, affluent, north Indian, Hindu, patriarchal, and upper caste. Indeed, it becomes clear from these films that it is only a certain kind of NRI who is of importance to Bollywood and to the nation. Other ways of being Indian and claiming Indianness are often marginalized.

The importance of Bollywood's role in defining "Indianness" in an age of global flows, of who can claim "cultural citizenship" in India, becomes particularly clear when we consider the Indian government's recent efforts to reach out to NRIs. In this new imagination of a "Global India," only people of Indian origin from "dollar and pound" countries like the United States, United Kingdom, and Canada are being offered dual citizenship. Others, either poorer migrants in these "dollar and pound" countries, or those from "third-world" countries like Fiji or Trinidad, are being excluded.

Thus, we need to approach the idea of "cultural citizenship" in the context of globalization and diasporic communities by acknowledging that media create spaces for people to work out notions of belonging and entitlement on a daily basis while remaining attuned to the ways in which "citizenship" gets circumscribed both by the workings of media industries and larger social and political forces.

See also Communication Rights in a Global Context; Cultural Appropriation; Cultural Imperialism and Hybridity; Global Community Media; Media and Citizenship; Nationalism and the Media; Runaway Productions and the Globalization of Hollywood; Tourism and the Selling of Cultures; World Cinema.

Further Reading: Appadurai, Arjun. *Modernity at Large: Cultural Dimensions of Globalization.* Minneapolis: University of Minnesota Press, 1996; Cohen, Robin. *Global Diasporas: An Introduction.* Seattle: University of Washington Press, 1997; Gillespie, Marie. *Television, Ethnicity, and Cultural Change.* London: Routledge, 1995; Gopinath, Gayatri. "Bombay, U.K., Yuba City: Bhangra Music and the Engendering of Diaspora." *Diaspora* 4 (1995): 303–21; Jenkins, Henry. *Convergence Culture: Where Old and New Media Collide.* New York: New York University Press, 2006; Lipsitz, George. *Dangerous Crossroads: Popular Music, Postmodernism, and the Politics of Place.* New York: Verso, 1997; Maira, Sunaina. *Desis in the House: Indian American Youth Culture in New York City.*

Philadelphia: Temple University Press, 2002; Morley, David. *Home Territories: Media, Mobility and Identity.* New York: Routledge, 2000; Naficy, Hamid. *The Making of Exile Cultures: Iranian Television in Los Angeles.* Minneapolis: University of Minnesota Press, 1993; Ong, Aihwa. *Flexible Citizenship: The Cultural Logics of Transnationality.* Durham: Duke University Press, 1998.

Aswin Punathambekar

BRANDING THE GLOBE

Global advertising is a double-edged sword. On the one hand, it has been credited with creating new markets, improving economies and connecting people worldwide through trade in consumer goods. On the other hand, it has been criticized for spreading consumer culture to every corner of the globe through the growth of multinational corporations and their advertising agencies as they preach the gospel of capitalist development. What are some of the intended and unintended effects of global advertising?

Globalization has been led mainly by economic interests in the Western world. During the closing decades of the twentieth century, helped in no small way by emerging digital communication technologies, international markets across the globe began to be opened up by multinational corporations and their advertising agencies. Modern media allow advertisers to spread unified branding campaigns, or global advertising messages around the world at a phenomenal rate through the global media. Because of this rapid communication and advanced transport and delivery systems, companies like eBay and Starbucks, for example, have been able to build in a few short years what corporations like Coca-Cola and General Electric took over a century to establish. Thus, Western multinational corporations were able to establish great wealth in the twentieth century through unprecedented global growth.

In a 2005 Interbrand study of the world's top 100 global brands, over 50 percent were U.S. corporations and 40 percent were European-based. Less than 10 percent of the top global brands were headquartered in Asia and none in Africa. However, the world is changing and as the markets in developing countries begin to grow, the effects of global advertising on consumer culture may have unintended effects.

THE ORIGINS OF THE MULTINATIONAL CORPORATION

The roots of the modern multinational corporation can be traced back to the 1600s, when the English monarch granted a charter to the British East India Company to establish overseas commercial and trade interests. Holland chartered the Dutch East India Company for the same purposes. These two companies were probably the first truly multinational corporations. These companies and others like them colonized their chartered territories on behalf of sponsoring monarchs. Before the twentieth century, economic expansion had been the exclusive domain of national governments either directly or through charters. But starting in the early 1900s, corporations began to take over this role.

By the twentieth century, the corporation had become the dominant type of business organization throughout the world. In the United States today, for example, while corporations account for only about 20 percent of all businesses, they generate about 90 percent of all business income.

During the 1920s, Henry Ford led the development of the modern manufacturing corporation by introducing assembly-line production. This allowed corporations to cut production costs and increase output. Manufactured products became more affordable for an increasing number of people. By the 1920s, the major industries in the United States that had evolved from clusters of small companies were taken over by major corporations. AT&T dominated the telephone industry; General Motors, Ford, and Chrysler produced the majority of automobiles; and Westinghouse and GE controlled the electrical equipment sectors. These competitive products were soon to be found around the world, and export earnings were responsible for an increasing share of U.S. corporate profits. It was not until after World War I that the United States began to emerge as a major world economic power. At the same time as Europe was recovering economically from the war and reestablishing its global trade through companies like Lever Brothers (soap and chemicals) and Royal Dutch Shell, the United States was building up its economic strength through the expansion of its own multinational corporations.

ADVERTISING AND GLOBALIZATION

Ben Bagdikian (1997) is one of the many who have recognized that advertising has always been a vital gear in the machinery of corporate power, arguing that "it not only helped create and preserve dominance of the giants over consumer industries, it also helped create a picture of a satisfactory world with the corporations as benign stewards" (p. 131). In 1926, the president of the United States, Calvin Coolidge, attributed the success of mass demand for products "entirely to advertising" and noted that advertising "is a great power...part of the greater world of regeneration and redemption of mankind" (p. 148).

While the Depression of the 1930s had a dampening effect on global industrial growth, the postwar boom from 1945 to 1960 saw the beginning of a huge influx of American corporations into the international arena. U.S. corporations like Coca-Cola, Colgate-Palmolive, Westinghouse, and General Motors built plants around the world. The Americans were soon joined in this expansion by European and later Japanese multinationals. Only 7,000 multinational corporations existed in 1970, but by 1994, their numbers had grown to 37,000 parent corporations—with over 200,000 affiliates worldwide. Multinational corporations currently employ over 73 million people around the world, and some are more economically powerful than many nation-states (Firth and Mueller 2003).

Multinational corporations have been able to achieve extraordinary growth during the twentieth century primarily because they had the assistance of multinational advertising agencies that assisted them in spreading the word about "the good life" (based on acquisition of material goods) around the globe.

THE SPREAD OF ADVERTISING AGENCIES

As multinational corporations extended their reach outside their national borders, they insisted that their advertising agencies set up branch offices in all the countries into which they expanded. The J. Walter Thompson advertising agency opened its first overseas office in Great Britain in 1899, and by the 1950s had 15 overseas agencies (Sivulka 1998). The Standard Oil and Coca-Cola accounts took the McCann Erickson advertising agency into Europe in the 1920s. By the 1960s, the expansion of U.S. agencies reached a peak. During this phase of ad agency expansion overseas, the international billings of the major U.S. advertising agencies began to outstrip the growth of their domestic billings. In 1960, some 36 American ad agencies had branches outside the United States and operated a total of 281 overseas offices. By the 1970s, international billings reached an annual US$1.8 billion and accounted for more almost 20 percent of total agency U.S. billings (Firth and Mueller 2003).

Establishing overseas branches and partnerships, U.S. advertising agencies were able both to service their multinational clients and to compete for the accounts of other U.S. firms operating abroad. Later, in the 1960s and 1970s, because U.S. domestic advertising business began to level off, overseas markets began to look even more appealing to the U.S. advertising agencies with multinational aspirations. As a consequence of this overseas expansion, the international billings of U.S. agencies with overseas operations more than doubled during the following decade.

A second major surge in international expansion by U.S. and European advertising agencies occurred during the 1980s—a decade of megamergers in the industry. These mergers involved a handful of large, highly profitable ad agencies operating at the global level. In 1986, for instance, three advertising giants—BBDO International, Doyle Dane Bernbach (DDB), and Needham Harper Worldwide—announced a three-way merger to create the world's largest advertising firm—the Omnicom Group. Further mergers and acquisition of agencies resulted in the creation of the British giant WPP Group. Today, four enormous advertising conglomerates or holding companies, the Interpublic Group, Omnicom Group, WPP Group, and Publicis Groupe SA, together control more than half the world's ad agencies. Table B.1 groups a small sample of the best known amongst the dozens of advertising agencies owned by these advertising behemoths.

Table B.1 Global Advertising Conglomerates and Selected Agency Holdings

Interpublic	Omnicom	WPP	Publicis
McCann Erickson	BBDO Worldwide	J. Walter Thompson	Publicis Worldwide
Lowe & Partners	DDB Worldwide	Ogilvy & Mather	Leo Burnett
Foote, Cone & Belding	TBWA Worldwide	The Batey Group	Saatchi & Saatchi

Source: Cappo, 2003.

GLOBAL BRANDS AND THE GROWTH OF CONSUMER MARKETS

As multinational corporations and advertising agencies have spread around the globe the concept of branding has also spread. Naomi Klein (2000a) wrote in *The New Statesman*:

> The formula for these brand-driven companies is pretty much the same: get rid of your unionized factories in the west and buy your products from Asian or Central American contractors and sub-contractors. Then, take the money you save and spend it on branding—on advertising.

Corporations like Nike, Reebok, and Tommy Hilfiger have moved their production outside the United States to the developing world's "free-trade zones"— free, that is, of taxes and wage or other labor regulations. In these developing countries, multinationals can produce goods at a fraction of the cost of manufacturing in a developed country. This successful formula has allowed the big image-makers like The Gap, Tommy Hilfiger, Ralph Lauren, and Nike, which were once satisfied with a 100 percent markup from the cost of factory production, to get closer to a 400 percent markup (Klein 2000b).

According to Klein, these profits are then pumped back into global advertising, which has resulted in these brands becoming global icons. Today, the top 10 global brands as identified by Interbrand include 8 U.S.-based firms, one Finnish, and one Japanese (see Table B.2).

While the expansion of Western brands throughout the world proceeded quite successfully during the twentieth century, bringing massive wealth to the West, at the beginning of the twenty-first century there are signs that the spread of global capitalism may have some unintended side effects. During the next 50 years, 97 percent of the world's population growth is expected to take place in the developing countries (e.g., India, China, Indonesia, and Brazil). The United

Table B.2 The World's Top Global Brands in 2005

Rank	Organization	Headquarters
1	Coca-Cola	USA
2	Microsoft	USA
3	IBM	USA
4	GE	USA
5	Intel	USA
6	Nokia	Finland
7	Disney	USA
8	McDonald's	USA
9	Toyota	Japan
10	Marlboro	USA

Source: Business Week Online, 2005.

Table B.3 World Population by Continent, 1998–2050

Continent	1998	%	2050	%
	(population in millions)			
Asia and Oceania	3,615	61	5,314	60
Africa	749	13	1,766	20
Europe	729	12	628	7
North America	305	5	392	4
Latin America and Caribbean	504	8	809	9
TOTAL	5,902		8,909	

Source: United Nations Population Information Network. http://www.popin.org/.

Nations Population Estimates and Projections also project that the populations of Europe and North America will shrink to only 11.5 percent of the total world population by 2050. Africa will grow to account for over 20 percent and Asia will make up 60 percent of the world's total population (see Table B.3).

These substantial shifts in the centers of gravity of global markets represent an interesting new phenomenon: the rise of global consumer culture fueled by global advertising and branding.

THE CASE OF CHINA

The People's Republic of China, for example, has a population of 1.3 billion people. While the overall gross domestic product (GDP) per capita is still relatively low, during the past two decades, China has been the world's largest and most rapidly developing country. China already has one-fifth of the world's consumers, and it has a rapidly growing middle class, hungry for consumer goods. Thus, developing countries like mainland China and India are destined to take center stage in the global bazaar.

This rapid economic growth in the developing world has resulted in a transformation of consumer behavior, and advertising is positioned at the epicenter of this transformation. In the past 10 years, over 100 million people in China moved up to the middle class and many others moved up to the wealthiest class. In fact, the figures on China's newly rich are staggering. China now boasts nearly 235,000 millionaires (US$ equivalency). At least 10,000 of these entrepreneurs are each worth US$17 million, according to researchers at the Chinese Academy of Social Sciences. In 2006, the 50th richest Chinese boasted an income of US$190 million, while in 1999, number 50 on the "rich list" had only $10 million. Economists forecast that in 10 years, China's middle class will be 400 million strong. While this economic growth has created unprecedented opportunities for Western multinationals—nearly 30 percent of all new McDonald's restaurants opened this year will be in China, and Starbucks, the huge U.S. coffee company, expects China to become their second largest market in the world—this rampant consumerism has also brought with it another phenomenon: piracy.

At the Shijingshan Amusement Park, which recently opened in the suburbs of Beijing, children are greeted by costumed figures like a large duck and a happily waving lady mouse. Are these Daffy Duck and Minnie Mouse? "No," says the management of the park, "the characters in our park just look a bit similar" to those in Disneyland.

Huge markets have sprung up in all the large cities in China selling fake branded items like Gucci bags, Mont Blanc pens, and pirated CDs and DVDs. The rise of consumerism and the Chinese ability to copy branded icons has strained ties between the wealthy countries in the West and China. The U.S. trade deficit with China, for example, soared to U.S. $232.5 billion in 2006. Thus, global advertising's success in creating new markets for branded Western consumer goods has created eager new consumers in the developing world, as well as opportunities for local entrepreneurs to capitalize on the rising tide of capitalism by producing an endless array of "fake global brands" for local consumption.

THE RISE OF GLOBAL MEDIA

The past few decades have also seen unprecedented growth in the global media to serve the needs of the global advertising industry. Western magazines like *Elle, Vogue, Maxim,* and *Seventeen,* for example, are now available in "local country" editions worldwide.

The unintended side effect of the growth in global media has also been to further stimulate consumer culture. Herman and McChesney (1997) point out that "the globalizing media treat audiences as consumers, not as citizens, and they are most attentive to those with high incomes." This, they show, has led to the erosion of the social and economic development role of the media in many developing nations. In country after country, commercial satellite and cable channels have captured the wealthier, urban viewers. These competitive market forces drive government media channels to cut back on "positive externalities of public service" and "at the same time give full play to audience-attracting programs featuring sex and violence." According to Herman and McChesney, the media in India, for example, "are being integrated into a global system that caters to those with effective demand and encourages them to want and to spend more." These authors go on to point out that India's globalizing media and the advertising community are promoting "an elitist consumerist culture within the larger society of what is still a Third World country" (p. 188). Their observations can be applied to many other countries in the developing world.

Thus, the linkages between the multinational corporations, global advertising, and the growth of commercial media channels are all interrelated. Agencies continue to lobby for media channels in which to advertise their corporate clients' products and services. The weight of evidence supports the contention that multinational corporations and global advertising interests throughout the world have clamored for the creation of commercial broadcasting to replace the existing public service systems.

CONCLUSION

Multinational corporations and their advertising agencies have a growing and essential role in the continued success of global capitalism. Globalization helped corporations spread the messages of consumption through global advertising and the global mass media have helped manufacturers and service providers to penetrate markets around the world. Global advertising spreads lifestyles and values along with the products being marketed. From their inception, the mass media have been commodities to be consumed in much the same way as hamburgers and cosmetic surgery.

Ironically, one major unintended side effect of the rise in consumer culture is the development of alternative markets in countries like China for locally produced "fake" branded items that are affordable to the rising masses of middle-class consumers. Meanwhile "real brands" like Haier and Lenovo from China are emerging on the international consumer market to challenge the Western giants like GE and IBM. Using the branding techniques they have learned from Western corporations, these new entrants to the marketplace can draw on over a billion local consumers to become a major presence in the global marketplace in the twenty-first century.

See also Advertising and Persuasion; Communication and Knowledge Labor; Communication Rights in a Global Context; Conglomeration and Media Monopolies; Cultural Appropriation; Cultural Imperialism and Hybridity; Global Community Media; Hypercommercialism; Pharmaceutical Advertising; Piracy and Intellectual Property.

Further Reading: Bagdikian, Ben H. *The Media Monopoly*. Boston: Beacon, 1997; Cappo, Joe. *The Future of Advertising: New Media, New Clients, New Consumers in the Post-Television Age*. New York: McGraw-Hill, 2003; Frith, Katherine T., and Barbara Mueller. *Advertising and Society: Global Issues*. New York: Peter Lang, 2003; Herman, Edward S., and Robert W. McChesney. *The Global Media: The New Missionaries of Corporate Capitalism*. London: Cassell, 1997; Khermouch, Gerry. "Special Report: The Best Global Brands." *Business Week Online*, http://www.Businessweek.com/magazine/content/02_31/63945098.htm; Klein, Naomi. "The Tyranny of Brands." *The New Statesman* 13, no. 589 (January 24, 2000a): 25; Klein, Naomi. *No Logo: Taking Aim at the Brand Bullies*. Toronto: Knopf Canada, 2000b; Ritzer, George. *The McDonaldization of Society: An Investigation Into the Changing Character of Contemporary Society*, 3rd ed. Thousand Oaks, CA: Pine Forge Press, 2000; Sivulka, Juliann. *Soap, Sex and Cigarettes: A Cultural History of American Advertising*. Belmont, CA: Wadsworth, 1998.

Katherine Frith

C

CABLE CARRIAGE DISPUTES

The transition from analog to digital television has rekindled an ongoing battle over the obligation of cable and satellite operators to carry local broadcast channels and cable companies to provide public access channels. Cable, satellite, and emergent video distributors, including telephone companies, have challenged these requirements, claiming government interference in their free speech rights. Does the proliferation of digital cable, satellite, and broadband Internet technologies mean that government intervention is no longer justified to support local television, despite ongoing support for local broadcast carriage rules by local communities? Does digital broadcasting change local commercial broadcasters' public interest responsibilities as they begin to offer more than one broadcast signal?

The Federal Communications Commission (FCC) established the "must-carry" rules in the early 1960s and Congress upheld them in 1992, applied them to direct broadcast satellite in 2002, and extended them to broadcasters' main digital signal in 2006 to take effect in February 2009. Cable and satellite operators have protested these requirements as unconstitutional breeches of their free speech rights. The courts found these rules unconstitutional in the 1980s but the Supreme Court upheld them by narrow 5 to 4 decisions in the 1990s. While these carriage requirements expose regulatory battles among competing industries, they also represent symptomatic solutions to broader structural issues regarding the emergence of new communications technologies and the role of governments, industries, and citizens in regulating them. Also exposed are broader conflicting cultural priorities from commitments to locally produced television, diverging tastes over national

LIFETIME

Carriage disputes have also erupted between national program networks and cable/satellite operators. One example of this occurred in January 2006 when the satellite company Echo-Star dropped the women's-oriented Lifetime network and Lifetime Movie Network from its service over a contract dispute, replacing them with a rival women's-oriented channel, Oxygen. Because Lifetime was partially owned by Disney, which also owned ABC, The Disney Channel, and ESPN networks, they had bargaining leverage over carriage rates. However, as the top-rated network among women viewers and an advocate for women's issues, Lifetime relied less on this corporate leverage than the public protests from their viewers.

Over 50 women's organizations, including the National Network to End Domestic Violence, the National Organization of Women, the YWCA, and the Breast Cancer Research Foundation, organized nationwide letter-writing campaigns and rallies to protest EchoStar and encourage subscribers to switch to a competing satellite service that carried the networks. A month later, EchoStar and Lifetime agreed on a contract, but the competing satellite company DirecTV sued Lifetime for failing to comply with a promise to pay $200 for each viewer who switched from EchoStar to DirecTV during the dispute.

---

commercial programs, and rosy forecasts for altogether different audiovisual cultures through broadband. The history of these disputes will continue to influence future debates over audiovisual policies.

PROTECTING LOCAL BROADCASTERS

Cable and broadcaster disputes began in the early years of television's expansion in the 1950s. Local cable systems consisting of hilltop microwave towers and cables strewn to homes emerged in the sparsely populated western states and hilly areas around the country where communities had poor or no broadcast reception. Broadcasters complained that this pirated their signals without paying for them and grew increasingly concerned as cable systems began importing signals from network-affiliated stations in distant cities, sometimes duplicating the programs on local stations. Evident at a series of FCC and congressional hearings on the matter were conflicting cultural values over the development of this new mass medium. The FCC's frequency allocation plan prioritized the development of local stations in every community despite the difficulty that sparsely populated areas might have in funding stations through advertising revenues. In 1962, under the newly appointed FCC Chair Newton Minow, who labeled network programming a "vast wasteland," the FCC required a Riverton, Wyoming cable operator to carry all local stations and prohibited it from importing distant signals that duplicated programs on local stations. The FCC extended these rules to all cable operators in 1965. But many residents in areas outside the signal reach of three-station markets (over 90 percent of households at this time) wanted access to more national network programming and the "local" television culture from distant cities—in some cases, communities created nonprofit cable and booster antenna systems to do so. In 1966, ostensibly to protect the potential growth of local UHF (ultrahigh frequency) stations in metropolitan areas, the FCC banned cable importations of distant broadcast signals into the top 100 TV markets, effectively stalling cable development there.

While these early cable systems were primarily antenna systems for better broadcast reception, in the late 1960s broadband cable offered more channel capacity and two-way interactivity. Rather than seeing it as a threat to local broadcasters, policy makers, nonprofit foundations, and social scientists found "Blue Sky" potential in cable to offer a variety of communication services such as job information, health and child care, distance education, and opportunities for citizen participation in local community affairs. The Johnson administration released the President's Task Force on Communication Policy, Ralph Lee Smith published the widely read *The Wired Nation*, and the Sloan Foundation circulated *On the Cable*, all championing broadband cable's potential to offer a wider array of programming, including the uplifting cultural programming dear to the critics of the vast wasteland, and a potential communication tool to address urban poverty and racial inequality.

LIFTING CARRIAGE RESTRICTIONS

In 1972, the FCC lifted the importation restrictions into major cities and required larger cable systems to offer at least 12 channels, two-way capacity, and three access channels for public, educational, and government use. However, the FCC retained its restrictions on pay-TV from two years earlier, which prevented pay-TV channels from using recent motion pictures, certain sports programming, and series with interconnected plots in anticipation that they might be otherwise siphoned away from free-to-air broadcasting. By the mid-1970s, the cable industry grew as did its lobbying power, FCC staff changes under the Ford and Carter administrations produced advocates of cable deregulation, satellites offered cable program producers national distribution, and the federal courts increasingly demanded factual evidence for cable restrictions. Ongoing disputes over the copyright liability of cable operators were settled in 1976 with the creation of a Copyright Royalty Tribunal that established compulsory licensing fees for programs. By the end of the decade, the federal courts found pay-TV and antisiphoning rules unfounded and the FCC lifted all cable programming restrictions.

With program restrictions lifted, carriage disputes shifted to the franchising process where municipal governments asserted their authority over channel capacities, franchise fees, local ownership rules, subscription rates, and public access provisions. In 1984, Congress addressed this with the first federal laws for cable television that gave cities authority over the franchising process and public access requirements, but limited franchise fees, forbade federal and state subscription rate regulations, and limited the powers of city government to regulate rates. With the stability of federal rules, cable penetration and new channels grew rapidly, but so did cable mergers, subscription rates, and service complaints. To redress this, in 1992 Congress enacted new legislation that established service standards and federal rate regulations as well as indecency rules for cable access channels (which were later found unconstitutional) and requirements to make cable programs available to competing providers including direct broadcast satellite. Because the federal appeals courts in 1986 and 1988 had struck down local broadcast carriage rules on free-speech grounds, the 1992 act reinstated must-carry requirements on up to one-third of cable systems' channel capacity, which the Supreme Court narrowly upheld a few years later. The act also gave local broadcasters the right to negotiate for compensation for carriage but larger cable operators refused to do so. Instead, broadcasters and their affiliated networks used this right to negotiate carriage of new cable channels, as did ABC with ESPN2 (both owned by Disney), NBC with CNBC, and Fox with FX.

In the late 1970s, Congress began to contemplate a more systemic rewrite of the Communications Act of 1934 to account for the emergence of new communications technologies. Industry and federal regulators moved toward a consensus that prioritized market competition and reduced government regulation to produce comprehensive legislation in 1996. The Telecommunications Act allowed telephone companies to offer video services, cable companies to offer telephone service, and broadcasters to own more stations nationwide and commit to timelines for converting to digital transmission. However, eight years later, telephone companies had yet to offer substantial competition in video, cable subscription rates had increased by 45 percent, and public interest groups and angry citizens had persuaded Congress that loosened broadcast ownership rules had given too much power to media conglomerates. In the late 1990s, direct broadcast satellites developed smaller dishes and digital compression technologies to offer local broadcast channels in addition to national networks, thus offering some competition to cable operators.

CABLE PROGRAM CARRIAGE TIMELINE

1952—Cable households, 14,000.

1960—Cable households, 650,000.

1961—A federal district court rejects restrictions on cable carriage on the basis of "unfair competition."

1964—A federal appeals court rejects right of broadcaster to restrict cable carriage.

1966—FCC asserts jurisdiction over cable and bans the importation of distant broadcast signals into largest 100 cities.

1968—U.S. Supreme Court finds that cable carriage of broadcast signal does not infringe on copyrights.

1970—Cable households, 4.8 million. FCC places content restrictions on pay cable.

1972—FCC lifts ban on distant broadcast signal importation into largest 100 cities and enacts nonduplication rules for these distant signals. Top markets must provide public, educational, government, and leased-access channels.

1974—A White House task force recommends separating cable operators from content providers.

1975—HBO launches using satellite distribution.

1976—Congress holds cable operators liable for broadcast copyrights and establishes compulsory licensing fees.

1977—Supreme Court strikes down pay-TV content restrictions.

1980—Cable households, 15 million.

1984—Congress enacts first federal cable TV laws, including granting cities franchising authority, restricting rate regulations, and reinforcing local broadcast must-carry rules.

1986 and 1988—Federal appeals court strikes down local broadcast must-carry rules as a violation of cable operators' First Amendment rights.

1990—Cable households, 53 million.

1992—Congress enacts laws for cable rate regulations, service standards, indecency rules, local broadcast must-carry requirements, and broadcaster rights to negotiate compensation for cable retransmission.

1994—Supreme Court upholds must-carry rules in a 5–4 decision.

1996—Congress enacts laws limiting cable rate regulations and loosening broadcast station ownership limits.

1997—Congress mandates a deadline of 2006 for converting to digital broadcasting.

2000—Cable households, 66 million. Satellite households, 12 million.

2002—Satellite operators required to carry local broadcast channels.

2005—Congress extends digital broadcast deadline to 2009.

2006—Congress debates federal video franchising for telephone companies and must-carry rules for broadcasters' multiple digital signals. FCC requires cable operators to carry broadcasters' main digital signal, effective 2009.

THE DIGITAL ERA

The most recent carriage disputes involve the transition to digital broadcasting. In 1997, Congress mandated that all broadcasters convert to digital broadcasting by the end of 2006. But cable operators' reluctance to carry broadcasters' analog and digital signals during the transition period slowed the process. In 2005, Congress extended the transition deadline to February 17, 2009, and provided $1.5 billion in subsidies to assist low-income households to purchase converter boxes. Because digital transmission makes more efficient use of the spectrum, broadcasters can offer multiple channels instead of just one. As of 2007, Congress has not required cable operators to carry broadcasters' additional channels. Absent these requirements, in 2005 public television stations entered an agreement with cable operators to carry four digital channels for each local PBS station. Local PBS affiliates have developed channels for kids programming, educational instruction, and local programming in addition to their main channels. Commercial broadcasters have lobbied for multicast carriage that some public interest groups have supported if additional public service requirements are enforced, such as channels for public affairs, educational children's programming, and community access.

Other carriage disputes include video franchising requirements for telephone companies. In 2006, the House passed a bill that stripped local municipalities of their authority to oversee the franchising process. The proceedings from the February 2006 Senate hearings on video franchising reveal a conceptual split between the public interest advocates in the television reform community and those with roots in Internet activism. The organizations that have worked in the trenches of local cable franchising for years, including the National Association of Telecom Officers, the National League of Cities, the National Conference of Mayors, and the Alliance for Community Media, made the case that without local oversight, national franchising would allow new entrants to redline their way to profitability and undermine local community participation in developing community-access television. However, Public Knowledge, the advocacy group focused on intellectual property issues and the defense of a "vibrant information commons," supported national video franchising to streamline the process and continue the deregulations set out in the 1996 Telecommunications Act (for the Senate hearings see http://commerce.senate.gov/hearings/witnesslist. cfm?id=1700; for Public Knowledge's hearing statement see http://commerce. senate.gov/pdf/sohn-021506.pdf). Similar debates have ensued at the state level (see http://www.freepress.net/news/21937).

The trajectory of these regulations over 60 years demonstrates the incremental approach that the FCC, Congress, and the courts have followed in addressing disputes between broadcasters and cable operators. Must-carry decisions were put in place, found unconstitutional, and then reintroduced to preserve free over-the-air local broadcasting as a primary public interest goal in television. But as broadband Internet technologies provide yet another distribution outlet for audiovisual programs, this history also reveals more structural issues regarding the property status of new technologies that can inform future debates. Government regulators have held broadcasters more accountable to community groups and citizens because broadcasters use the scarce public airwaves. Thus, the FCC, Congress, and the courts have favored citizen viewers' First Amendment rights to access diverse programming over the rights of commercial broadcasters. Conversely, regulators have treated cable wires as largely private property, favoring cable operators' First Amendment protections and limiting public interest requirements to must-carry rules and channel space for public access. Yet the private status of cable wires has been contested. Cable wires require public thoroughfares (such as city streets) and public airwaves to transmit national signals to local cable operators. Thus, in 1958 the Senate proposed a bill that applied the same public interest standards of broadcasters to cable operators, many state and municipal regulators in the 1960s and 1970s treated cable as a public utility, and telecommunications officials in the Nixon and Ford administrations recommended that cable be regulated as a common carrier with universal access requirements. More recently, the debate has turned to the Internet with a more market-oriented approach. In 2006, the FCC changed the property status of broadband Internet from a "telecommunications" service to an "information" service, which relieved Internet providers of universal access rules. A public-interest coalition fought back by calling on lawmakers to include "net-neutrality" provisions so that broadband service providers could not discriminate against content producers (see http://www.savetheinternet.com/=coalition).

CONCLUSION

A market-oriented consensus has driven communications policy since the FCC began deregulating cable television in the late 1970s. According to this consensus, new digital technologies hold the promise of solving public interest issues from expanding opportunities for local expression to uplifting the wasteland of popular commercial television, as long as the government steps out of the way to allow the "free market" to develop these new technologies. But in the wake of the failed market-oriented policies of the Telecommunications Act of 1996 that produced high prices, media conglomerates, and little competition, this consensus can be challenged through remembering that the property status of communications technologies is socially determined and open to contestation. From distant signal importation in the 1950s, local broadcast carriage in the 1960s, public access channels in the 1970s, rate regulations in the 1990s, and debates over video franchising jurisdictions and net neutrality in the 2000s, the lessons remain. Solutions require more than market-oriented approaches. Best practices have required regulatory frameworks where local, state, and federal governments; industry leaders; independent program producers; labor groups; public interest organizations; and concerned citizens have had a say in how communications technologies develop.

See also À La Carte Cable Pricing; Alternative Media in the United States; Conglomeration and Media Monopolies; Digital Divide; Media Reform; Net Neutrality; Online Digital Film and Television; Pirate Radio; Public Access Television; Public Broadcasting Service; Regulating the Airwaves.

Further Reading: Aufderheide, Patricia. *Communications Policy and the Public Interest: The Telecommunications Act of 1996.* New York: Guilford, 1999; Brown, Justin. "Digital Must-Carry and the Case for Public Television." *Cornell Journal of Law and Public Policy* 15 (Fall 2005): 74–109; Cooper, Mark. *Cable Mergers, Monopoly Power and Price Increases.* Washington, DC: Consumer's Union, 2003, http://www.consumersunion.org/pdf/CFA103.pdf; Gershon, Richard A. "Pay Cable Television: A Regulatory History." *Communications and the Law* 12, no. 2 (June 1990): 13–26; Horwitz, Robert. *The Irony of Regulatory Reform: The Deregulation of American Telecommunications.* New York: Oxford University Press, 1989; Le Duc, Don R. *Cable Television and the FCC: A Crisis in Media Control.* Philadelphia: Temple University Press, 1973; McChesney, Robert W. "Media Policy Goes to Main Street: The Uprising of 2003." *The Communication Review* 7 (2004): 223–58; Parsons, Patrick R., and Robert M. Frieden. *The Cable and Satellite Television Industries.* Boston: Allyn and Bacon, 1998; Parsons, Patrick. *Cable Television and the First Amendment.* Lexington, MA: Lexington Books, 1987; Shapiro, Andrew L. "Aiding the Final Push of the Digital Transition." *Cardozo Public Law, Policy and Ethics Journal* 5 (Fall 2006): 339–77; Sloan Commission on Cable Communications. *On the Cable: The Television of Abundance.* New York: McGraw-Hill, 1971; Smith, Ralph Lee. *The Wired Nation: Cable TV, the Electronic Communications Highway.* New York: Harper and Row, 1972; Snider, J. H. "Multi-Program Must-Carry for Broadcasters: Will It Mean No Public Interest Obligations for DTV?" *New America Foundation Spectrum Series Issue Brief no. 13*

(December 2003), http://www.democraticmedia.org/resources/articles/Pub_File_14pdf. pdf; Streeter, Thomas. "Blue Skies and Strange Bedfellows: The Discourse of Cable Television." In *The Revolution Wasn't Televised: Sixties Television and Social Conflict*, ed., Lynn Spigel and Michael Curtin, 221–42. New York: Routledge, 1997.

John McMurria

CELEBRITY WORSHIP AND FANDOM

The faces, fashionable figures, and extravagant lifestyles of media celebrities have become part of audiences' everyday lives. Proliferating entertainment news shows, Web sites, and magazines have created levels of familiarity and intimacy previously only shared with those in our immediate social environment. However, when celebrities become objects of fans' affection, the psychological bonds between fans and their favorite stars can rarely be described as worship or one-sided adoration, as fans and audiences negotiate and appropriate the media products through which they encounter the celebrity. They thus construct distinct meanings in their reading of mediated individuals.

A poignant and often echoed definition of celebrity was offered by Daniel Boorstin as early as half a century ago when he identified a celebrity as a "person who is known for his well-knownness" (1961, p. 58). Boorstin's definition highlights two key aspects of the cultural phenomenon of celebrity. First is its self-perpetuating nature in which media exposure breeds celebrity and celebrity furthers exposure. This inherent spiral of celebrity is unmasked in the recent rise of jet set—and reality television—celebrities, exemplified by Paris Hilton, whose celebrity status appears unrelated to any recognizable professional achievements. However, the difference between such recent examples of celebrity and more traditional manifestations of stardom such as film and sports stars in the first half of the twentieth century, the rise of pop musicians in the postwar period, and fashion models since the 1980s is one of degree rather than kind. Celebrity is thus a distinctly modern occurrence tied to the transformations of consumption, communication, and everyday life in industrial modernity. Second, Boorstin's definition points to the importance of audiences' sustained interaction with celebrities in media consumption allowing for degrees of familiarity and intimacy.

CELEBRITY AND INTIMACY

This perceived intimacy and its psychological consequences have been a focus of academic research on media power as well as the relationship between mass media and self. The presence and importance of celebrities in audiences' everyday lives has been viewed by early mass communication research as an indication of the power that media exercise over audiences: some have identified film stars as manifestations of "pseudo-individuality," which is maintained through shallow variations of physical appearance seeking to mask the inherent standardization of life and conformity in industrial societies (Horkheimer and Adorno 1972). The pretense and artificiality of the relationship between celebrities and audiences is in turn emphasized in Horton and Wohl's notion of "para-social interaction." According to Horton and Wohl, the interaction between stars and audiences "characteristically, is one-sided, nondialectical, controlled by the performer, and not susceptible of mutual development" (1956, p. 215), thus leaving audiences largely disempowered. To some, then, celebrity works as a powerful form of social and crowd control in the era of mass societies.

That such control has been *attempted* rather than successful (cf. Marshall 1997), however, reflects the complex power of relations between celebrities and their fans. John Thompson describes the relationship between fan and celebrity as "non-reciprocal intimacy at a distance" in which the celebrity does not "talk back." In contrast to face-to-face communication, audiences' encounters with celebrities are thus forms of "mediated quasi-interaction." Thompson suggests that audiences gain rather than lose control over such relationships: it is precisely because celebrities are so familiar to us, yet are not part of our daily face-to-face interactions or our social environment, that audiences have the capacity to shape their relationship with distant others. Celebrities are available at the press of a button or by opening a magazine when and where we like and require, while the communicative distance between celebrities and audiences creates the space for idealized readings of celebrities—a circumstance that explains the often profound disappointment of fans who meet their favorite celebrity face-to-face. Thompson thus describes an interest in given celebrities and the act of becoming a fan as a "strategy of self," a way to meaningfully build an identity in a mediated world.

FANDOM AS RELIGION?

The intense emotional attachment many fans display towards their favorite television show, sports team, band, or film star has triggered frequent comparisons between fandom and religion. Equally, stars and popular icons span the extraordinary world of media celebrity with the mundane life of audience members in ways similar to how religious iconography offers a link between the divine and the believer. Indeed, journalistic and academic discourses employ a range of religious terminology: "worship," "devotion," and "pilgrimage" are all popular concepts to describe fan practices. Even the word "fan" finds its etymological root in *fanaticus*, the Latin word for a member of a temple.

Despite such linguistic parallels, the differences between fandom and religion are profound: however intense the emotional bond between fans and stars, it is rarely attributed with transcendental significance by fans. Equally, while certain fan cultures employ religious symbols in fan art, as, for example, Jesus-like depictions of Elvis, such symbolism is employed by such fans to express their simultaneous fandom and faith. The link between religion and fandom is thus largely one of shared spaces identity construction: in today's mediated world, the consumption of popular media and icons has created an alternative space for identities to be formed and negotiated, thus filling a void created by the secularization of modern life.

CELEBRITY CULTURE VERSUS FAN CULTURE

Thompson's work reflects a shift of the pendulum from focusing on celebrities (media production) to focusing on fans and audiences (media consumption). Instead of concentrating on "celebrity culture," we might instead highlight the audience's power in creating meaning in the consumption of popular culture. In John Fiske's (1989a, 1989b) analogy, we could compare popular media products to jeans—they are mass-produced commodities that for all the standardization in their production become meaningful only through the way they are worn, made our own, and eventually torn by consumers. Far from uncritical worshippers of a particular celebrity, fans make "tactical" use of popular icons in ways that are empowering to themselves. Henry Jenkins's seminal study *Textual Poachers* further documents the degree to which audiences appropriate media texts for their own ends. In Jenkins's words, "I am not claiming that there is anything particularly empowering about the texts fans embrace. I am, however, claiming that there is something empowering about what fans do with those texts in the process of assimilating them to the particulars of their lives" (1992, p. 284). Crucially, rather than a bond between isolated audience members and their objects of affection, fans are often part of communities that share readings and ways of using media products, and hence that foster the critical rereading and appropriation of these products, as well as the creation of fan-authored materials such as fan fiction.

DESPERATELY SEEKING CELEBRITY

As part of his portrayal of postwar American consumer culture as suffering from a cultural pathology of narcissism, the historian Christopher Lasch identified the incessant need of individuals in such conditions to exercise their individuality by striving for fame and celebrity and thus seeking to separate themselves from the anonymous masses. The celebrity universe according to Lasch is a constant encouragement for the "common man" to identify with extraordinary and the spectacular, making the banality of our everyday existence difficult to bear.

In this approach, the contemporary fascination with celebrity is fuelled by the inherent focus on the self and self-fulfillment in contemporary culture. Crucially, however, such self-centeredness does not lead to the worship or adoration of a particular celebrity, which is always an act of subordination, but to the desire to achieve celebrity oneself, lucidly illustrated in the sheer endless supply of those seeking fame through participating in reality television programs, casting shows such as *American Idol*, or television talk shows. Fans and those striving for celebrity thus engage in opposing practices: while fans intersect themselves into media products through the distinct meanings they create in their readings underscored by admiration and appreciation of mediated stars and texts, celebrity seekers' interest does not lie with external objects (i.e., actual celebrities) but with their self and its ambition to achieve celebrity status.

FANS, ADMIRERS, OR WORSHIPPERS?

Just as with other media products such as television programs, celebrities too can become multifaceted objects that offer fans a range of readings and meanings, for pertaining to the rules and varieties of audience use, there is no fundamental distinction between the different forms of mediated popular culture. Admittedly, in their glamour, many celebrities reveal the inherent commercial logic of cultural production more pronouncedly than other popular texts. But at the same time, fan cultures focusing on particular celebrities are distinctly less common than phrases such as "celebrity worship" suggest. In Boorstin's definition of celebrity based on how well known a celebrity is, the boundaries between fame and notoriety are distinctly blurred. The dictum that there is no such thing as bad publicity has been taken to new levels by twenty-first century arrivals on the celebrity circuit such as Britney Spears and Paris Hilton. Yet, while their immense exposure ensures how well they are known, this presence does not automatically translate into being liked or even cherished. As Sconce notes, we are erroneous if we assume that "most Americans *like* Paris Hilton, when in fact, the vast majority of her media exposure is framed as negative irritation" (2007, p. 330). Celebrities can then serve not as object of worship or adoration but also as the focus of anti-fandom and displeasure. Moreover, in those cases where celebrities are at the center of fan cultures, they—at least from the point of view of the fan—take on other qualities than simply being well known and are valued for their musical, acting, or sporting talents; their appearance; or their actions and convictions.

Recent psychological and psychoanalytical approaches to the bond between fans and their fan objects further confirm that celebrity and media exposure provide a premise but not a sufficient basis for affection and adoration. In 1985, Vermorel and Vermorel collected a series of fan fantasies drawing on popular icons such as pop stars; their book documents how audiences' interests in stars are fed by sexual desires articulated in such fantasies. Desire and lust, however, do not equate to worship (and on occasion, the sexual fantasies they report point in the opposite direction) and can be assumed to be often fleeting and tied to particular physical attributes. Subsequent work examining fans of female Hollywood stars of the 1940s and 1950s (see Stacey 1994) and Anthony Elliott's analysis of the motives of Mark Davis Chapman's murder of John Lennon in December 1980 have suggested that fans engage in processes of "projection" and "interjection," in which an idealized reading of the star allows for the externalization of positive and negative attributes of the fan him or herself, and thus provides the basis for the emotional bond between fan and star. Stars and other fan objects might then function as a "mirror" to fans' self-image, offering a bond between fan and star that is grounded in the fan's unrecognized self-reflection. In all such scenarios, the celebrity is thus not the object of abject adoration or worship, but subject to complex processes of identification, projection, and reflection and can be ascribed with positives (fandom) or negative connotations (anti-fandom). While how well the celebrity is known is the premise for such processes to take place in acts of "mediated quasi-interaction," they also require subjectively recognized qualities beyond simple celebrity status. Celebrity by itself therefore does not guarantee public affection and adoration, and celebrity status doesn't automatically translate into popularity, much less worship.

See also Audience Power to Resist; Cultural Appropriation; Paparazzi and Photographic Ethics; Sensationalism, Fear Mongering, and Tabloid Media; Transmedia Storytelling and Media Franchises; User-Created Content and Audience Participation.

Further Reading: Boorstin, Daniel. *The Image: A Guide to Pseudo Events in America*. New York: Atheneum, 1961; Cavicchi, Daniel. *Tramps Like Us; Music and Meaning among Springsteen Fans*. New York: Oxford University Press, 1998; Elliott, Anthony. *The Mourning of John Lennon*. Berkeley: University of California Press, 1999; Fiske, John, *Reading the Popular*. Boston: Unwin and Hyman, 1989a; Fiske, John, *Understanding Popular Culture*, Boston: Unwin and Hyman, 1989b; Gray, Jonathan, Cornel Sandvoss, and C. Lee Harrington, eds. *Fandom: Identities and Communities in a Mediated*. New York: New York University Press, 2007; Hills, Matt. *Fan Cultures*. New York: Routledge, 2002; Horkheimer, Max, and Theodor W. Adorno. "The Culture Industry: Enlightenment as Mass Deception," in *Dialectic of Enlightenment*, New York: Seabury, 1972; Horton, Donald, and R. Richard Wohl. "Mass Communication and Parasocial Interaction: Observation on Intimacy at a Distance." *Psychiatry* 19, no. 3 (1956): 215–29; Jenkins, Henry. *Textual Poachers: Television Fans and Participatory Culture*. New York: Routledge, 1992; Lasch, Christopher. *The Culture of Narcissism: American Life in an Age of Diminishing Expectations*. New York: W. W. Norton, 1979; Marshall, P. David. *Celebrity and Power: Fame in Contemporary Culture*. Minneapolis: University of Minnesota Press, 1997; Rojek, Chris. *Celebrity*. London: Reaktion, 2001; Sandvoss, Cornel. *Fans: The Mirror of Consumption*. Malden, MA: Polity, 2005; Sconce, Jeffrey. "A Vacancy at the Paris Hilton," in *Fandom: Identities and Communities in a Mediated World*, ed. Jonathan Gray, Cornel Sandvoss, and C. Lee Harrington. New York: New York University Press, 2007; Stacey, Jackie. *Stargazing: Hollywood Cinema and Female Spectatorship*. New York: Routledge, 1994; Thompson, John B. *The Media and Modernity: A Social Theory of the Media*, Cambridge: Polity, 1995; Turner, Graeme. *Understanding Celebrity*. Thousand Oaks, CA: Sage, 2004; Vermorel, Fred, and Judy Vermorel. *Starlust: The Secret Fantasies of Fans*. London: Comet, 1985.

Cornel Sandvoss

CHILDREN AND EFFECTS: FROM *SESAME STREET* TO COLUMBINE

Children are generally considered to be a vulnerable audience, and fears about the possible negative effects that media might have on them have circulated since the spread of mass-produced culture in the nineteenth century. At the same time, there have always been progressives who have assumed that "proper" media could have positive effects on children. What roles should parents, educators, the government, and media producers themselves play in guaranteeing that children have access to appropriate media? And who decides what is appropriate?

THE TELEVISION RATINGS SYSTEM

A voluntary ratings system for television was established in 1997, and all programs except for news and sports are now rated Y (suitable for children aged 2 to 6), Y7 (may not be suitable for children under 7), G (suitable for general audiences), PG (parental guidance suggested), 14 (may not be suitable for children under 14), or MA (suitable for mature audiences). There are also specific content indicators. Y7 shows, for example, are frequently labeled FV for "fantasy violence"; the label is considered less strong than the plain V given to programs for older viewers. Other content labels include: S (sexual situations), L (coarse language), or D (suggestive dialogue). Studies have shown, though, that many parents are unfamiliar with the ratings and that very few use their V-chips.

Anxieties about the possible effects of media on children spring in large part from the adult desire to uphold a sacred ideal of childhood innocence. Adults fear that media may have a wide range of effects on children, making them violent or sexually active, for example, or inculcating them with racist, sexist, or homophobic prejudices. Of course, what is "negative" depends on the point of view of the adult. Traditionalist parents, such as members of conservative religious groups, are likely to want their children to consume very different media than that which would be favored by more liberal parents.

Unlike many concerned parents, most producers of media see children not as endangered innocents but as savvy consumers capable of making their own decisions about media consumption. If, from the point of view of video game, TV, movie, and comic book producers, media are to be censored by anyone, it is clearly parents who should be in the driver's seat, not the government.

Activists tend to disagree, feeling that government should take a more active role in regulating children's media. However, activists vary widely in their definitions of what is dangerous. Liberals like Action for Children's Television focused on eliminating excessive commercialism. Conservative groups like, in the 1980s, the born-again Christian group the Moral Majority, and, more recently, the evangelicals of Focus on the Family, have focused almost exclusively on advocating the censorship of sexuality.

HISTORICAL OVERVIEW

Perhaps the most famous opponent of putatively dangerous children's media was Anthony Comstock, a late nineteenth- and early twentieth-century moral reformer who was particularly concerned about dime novels—cheap storybooks for working-class kids that emphasized criminal adventures. In the 1930s, the social-scientific Payne Fund Studies also addressed the issue of the teaching of crime to minors. One of the most widely publicized of the studies examined the film-going habits of juvenile delinquents. Not surprisingly, when asked if they had turned to crime because of gangster films, many boys were eager to oblige the researchers and say yes. The girls studied were runaways, many of whom had

had sexual relations; these subjects, too, were happy to blame their adventures on the scenes of seduction they had observed in Hollywood films.

By 1934, Hollywood's self-censoring organization, the Production Code Administration (PCA), had perfected a system for previewing all scripts and completed films with an eye for making them "safe" for general consumption. Children (and "immature" adults) were to be shielded from images of sex and violence. In the 1950s, as the PCA began to lose power, a new bogeyman emerged: crime and horror comics. Psychologist Frederick Wertham spearheaded a movement against violent comics, claiming they schooled children in sadism and sexual perversion. In 1954, the Comics Code Authority was set up by the comics industry to censor itself. Though the Code was theoretically voluntary, the industry feared that if it didn't censor itself the government would step in and do the job.

Of course, comics were not considered the only source of juvenile delinquency in the 1950s: TV was also singled out. Shows like *The Untouchables* were attacked for their violence, but it was not just television's images that were seen as the problem; TV itself became a new member of the family, a device that could bring families together around a "wholesome" program or divide families who fought over viewing decisions. TV might even do ill to children, adults worried, by harming their vision or diverting their time from wholesome outdoor play.

In the post–World War II years, anxieties about the sexual content and, more generally, rebellious attitude of rock 'n' roll were also on the rise. These kinds of anxieties would surface again in 1985 when the Parents Music Research Council would successfully advocate for warning labels to be put on sexually explicit (or explicitly violent) albums. Youth-targeted music had contained risqué lyrics for years, but anxieties came to a head in the 1980s due in large part to the dramatic commercial success of rap music and the rise of the Walkman, which enabled kids to listen to music in utter privacy. Anxious parents worried about

SESAME STREET

Sesame Street was the first American educational children's program to receive government funding and the first to be produced with input from psychologists and educators. It was also a breakthrough show for its aggressive targeting of minority viewers, and part of its enduring legacy is the idea that multiculturalism should play a role in children's television. Each season, a curriculum is rigorously plotted out and segments are tested on the target audience (3- to 5-year-olds); segments that do not successfully hold viewers' attention or convey lessons are revised or discarded before broadcast. In the early years, a relatively small amount of *Sesame Street* merchandise existed, but today the show's characters are widely marketed; such commercialization is a symptom of PBS's overall commercialization in the wake of dramatically reduced government support for public broadcasting. When *Sesame Street* first premiered, it was controversial; developmental psychologists worried about the show's fast pacing and questioned the idea of using television to teach, and right-wingers attacked the show for its picture of racial integration. Today, however, there is probably no program more widely acknowledged as having positive effects on young viewers.

what their children might be secretly listening to and whether that private music might have negative consequences.

Though anxieties about the effects of music, television, and film on children still bubble up, video games and the Internet are today seen as the biggest threats to children. Video games are assumed to make children violent and sexually precocious; the Internet is often assumed to be swarming with sexual predators. To keep children "safe" from the Internet, conservative politicians and activists fought for the inclusion of the Communications Decency Act (CDA) in the Telecommunications Act of 1996. The CDA was intended to make the entire Internet devoid of content that might harm minors. This proved both unfeasible—given the Internet's vast, decentralized, international sprawl—and unconstitutional. The courts struck down the CDA as a First Amendment violation almost immediately.

GOVERNMENT REGULATION OF TELEVISION

In the 1950s, Senator Estes Kefauver led hearings on juvenile delinquency, which included testimony on the possible effects of TV, radio, and comics on children, and Senator Thomas Dodd held hearings specifically on television violence in the early 1960s. Senator John Pastore held hearings on TV violence in 1972 in response to a series of studies on "Television and Social Behavior" that had been commissioned by the Surgeon General's Office. The studies' results were inconclusive: it was clear that viewing violent images might have short-term effects on children's behavior, but whether the images could cause damage over time remained very much an open question. In any case, the government did not attempt to directly regulate television content as a result of the studies.

ACT fought a long battle for the regulation of children's television, and in the 1970s the Federal Communications Commission (FCC) instituted a number of rules for children's television, regulating the ratio of program to commercial content, adding separators ("bumpers") between programs and ads, and eliminating "host-selling," the practice of television hosts (lead actors on children's shows) directly hawking goods to their young viewers during programs. These regulations were clearly designed with the assumption that excessive commercialism had negative effects on child viewers. The regulations were undone in the 1980s by President Ronald Reagan's FCC.

In the 1990s, politicians debated the V-chip, a device to be implanted in all televisions that would enable parents to block out inappropriate content. The V-chip requirement was included in the Telecommunications Act of 1996. "V" stood for "violence," as promoters of the chip assumed that violent material was the content that parents were most concerned about. Conservative religious activists opposed the chip, advocating instead (without success) that TV should simply be cleaned up across the board so that V-chips were unnecessary.

As a result of persistent activist pressure, the Children's Television Act (generally supported by Democratic politicians and opposed by Republican politicians) was finally passed in 1990. The Act requires broadcasters—but not cable providers—to provide three hours of educational or informational programming

COLUMBINE

The teenagers who shot and killed their classmates at Columbine High School in 1999 were alienated youths in long, black trench coats. Though they did not sport the make-up, jewelry, and other dark markers of the Goth subculture, the boys were widely identified as Goths, and a national hysteria about the dangers of youth culture ensued. Goth influences range from horror films to Romanticism and Gothic literature, and Goths express their loneliness and feelings of alienation through their theatrical, vampire-like appearance and their taste for dark music. In the wake of Columbine, adults were quick to blame musicians like Satanist Marilyn Manson for his corrupting influence on Goths. Less attention was paid to the important sociological conditions that cause nonconformist youth (those with no interest in sports and unusual tastes in music, clothes, or books) to feel lonely and alienated in the first place. A handful of liberals observed that easy access to guns obviously enabled the Columbine killers, but most irate adults felt that media—which was assumed to turn kids into Goths—was the more pressing problem. One Republican cited in *Time* magazine went so far as to say that our country needed "Goth control" not "gun control."

---

to children each week. The rationale for imposing such obligations on broadcasters is twofold: (1) Children are a vulnerable minority audience, and broadcasters have an obligation to provide something of value to this vulnerable audience rather than simply manipulating it. (2) The broadcast spectrum (the air through which broadcast signals are sent) is, in principle, owned by the public, and broadcasters are legally obliged "to serve the public interest, convenience, and necessity." Free market proponents argue that the Nielsen ratings are a sufficient gauge of which programs serve the public, and that government has no place interfering with broadcasters' business practices. Those favoring regulation, conversely, argue that children's special needs cannot be assumed to be met by whatever program is able to garner the highest rates for candy and toy ads; excessive commercialism, from this perspective, has a very negative effect on children.

ASSUMPTIONS AND MISUNDERSTANDINGS UNDERPINNING ADULT ATTACKS ON CHILDREN'S MEDIA

Adult-led attacks on media consumed by children have shifted their focus over time, but certain elements seem to recur, underpinning the activities of anxious adults. First, adults have tended to exaggerate the vulnerability of children while, conversely, imagining themselves mysteriously immune to being negatively affected by media. Second, adults have assumed that children are naturally innocent and pure, and are only corrupted when introduced to mass media. That children might be naturally greedy, violent, or sexually curious is rarely considered because such an idea would conflict with very strong cultural assumptions (which only emerged in the Victorian era) that children were inherently good and pure. Third, media have become scapegoats. If a child is excessively hostile, it is easier to blame television or video games than to look elsewhere (the family or school) for causes. Fourth, would-be censors speaking in the name of children often really want to clean up *everybody's* media. Such censors, in effect, end up treating all media consumers as if they are children. Fifth, attacks on children's media, whether undertaken by activists, politicians, or social scientists, have tended to decontextualize media, especially media with violent content. "Violence" is rarely understood as one narrative component among others, or seen has having a potentially positive valence.

For example, journalistic attacks on *Buffy the Vampire Slayer* shortly after the shootings at Columbine in 1999 emphasized that one episode (whose broadcast was deferred after Columbine) pictured a miserable teenager with a gun, isolated in a tower within shooting range of his classmates. That the episode centered, with great sensitivity, on the real pain of adolescence, and that the boy with the gun was driven to consider not mass murder but rather suicide, was simply ignored. It did not matter to angry grown-ups that *Buffy* examined violence in a thoughtful way; they were sure that popular culture—especially video games and Goth music—were the root cause of the Columbine incident, and they were eager to attack any youth media that dealt with violence, regardless of its approach (see "Columbine" sidebar).

The important thing to remember is that every generation witnesses hysteria about whatever media is most popular among children. Such hysteria tends to subside when the next big thing comes along. Waves of hysteria are also shaped by shifting political climates. With President George W. Bush, a conservative born-again Christian, in the White House, and a Republican Congress, Janet Jackson's breast-baring "costume malfunction" at the 2004 Super Bowl snowballed into a national conservative Christian campaign to sanitize the airwaves in order to keep children safe from profanity and sexually charged images. Suddenly, the FCC was deluged with complaints about "indecent" material, and it responded by fining radio and TV broadcasters at a previously unheard of rate. When Democrats have dominated Congress or the White House, concerns about media effects have focused less on sex and more on commercialism and the advocacy of educational programming.

EDUCATIONAL TELEVISION

Alarmist declarations about the purported negative effects of media on children will always, unfortunately, receive more attention than attempts to use media to educate, edify, or simply entertain youth in a positive manner. Yet there have always been a minority of educators, activists, politicians, parents, and media producers themselves who have stood up for the potentially positive effects that media might have on children. The FCC's first female commissioner, Frieda Hennock, was a strong advocate for educational programming (directed to both adults and children) in the late 1940s and early 1950s. In the 1960s, FCC chairman Newton Minow and Attorney General Robert F. Kennedy encouraged broadcasters to create more educational programming. At the time, "educational" children's shows like *Romper Room* and *Captain Kangaroo* focused on socialization and basic skills like tying one's shoelaces. That all changed with the premiere of *Sesame Street* in 1969, which shifted the focus to teaching cognitive skills (see "*Sesame Street*"). Today, most educational programming is shown on PBS and on the children's cable channel Nickelodeon. *Blue's Clues* and *Dora the Explorer* are among Nickelodeon's most popular educational shows.

See also Government Censorship and Freedom of Speech; Media Literacy; Media Reform; Media Watch Groups; Public Broadcasting Service; Regulating the Airwaves; Television in Schools; Video Games; Violence and Media; Youth and Media Use.

Further Reading: Buckingham, David. *After the Death of Childhood: Growing Up in the Age of Electronic Media.* Cambridge: Polity Press, 2000; Hendershot, Heather. *Saturday Morning Censors: Television Regulation before the V-Chip.* Durham: Duke University Press, 1998; Jenkins, Henry, ed. *The Children's Culture Reader.* New York: New York University Press, 1998; Jenkins, Henry, ed. "Professor Jenkins Goes to Washington." *Harper's Magazine* (July 1999): 19–23; Kunkel, Dale. "From a Raised Eyebrow to a Turned Back: The FCC and Children's Product-Related Programming." *Journal of Communications* 38, no. 4 (August 1988): 90–108; Morrow, Robert W. *Sesame Street and the Reform of Children's Television.* Baltimore: Johns Hopkins University Press, 2006; Seiter, Ellen. *Sold Separately: Children and Parents in Consumer Culture.* New Brunswick: Rutgers University Press, 1993; Singer, Dorothy G., and Jerome L. Singer, eds. *Handbook of Children and the Media.* Thousand Oaks, CA: Sage, 2001; Spigel, Lynn. "Seducing the Innocent: Childhood and Television in Postwar America" in *Welcome to the Dreamhouse: Popular Media and Postwar Suburbs,* ed. Lynn Spigel. Durham: Duke University Press, 2001.

Heather Hendershot

COMMUNICATION AND KNOWLEDGE LABOR

In the information age, contemporary advanced societies are no longer organized around agriculture or manufacturing. Instead, an increasing amount of work is directed toward production and distribution of information, communication, and knowledge. This shift has changed the occupational structures of developed societies and is beginning to be felt in some less developed ones as well. As job opportunities and working environments change with the development of new technologies, telecommunication companies have benefited from reducing the skill component of jobs or eliminating jobs entirely and replacing them with automated systems. This especially applies to jobs traditionally filled by women. Global telecommunication technology also allows outsourcing of knowledge workers to cheaper labor markets in the developing world. With these changes, the question facing scholars of communication and information technology is not how such changes will continue, but if knowledge workers will realize their strength and organize around their common interests.

The study of knowledge labor has raised important questions for academics and policy makers. Because they have such an important impact on research and intervention, the most fundamental questions have to do with how we define and make use of the terms. Since there is extensive debate on this topic, it is more useful to provide a range of definitions for each term than imagine and impose one ostensibly correct meaning.

DEFINING KNOWLEDGE LABOR

Knowledge work has been defined in the narrow sense as involving creative labor or the direct manipulation of symbols to create an original knowledge product or to add obvious value to an existing one. According to this view, knowledge work would include what writers, artists, Web page designers, and software creators do. A more expansive definition encompasses the work of those who handle and distribute information, including people like librarians and postal workers. The reason for considering these jobs to be knowledge occupations is because an increasing amount of the work performed involves making use of information to efficiently and effectively deliver an information product. By including this work, one acknowledges that the line between what is and is not creative labor in the knowledge field is very fuzzy and that a good case can be made that workers who appear to be more marginal to knowledge production nevertheless add tangible value to the information product. There is also a practical purpose to expanding the definition. The meaning of knowledge labor is not just measured by external criteria but by how it is subjectively experienced by workers themselves. Creative work is distinguished from information handling or distribution because it is felt to be different in the lives of workers. But that is less the case today as evidenced by the growing "convergence" of different kinds of workers organized under the same union umbrellas. Finally, the most expansive definition of knowledge work would include all workers involved in the chain of producing and distributing knowledge products. This view maintains that workers involved in the production of computer hardware, including low-wage immigrant women workers in Silicon Valley and abroad, are knowledge workers because they are an integral part of the value chain that results in the production of the central engine of knowledge production, the computer. Similarly, call-center workers who sell communication products and services would also fall within this broad definition of knowledge work because they are central to marketing information and make use of the products of communication technology to carry out their work. Moreover, the management and control of their work would not be possible without the advanced surveillance technologies made possible by developments in communication and information technology.

THE RISE OF KNOWLEDGE WORKERS

Discussion and debate about the relationship between the technologies of communication and information, work, and social development is not new. An extended history of the subject in the West would include the work of Comte de Saint-Simon, who speculated on the transformation from manual to mental labor in the eighteenth century; of Karl Marx. who referred to the formation of a "general intellect" in the course of capitalist development; and of Charles Babbage, whose difference engine gave us one of the first serious designs for a computer in the nineteenth century. These and others have had a substantial impact on how we think about work and information technology. In the last 50 years, the academic emphasis has been on developing measures to track the growth of the information sector as an economic force. Jean Fourastié provided the first sustained analysis of the division between agriculture, manufacturing, and the expanding services sector. Fritz Machlup was among the leaders in charting the expansion of the data and information components of the economy, and Marc Uri Porat built on this work to document the shift from an economy based on the primary (agriculture) and secondary (manufacturing) sectors to one rooted in services (tertiary) and information (quaternary) occupations. Neither Machlup nor Porat addressed the political, social, and cultural implications of this transformation in anything approaching the theoretical sophistication of Daniel Bell.

According to Bell, we were not merely experiencing a growth in data and information, nor merely a shift in the major occupational categories, but a transformation in the nature of capitalist society. Capitalism had been governed for two centuries by industrialists and their financiers, who comprised the capitalist class. Now, with the rise of a society dependent on technology and particularly on the production and distribution of information, Bell maintained that a new class of leaders, a genuine knowledge class of well-trained scientific-technical workers, was rising to prominence and ultimately to leadership of a postindustrial capitalism. Inherited wealth and power would shrink in significance and a genuine meritocracy would rule. Such a society would not necessarily be more democratic, but it did portend a shift in power from its traditional base in family inheritance to technical and scientific knowledge. The ranks of knowledge workers would literally power and manage this new postindustrial economy, leading to steady economic growth and the decline of historic ideologies. For Bell, political battles over public policy would diminish as technical algorithms and knowledge-based measures would govern. There would no doubt be tensions in such a society, but these would be technical and not ideological.

KNOWLEDGE COMPANIES DOMINATE
AND DE-SKILL WORKERS

It did not take long for others to conclude that, cultural issues aside, postindustrialism itself was not inherently progressive. For Herbert Schiller, postindustrialism meant the rise of transnational media and communication businesses that would pump out support for American values, including its military and imperial ambitions, and eliminate alternatives through increasingly concentrated market power. According to Harry Braverman, for the vast majority of workers in the service, retail, and knowledge professions, labor would be as regimented and ultimately de-skilled, as it had been in assembly-line manufacturing. Indeed, given the immateriality of knowledge work, it would be easier than in the industrial era to separate conception from execution, and to concentrate the power of conception (e.g., design and management) in a dominant class.

There has been widespread debate ever since Bell, Braverman, and Schiller addressed these issues, but there is some agreement in key areas. There is consensus that a shift has occurred in developed societies, and that one is beginning in some less developed ones, from manufacturing to knowledge work. Yes, people agree, there was and still is considerable knowledge required in much of

CONVERGENCE BITES BACK

On August 15, 2005, Canada's national broadcaster, the CBC, locked out all of its employees in a labor dispute. The company decided to contract out much of its work to temporary, part-time, and freelance employees in order to save on labor costs as well as to hire and lay off workers as it wished. The union representing permanent employees refused to sign a new agreement with these provisions and the battle was on.

CBC management expected victory because it had succeeded in convincing the Canadian government that all of its employees, once members of numerous unions, should be brought together in one bargaining unit. It expected that members of a union containing newsreaders, writers, camera operators, and skilled and semi-skilled technical personnel would not get along and would certainly not hold out together in a long labor dispute. The company was wrong.

In one of the first successful labor actions of its kind, a diverse group of knowledge workers held out together for seven weeks and used their communication skills to rally the CBC audience to its side. Most notably, they organized a national caravan dubbed CBC Unlocked, and broadcast "lockout" versions of favorite programs on community stations across the country. When the company succeeded in securing one bargaining unit, workers chose to join the Communication Workers of America (CWA), the leading example of a converged union. Canadian nationalists were upset, but the CWA used its large membership base to provide $7 million in strike benefits and drew on its international networks to organize pickets at Canadian embassies around the world.

The company eventually gave in to the pressure of its workers, its audience, and the Canadian government, and settled for far less than it wanted, thereby demonstrating the power of a converged union and of knowledge workers to unite and use their communication skills effectively.

---

manufacturing as well as in agricultural work. But the difference today is that an increasing amount of work is taken up with the production and distribution of information, communication, and knowledge. Furthermore, there is agreement that a dynamic process of de-skilling, up-skilling, and re-skilling is taking place in the occupational hierarchy. At different times and in different sectors one or another of these processes predominates, but the labor process, most concur, cannot be reduced to the singularity of one process. Nevertheless, there is also agreement that companies have benefited from reducing the skill component of jobs or eliminating jobs entirely and replacing them with automated systems, and this especially applies to jobs traditionally filled by women.

OUTSOURCING KNOWLEDGE LABOR

Where de-skilling or job elimination is not possible, companies have accomplished the same objective by moving jobs to low-wage areas within a country or by shipping them abroad. Since knowledge work typically does not require moving material things over long distances (e.g., call centers and software engineering contain little or no bulk), the production process requires the use of global telecommunications systems whose costs have been declining over years of technological development. This process of outsourcing enables, for example, an American company to use data-entry workers in China, call-center employees in Canada, and software programmers in India and incur a fraction of the labor costs that it would by employing workers in the United States. This process is by and large an extension of the general predominance of a business-led neoliberal agenda that has transformed the business-labor social contract of the 1950s and 1960s (guaranteed jobs at a living wage with a package of benefits) to a business-first agenda that, in the name of productivity, has made jobs, wages, and certainly benefits far from a guarantee in today's developed societies. Because outsourcing is part of a wider business agenda that has also attacked the social policy instruments that protected labor and trade unions, it has been all the more difficult for working people to mount a successful defense.

KNOWLEDGE WORKERS UNITE

Out of necessity and often using the tools of their trade, knowledge workers are increasingly organizing to defend creative work and its public purpose. Across the converging communication and information technology sectors, they are organizing trade unions that respond to technological convergence and the convergence of companies that have created massive concentration in the knowledge industry. For example, the Communication Workers of America (CWA) represents 700,000 workers in the media, telecommunication, and information technology sectors. A similar convergent union, the Communication, Energy and Paperworkers of Canada, now represents about 80,000 workers in these and other occupations. Demonstrating the value of labor convergence across borders, the CWA used its power to successfully unite on-air and technical workers to defeat the 2005 lockout of workers at Canada's national broadcaster. At the international level, the Union Network International (UNI), a global federation spanning the converging knowledge arena, calls itself "a new international for a new millennium." UNI was founded in 2000 and includes 15.5 million workers from 900 unions in 140 countries. Finally, even high-tech workers, typically an enormous challenge to organize, have, with the help of the CWA and other unions, revived social movement unionism in the United States by organizing disgruntled workers who write code and produce content at Microsoft, IBM, and other big firms.

WILL ACADEMIC KNOWLEDGE WORKERS FOLLOW?

University and college professors long ago recognized that technology, education, and professional status did not lift them out of the realm of workers. Many responded by organizing trade unions that follow the craft model. This has provided a privileged status and academics are arguably the new aristocracy of labor. But it has separated teachers in higher education from the process of labor convergence. As a result, they cannot enjoy the benefits of joining workers across the knowledge arena and the opportunity to extend to other knowledge workers the principles that university faculty have fought with some success to maintain: full-time, secure jobs, with tenure and good pensions. Instead of setting the standard for knowledge workers worldwide, university faculty have hoarded their privileged status. But commercialization with new technologies continues to nip at the heels of academic labor and threatens to shred that status. Indeed, the future of knowledge and communication labor is likely to depend less on the next new thing and more on whether knowledge workers of the world, including academic workers, will unite.

See also Bollywood and the Indian Diaspora; Branding the Globe; Communication Rights in a Global Context; Conglomeration and Media Monopolies; Digital Divide; The DVD; Global Community Media; Google Book Search; Hypercommercialism; Online Publishing; Piracy and Intellectual Property; Pirate Radio; Public Access Television; Runaway Productions and the Globalization of Hollywood; Tourism and the Selling of Cultures; World Cinema.

Further Reading: Bell, D. *The Coming of a Post-Industrial Society*. New York: Basic, 1973; Blok, A., and G. Downey, eds. *Uncovering Labour Relations in Information Revolutions, 1750–2000*. Cambridge: Cambridge University Press, 2003; Braverman, H. *Labor and Monopoly Capital*. New York: Monthly Review, 1974; Brint, S. "Professionals and the Knowledge Economy: Rethinking the Theory of Postindustrial Society." *Current Sociology* 49, no. 4 (2001): 101–32; Elmer, G., and M. Gasher, eds. *Contracting out Hollywood*. Lanham, MD: Rowman and Littlefield, 2005; Head. S. *The New Ruthless Economy*. New York: Oxford University Press, 2003; Huws, U., ed. *The Transformation of Work in a Global Knowledge Economy*. Leuven: Katholieke Universiteit Leuven, 2006; Huws, U. *The Making of a Cybertariat*. New York: Monthly Review Press, 2003; McKercher, C., and V. Mosco. "Divided They Stand: Hollywood Unions in the Information Age." *Work Organization, Labour and Globalisation* 1 (2007): 130–43; Mosco, V. "Knowledge Workers in the Global Economy: Antimonies of Outsourcing." *Social Identities* 12 (2006): 771–90; Mosco, V., and C. McKercher. "Convergence Bites Back: Labour Struggles in the Canadian Communications Industry." *Canadian Journal of Communication* 31 (2006): 733–51; Schiller, H. I. *The Mind Managers*. Boston: Beacon, 1973; Smith, T., D. A. Sonnenfeld, and D. N. Pellow, eds. *Challenging the Chip*. Philadelphia: Temple University Press, 2006.

Vincent Mosco

COMMUNICATION RIGHTS IN A GLOBAL CONTEXT

Over the past six decades "communication rights" has been a recurring theme in global discussions about democratic freedoms. Advocates argue that a more democratic communication system providing equal access and diverse information will help create a more peaceful and humanistic world, preserve indigenous culture, and sustain democratic institutions. Yet, establishing universal codes and implementing their protection in global policy regimes has proven to be an ongoing struggle.

The first official proposal for "communication rights" can be traced to the French civil servant Jean d'Arcy in 1969. This proposal built on earlier principles that began to take shape in the aftermath of World War II. The first global articulation of what eventually became known as the "right to communicate" occurred in Article 19 of the 1948 Universal Declaration of Human Rights. Article 19 states: "Everyone has the right to freedom of opinion and expression; this right includes freedom to hold opinions without interference and to seek, receive and impart information and ideas through any media and regardless of frontiers." The boldest and most innovative component in this statement is the "freedom to impart information." Also noteworthy is the positive rendering of this wording that is largely missing from the negative freedoms outlined in influential standards such as the U.S. First Amendment: "Congress shall pass no law..." Instead, communication rights are often articulated in ways that assume people are not simply passive consumers, but also have a *right of access* to diverse sources of information within a democratic media system. That is, communication rights are not merely about "freedom from" but also "freedom for," and require at least a two-way communication flow based on principles of balance, equal access, and democratic participation. Like other official statements of human rights and democratic norms that we often take for granted, this codification is a significant achievement for its role in shaping debates and determining global norms and policies. However, such codes are often ignored or interpreted in different ways, which sets the stage for contestation. Struggles around the meaning and protection of communication rights have risen to the fore during a number of historic and contemporary forums.

FREE FLOW OF INFORMATION VS. RIGHT TO COMMUNICATE

Historically, the idea of communication rights has clashed with an emphasis on "information" extricated from its communicative context. In other words, while information is often treated like a commodity, communications is a crucial human process that cannot be bought and sold on the market. Likewise, systemic problems like the "digital divide" cannot be easily remedied by some technical fix, but instead require processes that are by nature social and political. Many advocates argue that communication rights should be considered an inalienable human right, protected by international law.

Differing from communication rights in terms of its emphases and objectives, the free flow of information doctrine first became prominent in U.S. foreign policy in the mid-1940s, reflected in statements made in 1946. U.S. Assistant Secretary of State William Benton said, "The State Department plans to do everything within its power along the political or diplomatic lines to help break down the artificial barriers to the expansion of private American news agencies, magazines, motion pictures, and other media of communication....Freedom of the press—and freedom of exchange of information generally—is an integral part of our foreign policy." John Foster Dulles, who would become U.S. secretary of state in the 1950s, stated, "If I were to be granted one point of foreign policy and no other, I would make it the free flow of information."

In the1940s, liberals and conservatives alike, though perhaps for different reasons, pushed for the free flow of information. Given the ascendance of Western

COMMUNICATION RIGHTS TIMELINE

1948—United Nations Declaration of Human Rights established.

1978—"The Declaration on Mass Media" formally issued at the UNESCO General Assembly.

1980—The MacBride Commission's report "Many Voices, One World" published.

1984 (December 31)—United States pulls out of UNESCO.

1985—United Kingdom pulls out of UNESCO.

2003—World Summit on the Information Society Phase I held at Geneva.

2005—World Summit on the Information Society Phase II held at Tunis.

commerce and U.S. global dominance, the postwar era was an especially propitious time to be promoting the virtues of unrestricted movement of information. Critics argue that U.S. corporations continue to use the language of free flow of information to rid themselves of regulatory constraints. What is noticeably missing from the free flow language is concern for information quality and questions of access, which were raised in the United States during the 1940s Hutchins Commission on Freedom of the Press, but largely faded from Western discourse until its reemergence during global debates in the 1970s.

COMMUNICATION RIGHTS DURING NWICO

In the decades following World War II, communication rights served as a global counternarrative to the prevailing "freedom of information" rhetoric. These two visions clashed within UNESCO during what became known as the New World Information and Communication Order (NWICO) debates. The NWICO debates raged in and outside the United Nations from the mid-1970s through the mid-1980s, allowing for the first time a wide range of media and telecommunications-related issues to be argued in a relatively open and global context. Unfolding within the polarity of the Cold War era, NWICO was spearheaded by the Non-Aligned Movement (NAM) of U.N. countries, whose membership had increased with dozens of newly independent countries following decolonization. This sudden swell in so-called third-world countries led to a rebalance of power in the United Nations, forming a third force between the Soviet Union and the United States. The developing world's strengthened position fueled reform efforts concentrating on cultural identity, imperialism, and communication rights.

The NWICO debates led to "The Declaration on Mass Media," which was introduced in 1972 and formally issued at the 1978 UNESCO General Assembly. It caused acrimonious debate around the dominance of Western news content and the increasing importance of Western-controlled technologies that kept non-Western countries in a state of "forced dependency." The biggest conflict centered on proposed amendments to the free flow of information doctrine, which the Western press cast as a life or death struggle for press freedom. After fierce contestation and a watered-down final product, the free flow doctrine was amended to read: "free-flow and wider and better balanced dissemination of information."

The MacBride Commission's report to the 1980 UNESCO general assembly built upon these earlier provisions with a wide range of recommendations that would effectively redistribute global media power, such as television imagery, the distribution of radio receivers, and the journalistic right of reply, to name several. By suggesting structural changes, including regulations on information flow, UNESCO invited the wrath of a burgeoning pro-market neoliberal order championed by Ronald Reagan and Margaret Thatcher. By the early 1980s anti-UNESCO fervor in Western elite circles reached a feverish pitch, abetted by right-wing groups such as the Heritage Foundation. The United States and United Kingdom subsequently pulled out of UNESCO in 1984 and 1985, respectively. Following the pull out of UNESCO's largest sponsors, NWICO gradually receded into relative obscurity. However, annual MacBride panels persisted for many years and helped bring together a new civil society coalition that would form the basis for a new theater of contestation. Indeed, two decades following the lost alternatives of NWICO, the crystallization of a new civil society alliance was evident when similar issues involving democracy and communication reemerged at the World Summit on Information Society.

COMMUNICATION RIGHTS AT THE WSIS

Recent years have witnessed a resurgence in reform efforts around communication rights. During the International Telecommunications Union (ITU)–sponsored discussions known as the World Summit on the Information Society (WSIS) in 2003 and again in 2005, communication rights emerged as a rallying theme for global media reform groups. The original goal of the WSIS was to "define a common vision of the information society." Given the summit's initial focus on important social problems like the global digital divide, the coalition behind the Campaign for Communication Rights in the Information Society (CRIS), the World Forum on Communication Rights (WFCR), and other reform groups saw opportunities for advancing communication rights. However, initial hopes for the WSIS to seriously address communication rights were dashed early on when discussions devolved into a technical dispute over Internet governance. Nonetheless, both phases of the WSIS saw a genuinely progressive presence. Groups like the World Association for Christian Communication (WACC) and the Association for Progressive Communications (APC), among others, articulated alternative policy visions based on social justice and human rights, and worked hard to get less technocentric language into official WSIS documents, focusing on structural inequities such as lack of access to new communication technologies. Drawing heavily from Article 19 language, the continuity between NWICO-era and WSIS rhetoric was partly due to the involvement of similar groups and individuals. For example, people associated with WACC participated in both movements, as did many veteran activists and academics.

Arguably the most significant alternative vision to emerge at phase one of the WSIS was the "civil society declaration." Overall, this wording is very similar to NWICO-era manifestos with references to communication rights. A significant symbolic victory for communication rights advocates and progressive non-governmental organizations was the inclusion of similar language in the official WSIS Declaration of Principles document:

> We reaffirm, as an essential foundation of the Information Society, and as outlined in Article 19 of the Universal Declaration of Human Rights, that everyone has the right to freedom of opinion and expression; that this right includes freedom to hold opinions without interference and to seek, receive and impart information and ideas through any media and regardless of frontiers. Communication is a fundamental social process, a basic human need and the foundation of all social organization. It is central to the Information Society. Everyone, everywhere should have the opportunity to participate and no one should be excluded from the benefits the Information Society offers. (ITU, 2003, ¶4)

Anchoring information to crucial communication processes, this statement challenged the otherwise technocentric thrust of official WSIS documents. Nevertheless, many participants saw this inclusion as inadequate. Although it suggests everyone's communication needs should benefit from the information society, it does not address preexisting global inequities or the means by which disadvantaged people will be given the opportunity to participate in the brave new world of the "Information Society." An alternative approach advanced by communication rights advocates focuses less on easy technological remedies, and more on social needs that require a redistribution of crucial resources.

The emphasis on information is itself an ideological turn, and continues to draw from the free flow of information rhetoric that, in many cases, is as much about allowing commercial interests to operate unimpeded as it is for creating a truly democratic communication system with equal access for all. The increasingly corporate-dominated Internet arguably represents a major triumph of this antiregulation view.

COMMUNICATION RIGHTS TODAY

Various advocacy groups continue to fashion a post-WSIS strategy to mobilize civil society around communication rights. During and immediately following the WSIS, new attempts were made to help further define communication rights. For example, a statement delivered at the World Forum on Communication rights, which was held in conjunction with the first phase of the WSIS, characterized communication rights as a "universal human need" based on "the key principles of Freedom, Inclusiveness, Diversity and Participation." A CRIS document titled "Assessing Communication Rights" defined communication rights in terms of human dignity that goes beyond protections of opinion and expression to include areas like "democratic media governance, participation in one's own culture, linguistic rights, rights to enjoy the fruits of human creativity, to education, privacy, peaceful assembly, and self-determination." This same document divided communication rights into four pillars: communication in the public sphere; communication of knowledge; civil rights in communication; and cultural rights in communication.

Despite the renewed interest in communication rights and the promising signs of global mobilization, there are also many troubling developments. Autocratic governments around the globe continue to suppress the most basic communication rights. Countries like Burma and China are prime culprits, but even Western democracies like the United States recently have witnessed state infringements against civil liberties, such as covert government surveillance. These developments do not bode well for communication rights.

At the same time, however, media reform efforts with a focus on communication rights have taken on a new urgency. In the United States, public uprisings manifested around media ownership issues in 2002–03, and Internet policies such as net neutrality in 2006–07. A possible silver lining to various political and media crises is the increasingly mainstream notion that communication rights require structural safeguards. Despite the ascendance of the blogosphere, a well-funded, vibrant public media system is still necessary. Although many U.S. media reform groups tend to focus on domestic issues, there is also a growing awareness that communication rights are a global issue. Increasingly, advocates within North America and abroad are calling for a more internationalized media reform movement, encouraging greater coordination around global intellectual property regimes, media concentration, and other contentious communication issues.

Since their first articulations in the mid-twentieth century, communication rights have figured prominently in progressive global reform efforts to create a more democratic world. Then as now, on multiple fronts, the global struggle for communication rights continues.

See also Al-Jazeera; Blogosphere; Cultural Imperialism and Hybridity; Digital Divide; Global Community Media; Government Censorship and Freedom of Speech; Internet and Its Radical Potential; Media Literacy; Media Reform Net Neutrality; Regulating the Airwaves.

Further Reading: Calabrese, Andrew. *Many Voices, One World: Towards a New, More Just, and More Efficient World Information and Communication Order.* New York: Rowman and Littlefield, 2004; Cammaerts, Bart, and Nico Carpentier. *Reclaiming the Media: Communication Rights and Democratic Media Roles.* Bristol: Intellect Books, 2007; Costanza-Chock, Sasha. WSIS, the Neoliberal Agenda, and Counterproposal from "Civil Society" presentation for Our Media III, Barranquilla, Colombia, May 20, 2003; McLaughlin, Lisa, and Victor Pickard. "What Is Bottom Up about Global Internet Governance?" *Global Media and Communication* 1, no. 3 (2005): 359–75; Nordenstreng, Kaarle. *Mass Media Declaration of UNESCO.* Norwood, NJ: Alex Publishing Corporation, 1984; Ó Siochrú, Sean, and Bruce Girard. *Global Media Governance: A Beginners Guide.* New York: Rowman and Littlefield, 2003; Ó Siochrú, Sean. "Will the Real WSIS Please Stand-Up? The Historic Encounter of the 'Information Society' and the 'Communication Society.'" *Gazette—The International Journal for Communication Studies* 66 (2004): 203–24; Pickard, Vincent. "Neoliberal Visions and Revisions in Global Communications Policy from NWICO to WSIS." *Journal of Communication Inquiry* 31, no. 2 (2007): 118–39; Preston, William, Edward Herman, and Herbert I. Schiller. *Hope and Folly: The United States and Unesco, 1945–1985.* Minneapolis: University of Minnesota Press,

1989; Schiller, Herbert. *Communication and Cultural Domination.* White Plains, NY: International Arts and Science Press, 1976; Schiller, Herbert. *Living in the Number One Country.* New York: Seven Stories Press, 2000; Thussu, Daya Kishan. *International Communication: Continuity and Change.* New York: Oxford University Press, 2000.

Victor W. Pickard

CONGLOMERATION AND MEDIA MONOPOLIES

Conglomeration poses a range of issues for citizens and consumers. Does the presence of prominent news outlets in multinational conglomerates influence the coverage of contentious social and political issues? What effect does industry concentration have on media content—motion pictures, television programs, music, and so on? Does the loss of diversity in ownership result in the replication of money-making formulas that promote a corporate ethos at the expense of original ideas? Overall, does consolidation make it impossible or at least improbable for independent voices and viewpoints to reach citizens and consumers? These are just a few of the questions that surround the ownership controversy.

The focal point in the battle over media conglomeration is the concentration of prominent news and entertainment firms in a handful of corporations. Free market advocates argue that centralized ownership is necessary if companies are to remain profitable. They point to the explosion in the number of programming outlets, arguing that consolidation has not restricted the variety of media content. But opponents contend that conglomeration eliminates alternative viewpoints and empowers corporate media to promote dominant ideas and frame public discussion and debate.

DEFINING CONGLOMERATION

Conglomeration is the process through which distinct companies come under common ownership within a single corporation. There are two different models of conglomeration, and prominent media firms fall within each of them. The traditional definition of conglomeration involves the grouping of wide-ranging, unrelated businesses from various industrial sectors. This model involves unrelated diversification, which is the expansion into industries that are not related to the core business of a conglomerate. The General Electric acquisition of NBC in 1986 is a classic example of that type. A second model of conglomeration builds through related diversification, which involves the acquisition of firms that are connected to the core business in critical areas. The evolution of Viacom is an example of that form. Cable television was its core business in the 1980s, with ownership of MTV, Nickelodeon, and Showtime, before it expanded into motion pictures and broadcast television with the acquisitions of Paramount Pictures in 1994 and CBS in 2000.

MONOPOLIES

Conglomeration is one factor that leads to concentration, and ultimate consolidation results in monopolies. That structure exists when there is just a single

CONGLOMERATION AND THE LOSS OF LOCALISM

The headlines about conglomeration are often written when studios and networks combine, but less discussed is the potential impact at the local level. Local ownership of newspapers was once common, but as newspaper chains expanded, local ownership became rare and the number of cities with multiple dailies declined. The nature of local television and radio ownership also changed, as Congress and the Federal Communications Commission (FCC) relaxed one-to-a-market rules and allowed groups to reach a higher percentage of households nationwide. These changes transformed the marketplace with massive station groups and less local ownership, and more appear to be on the horizon. In 2003, the FCC voted to relax its prohibition on the cross-ownership of newspapers and television stations in the same market. The justification was the numerical increase in the number of available outlets, including the Internet. The firestorm that followed made clear that there was not universal agreement and courts blocked their implementation, but the FCC started down a similar path in 2006.

seller of a given product in a market. True monopolies are most common in the newspaper business. Countless cities have just one daily, like Atlanta's *Journal-Constitution*. Far more common are media markets that are oligopolies, which feature a few giant sellers of a product with each having a significant share of the market. In 2005, for example, four global giants—Universal Music, Sony BMG, Warner Music, and EMI Group—combined for over 80 percent of music sales in the United States and worldwide. Some use the phrase media monopolies to describe the small collection of corporations that are dominant in various media markets.

ISSUES OF OWNERSHIP AND CONTROL

One of the battle lines in the debate over conglomeration is whether ownership and control matters or not. From a free market perspective, ownership of a firm is not a concern unless combinations create market structures that lead to anticompetitive conditions. The Sherman Antitrust Act was enacted in 1890 to address such behavior in the United States, and it has shaped media markets. In 1938, the federal government launched a decade-long legal battle with the Hollywood studios, accusing the majors of "combining and conspiring" to "monopolize the production, distribution and exhibition of motion pictures." When the same corporation owns production studios as well as the theaters that show the movies it makes, the control of production, distribution, and exhibition could effectively close out competition. The so-called Paramount consent decrees, a series of agreements between the government and studios, prohibited anticompetitive behavior and forced the "divorcement" of production and distribution from exhibition. Free market advocates argue that this is as far as the government should delve into the marketplace.

The question is whether the nature of media products raises more significant concerns and demands additional government action. The attention to such issues has shifted over time as new ideas and ideologies come to the fore.

In 1966, International Telephone and Telegraph (ITT) attempted to acquire the ABC television network, and despite claims that the network would remain independent, the Department of Justice and others questioned the impact ITT's international operations might have on ABC News and blocked the merger. Two decades later, the regulatory climate was altogether different, and there was little opposition to the combination of General Electric and NBC, although the issues were very similar.

The focus on ownership and control hinges, in part, on the potential impact of media content. Mark Fowler, chair of the Federal Communications Commission (FCC) in the 1980s, once stated that a television is nothing more than a "toaster with pictures." This, in turn, meant that the government could treat television the same as other industries. Scholar Douglas Kellner, however, argues that television assumes a critical role in the "structuring of contemporary identity and shaping thought and behavior." In his view, television has undertaken functions once ascribed to "myth and ritual," including "integrating individuals into the social order, celebrating dominant values," and "offering models of thought, behavior, and gender for imitation." From this perspective, media play a significant role in society and conglomeration becomes a far more serious issue.

TYPES OF CONGLOMERATION

There are multiple incentives for conglomeration. The expansion into diversified businesses creates opportunities for growth and allows a conglomerate to cushion the impact of downturns in core business sectors. General Electric is often cited as the model of a diversified conglomerate, and its collection of businesses makes it, among other things, a military contractor and designer of nuclear power plants. NBC Universal contributes less than 10 percent of the total revenue of General Electric, but with a number of news outlets, among other things, NBC might be far more important to the parent company by helping shape public debate over contentious issues, such as militarism and energy production, through NBC News, MSNBC, and CNBC. In 1987, for example, less than a year after the meltdown of the nuclear reactor in Chernobyl, NBC News aired an hour-long show entitled "Nuclear Power: In France It Works."

SYNERGY

More common in media industries is related diversification. This allows a conglomerate to build upon a strong business though the diversification into areas that are close to the core. This can create synergies that enable it to increase revenues and decrease costs through the common management of multiple businesses. This is evident in the conglomeration of media assets in corporations such as The Walt Disney Company, Time Warner Inc., and News Corp. Motion picture production and distribution remain important contributors to the Disney bottom line, for example, but the most successful unit in Disney is the Media Networks division, which includes both ABC and ESPN. Disney's corporate expansion into related fields proved to be quite lucrative.

Horizontal and vertical integration are defining characteristics in media consolidation since the 1980s. With horizontal integration, firms acquire additional business units at the same level of production, distribution, or exhibition. Such consolidation enables conglomerates to extend their control and maximize economies of scale through the use of shared resources. With vertical integration, firms acquire additional business units at different points in the process. This allows them to control the supply and cost of essential materials and enables them to rationalize production and increase their control over the market.

Using vertical and horizontal integration, media conglomerates gain far greater control over the marketplace, but such economic strategies limit market access for independent producers and distributors. This is most evident in the motion picture and television industries. Independent film distributors were prominent in the late 1980s, but a decade later the major conglomerates had swallowed most of these firms while large theater chains had overtaken small movie houses. By 1997, six corporations accounted for over 92 percent of box office revenue, and the blockbuster and the multiplex came to define the American moviegoing experience. The same pattern is evident with prime-time television. As networks exerted greater control over television production, fewer programs originated from outside of conglomerates focused on financial control and less risky programs became appealing. Numerous versions of profitable formulas multiply in seemingly endless spin-offs, as the dearth of original, innovative television productions become more evident.

These practices extend to foreign markets as well, and the impact of Hollywood on indigenous production is a long-standing concern. The U.S. government promotes the export of media products across borders, and one of the justifications for the relaxation of ownership restrictions at home is the argument that the media conglomerates need to be massive to succeed overseas. This contributes to a general mindset that firms that do not grow through mergers

THE CONGLOMERATION OF MICKEY MOUSE

The transformation of The Walt Disney Company from a struggling studio operating in the shadow of its related theme parks into a sprawling corporation provides one of the clearest examples of conglomeration. The first step was the creation of production units to develop a diversified slate of films. In 1983, combined domestic and foreign box office receipts for its motion pictures totaled just $82.5 million. A decade later the filmed entertainment division of Disney generated $3.67 billion in revenue. The diversification into related businesses was the next and most significant step. The biggest headlines came in 1996 with the acquisition of Capital Cities/ABC Inc. This created vertical integration between ABC and the production units within Disney, links that were most evident a decade later when three shows from Touchstone Television, *Lost*, *Desperate Housewives*, and *Grey's Anatomy*, fueled a resurgence of the network. That merger also included ESPN, which became the most lucrative unit in the Disney empire. In 2004, the diversified conglomerate generated over $30 billion in revenue, 20 times what it did in 1984.

and acquisitions will be swallowed. Ted Turner's pursuit of both broadcast networks and motion picture studios before Turner Broadcasting became part of Time Warner in 1996 is testament to this way of thinking. Turner summarized the goal in simple terms: "The only way for media companies to survive is to own everything up and down the media chain.... Big media today wants to own the faucet, pipeline, water, and the reservoir. The rain clouds come next."

CHANGES IN THE NATURE OF CONGLOMERATION

The change in the corporate control of the three major broadcast networks—ABC, CBS, and NBC—illustrates how conglomeration transformed media assets since the 1980s. In 1985, two of the networks were still linked to the individuals who created them, ABC and Leonard Goldenson and CBS and William Paley, while NBC remained in the hands of the corporation that launched its radio network in the 1920s, RCA. At that time, the networks remained the core businesses of their corporate parents, and the news divisions supported the public interest mandate that came with broadcast licenses. In 2005, all three shared ownership with a major motion picture studio—ABC and Walt Disney, CBS and Paramount Pictures, and NBC and Universal Pictures—and the news divisions were important revenue centers. These combinations raise various concerns, not the least of which is the coverage of the conglomerates themselves. Michael Eisner once put it in simple terms: he did not want ABC covering Disney.

Not all combinations prove to be successful and some argue that modern conglomerates are too unwieldy to react to changes in the marketplace. The most notable failure is the merger of America Online and Time Warner in 2001.

MOTION PICTURE AND TELEVISION CONGLOMERATION, 1985–2006

1985—News Corp. acquires Twentieth Century Fox.

1986—Capital Cities and ABC merge to create Capital Cities/ABC Inc.; General Electric acquires NBC.

1989—Time Inc. and Warner Communications merge to create Time Warner Inc.; Sony acquires Columbia Pictures.

1990—Matsushita Industries acquires Universal Pictures.

1993—Walt Disney Co. acquires Miramax Films.

1994—Viacom Inc. acquires Paramount Pictures.

1995—Seagram Co. Ltd. acquires Universal Pictures.

1996—Walt Disney Co. acquires Capital Cities/ABC Inc.; Time Warner Inc. acquires New Line Cinema.

2000—Viacom Inc. acquires CBS Inc.; Vivendi SA acquires Universal Pictures.

2001—Time Warner and America Online merge to create AOL Time Warner.

2004—General Electric and Vivendi Universal merge assets to create NBC Universal.

2006—Viacom and CBS split and form two corporations, with Sumner Redstone retaining majority ownership of each of them; Viacom Inc. acquires DreamWorks SKG.

The melding of old media and new media did not reap the promised rewards and AOL was dropped from the corporate letterhead in 2003, but it was not just the size of Time Warner that was its undoing as pundits point to various problems. And some changes are more cosmetic. In 2006, Viacom split its assets into two corporations, Viacom Inc. and CBS Corp., but Sumner Redstone remained in control of both of them, so ownership and control did not change hands. The rationale for the split was not the size of the conglomerate but the price of Viacom stock, with Redstone and others contending that the true value of the motion picture and cable television assets would be realized after the split from the slower-growing broadcast interests.

CONGLOMERATION: MULTIPLICITY OR DIVERSITY

When Ben Bagdikian published the first edition of *The Media Monopoly* in 1983, he estimated that ownership of most of the major media was consolidated in 50 national and multinational conglomerates. When he published *The New Media Monopoly* two decades later, Bagdikian concluded that the number had dwindled to just five. The degree of conglomeration in media industries is evident across the board. In 1985, there were six major motion picture studios and three major broadcast television networks, and nine different conglomerates controlled one of each. In 2005, the number of broadcast networks had doubled with the addition of Fox, The WB and UPN, but the number of corporations that owned a studio or network had dwindled to just six. Those corporations—Disney, NBC Universal, News Corp., Sony, Time Warner, and Viacom—also held an ownership interest in over 75 percent of the cable and satellite channels with over 60 million subscribers, as well as the most prominent premium movie channels, HBO and Showtime.

Therein rests an important battleground in this debate. Since the 1980s, Congress and the FCC relaxed ownership rules based on the argument that increases in outlets rendered such regulations needless interference in the marketplace. When the FCC announced the relaxation of various rules in 2003, chair Michael Powell argued that the "explosion of new media outlets" demanded change so the commission did not "perpetuate the graying rules of a bygone black and white era." There is little question that the number of outlets has increased. Less certain is whether this growth resulted in more independent voices and diverse viewpoints.

Central to this debate is the distinction between multiplicity and diversity, since it is possible to increase the number of available outlets without a parallel expansion in the range of ideas and values in the public commons. The rise of cable news services, for example, diluted the influence of the broadcast network news divisions and created the impression of abundance. This could be quite significant, since the dissemination of news and information from diverse and antagonistic sources is considered a pillar of self-government in democratic societies. When one traces the ownership and control of the cable news services, however, the promised excess is nowhere to be found. The five prominent cable news services—CNN, CNN Headline News, CNBC, MSNBC, and Fox News

Channel—are all part of major media conglomerates, as are the broadcast networks. These are far from diverse and antagonistic sources of news and information, so the debate on media conglomeration rages on.

See also Branding the Globe; Communication and Knowledge Labor; Communication Rights in a Global Context; Hypercommercialism; Media and the Crisis of Values; Media Reform; Minority Media Ownership; Net Neutrality; Piracy and Intellectual Property; Pirate Radio; Regulating the Airwaves; Runaway Productions and the Globalization of Hollywood.

Further Reading: Bagdikian, Ben. *The New Media Monopoly.* Boston: Beacon Press, 2004; Croteau, David, and William Hoynes. *The Business of Media: Corporate Media and the Public Interest,* 2nd ed. Thousand Oaks, CA: Pine Forge Press, 2006; Herman, Edward S., and Noam Chomsky. *Manufacturing Consent: The Political Economy of the Mass Media.* New York: Pantheon Books, 1988; Kellner, Douglas. *Television and the Crisis in Democracy.* Boulder, CO: Westview Press, 1990; Kunz, William M. *Culture Conglomerates: Consolidation in the Motion Picture and Television Industries.* Boulder, CO: Rowman and Littlefield Publishers, 2006; McChesney, Robert. *The Problem of the Media: U.S. Communication Politics in the Twenty-First Century.* New York: Monthly Review Press, 2004; Turner, Ted. "Break Up This Band." *Washington Monthly* (July/August 2004): 33–44; Wasko, Janet. *Hollywood in the Information Age: Behind the Silver Screens.* Austin, TX: University of Texas Press, 1995.

William M. Kunz

CULTURAL APPROPRIATION

When the mass media and information technology became increasingly central parts of everyday life during the last century, they produced an extraordinary increase in the volume of cultural material available to us. The symbolic forms that media and the Internet generate—TV programs, blogs, movies, radio personalities, podcasts, and so on—have become some of the most recognizable and influential elements of culture, and human involvement with the full range of cultural forms that surround us has also become more diversified, flexible, and intense. Some worry that citizens consume such forms passively, and that culture as such is manufactured by the industries that create the media. But people have greater opportunities than ever before to actively shape the meanings of cultural institutions and experience. They do so as individuals and members of groups by creatively engaging their cultural environments in ways that promote their own interests.

Our cultural worlds have become increasingly complex. In particular, the symbolic aspects of culture have become much more common and widespread. In the face of what might seem to be considerable prospects for creative engagement with the media and popular culture, however, some critics contend that we are all being fed a homogenous, prefabricated culture. To such critics, corporations create, control, and regulate culture and thus our very means of expression.

But culture cannot be so easily contained. The remarkable growth of media, information technology (IT), and the culture industries demonstrates one fundamental fact—culture is dynamic, always changing. Why is this so? Certainly economic motivations explain part of the changing nature of culture. The media, information, and culture industries constantly search for new ideas and personalities they can sell to potential audiences. Audiences play their part too, though, by demanding constant cultural stimulation. Novelty and change are important parts of human nature.

Culture is not limited to what is offered up by the media, IT, and culture industries, of course. Culture has more traditional features too—language, religion, typical food, and gender relations, for instance, all help define us culturally. But even these traditional anchors of culture are represented symbolically in the Information and Communication Age. For instance, language is a symbol system in and of itself. Religion depends on symbolic imagery—the Christian cross, Jewish star of David, and Muslim crescent moon, for example—as well as music, mythology, holidays, and rituals, to maintain its cultural influence. Food is inherently visual and often represented in advertising. The way the mass media present images of men and women contributes much to our understanding of gender roles.

Without question, much of what we come to believe about our culture is conditioned by repeated exposure to the communications and culture industries, and to more traditional sources of information—especially religious institutions, schools, government, political parties, and civic organizations. We know how pervasive and powerful these influences can be, but do they determine our sense of culture and cultural identity?

Not entirely. Humans are not just passive recipients of cultural information. Although the tendency to conform to cultural norms and expectations is always there, and the norms and expectations are backed up by all kinds of rules and regulations, most people—especially more independent-minded individuals—do not simply accept the cultural values, norms, and habits they inherit. People and groups often resist the cultural framing and conditioning to which they are exposed. That resistance sometimes leads to the creation of alternative cultural expressions.

A DEFINITION

The key battleground concept of cultural appropriation refers to how people take something that is given to them by culture and use it for their own purposes, sometimes in direct contradiction to the intention of the creator of the original idea. By culturally appropriating a cultural resource, people "re-signify" the object or idea in question. They give it a different meaning.

To understand the usage of the concept being described here, it is best to think of the word "appropriation" as a noun that is being modified by an adjective, "cultural." A "cultural appropriation" is an act of cultural modification that is performed by individuals or groups. The term "appropriate" can also be used as a verb to communicate the idea being discussed here, as in "people appropriate cultural materials for their own reasons." Don't let the more familiar definition of the adjective "appropriate" throw you off. For our purposes, "appropriate"

CULTURE AND SUPERCULTURE

The cultural creativity we see everywhere is not limited to what is presented by the mass media and the cultural industries, or to public appropriations made within alternative social or cultural movements like punk rock or religion. Culture is becoming more and more personalized today—think YouTube, MySpace, iPod. The driving force behind this decentralization of culture is modern communications technology. Access to Internet and satellite TV, mobile (camera) phones, and computer software, for example, gives people in more developed countries and middle-class individuals in less wealthy parts of the world unprecedented sources of inspiration and tools for expanding their worlds as consumers and producers of culture. Through acts of individual "cultural programming," enterprising individuals today create their own dynamic, personal "supercultures"—personalized matrices of material and cultural resources.

does not mean "proper" or "fitting to the occasion." What cultural appropriation means and how it works becomes much easier to grasp with some examples.

THE CLASSIC EXAMPLE: PUNK ROCK

The quintessential case of cultural appropriation can be found in popular culture of the turbulent 1970s, a stressful period in world history. Fierce resistance to the Vietnam War was raging across the globe. Civil rights struggles, the emergence of modern feminism, and increased use of illegal drugs by middle-class youth were taking place. In England, other problems were developing. Much of England's industrial economy—mining and manufacturing—was declining. Working-class jobs were evaporating. British youth—especially young men—found their job opportunities shrinking and their lives becoming increasingly bleak.

At the same time, changes were taking place in the popular music industry in England and the United States. Music fans had become bored with pretentious "progressive rock" or "art rock" bands like Yes, Genesis, King Crimson, Jethro Tull, and Rush. The poetic lyrics, lush arrangements, long solos, and concert hall venues of these "super groups" were being rejected by more and more popular-music fans. The virtuoso groups were being replaced by bands that played short, simple, angry songs to smaller audiences in clubs. Punk rock was born.

The cultural emblem of the punk movement was a striking act of cultural appropriation—safety pins that were stuck through facial skin as simple piercings. The original function and significance of the safety pin for everyday domestic purposes had been appropriated by disenfranchised youth for cultural and political reasons—rejection of a life of boredom and meaninglessness. Piercing the skin with a safety pin—meant to shock and disgust mainstream society—became a highly recognizable sign of resistance to the dominant culture. The symbolic effect has had lasting effects. The contemporary body piercing craze began as an iconic symbol of a social and musical revolution that raged from the mid-1970s through the early 1980s.

COLLECTIVE APPROPRIATION: RELIGION

Cultural appropriation often reflects resistance to or the projection of an alternative solution to the massive power that is wielded by government, industry, and religion, and other social institutions. Let us consider the supremely important case of big religion. Because faith has proven to be so important to so many people in nearly every world culture, religious ideology, institutions, and iconography—often in mediated form—have become familiar objects available as popular resources for cultural appropriation. Some examples can help illustrate how this works. Catholics everywhere make their own nontraditional Catholicism, often to the horror of Church authorities. In Latin America, for example, people have invented various hybrid local religions composed of traditional Vatican dogma and liturgy, but also reflecting local customs, beliefs, superstitions, and rituals, including African voodoo. In recent years, many Latin American Catholics have adapted and transformed Catholic ideology, authority, rules, and rituals to better fit their own personal, group, and cultural orientations in massive processes of "collective appropriation." The "Black Saints" were created by African slaves and their progeny in Brazil in order to make the bible more ethnically relevant, as another example, and Venezuelan residents of a poor Andean village have replaced Jesus on the cross with a local hero, a medical doctor who saved many lives in the area a century ago. All these particular images gain power and popularity because they are picked up and circulated by the mass media, also known as the "cultural media," and become part of the common consciousness.

A particularly striking example of collective cultural appropriation in the realm of religion in Latin America is the Santa Muerte (Saint of Death) movement in Mexico. This social movement was started by poor people who felt their spiritual and social needs weren't being sufficiently met by the traditional Church. To develop an alternative faith, people appropriated virtually all of the main symbols of Catholicism. Most importantly, the Virgin Mary, a cultural symbol of great importance to Catholics everywhere but especially within the Mexican interpretation of the religion, was transformed into La Santa Muerte, the "saint of death." She appears as a skeleton cloaked in a shroud. That particular symbol was created because one philosophical tenet of the movement is that only in death do all people truly become equal. Only then, at the imagined moment of meeting God, can poor people become properly recognized and valued. Other religious symbols have been culturally appropriated too, often for less serious reasons. Madonna popularized the cross as a decorative object for her shows and videos, and the Jewish Kabala became a symbol of her celebrity lifestyle. Goth rocker Marilyn Manson made religious iconography, including the cross, part of his purposefully "demonic" stage show.

INTENTION

Not all instances of cultural re-signification are intentional or even consciously recognized by those who do the work. Homeless people in the United States, for example, have turned supermarket shopping carts into personal storage vehicles.

Doing so, they take a material resource and cultural symbol of middle-class abundance—the metal shopping cart—and transform it ironically into something they feel they need for sheer survival. In the process, a new cultural meaning of the shopping cart is created. During the Vietnam and Iraq wars, some soldiers used military gas masks as inhaling devices to heighten the effect of marijuana smoke, certainly not the reason the troops were issued the masks in the first place. The gas mask, a symbol of war, was used for a purpose that stood in direct contradiction to the fighting, although communicating that alternative meaning was not intended. These are acts of cultural re-signification, but *not* of cultural appropriation. To appropriate a cultural resource requires some degree of conscious awareness of the action being taken on the part of the responsible individual or persons.

Even when cultural materials are consciously repackaged to create new meanings and send new messages, those actions don't change the original meaning or meanings of the cultural object for everyone. Culture is not a finite concept; there is plenty of room for many possible meanings of all cultural goods and representations. Safety pins are still understood and used for their original purposes, for example. The traditional Catholic Church still maintains a strong presence in global culture. Shopping baskets and gas masks continue to function for the practical reasons they were invented.

THE CULTURAL HYBRID

As we've seen, acts of cultural appropriation often create cultural hybrids—the fusing of cultural forms. Rap music and hip-hop culture, for instance, have been appropriated by individuals and groups around the world in ways that suit their own purposes. Rap began as a cultural expression of stressful American inner-city culture. But consider what happens when rap is exported to a place like Hong Kong, Indonesia, or Spain. The cadence, sound, and style of rap are appropriated by local musicians in these places, where it is sung in local languages with lyrics that refer to local personalities, conditions, and situations. The resulting musical hybrid is an amalgam of American inner-city black culture and Hong Kong, Indonesian, and Spanish youth culture. Cultural resources—rap music and all the attendant features of hip-hop culture—have been appropriated and the result is a variety of cultural hybrids.

CULTURAL APPROPRIATION IS CREATIVE WORK

Individuals and groups who attempt to alter or expand the meanings of the cultural institutions and resources around them participate in highly creative work. The ability to interact imaginatively with the endless array of material and symbolic cultural resources in our world represents a crucial part of what separates humans from other animals. We are active agents of our cultural lives. We don't just passively inherit our cultural surroundings; we engage, modify, and transform them. The symbolic consequences of cultural appropriation can be enormous—at times even leading to revolutionary cultural developments like the punk rock phenomenon or the creation of alternative religions.

See also Audience Power to Resist; Cultural Imperialism and Hybridity; Innovation and Imitation in Commercial Media; Online Digital Film and Television; Tourism and the Selling of Cultures; User-Created Content and Audience Participation; World Cinema; Youth and Media Use.

Further Reading: Fiske, John. *Understanding Popular Culture.* Boston: Unwin Hyman, 1989; Garcia Canclini, Nestor. *Hybrid Cultures.* Minneapolis: University of Minnesota Press, 1995; Giddens, Anthony. *Modernity and Self Identity.* Cambridge: Polity, 1991; Hannerz, Ulf. *Cultural Complexity.* New York: Columbia University Press, 1992; Hebdige, Dick. *Subculture: The Meaning of Style.* London: Methuen, 1979; Lull, James. *Culture-on-Demand.* Oxford: Blackwell, 2007; Lull, James. *Media, Communication, Culture:* New York: Columbia University Press, 2000; Willis, Paul. *Common Culture.* Boulder, CO: Westview, 1990; Willis, Paul. *The Ethnographic Imagination.* Cambridge: Polity, 2000.

James Lull

CULTURAL IMPERIALISM AND HYBRIDITY

Hollywood movies, television shows, and music CDs are just some of the U.S. media exports that can be found in almost every corner of the globe, however remote. As soon as U.S. programs were sold overseas, the export of American media stirred controversy. In the twenty-first century, critics continue to charge that the massive exporting of U.S. media and consumer goods harms indigenous cultures by influencing attitudes and edging out local producers in a process that leads to the domination of U.S. products and values. Other scholars see evidence of cultural mixing and a process of sharing that results in hybrid genres and cultural fusion in an age of globalization.

The charge that the United States was practicing cultural imperialism was heard frequently from the 1960s through the end of the twentieth century. Scholars, political activists, and policy makers asserted that Western films, TV shows, and commodities were promoting a social model of consumer-based capitalism. They lodged the central claim of cultural imperialism: that through the media, U.S. business and political leaders were trying to influence audiences in receiving countries and create overseas environments favorable to Western political and economic interests. In the process, the argument goes, the autonomy of receiving countries, as well as their cultures, values, and identities would be weakened or destroyed.

HISTORY OF A CONCEPT

The idea that an imperial power exports its culture as part of a process of domination is not limited to the modern setting. It has been applied to past practices of European countries such as Britain, France, and Spain, and also to the Japanese and Ottoman Empires, as well as other imperial regimes throughout history. The cultural imperialism thesis states that with politico-military imperialism on the wane, powerful countries use cultural means rather than

HOW TO READ DONALD DUCK

How To Read Donald Duck: Imperialist Ideology in the Disney Comic was a seminal study by Latin American author Ariel Dorfman and European scholar Armand Mattelart. First published in Chile in 1971, the book was an analysis of popular U.S. comic books that were sold in Spanish translation in Latin America. These comics contained stories set in imaginary third-world countries such as "Aztecland," and depicted the natives of these lands as backward savages. In one comic book Donald Duck goes to Africa, where the inhabitants are happy to trade their valuables for trinkets because they are in awe of the trappings of "civilization." Reading between the lines, Dorfman and Mattelart found messages of corporate capitalist ideology and native inferiority that they argued would influence Latin American readers of these comics to discard their own values and identities and accept U.S dominance.

armed force and occupation to achieve their political and economic goals. In this view, cultural products can smooth the way for domination by exposing people to products they may desire, the values that are seen to accompany those products, and ultimately even new sources of allegiance. In short, the cultural imperialism argument is that if people in other countries consume a lot of U.S. television shows, films, and other media products, they are likely to forget or reject their own cultural roots and instead try to emulate the characters and practices they are exposed to through imported media.

In *Mass Communication and American Empire*, well-known media scholar Herbert Schiller argued that the United States was extending its already sizeable power through economic dominance of other countries' communications systems and through the cultural influence carried by exported media. With this book Schiller set forth a fundamental claim that cultural imperialism constituted a threat to traditional cultures. Schiller went on to argue that the mass media were the principal vehicles for promoting Western values, and that the U.S. government and business sectors were deliberately attempting to mold developing countries' values and institutions to benefit U.S. objectives.

The term cultural imperialism carries with it certain assumptions about the relationship between the developed and developing worlds. It follows Immanuel Wallerstein's world systems model that places the developed countries in the center, dominating the peripheral nonindustrialized countries in ways that do not allow those countries to develop independently. Cultural imperialism also draws from dependency theory, which states that underdevelopment has not been simply a matter of some countries progressing more slowly than others, as some have suggested, but rather that the developed countries derive economic benefits from this unbalanced relationship.

ONE-WAY FLOWS

Analysis of the global trade in entertainment products confirms that the United States has been the world's principal exporter of films and television programs, while importing very little. The recognition of this "one-way flow" of film and TV internationally has contributed to the charge that in their search for worldwide markets and sympathetic populations, transnational corporations, most based in the United States, are practicing cultural imperialism.

Objections to cultural imperialism have been voiced in international debates about the regulation of media imports in the interest of national development. Such controversies pitted the U.S./U.K. conception of the "free flow of information," which promoted unregulated markets in news and entertainment, against many other countries' insistence on the need for balance in media exchanges, particularly of news. This position was expressed in the UNESCO-based call for a New World Information and Communication Order. Addressing concerns related to cultural imperialism, the 1980 report of the UNESCO International Commission for the Study of Communication Problems, known as the MacBride Commission, reiterated the claim that Western countries' domination of international media and culture were endangering national identities of less powerful countries.

COUNTER-ARGUMENTS

While the concept of cultural imperialism challenges existing global inequities, it has many critics. One major critique of the cultural imperialism thesis is that it disregards the role of audiences in interpreting media. The claim that audiences are affected in specific, predictable ways by media content has been widely challenged. In the context of cultural influence, some studies have shown that people interpret the messages of television programs and other media fare in ways that are consistent with their own cultural backgrounds. Therefore, any television program can have multiple interpretations. This dilutes the claim that imported audiovisual material consistently shapes audience members' attitudes and behaviors in ways favorable to Western values. The cultural imperialism claim that exposure to imported images and ideas weakens cultural identities has also been challenged along the lines that audience interpretations vary. Some studies have shown that imported media can have a strengthening effect on people's identities because audience members may react to the unfamiliar images and practices depicted in imported TV and films by becoming more aware of their own traditions and symbols, and more loyal to their cultures.

Another major critique of the claim that imported media products weaken receiving cultures is that this claim overlooks the complexity of cultural interactions. Cultural exchange is a multifaceted process. As a way of conceptualizing and analyzing the intricacies of cultural interactions, the concept of cultural hybridity has gained attention. This concept recognizes that cultures draw from one another and blend in unplanned ways to produce new cultural manifestations. This process is multidirectional—it does not occur solely as a one-way imposition of elements of dominant cultures on less powerful cultures. For example, the quintessentially U.S. musical style of rock 'n' roll—which is exported and emulated around the world and which has itself engendered accusations of cultural imperialism—would not exist without the abundant contribution of African influences. Similarly, the Latin American influence on U.S. popular music and TV—and on U.S. culture in general—is growing.

In an age of corporate globalization, some scholars and economists have come to criticize more overt forms of unequal global distribution of wealth and the policies, trade agreements, and legal structures that sustain this situation. As international military conflict continues to characterized the early twenty-first century, the importance of shared culture and its potential contribution for mutual understanding is gaining interest as one pathway to a more peaceful and stable world.

HYBRIDITY AND GLOBALIZATION

While it is still true that the U.S. dominates global media exporting, and imports very little media material from other countries, in the twenty-first century the term cultural imperialism is seldom used. It has been overtaken by the concepts of hybridity and globalization, the understanding that through communication and transportation technologies, the world has become increasingly interconnected. The concept of media globalization recognizes that media are central to the ongoing growth of international interaction and interdependence, and it lacks the implication of deliberateness that is built into the notion of cultural imperialism.

See also Audience Power to Resist; Bollywood and the Indian Diaspora; Branding the Globe; Communication Rights in a Global Context; Cultural Appropriation; Global Community Media; Piracy and Intellectual Property; Tourism and the Selling of Cultures; World Cinema.

Further Reading: Dorfman, Ariel, and Armand Mattelart. *How to Read Donald Duck: Imperialist Ideology in the Disney Comic,* trans. David Kunzle. New York: International General, 1971; International Commission for the Study of Communication Problems. *Many Voices, One World.* Paris: UNESCO, 1980; Kraidy, Marwan M. *Hybridity.* Philadelphia: Temple University Press, 2005; Nordenstreng, Kaarle, and Tapio Varis. *Television Traffic: A One-Way Street.* Paris: UNESCO, 1974; Schiller, Herbert I. *Mass Communications and American Empire.* New York: Beacon, 1969; Tomlinson, John. *Cultural Imperialism.* Baltimore: Johns Hopkins, 1991; Wallerstein, Immanuel. *The Modern World System: Capitalist Agriculture and the Origins of the European World Economy in the 16th Century.* New York: Academic Press, 1974.

Nancy Morris

DATING SHOWS

From *The Dating Game* and *Love Connection*, to *Temptation Island, The Bachelor*, and *I Love New York*, dating games have been a staple of television for many years, offering mild fun, occasional titillation, and scripts of romance to be or not to be. Many have been resoundingly criticized for their normalization of heterosexual romance, and for the roles that they seemingly propose that men and women play in real life's dating games, but some have also been praised for opening up a space on television in which gender norms and expectations can be challenged, played with, and interrogated.

HISTORY

While today's post-*Bachelor* explosion of dating games might suggest that the genre is relatively new to television, the genre "dates" back to the 1970s' *The Dating Game* and its 1980s copycat, *Love Connection*, both of which asked singles to select from a group of three suitors based on a series of rather staged questions and even more staged answers. Audience members could laugh at the inappropriate answers or suitors, or root for the "right" connection, and thus the genre neatly married comedy and romance, offering idle fun in half-hour chunks.

A new sort of dating show then began with the rise of reality television programming in the late 1990s. *Blind Date*'s cameras followed dates, while producers added snarky comments and criticism in the form of animated pop-ups, supposed thought bubbles, or analysis by a range of commentators in a comment bar at the bottom of the screen. Also, since *Blind Date* was sold to fill late evening timeslots, it also sexed the genre up considerably, featuring contestants in skimpy bikinis, bumping and grinding at night clubs, engaging in long and sloppy kisses, and so forth. *Blind Date*'s followers, such as *Elimidate* and *Fifth Wheel*, later added a competition element, whereby singles would date multiple suitors at one time, inspiring contestants to one-up each other in dancing, kissing, and stripping.

This competition met its nadir with FOX's *Who Wants to Marry a Millionaire?* in 2000, a show that while roundly criticized, whet the network's appetite for prime-time, hour-long versions of the *Elimidate* formula of young people, sexy locations, lots of alcohol, and open invitations to cavort. Thus, *Temptation Island* followed, a show that split four couples up, placing the women on a tropical island with 20 young men, and the men with 20 young women, to see if anyone would be "tempted" to cheat. *Temptation Island* opened the floodgates for prime-time dating shows, with the less tawdry and significantly more popular *The Bachelor* starting on ABC in 2002. *The Bachelor* took a bachelor to a secluded mansion filled with 25 women in evening gowns, and then proceeded to arrange "fantasy dates" for them, as the bachelor was required to whittle the 25 down to a final winner. The show also inspired multiple variations, from FOX's *Joe Millionaire* and NBC's *Average Joe* and *For Love or Money*—all of which "tricked" the bachelor/ette or suitors in some way—to

A SELECTIVE TIMELINE OF DATING SHOWS

The Dating Game	ABC, 1975–83; syndication, 1978–80, 1986–89, 1996–99
Love Connection	syndication, 1983–94, 1998–99
Blind Date	syndication, 1999–2006
Who Wants to Marry a Millionaire?	FOX, 2000
Elimidate	syndication, 2001–06
Fifth Wheel	syndication, 2001–04
Temptation Island	FOX, 2001, 2003
The Bachelor/The Bachelorette	ABC, 2002–
Average Joe	NBC, 2003–05
Boy Meets Boy	Bravo, 2003
Cupid	CBS, 2003
For Love or Money	NBC, 2003–04
Joe Millionaire	FOX, 2003
Date My Mom	MTV, 2004
The Player	UPN, 2004
Next	MTV, 2005
Parental Control	MTV, 2006
Flavor of Love	VH1, 2006
I Love New York	VH1, 2007

CBS's *Cupid*, which allowed audience voting, and UPN's *The Player*, which pimped out the formula. In spring 2007, *The Bachelor* was in its tenth cycle, still going strong.

Meanwhile, MTV and VH1's move into the world of reality television produced yet another subgenre of the dating show, with over-the-top, outrageous comedies with quirky twists. *Date My Mom* required suitors to go on a date with the bachelorette's mother, *Next* allowed the bachelor/ette to end the date and replace the suitor at any time, *Parental Control* gave parents the chance to choose two alternatives to their child's current significant other, and *The Flavor of Love* and spinoff *I Love New York* tried to find love for the comical characters Flavor Flav and Tiffany Pollard.

PLAYING FOR THE CAMERA: CRITICISM

A common criticism of many dating shows is that they perpetuate tired and regressive notions of how men and women should behave, especially while dating. First, with all but a few exceptions, most shows take heterosexuality as the assumed norm, immediately marginalizing gay or lesbian sexuality or romance. Such a move occurs at blinding speed, though, precisely because dating shows often espouse rigid ideals of ideal masculinity and femininity. Women on *The Bachelor*, for instance, are rewarded for being demure, quiet, and submissive, as many seasons of the show have featured a loud and assertive woman in the first episode who is cut from the pack, and is shunned by her fellow contestants, for daring to behave as she does. Women are assumed to want a rich, muscular, take-charge man, while men are assumed to want a slim, demure woman who will let him take the lead. Moreover, the women often appear to privilege finding romance above all other activities in their lives, suggesting that finding a spouse is a single woman's first and most important task in life. Even when the bachelor is in theory the one seeking companionship, shows such as *The Bachelor* often depict him as the "missing piece" of the puzzle for the women, positing a clearer sense of lack with the women than with the man, and hence implying that women need validation and completion from men. Certainly, since many such shows depict the women willing to back-stab each other, or to gloat in victory, they paint a picture of fiercely competitive, even desperate women, that is often contrasted to the relaxed friendliness and composure of the man or men.

Of particular concern too is the degree to which many dating shows require women to perform for the bachelor significantly more than their gender-flipped variants require men to perform for women. Women are encouraged to conform to a slim body image, and to render their body as a spectacle for the men to enjoy. Whether this takes the form of dancing competitively on bar tables or poolside on *Elimidate*, or of the prolonged set piece of the "rose ceremony" in *The Bachelor*, in which the man, the male host, and the camera gaze continuously at the women while trying to decide who to pick, as if from a catalog. Feminist critics express concern with television (and film) images such as this where the camera's "eyes" are gendered as heterosexual male, with the woman performing for the camera; the concern is that such shows normalize the act of turning women into sexual objects perpetually on show, and that such normalization will also encourage women to look at themselves as might a (horny) man, and hence both to welcome and solicit the male sexual gaze at all moments. The shows invite audiences to criticize the harem of female suitors as unworthy, determining who will be unlikely to garner the man's favor, and so forth, hence reducing a woman's value to her "usefulness" to men.

Some feminist critics also detect a worrying misogynistic vein to some dating shows, given that they often encourage viewers to enjoy the site of women defeated. *Average Joe*, for instance, promised a bachelorette a house full of eligible suitors and then delivered a bus full of "geeks," and overweight or otherwise conventionally unattractive men. The camera then relished in her horror as one by one the men stepped off the bus, and much of the show continually berated her for being so superficial—even as it never problematized its own choice of a conventionally attractive woman as the ideal date. *Joe Millionaire* deceptively told its female suitors that the bachelor was a millionaire, and yet audience members knew the truth all along, and hence were invited to enjoy the spectacle of "gold-diggers" being belittled and punished for their greed—even when women are positively encouraged to seek men for such reasons in many other dating shows and products of mass culture.

THE RACIAL POLITICS OF DATING SHOWS

Dating shows also offer messages about interracial dating, and about race and beauty. *The Bachelor*, for instance, is particularly fond of the stereotypical beauty pageant blonde, rarely adding more than one or two obligatory minority woman, and to date no minority bachelors. The number of nonwhite suitors on dating shows only tends to go up when the bachelor/ette is nonwhite. Thus, when the supposed paragons of beauty and attractiveness tend overwhelmingly to be white, or else a special exception to the bachelor/ette's racial background (as though competition now occurs in a minor league), the racial politics of beauty are pronounced on dating shows.

Enter Tiffany Pollard, also known as "New York," star of VH1's *Flavor of Love* and *I Love New York*, who became a veritable "unruly woman," much loved by fans for her decidedly "unfeminine" behavior: speaking her mind at volume, loving to eat, mocking or belittling men, and refusing to be any man's trained puppy. While a glorious rejection of and play with expectations of gender on one level, as an African American woman, Pollard's racial characterization was less clear, galvanizing audience reaction into those who found her yet another offensive replication of the stereotypical sassy African American woman, and those who found her performance so over-the-top and excessive as to gleefully poke fun at and disable the racial caricature, much as did the entire genre of blaxploitation films in the 1970s.

PLAYING WITH THE CAMERA: BREAKING THE MOLD

However, the dating show is a more complex genre than its surface of outright sexism suggests. In particular, as *Average Joe* or *Joe Millionaire* suggest, dating shows have long been loved for showing *bad* matches, and while the audience member's criticism of those on screen may at times be misogynistic, it might at other times allow audiences a chance to distance themselves from prevalent scripts of romance. Here, then, it is the very cheesiness of suitors, of dates, and of cast members' long confessionals that amuse, and instead of engaging with dating shows as romances, we might instead engage with them as comedies. As comedies, some dating shows invite us to laugh at the silliness of dating expectations, to roll our eyes at those who endlessly seek to live up to the expectations, and hence to create different dating norms. Just as watching *Jerry Springer* might bring amusement to audiences, yet no role models for future behavior, so too might watching dating shows allow a space for play with and mockery of those on screen.

In particular, the MTV and VH1 shows so obviously mix scripted behavior, and outrageous premises, in a way that encourage little identification, and much mirth. *Parental Control*, for instance, shows very little of the actual dates, and instead focuses a lot of the screen time on verbal sparring between the parents and the unwanted significant other, the three of whom must watch video footage of the dates together. Here, the unwanted significant other often becomes a comic hero, with the parents' traditional expectations flouted and abused by the often free-spirited significant other. Similarly, when the parents first interview prospective dates, the producers always litter the pool with yet more comic characters. While we might see their comic misbehavior as policing and disciplining a very firm notion of how one *should* behave, it is also such characters who become the life of the show, and who make it enjoyable to watch, and thus we will often support that behavior rather than chastise it.

Quite apart from the more riotous and comic dating shows, we might also observe that identification is never secure even with shows such as *The Bachelor*. While the bachelor is selecting from a group of 25 women, for instance, this may well salt wounds of past rejection and public humiliation for viewers, who might therefore identify with the rejected women, not the bachelor. In such a situation, the bachelor's seemingly "dreamy" qualities might therefore be inverted, as he becomes yet another cardboard cut-out man who the viewer would be best to avoid. As with all reality television, much of the work of the dating shows takes place in the conversations and criticisms they inspire, not solely on the screen. Just as *American Idol* or *America's Next Top Model* do not require that viewers validate the ultimate winner, neither does *The Bachelor* require that one either agree with the bachelor or even agree that he is a worthy catch in the first place.

Finally, dating shows can also challenge the norms of patriarchal, heterosexual romance. Most notably, many shows focus more on "hooking up" than on meeting one's actual spouse, thereby refuting the supposed purpose of traditional dating. None of the MTV or VH1 shows seem to express hope in relationships lasting beyond a few months, and UPN's *The Player* was particularly insistent on celebrating "players" and those who reject notions of ideal love, marriage, and long-term relationships. MTV's shows have even offered gay or lesbian episodes, and Bravo's *Boy Meets Boy* staged an all-male dating show. Viewers, meanwhile, are becoming increasingly aware that contestants on most reality television shows are often there for the fame and exposure, willing to play whatever role necessary, yet rarely likely to stay with their television-arranged partnership longer than the date of broadcast. Hence, many dating shows are framed as games first and foremost, not as decisively real, and thereby in turn might suggest the degree to which real-life dating and gender role-play are themselves highly peculiar games.

CONCLUSION

Ultimately, in the dating show, we have an odd genre, one that is occasionally progressive, offering the tools and images to reject scripts of patriarchal, heteronormative romance, that sometimes equates to little more than a postmodern play with little embedded meaning, and yet that at other times perpetuates a model of romance and gendered behavior that hearkens back several centuries. Rather than alternate between these options at different times, though, dating shows are often all of the above at the same time, making it particularly difficult to evaluate or even to parse out their gender politics, instead requiring a purposive viewer to read around and through its various gender blockades.

See also Audience Power to Resist; Body Image; Gay, Lesbian, Bisexual, Transgendered, and Queer Representations on TV; Reality Television; Representations of Masculinity; Representations of Race; Representations of Women.

Further Reading: DeRose, Justin, Elfriede Fürsich, and Ekaterina V. Haskins. "Pop (Up) Goes the *Blind Date:* Supertextual Constraints on 'Reality' Television." *Journal of Communication Inquiry* 27, no. 2 (2004): 171–89; Fiske, John. *Reading Popular Culture.* London: Unwin Hyman, 1989; Galician, Mary-Lou. *Sex, Love, and Romance in the Mass Media: Analysis and Criticism of Unrealistic Portrayals and Their Influence.* Mahwah, NJ: Lawrence Erlbaum, 2003; Graham-Bertolini, Alison. "*Joe Millionaire* as Fairy Tale: A Feminist Critique." *Feminist Media Studies* 4 (2004): 341–43; Gray, Jonathan. "Cinderella Burps: Gender, Performativity, and the Dating Show." In *Reality Television: Remaking Television Culture,* 2nd ed., ed. Susan Murray and Laurie Ouellette. New York: NYU Press, 2008; Mendible, Myra. "Humiliation, Subjectivity, and Reality TV." *Feminist Media Studies* 4 (2004): 335–38; Mulvey, Laura. *Visual and Other Pleasures.* Bloomington: Indiana University Press, 1989; Rowe, Kathleen. *The Unruly Woman: Gender and the Genres of Laughter.* Austin: University of Texas Press, 1995.

Jonathan Gray

DIGITAL DIVIDE

Many have argued that inequalities of access to the Internet in an information-driven society pose a serious social problem and that public investment is needed to solve it. Others contend that the digital divide is a minor concern that will resolve itself without government involvement and spending. The positions we take on this debate depend upon our understanding of how new technologies spread throughout society, whether we think Internet access is a frill or a necessity, and our vision of whether government can and ought to help broaden access.

Concerns over the digital divide, and the origins of the term itself, stemmed mainly from studies of who used computers and the Internet that were conducted in the mid-1990s by the U.S. government. This research found dramatic inequalities of access to digital technologies at a time when the Internet was being popularized and the U.S. economy was emerging from recession. The digital divide sparked concerns about whether broad participation in the economic and educational benefits of the information age would be possible. In response, President Bill Clinton's administration, local governments, and private charities invested in efforts to make Internet access widely available in schools, libraries, community centers, and health care facilities. Within a few years, critics of this investment argued that the digital divide had never been a large problem and that it had shrunk so quickly that it no longer required public attention.

Although the terms of the debate over the digital divide have changed, the controversy itself remains relevant. As late as 2005, around 1 in 5 Americans had never accessed the Internet or used e-mail (Pew Internet & American Life Project 2006). Many people around the world lack access to basic information and communication technologies, so the divide is not simply an American phenomenon, nor is it merely about access to the Internet. In addition, as high-speed broadband Internet service was introduced in the United States and other developed countries, inequalities arose between Americans who could afford this enhanced service and those with slower dial-up Internet service. High-speed service became a necessity for making full use of what the Internet had to offer—video, audio, telephony, games, and so on. Because ongoing technological innovation is likely, the debate over unequal access to these technologies will probably always be with us.

The digital divide may be defined as the gap between those who have access to information and communication technologies and use them effectively for educational, economic, civic, and cultural needs, and those who do not. Effective use involves not only the ability to receive information, but also to adapt it to one's needs, and to create and communicate one's own knowledge and views to others. Advocates for equal access see the abilities to send and receive information via new media as necessary conditions for full participation in society. Thus, those who are concerned about inequality tend to call for *digital inclusion* for those who are least likely to have high-speed Internet connections, or any access. These underserved groups include people with less education, those with lower incomes, African Americans and Latinos, people with physical disabilities, the elderly, and rural residents.

Given the many factors that shape Internet access, advocates for digital inclusion argue that it requires more than simply providing computers and Internet service. Offered the bare physical resources that allow one to get on the Internet, many people will be unable or unwilling to use it, or to use it to its fullest potential. They also need training in how to use computers and navigate the Internet.

WHAT INFLUENCES INTERNET ACCESS?

Availability: Service providers prefer to reach areas that are densely populated, affluent, and lack competing providers, because these areas are most profitable. Individuals are more likely to use the Internet if it is accessible in their home, school, or a nearby library.

Technology: The reach, complexity, and cost of maintaining computers and Internet service shape access. For example, some Internet service technologies, such as Wireless Fidelity (Wi-Fi) have limited reach or are too expensive to deploy everywhere.

Affordability: Access is shaped by the costs of Internet service, the devices used to receive it, and, in the developing world, electricity.

Government Regulation and Resources: Widespread, affordable provision of service often depends on government permission to lay cables along public streets or to use public airwaves to transmit signals; subsidies and loans to persuade companies to offer service in low-profit areas or to allow individuals to subscribe more cheaply; and laws that encourage freedom of speech.

Training: Instruction in literacy and computer literacy must be available.

Appropriate Content: Culturally relevant content in users' own language is necessary.

Trust: New users need sufficient protection from cybercrime, breaches of privacy and security, and unwanted content (pornographic or violent material).

Social Norms: Globally, many people are discouraged from using the Internet based on gender, ethnicity, and other inequalities. Support from family, friends, or community institutions is often needed to encourage people to use the Internet fully.

They need support from family, friends, and the larger culture in which they live to use a technology that can seem bewildering, threatening, or merely irrelevant to one's way of life. People need relevant content in a language they speak and read. Whether societies should help provide these benefits to their citizens hinges on three issues: new technologies' ability to spread to all members of society, the significance of ensuring that people have equal opportunities to communicate, and the role of government in the information age.

DIFFUSION AND INNOVATION

Those who minimize the significance of the digital divide contend that disparities work themselves out over time as technologies diffuse throughout the population. The early adopters of the Internet may have been more white, male, affluent, and educated than the norm, but this is less the case now that Internet usage is permeating societies, at least in the developed world. Prices for computers and basic Internet service have fallen dramatically. People can log on for free in public libraries, schools, and even coffee shops. As a generation of youth who have grown up online mature into adults, any meaningful differences in Internet use are likely to disappear.

However, others argue that true digital inclusion requires keeping up with a set of technologies that are in perpetual motion. Advances in hardware used to access the Internet, from mobile phones to personal digital assistants, confer greater benefits on those who can afford to buy the latest devices. Facility with rapidly developing applications, from instant messaging to blogs to wikis, empowers some denizens of cyberspace to express themselves more widely and powerfully than others. New forms of Internet service, including high-speed service and wireless access, allow some to connect faster, more conveniently, and more productively than others. Some of us will always fall behind without support because as some technologies that shape Internet usage are widely adopted others are introduced that transform access anew.

COMMUNICATION RIGHTS

Critics of efforts to close the digital divide maintain that a market economy requires us to accept some inequality of outcomes in life. As long as a society makes some effort to provide equal opportunity to meet basic human needs, it is not a problem that some will end up earning more than others and therefore be able to afford more luxuries. From this standpoint, people may have fundamental rights to public schooling, basic health care, or national security, but not to most communication technologies and services. Perhaps the poor should pay less for local telephone service so that they can call 911 for help in emergencies, but they do not deserve free or low-cost broadband Internet service subsidized by higher rates on other users. Furthermore, the critics argue, most people who still lack home Internet connections do not want them either because they find the Internet unnecessary or objectionable. For some, being an Internet have-not is a choice.

DIGITAL INCLUSION PROJECTS

There are many examples of efforts to extend the benefits of full Internet access to underserved communities. For example, when the city of Philadelphia commissioned a municipal broadband network, it required the private company that offered Internet service over the city's network to set aside 5 percent of annual revenues earned in the city to pay for computers and training for low-income families and minority-owned businesses. The city also required that service be offered at a discount to poor families and that free access be available at numerous "hotspots" around Philadelphia. Some nonprofit organizations have gone further by developing Web sites that attract underserved groups to use the Internet by offering informational, educational, and job training resources targeted to these groups' interests. For example, One Economy, an organization that provides computers, Internet service, and training in public housing developments, created its own World Wide Web site in English and Spanish called The Beehive, which includes information tailored to low-income people about money, health, jobs, school, news, voting, citizenship, and family issues. The Beehive also offers free e-mail accounts and many local sites focused on users' home cities to connect people to their communities.

In contrast, others contend that in a society that relies on information for its lifeblood, communication technology has become a necessity for equal opportunity and social inclusion. In this view, communication should be considered less like income (where capitalist societies tolerate stark inequalities) and more like education or voting—a fundamental component of a basic standard of living and citizenship. For example, increasingly people are likely to receive their telephone, television, radio, and Internet service via a single broadband connection. Free or low-cost broadband service for the poor has been hailed as a crucial tool for education, a potential economic engine for reviving low-income communities, a means for receiving better medical care and emergency services, increasingly necessary for applying for government services and engaging in effective political participation, and the main medium for twenty-first-century news and entertainment. Therefore, some view broadband as a basic public need comparable to utilities such as roads, water, and electricity.

ROLE OF GOVERNMENT

Even if the digital divide is a problem, can government solve it efficiently and effectively? Skeptics accuse programs such as the U.S. e-rate program, which introduced new fees on telephone subscribers' bills and used the money to help fund Internet service in public schools, libraries, and clinics, of being wasteful and unnecessary. Some private efforts to connect low-income villages and neighborhoods around the world have been well-intended failures because they neglected to do more than provide computers and modems to people who had no training or money to maintain the equipment. Some have argued that government should not burden the telecommunications industry by requiring it to offer service in unprofitable areas. Telecommunications companies have strongly objected to competition from municipal broadband projects, in which cities build their own high-speed networks in part to offer cheaper service to residents.

However, others see public regulation and investment as necessary for expanding access to information. They note that high-speed Internet service is most widely available in countries where governments have taken a greater role in requiring private providers to deploy service to all areas or helped subsidize the building of broadband networks. The U.S. government did little to support broadband deployment in its early years and broadband was therefore less widely available and slower than in many other wealthy countries. Supporters of public involvement in Internet provision argue that telecommunications companies have failed to offer affordable service and have refused to extend their networks to serve unprofitable communities. The federal government's stance was different during the advent of the telephone industry in the late 1800s, when the same problems arose. Regulations compelled telephone companies, many of which held monopoly control over their markets, to serve all communities and to charge lower rates to rural, low-income, and household subscribers so that everyone could be connected via the new medium. Some cities built their own telephone networks to achieve these ends. The voices of those who supported universal service requirements and public networks in the early days of telephony echo in contemporary debates over broadband and the digital divide.

See also Blogosphere; Communication Rights in a Global Context; Internet and Its Radical Potential; Media Reform; Minority Media Ownership; Net Neutrality; Public Sphere; Regulating the Airwaves; Representations of Race; User-Created Content and Audience Participation.

Further Reading: Bagga, R. K., Kenneth Keniston, and Rohit Raj Mathur. *The State, IT and Development.* London: Sage, 2005; Bridges.org. "Spanning the Digital Divide." *Bridges. org* (May 2001). http://old.bridges.org/spanning/pdf/spanning_the_digital_divide.pdf; Compaine, Benjamin M. *The Digital Divide: Facing a Crisis or Creating a Myth?* Cambridge, MA: MIT Press, 2001; Digital Divide Network. http://www.digitaldivide.net/. Navas-Sabater, Juan, Andrew Dymond, and Niina Juntunen. *Telecommunications and Information Services for the Poor: Toward a Strategy for Universal Access.* Washington, DC: World Bank, 2002; Norris, Pippa. *Digital Divide: Civic Engagement, Information Poverty, and the Internet Worldwide.* Cambridge: Cambridge University Press, 2001; Pew Internet & American Life Project, *Home Broadband Adoption 2006.* Available at: http://pewinternet.org/pdfs/PIP_Broadband_trends2006.pdf. Servon, Lisa J. *Bridging the Digital Divide: Technology, Community, and Public Policy.* Malden, MA: Blackwell Publishing, 2002; Solomon, Gwen, Nancy J. Allen, and Paul Resta. *Toward Digital Equity: Bridging the Divide in Education.* London: Allyn and Bacon, 2003; Warschauer, Mark. "Reconceptualizing the Digital Divide." *First Monday* 7, no. 7 (July 2002). http://firstmonday.org/issues/issue7_7/warschauer/index.html.

Chad Raphael

DISABILITIES AND THE MEDIA

Representation of persons with disabilities in the media reveals societal attitudes as well as the limits and fears of society's understanding toward persons with disabilities. Media depictions have real repercussions on the lives of persons with disabilities, and all the more so when they are physically unable to speak for themselves, or if they lack access to media tools of representation. It can be said that we will all one day be disabled at some time in our lives. In light of continuing scientific developments in medicine, reproductive technology, prenatal genetic testing, and much more, we need to seek ways to change ourselves to make the world a better place for persons with disabilities.

MEANINGS AND MODELS OF DISABILITY

Although disability is a distinctly modern concept, representations of disability—of the human body injured and diseased—have been with us as long as the human body has been represented in painting and in sculpture. Along with the numerous technological innovations of the modern age—photography, the rapid and widespread distribution of text and images first via newspapers and magazines, then via television and film, and now via the Internet—have arisen more images of disability. Images of persons from war zones and from foreign countries that do not have access to the same medical care as in the West

NORMS AND NORMALITY

The word *normal* as "constituting, conforming to, not deviating or different from, the common type or standard, regular, usual" only enters the English language around 1840. (Previously, the word had meant "perpendicular"; the carpenter's square, called a "norm," provided the root meaning.) Likewise, the word "norm," in the modern sense, has only been in use since around 1855, and "normality" and "normalcy" appeared in 1849 and 1857, respectively. If the lexicographical information is relevant, it is possible to date the coming into consciousness in English of an idea of "the norm" over the period 1840–1860.

On the "Normal" from Lennard Davis, "Constructing Normalcy: The Bell Curve, the Novel, and the Invention of the Disabled Body in the Nineteenth Century," in *Disability Studies Reader*, 2nd ed. New York: Routledge Press, 2006.

have brought more graphic visual representation of physical injury and disease right into one's living room and onto one's computer screen. The media can be said to have, on the one hand, contributed to familiarizing disability and making it seem less strange. On the other hand, the very showing of images of "others" can have the effect of turning persons with disabilities, whose visual appearance is somehow different, into a "freak" on display.

The medical model of disability and the social model are two frameworks in which disability can be understood. The term *disability* is itself a medical term that suggests injury and that denotes and is connected to notions of *cure*. Therefore, the term is often conceived of as a condition that can be fixed. In this model, to be disabled is to be sick or physically ill; to be broken and in need of recovery from the disability. Another model of disability is the social model, according to which disability is socially and culturally constructed. The social construct model takes into account societal and cultural meanings of impairment, health, and disease; of how material conditions and the environment contribute to the experience of being disabled; of what it means to have a physical, mental, or cognitive condition that makes participation in so-called normal acts of society, of human beings, difficult and even not possible.

Both models have limits. There are real physical and health aspects for persons with disabilities, but societal perceptions of what it means to be disabled also play into how persons with disability are viewed and treated, how decisions about research are made, how services are devised and delivered, and how political policy is created and implemented.

REPRESENTATION, ADVOCACY, AND SELF-ADVOCACY

Persons with disabilities have often been seen as not only physically weak but also cognitively and mentally impaired, as if cognitive and physical impairment occur together. Advocates for disabled persons were first "able-bodied" or nondisabled persons because it was thought that disabled persons lacked the capacity to advocate and speak up for themselves. Charity organizations and advocacy organizations for disabilities can shape not only understanding about disabilities and about persons with disabilities, but can also significantly influence the course of research and therefore of new developments and treatments about a disability due to their fund-raising capacity.

In the wake of the Civil Rights movement in the 1960s, persons with disabilities began to advocate for themselves. In 1977, members of the disability community participated in a four-week sit-in in the offices of San Francisco's Department of Health, Education, and Welfare, to call for the enforcement of Section 504 of the Rehabilitation Act of 1973. The protesters were successful and Section 504 is regarded as a precursor to the Americans with Disabilities Act (ADA) of 1990. Advances in technology and in medical care have assisted persons with disabilities in self-advocacy. The development of new technologies from motorized wheelchairs to computers and the Internet to augmentative communication devices has enabled persons with disabilities to have greater mobility, to communicate more readily, and to more fully participate in their communities. As a result, persons with disabilities are more and more seen; are more and more visible, and seek more and more to represent themselves and to (rightfully) be the authority about how they are represented. More and more memoirs and other writings by persons with disabilities are now available, and by persons whose communicative and cognitive impairment (i.e., those with Down Syndrome) would in the past have been seen as making this impossible.

It is crucial that the persons who have the disability be in charge of their own representation. Stereotypes about disabled persons as a "burden" and less than normal are so deeply entrenched that people do not realize they are perpetuating discriminatory attitudes at the moment when they believe themselves to be advocating for positive change. This is in no small part because, too often when it comes to the media, those with disabilities are not in charge of the tools of the media. An example of this is the autism advocacy efforts of talk radio host Don Imus. Imus has been both praised for his speaking about autism on the air and criticized. In his broadcasts, Imus presented one theory of autism causation that, accordingly, offered a one-dimensional representation of autism: Imus spoke of autism as being caused by vaccines and of autistic children as damaged and injured. (Imus's wife, Deirdre Imus, is herself an advocate for environmental causes and has created her own line of environmentally friendly cleaning products.) Due to the popularity of Imus's talk show (until his ouster in April 2007 as a result of his racist comments with regard to the Rutgers University women's basketball team), whatever he might say about autism, and about the causes of and potential treatments for autism—however one-sided and simply inaccurate—reached a much broader audience and perpetuated misunderstanding of autistic persons.

The Internet has leveled the playing field in giving persons with disabilities not only a voice but a constant presence. Via e-mail, chat rooms, and blogs, the Internet has made it possible for persons with disabilities who might have difficulties in physically transporting themselves to a meeting, a support group, or a rally, to find each and to find support, and to band together to be a growing political presence. By putting up their own Web sites and other media publications, disability advocates like Not Dead Yet have taken on more and more of a part

DEFINING DISABILITY

The federal government defines disability:

> For purposes of nondiscrimination laws (e.g. the Americans with Disabilities Act, Section 503 of the Rehabilitation Act of 1973 and Section 188 of the Workforce Investment Act), a person with a disability is generally defined as someone who (1) has a physical or mental impairment that substantially limits one or more "major life activities," (2) has a record of such an impairment, or (3) is regarded as having such an impairment. With this definition, we see how important the social construction of a disabled person can be to policy, perceptions and even behavior.

in the discussion about their disabilities. Disability advocates argue that there is a unique disability culture that is outside of normal and normative mainstream culture. For instance, deaf culture argues against teaching deaf children to use spoken language and to use sign language, and critiques the use of cochlear implants. Why not enable deaf persons to communicate with a means (sign language) that is more readily accessible for them, rather than requiring them to use verbal language, which might be easier for those of us who are not disabled to understand, but which emphasizes deaf persons' disability?

DISABILITY IN THE MASS MEDIA

One example of how media accounts of disability have shaped societal understanding, and misunderstanding, of disabled persons can be seen in the example of Dr. Jack Kevorkian and the creation of Not Dead Yet. Not Dead Yet is a disability rights advocacy group which was founded on April 27, 1996, shortly after Kevorkian was acquitted in the assisted suicides of two women with nonterminal disabilities.

Kevorkian was convicted of second-degree murder in the death of Thomas Youk, 52, a Michigan man suffering from Lou Gehrig's disease. Referring to his release after eight years in prison as "one of the high points of his life," Kevorkian was met by Mike Wallace of *60 Minutes* on his release. In 1998 Wallace's reporting on the filming of Youk's death "played a key role in Kevorkian's conviction"; an interview with Kevorkian was broadcast on *60 Minutes* on the Sunday following his release in June 2007. "They'll downplay his history of helping non-terminally ill disabled people commit suicide and portray him as some kind of martyr," Not Dead Yet wrote in December 2006. "They won't mention his advocacy of lethal experimentation on death row prisoners or disabled infants at all." Many disability rights advocates have long opposed Kevorkian and his public crusade to legalize assisted suicide. They have argued that doing so would essentially make it "open season" for people with disabilities who are often considered a burden on society, particularly at a time when the cost of health care is high. They have also noted that many people Kevorkian "helped" end their lives were not in the final stages of terminal illnesses, but instead had disabilities and were in "emotional, psychological or social crises, which made them more vulnerable."

Another disability that has been grossly misrepresented in the mass media is autism, a neurological disorder characterized by impairments in social skills, communication, and behavior. Despite the fact that today we know more than we ever have about autism since Leo Kanner first identified the disorder in 1943 and since 1967, when Bruno Bettelheim's *The Empty Fortress: Infantile Autism and the Birth of the Self* was published, we still talk about autism the same way that we did in the days of both men. Much of what is said about autism in the mass media presents a view of autism that still draws on the metaphors and images of autism used in the 1960s. Autism is still said to be "mysterious" and treatment a "mystery." Similarly, the causes of the disorder, and life with autism, is often considered "hopeless." Despite significant advances in scientific research and in educational methods, the popular representation of autism has not changed from that of earlier decades, and shows little sign of changing. This disconnect between what we actually know about autism and popular representations of autism, persists and is ultimately not beneficial for our understanding of autism, of disabled children and adults, and of disability as a whole.

It is necessary to foster more positive representations of autism and life with autism in order to stop seeing autistic persons as broken and diseased beings who need to be fixed and made nonautistic. This task is easier said than done; attempts to change stereotypes about autism can sometimes result in more misunderstanding. In "Autism: The Art of Compassionate Living," Jennifer Liss of *WireTap* writes about the efforts of parents to battle stereotypes about autism and to raise understanding. In her video, *Autism Every Day,* autism mother and ex-CNN news anchor Lauren Thierry describes how she tried to capture "autism every day" to combat myths of autistic persons as "idiot savants" and of autism as caused by bad parenting. Said Thierry: "The party line is supposed to be that anything that raises awareness you're supposed to be happy about. That notion is 10 years old. At this point we need to be showing the world what the vast reality truly is." That reality, according to Thierry, includes images of kids not sleeping through the night, banging their heads against the wall or running into traffic, not images of kids setting basketball records or passionately playing the violin. However, as Liss writes in her article, it seems that Thierry sought a particular image of life with an autistic child in her video, one which emphasized only the negative. Before filming, Thierry told her subjects not to vacuum the house or do their hair. The camera crew showed up unexpectedly, so her subjects had no therapists present; the cameras rolled as a mom struggled with her son to brush his teeth, as a 9-year-old was in severe distress, and as a 5-year-old was having his diaper changed. Though Thierry undoubtedly wanted to tell the truth, much of the footage of *Autism Every Day* is characteristic of nonfiction programming designed to attract ratings. And such dark and uncomfortable revelations are only one side of living with children with autism.

One of those dark and uncomfortable truths that the article "Autism: The Art of Compassionate Living" refers to is the killing of autistic children by their parents. Dr. Karen McCarron, who allegedly killed her 3-year-old daughter,

Katherine McCarron, is mentioned, as is Alison Tepper Singer, senior vice president of Autism Speaks, an organization that seeks to provide information about autism and raise funds for research. Autism Speaks featured the *Autism Every Day* video on its Web site, http://www.autismspeaks.org, and showed it at fund-raising events. Tepper Singer is herself an autism mother who, in the *Autism Every Day* video, talks about wanting to drive off the George Washington Bridge with her autistic daughter. Many autistic persons and families with autistic children have reacted with outrage and disgust to Singer's statement and have even drawn a connection between her and Karen McCarron. Thierry called Singer "gutsy and courageous" and noted that "you don't say stuff like that—camera rolling—unless you are truly ready to play ball with the entire world."

My son, Charlie, is autistic and our family has been through every autism experience including the "terrible" ones—the screaming at the doctor's visits, the feces where they shouldn't be, the bruises, the dwindling bank account. But these experiences are only so terrible as we choose to represent them as such. While it is necessary to show compassion for parents who have difficult lives and have made sacrifices for their autistic children, the majority of our concern needs to start with the autistic child, with autistic persons, and to think about how we represent them. Otherwise, we are only reinforcing myths and stereotypes about autism. Desperation is one perception of raising a disabled child, and not necessarily as fact, and to represent life with a disabled child as "desperate" or a "tragedy" can have real repercussions.

REPRESENTATION AND PRENATAL GENETIC TESTING

The representation of disability matters because what people think about a disabled person can influence decisions about having, or not having, a child with a disability such as Down Syndrome. Due to new, less invasive screening techniques—an ultrasound exam that can detect whether a child might have Down Syndrome as early as 11 weeks into pregnancy—the American College of Obstetricians and Gynecologists (ACOG) is recommending that all women who are expecting be screened. Previously, only women 35 years of age and older have been routinely tested for chromosomal abnormalities in their fetuses. The new ultrasound exam, a nuchal translucency test, measures the fluid that accumulates in the back of a fetus's neck: There is a "strong association" between this thickening of the back of a fetus's neck and Down Syndrome, and studies that use this measurement along with two blood tests have been shown to detect 82 to 87 percent of Down Syndrome cases.

Parents-to-be who discover that they may have a child with a disability are likely to consider the views of medical professionals and of medical and charity organizations in making their decision to have, or not to have, a child. With regard to prenatal testing for Down Syndrome, some professionals represent life with a disability in a negative light. For instance, Dr. James Goldberg, the former chair of the ACOG's committee on genetics, notes that it is "not as problematic" to lose a normal pregnancy as to give birth to a Down syndrome child. Such a statement implies that a child born with Down Syndrome—that a disabled child—can be "problematic" to a family, and that having the information in one's first trimester of pregnancy that one is carrying a child with Down Syndrome—a disabled child—will do, in the words of Dr. Nancy Green, medical director of the March of Dimes, "the most good for the biggest number." Given that the population of children with Down Syndrome—of children with a disability—does not comprise "the biggest number" in society, one might wonder what form "the most good" might take: Is it suggested that "the most good" would be for fewer disabled persons to be born, so that those who do not have a disability do not have to take care of them?

English and disability studies professor Michael Bérubé offers a different picture about "the good" of life with a disabled child. Bérubé's son Jamie has Down Syndrome. In his book, *Life As We Know It: A Father, a Family, and an Exceptional Child,* Bérubé represents his son by narrating his early struggles to learn to eat and talk and learn; he has continued to write about Jamie growing up and becoming a teenager who loves Harry Potter books and traveling. Bérubé understands the significance of images and words, our "social constructions" of disabled persons, when he writes in the Epilogue to his book. "That's why advocates of the disabled are so concerned about polite words, popular movies, and visual and textual representations of every kind. We need to deliberate the question of how we will represent the range of human variation to ourselves" (p. 260).

CONCLUSION

As more tests for screening for chromosomal and genetic abnormalities in a fetus are developed, we will be faced with more difficult questions about having a child with a disability. If life with a disabled child is represented as terrible and tragic, people may be more likely to choose not to have such a child. If life with a disabled child is represented as full of hope and new discoveries amid the difficulties, people can understand that life with disability, while different, can be very good indeed.

The metaphors and the language that are used to refer to people with disabilities have a direct impact on how they are understood and treated by society. It is crucial to pay attention to how persons with disabilities are represented in the media because, as disability studies scholars Sharon Snyder, Brenda Jo Brueggemann, and Rosemary Garland-Thomas write, "Disability as both a bodily condition and a social category either now or later will touch us all. The fact that many of us will become disabled if we live long enough is perhaps the fundamental aspect of human embodiment." Each one of us is likely to one day become disabled as we age and our bodies change and it is therefore all the more crucial to pay attention to how disability is represented in the media today.

See also Bias and Objectivity; Internet and Its Radical Potential; Narrative Power and Media Influence; Paparazzi and Photographic Ethics; Public Access Television; Sensationalism, Fear Mongering and Tabloid Media; Shock Jocks.

Further Reading: Bérubé, Michael. *Life As We Know It: A Father, a Family, and an Exceptional Child.* New York: Vintage, 1998; Burke, JoBeth McDaniel. *A Special Kind of Hero: Chris*

Burke's Own Story. Backinprint.com, 2001; Davis, Lennard. *Disability Studies Reader*, 2nd ed. New York: Routledge, 2006; Fries, Kenny. *Staring Back: The Disability Experience from the Inside Out*. New York: Plume, 1997; Grandin, Temple. *Thinking in Pictures: My Life with Autism*. New York: Vintage, 2006; Grinker, Roy Richard. *Unstrange Minds: Remapping the World of Autism*. New York: Basic Books, 2007; Longmore, Paul, and Lauri Umansky, eds. *The New Disability History (American Perspectives)*. New York: New York University Press, 2001; Mitchell, David. *Narrative Prosthesis: The Body and the Dependencies of Discourse*. Ann Arbor: University of Michigan Press, 2001; Osteen, Mark, ed. *Autism and Representation*. New York: Routledge, 2007; Rose, Martha L. *The Staff of Oedipus: Transforming Disability in Ancient Greece*. Ann Arbor: University of Michigan Press, 2003; Snyder, Sharon L., Brenda Brueggemann, and Rosemary Garland-Thomas, eds. *Disability Studies: Enabling the Humanities*. New York: Modern Language Association, 2002; Sontag, Susan. *Illness as Metaphor and AIDS and Its Metaphors*. New York: Picador, 1990.

Kristina Chew

THE DVD: HOME VIEWING OF MOVIES COMES OF AGE

The DVD has revolutionized home viewing of movies and television programs and is an important part of the high-tech media development of the twenty-first century. Far cheaper to produce, easier to store, and capable of housing much more information than a VCR tape, the DVD also offers interactive possibilities for the viewer that have changed the way people relate to films and many television series. The DVD is part of a long series of technological developments, starting back in the 1920s, that have ironically been resisted, at least since the dawning of the television era, by the very people destined to make the greatest profits from them.

WHAT IS A DVD?

A DVD, or "Digital Video Disc" (sometimes "Digital Versatile Disc"), is an optically read storage device that can be used to house images (both still and moving) and sound for playback. Its size, the same as the older compact disc (CD), was chosen because it allowed manufacturers to use the same carriers they were making for CD players. Though primarily used for movies and games, it can be used for much more, providing a discrete and portable vehicle for the storage of data of all sorts.

By 1999, just two years after the DVD was first offered for sale in the United States as a vehicle for movies, thousands of titles had been transferred to the new technology. As the price of players (thanks to the decision to use the CD size) was low, people were quick to switch to the DVD format for home viewing. In addition, the DVDs proved easier to store than much bulkier videotapes, could provide movies in their original aspect ratio (the height/width ratio of the studio release), could be easily accessed at any point in the movie (while VCRs required rewinding and fast-forwarding), and could contain much more information, making it possible to add attractive extras that convinced many people to replace their old videotapes completely.

Not only were the DVDs attractive to the consumer, but the manufacturers liked them as well. Costing less than half as much to produce as a videotape, the DVDs could sell for as much if not more (especially when packaged as "special editions"). This made it financially attractive for the manufacturers to produce as many movies on DVD as possible, leading to a renewed popularity of old movies. Restored Hollywood musicals, films noir, romantic comedies, and even silent films have found their way to DVD, creating an entirely new fan base for films that had not been seen by the general public for years.

BACKGROUND AND HISTORY

Home viewing of commercial movies began on the heels of World War I with the introduction of the Pathé Baby with its 9.5-millimeter center-sprocket film in 1922 and the transfer of professional films to that gauge. The Kodascope, Kodak's first 16-millimeter home system, soon followed. Though these were more curiosities than anything else, they gave people a taste for home viewing that was only to grow over the next decades up to the point where, by the end of the century, home viewing had become the driving financial force behind the American film industry.

Just as cinema has gone through numerous revolutions since the 1920s, so has home viewing. In keeping with the technology of the time, the Baby and the Kodascope of the 1920s had no ability to produce sound. When sound finally came to the movies in 1927, it did not also come to home viewing. For home projectors, that came a few years later—in 1932, with the introduction of an RCA Victor sound system.

The popularity of television, starting in the late 1940s, led to a new way of watching movies at home. No longer did people need projectors and their own film libraries; now, they could simply turn on the set, sit down, and watch. Unfortunately for home viewers anticipating first-rate movies on the small screen, the movie studios of the day saw television as a threat, as competition. They would not release their major pictures to the television stations or networks, forcing television, when showing movies at all, to rely on B-westerns, science fiction, and horror movies, leading to a nostalgia for such films that remains to this day among the baby-boomers growing up at the time. It wasn't until the early 1960s that recent feature films were regularly shown on television, starting with NBC's Saturday Night at the Movies. Before that time, only a few major feature films were aired regularly on television, most notably *The Wizard of Oz* at Thanksgiving and *It's a Wonderful Life* at Christmas. It was television that made both films the cultural icons they now are, something that studio executives, anxious and protective, were not able to appreciate until years later.

By the 1970s, having finally proved they could augment studio profits when shown on television, movies were a staple of both network and local-station fare. They had established themselves as an important part of home entertainment for the average American, not just those who could afford film projection equipment. Soon, movies would become one of the *most* important parts of home entertainment with the introduction of inexpensive systems that could record whole movies for playback later, such as the Video Home System (VHS) and

BRAZIL

One of the most interesting DVD releases is the Criterion (the most respected of the DVD manufacturers) version of Terry Gilliam's 1985 film *Brazil*. The multi-DVD set includes two complete versions of *Brazil*. One of these is a "director's cut" with an optional commentary by Terry Gilliam. It is the film as Gilliam wanted it to be. It was prepared with care for the DVD with all of the care and devotion that has become the hallmark of Criterion. The other is a pan-and-scan version of the movie, the version first shown on television and including a "love conquers all" ending that Gilliam did not create (it was done by the studio without his permission). Significantly, Gilliam does not provide commentary for this version.

The significance of having both versions in one set is that one is able to see quite clearly the difference between pan-and-scan and the film in its original aspect ratio. This, perhaps even more than the butchering of the film by the studio, is what makes this set interesting to the film buff and historian. However, the ability to compare a director's version of a movie with what the studio wanted is also a boon to the viewer.

Included in the set are documentaries on the making of the movie and even a sequence of storyboards used in the making.

---

the ill-fated Betamax. The introduction of home taping systems scared the film studios. They believed that amateur home recordings would eat away at their profits. It took them some years to realize that the VHS was a boon to them, not something that would starve them. Rental of videotapes had become big business by the end of the 1970s. Soon after that, *sales* of prerecorded movies on videotape began to take off as people began to understand and demand the higher quality of professionally dubbed tapes as compared with home recordings.

Even on prerecorded tapes, however, the quality of videotape was never very high. There was at least one alternative that did gain a little momentum, the laserdisc, but it was unwieldy (as large as a long-playing record) and, like the Sony tapes, could not hold an entire movie. Even so, a number of films were transferred to laserdisc in the 1980s and early 1990s, bought mainly by serious film fans who objected to the alterations of films made for presentation on videotape. The warning inserted on the screen before the start of most videotapes, "This film has been modified from its original version. It has been formatted to fit your screen," began to irritate more and more viewers. By the 1990s, the demand for films presented in their original and with even higher quality had grown sufficiently so that manufacturers finally started to seriously develop alternatives to the videotape.

ADVANTAGES OF THE DVD

At the time that television was introduced, it used an aspect ratio of 1.33:1, just slightly narrower than the movies of the era. Partly in response to television (wanting a more dynamic look that could not be reproduced on television) and partly because new technologies allowed it, movies soon moved to what would come to be called "widescreen." Today, most films are produced either in a ratio of 1.85:1 or 2.35:1 (CinemaScope). In either case, reproducing that ratio on a television required letterboxing, strips of black above and below the image on the screen. In the early days of videotape, people objected to this, partly because videotapes were not very sharp to begin with, and reducing the size of the image made it even harder to see.

To get rid of the letterbox effect, videotape manufacturers utilized a process called "pan and scan," effectively cutting off a part of each shot, capturing only what was deemed essential to the scene. This appalled film enthusiasts, but there was little they could do about it aside from buying the expensive and ungainly laserdiscs—until, that is, the advent of the DVD and, at the same time, developments in television sets that allowed for sharper image reproduction. Initially, most DVDs were offered in both letterbox and full-screen editions, but most viewers no longer feel the need for the larger image *in* the screen—and not simply because the image is now sharper. Televisions are larger and, because of the popularity of the DVD and the desire they have sparked for seeing films as they were originally intended, many are offered with an aspect ratio just slightly narrower than that (1.85:1) of most commercial films.

Other advantages of the DVD are increased sound possibilities, the ability to turn subtitles on and off, the ability to switch to dubbing in other languages, and the possibility of listening to a commentary on the film or television episode while it is playing. And, of course, there are the extras. Sometimes additional full-length films are added, biopics of directors and actors, documentaries on the making of the movie or television show, or even another film of the same name (as in the case of one DVD release of the Stanley Donen film *Charade*). Outtakes and deleted scenes also show up, as do music videos and a wide range of other items—all added to entice consumers away from their videotapes.

Even with the immediate popularity of the DVD, the film studios, once again, did not understand clearly that the DVD, like showings on television and the videotapes the DVD superseded, *augmented* their films instead of replacing them. This time, though, the evidence of the value of the DVD came quickly. By 2004, according to the *New York Times*, income from home viewing of movies (including television broadcast rights, cable rights, videotapes, and DVDs) was nearly triple that of theater showings. To the surprise of studio executives, home viewing had become the driving engine of the movie industry.

The producers of televisions shows, however, came to an understanding of the possibilities and advantages of the DVD much more quickly. The ability to offer "complete season" sets of shows was potentially as lucrative as syndication of reruns, providing an after-market with a power to extend the life of a show well beyond broadcast runs. DVDs have allowed viewers the chance to escape the ad breaks of broadcast television, and to watch multiple episodes at once, and hence along with such devices as TiVo, they are revolutionizing how viewers can watch and engage with television on their own terms.

The DVD has also provided new power for producers in their battles with networks. *The Family Guy*, for example, was cancelled twice—but was brought back each time in part because DVD sales of the shows were so strong that the

THE CHAPLIN COLLECTION

Each volume of *The Chaplin Collection* contains multiple DVDs, together providing an overlook of Chaplin's career from his early days to his late sound films. Each major movie is accompanied by an introduction by Chaplin biographer David Robinson along with chapters from Serge Toubiana's *Chaplin Today* series. The prints of the movies used in the transfer to DVD are those held by Chaplin's family from his own vault, providing a chance to see the movies without the wear and tear we have come to associate with the viewing of silent films.

Each volume contains a great deal of additional material, from separate presentation of scores to recordings of Chaplin reading. There are also pieces of home movies made by one of Chaplin's sons and shorts relating to the topics of the Chaplin films.

FOX network was forced to recognize the sustained drawing power of the show. Another FOX show, *Firefly*, though cancelled in its first season, produced DVD sales so powerful that Universal Pictures willingly backed a movie based on it. Though only one of the elements leading to the diminution of network power, the DVD has contributed to the broadening of viewing possibilities within an arena once dominated by just three networks.

DISADVANTAGES OF THE DVD

The DVD is *not* film. To a cinema purist, this will always be a disadvantage. Even when projected, it does not have quite the feel of film. The image from a DVD can also break up, its own version of the scratches that mar film, and the shelf-life of a DVD is not expected to be particularly long (though this may not matter, as new technologies may replace them before this ever becomes a problem).

The greatest danger posed by the DVD and by digital technology in general is that, as it replaces film, the originals may not be preserved. Already, the reserve of 16-millimeter prints is quickly disappearing. Soon, all movies may exist only digitally, something at which film scholars and restorers shudder. Though there are enough advantages to the digital that some filmmakers (such as David Lynch) now shoot exclusively in a digital format, the fact remains: most films were (and still are) shot on film with the intent that they be shown on film. As we move away from film, the possibility of seeing these movies in the format they were created for (and thus of seeing them exactly as they were meant to be) is disappearing.

Like the videotape before it, the DVD changes the way movies are made, something many filmmakers view with caution. As VHS systems became increasingly important to industry profits, filmmakers started shooting differently, constructing their scenes with an eye towards eventual pan-and-scan cropping—grouping the most important elements of a shot at the center of the image, for example. Since the advent of the DVD, with its easy accessibility and much clearer images,

A HOME VIEWING TIMELINE

1922—The Pathé Baby, the first home movie projector, appears.

1923—Kodascope 16-mm projector and Cine-Kodak 16-mm motion picture camera introduced.

1925—Kodascope Libraries, the first of a number of similar enterprises, began offering 16-mm films for rental.

1930—First regular television transmissions, by the BBC.

1933—The first 16-mm projector with sound, the RCA Victor Photophone Junior Portable, comes on the market.

1946—Home sales of television sets begin to show commercial possibilities of the medium.

1948—First cable television system introduced.

1949—William Boyd, who had bought the rights to his "Hopalong Cassidy" movies, edits them and offers them to television stations.

1953—Admiral introduces the color television set.

1956—AMPEX introduces first videotape recorder.

1958—Optical video disc invented.

1961—Saturday Night at the Movies debuts on NBC.

1972—Philips introduces the first home videocassette recorder.

MCA/Philips LaserDisc demonstrated.

1975—Sony Betamax marketed.

1977—JVC introduces the first VHS VCR with two-hour tapes.

1996—First DVD player sold (in Japan).

---

set designers and directors have found themselves concentrating more on the details in their shots, sometimes to the detriment of the whole, as happened in Peter Weir's 2003 film *Master and Commander*, where even the buttons on the costumes were faithful reproductions of early nineteenth-century buttons, but where more significant historical gaffes went undetected.

CONCLUSION

Though the DVD may not have a long life as a vehicle for movies or television (or even for games), it has helped change viewer relations to films—and has finally convinced studio executives that home viewing of movies is not something to be fought, but encouraged, and that non-advertiser-driven television can be lucrative. Collectors of videotapes were always a little shy about their hobby, knowing that the versions of the movies that they cherished were not of high quality, due to limitations in the technology and the editing (including pan-and-scan) that generally accompanied them. The DVD has changed that. With the DVD has come not just improvement in quality, but the extras have sparked a new interest in the history of movies as well as in genres that have been long considered almost dead. DVD collectors have become students of movies and television, of their histories and their versions. At no time have so many people known so much about so many movies in particular—many of which had come close to being completely forgotten by the end of the twentieth century.

Today, studio executives still worry about the loss of control that home viewing represents. Because they are so cheap to produce, DVDs are pirated and sold, often for a quarter of the price of the legitimate release. Studios try to stop this, but do not want to do the one thing that would really counter piracy: bring down their own prices. They are also trying to stop copying and altering of DVDs by home viewers through technological blocks, but this is proving extremely difficult in the face of the ingenuity of home viewers.

Whatever form movies may be brought into the home by in the future, the impact will probably not be as great as that of the DVD. The new technology probably will not be packaged as discrete entities as DVDs are, allowing each movie to be surrounded by commentaries, alternate endings, and related material of all sorts (these will be available, certainly, but probably through links on the Internet and not as part of a package). But the impact of the DVD will remain; knowledge of movies will probably never fall back to its pre-DVD level.

See also Alternative Media in the United States; Online Digital Film and Television; Political Documentary; Piracy and Intellectual Property; TiVo; Transmedia Storytelling and Media Franchises; World Cinema.

Further Reading: Abramson, Albert. *The History of Television, 1942–2000.* Jefferson, NC: McFarland, 2003; Barlow, Aaron. *The DVD Revolution: Movies, Culture, and Technology.* Westport, CT: Praeger, 2005; Bordwell, David, and Kristin Thompson. *Film History.* New York: McGraw Hill, 2002; Briggs, Asa, and Peter Burke. *A Social History of the Media: From Gutenberg to the Internet.* Cambridge: Polity Press, 2002; Lewis, Jon, ed. *The End of Cinema as We Know It: American Film in the Nineties.* New York: New York University Press, 2001; *The Velvet Light Trap* no. 56 (2005), special issue on DVDs.

Aaron Barlow

EMBEDDING JOURNALISTS: HOW CLOSE IS TOO CLOSE?

The U.S. invasion of Iraq marked a new era in the evolving relationship between the media and their military sources. Prevented from access to the battlefield in previous conflicts, journalists were invited by the Pentagon to accompany troops into the theater of operation during Operation Iraqi Freedom. During the invasion of Iraq, over 700 embedded war correspondents from the United States rode with American and British soldiers across the Iraqi desert and reported from remote locations, sometimes using new cell-phone video technology, making the Iraq war the first to be broadcast live, in real time. Critics questioned the wisdom of what they called a loss of journalistic independence while Pentagon officials proclaimed they wanted the public to see what war was really like. Embedding was a profound historical development for communication and war reporting, and had significant influence on the way the war was reported. Coverage of the Iraq invasion will have enduring effects on the ways in which the media tell the story of war.

WAITING FOR WAR STORIES: ANTICIPATING AN INEVITABLE WAR

With the invasion of Iraq, the Pentagon promised media access to the battlefield unseen since Vietnam. Journalists gauge their freedom to report war based on their ability to cover military units in actual combat. In what was being heralded a new era of military openness, reporters expressed hopeful skepticism about Pentagon promises to accompany troops into Iraq. In the weeks before the

war started, hundreds of journalists were embedding with military units anticipating their new access to close-up views of combat. At the same time, protests against the war took place in major cities across the globe, demonstrations
that were largely ignored by the American mainstream media. Instead, the news
agenda was filled with stories showing "embeds" training at media boot camps,
learning about gas masks, and running with heavy backpacks while holding
cameras taking footage on the run. Network anchors prepared audiences for
what they said would be an uncensored war. Overall, the early coverage of the
embedding process set the tone and created a media atmosphere that made war
seem inevitable.

POSITIVE IMAGES

News reporting of the conflict seemed to be under way even before the fighting started. Prewar news coverage was dominated by positive stories about the
military from reporters embedded with troops along bordering countries who
were "waiting for war." U.S. network anchors Dan Rather and Tom Brokaw were
already wearing khakis in the desert, driving Humvees, profiling soldiers, hitch-
ing rides on helicopters, and previewing high-tech weaponry. "With all this fire-
power and all these forces primed and ready to go, how long can they stay in peak
condition?" worried NBC's Tom Brokaw (NBC, February 18, 2003). Other topics important for public discussion before the war started, such as the potential
humanitarian crisis, the validity of the charge that Saddam Hussein had weapons of mass destruction, and diplomatic proposals that might have prevented
the conflict, were downplayed, discounted, or left outside the news agenda.

THE CRITICS

In the United States, discussions in the alternative media took on a different, more critical attitude to embedding than those in the mainstream media.
Veteran war correspondent Chris Hedges was one of the most outspoken critics
of the idea. In cautionary statements to the press before the war, Hedges argued
that the idea that reporters would have unfettered access was based on wishful
thinking. He went on to say that the practice of embedding was insidious and
predicted that it would produce a loss of distance as reporters gained a sense of
loyalty to the troops they covered.

Hedges was referring to a commonly held attitude about reporters and officials. Many journalism texts spend time recounting cautionary tales about how
journalists should avoid the loss of professional and emotional distance from
their sources. Accurate reporting demands journalistic independence.

THE HISTORICAL PERSPECTIVE

Many analysts and journalists understood from the beginning that embedding would create a different dynamic between reporters and soldiers than existed in previous wars. Vietnam has been referred to as the "uncensored" war

largely because of the frontline access afforded war correspondents. Photojournalists and "renegades" covering the war moved freely through the country, found their own units, and buddied up with soldiers and officers alike. They covered them for a time, then moved on. "Embeds" in Iraq, on the other hand, had no independence, no vehicles, and were required to stay with the assigned unit for the duration of the war. There were lists of restrictions and rules to be followed. Assignments were centrally organized by the Pentagon, and there was no "cutting deals" in the field. Journalists covering Iraq were totally dependent on the military, not only for access, but also for equipment, medical supplies, and their own protection. Indeed, Iraq became a dangerous conflict for all reporters, and numerous journalists continue to be killed.

In addition, some officers made it clear from the beginning that journalistic independence would be undesirable in the field. At briefings in Kuwait City, embeds were told they would be made part of the unit, and a member of the team. The *Washington Post* (March 7, 2003) quoted Lt. Col. Rick Long who said, "Reporters shouldn't be…independently probing for facts.…If something bad happens, it's the military's job to investigate."

PRESS POOLS AND THE FIRST GULF WAR

War correspondents Chris Hedges and John MacArthur both covered the first Persian Gulf War in 1991, and were outspoken critics of the "pool system." Their experiences made them highly skeptical about embedding. During the first Gulf War, the press had been promised access through a pool system, in which teams of reporters would accompany troops and share footage and information with each other. But from the beginning, war correspondents were highly restricted, and many journalists were blocked from the field of operation when the ground war started. In addition, official military escorts followed journalists as they interviewed troops, and pubic affairs personnel attempted to manage information between the media and the military. Alternative news outlets took the military to court and the Center for Constitutional Rights filed a lawsuit against the Pentagon for censorship during the Desert Shield and Desert Storm operations (The Center for Constitutional Rights 1991, pp. 10–11). The lawsuit documented the ways public affairs "escorts engaged in arbitrary censorship of interviews, photography and altered the activities of the soldiers when reporters came into their presence, not for security reasons, but to ensure favorable coverage of the military presence."

THE MILITARY PERSPECTIVE

The Pentagon had learned from the first Gulf War that U.S. journalists were unlikely to be critical of military operations if they felt it would jeopardize their future access to combat. In addition, press restrictions over the years had blocked what the military perceived as positive stories of battle along with the negative. General Wesley Clark, working as a CNN analyst, admitted that restricting journalists during the Persian Gulf War was a huge mistake. He noted that there was no reporting, images, or even documentation of one of the biggest armored battles ever fought. In addition, the Pentagon had been criticized for restricting the press, first during the invasion of Grenada in 1983 by the Sidle commission, and again by a Defense Department report after the Panama invasion that concluded that the failure of the pool arrangement resulted in stories and pictures of dubious quality. Though the media coverage of the first Gulf War was highly positive, particularly after the fighting started, the Pentagon was roundly criticized for press restrictions. Embedding was viewed as the solution to the problem of battlefield access. It was seen as a process that would be able to take advantage of the considerable resources of the media, but under controlled conditions more favorable to the military.

PUBLIC RELATIONS

Since World War II, the distinctions between military information operations (psyops), public diplomacy, and public affairs have been blurred with each new war, but the evidence is that the development of the embeds policy and its implementation in the United States was largely driven by a public relations agenda. Even as it promised a lack of "blanket censorship," the Pentagon did not hide its desire to shape positive coverage of the invasion of Iraq. As former war correspondents and alternative media were reporting stories critical of the new relationship between the Pentagon and the media, embedding, it was discovered, was the brainchild of Assistant Defense Secretary Victoria Clarke. Clarke's public relations experience included working for Hill and Knowlton, the PR firm responsible for promoting the false baby-incubator story from the first Gulf war.

THE EXCITEMENT OF INVASION

With embedding, the invasion of Iraq resembled other television productions in which journalists and media producers follow their subjects in unscripted shows designed to give a sense of authenticity and excitement. On U.S. television, war coverage mirrored reality shows (such as *Cops*) and camera and journalistic perspectives merged into a point of view united with the military effort. Empowered by riding shotgun with the soldiers, journalists on U.S. media barely contained their excitement. They wore goggles, flack jackets, and even reported through gas masks as they adopted military jargon; "There are boots on the ground." They interviewed top-gun pilots and crawled along the ground with gunfire in the distance, pressing microphones into soldiers' faces as they pointed their weapons.

So surreal was the experience that newscasters felt compelled to tell viewers that the images they were seeing were live, not a movie. Coverage of the Iraq invasion in the United Kingdom, where journalists covered British troops, had similar effects. There is an irony here, of course, in which the verisimilitude of frontline reporting appears to create a sense of unreality. It explains, nonetheless, the findings of an Independent Television Commission survey in

FROM IRAN-CONTRA FALL GUY TO EMBEDDED REPORTER FOR FOX NEWS

One former marine who became an embedded U.S. reporter during the invasion of Iraq is of particular interest. Oliver North achieved notoriety during the televised Iran-Contra hearings in the summer of 1987. A little-known Vietnam veteran who worked at the National Security Council under the Reagan administration, Lieutenant Colonel Oliver North was implicated as a key player in the scandal. He worked with former General Richard Secord and others to supply arms to the "contras," or counterrevolutionaries, fighting to overthrow the Sandinista government in Nicaragua. Because the contras attacked Nicaraguan civilians and were charged with human rights abuses, Congress had denied them military aid.

Oliver North, or "Ollie" as President Reagan called him, resigned his post along with National Security Advisor Admiral John Poindexter in November 1986, when Attorney General Edwin Meese announced that sophisticated weapons systems had been sold to Iran and money from the sales had been diverted to buy weapons for the contras.

When congressional hearings investigating the scandal were carried live on television, the media spotlight cast an unusually favorable glow over North who, just as easily, could have been cast in the role of villain. Though North admitted to supplying the contras against congressional mandate, activities that were illegal and unconstitutional, his felony conviction was overturned on a technicality because he had been granted immunity for his testimony before congress. Sixteen years after being called before Congress for his role in the Iran-Contra Affair, Oliver North was accepted as a legitimate journalist and hired by FOX News, becoming one of the most visible embedded U.S. TV reporters covering the push into Baghdad during the invasion of Iraq in 2003.

the United Kingdom in which a majority—52 percent—said that this kind of reporting can make war seem too much like fiction, and too easy to forget people are dying. This idea was echoed in focus groups, in which people repeatedly referred to the coverage as being like a "war film." And indeed sometimes it was a war film, as in the case of the Jessica Lynch story, or the various mooted involvements of Hollywood in the Pentagon's public affairs or psyops operations.

WAR WITHOUT CONSEQUENCES

Broadcasters found themselves irresistibly drawn into the action-packed drama of a war against an almost invisible enemy (if Iraqi civilians were enigmatic, the Iraqi soldiers were almost completely absent—rarely seen or discussed, but generally assumed to be supportive of Saddam Hussein). From the pro-war perspective, the norms of taste and decency made it difficult for broadcasters to show the more graphic images of death and destruction, giving the narrative an almost fictional quality.

Journalists and critics had predicted that embedding would result in stories biased toward the military's perspective. Investigative reporter Greg Palast noted before the invasion that media coverage almost never mentioned the possibility that people would die when bombs were dropped on Baghdad. "We've forgotten about the Iraqis. Who will document the effects of the bombing?" (personal communication with the author, February 2003). When another journalist, soon to embed with the U.S. military, was asked if they would be allowed to take pictures of Iraqi civilian casualties, the response was, "We're telling the U.S. military's story, that will be up to other journalists" (personal communication with the author).

EMBEDDING AS A NARRATIVE FRAMEWORK

The news value of the battlefield footage that embeds provided was so compelling that while there were many more complex stories to tell—about the wider international context, the Iraqi people, the economic implications, the reaction of the Arab world, public opinion, debates about the rationale for the war and its aftermath—these were eclipsed by a narrow focus on the fighting itself.

In the aftermath of the invasion, it is widely understood that the U.S. media did not take an independent position with regard to the military operation, and that critical coverage came only after the war continued to devastate Iraq and kill American soldiers. But during the invasion, British broadcasters were aware of the divided attitudes about the war in the United Kingdom and made efforts to be impartial. So, for example, while the U.S. networks—following warnings from the Pentagon—pulled their teams from Baghdad, British reporters steadfastly remained. And there is little evidence that broadcast journalists in the United Kingdom were seduced by the embed program to become cheerleaders for the U.S. forces. Research on the U.K. coverage suggests that more pro-war accounts came from studios in London, not from the embeds in Iraq, whose reports were much more nuanced.

One of the most significant changes brought about by embedding is that in previous conflicts when war reporters had little access to the field, broadcasters were heavily dependent on military briefings. During the 1991 war with Iraq, media coverage was dominated by military briefings from Riyadh and Dhahran, Washington and London. Especially in the case of British media, coverage of the 2003 conflict represented a significant point of departure, with fewer reports coming from central command ("CentCom") headquarters in Qatar. Reports from embeds, on the other hand, played a more significant role, providing a great deal of the footage from the region.

Not only did the embed program thereby allow British viewers to get closer to the front lines than in previous wars, it meant that, at least in the U.K. media, there was more space for independent verification of information and that information about the progress of the war was less clearly controlled by the military.

What the embed system did do, however, was bind journalists into a focus on the progress of the war at the expense of broader contextual issues. The fact that there were no embeds with Iraqi forces (for obvious reasons) combined with traditions of taste and decency to humanize the U.S.-led forces and dehumanize the Iraqis. This war narrative then created its own momentum, making "liberated" Iraqis more newsworthy than the many who had, at best, mixed feelings about the war. In the case of U.S. coverage, a concerted effort was made to avoid viewer empathy for wounded Iraqis through various verbal and visual strategies. In the rare case the wounded Iraqis were shown on American TV, the images were identified as propaganda for Saddam Hussein. Dead and wounded American soldiers were also rarely seen.

CONCLUSION

Embedded reporting, precisely because it provides such newsworthy reports, forces the coverage towards a simplistic narrative in which wider questions about the war are excluded. Indeed, it could be argued that to the degree that embeds succeeded in providing objective, exciting, relatively uncensored British reports, such reporting made the story of war more compelling. This explains the Pentagon's enthusiasm for the program. In short, if the details did not always go their way, the thrust of the coverage was very much on their terms.

Both in Britain and the United States, the historical significance of the role of embedding was in constructing a narrative confined to the progress of the war. Telling an exciting, real-time, visually stimulating narrative of conflict forced the wider questions about the war to the background, and made the moment of victory, rather than, for example, the long-term welfare of the Iraqi people, the climax of the narrative. Even when British embedded reporters were demonstrably impartial, it was within the confines of a limited perspective—a focus on the progress of the fighting rather than why the war was being fought or what its consequences might be. Without that discussion, the media did not fulfill their role in a democratic system, to provide the public with the information it needed to understand the national security policies, and the long-term effects of military actions taken by its government.

See also Alternative Media in the United States; Anonymous Sources, Leaks, and National Security; Bias and Objectivity; Journalists in Peril; Narrative Power and Media Influence; Nationalism and the Media; Paparazzi and Photographic Ethics; Parachute Journalism; Presidential Stagecraft and Militainment; Propaganda Model; Reality Television; Sensationalism, Fear Mongering and Tabloid Media.

Further Reading: Andersen, Robin. *A Century of Media, A Century of War*. New York: Peter Lang. 2006; Bennett, W. Lance. *News: The Politics of Illusion.*, 6th ed. New York: Pearson, 2005; Center for Constitutional Rights. Federal Lawsuit, US District Court: Southern District of New York, January 1991; Hedges, Chris. *War Is a Force That Gives Us Meaning*. New York: Anchor Books, 2002; Knightly, Phillip. *The First Casualty: The War Correspondent as Hero and Myth-Maker from the Crimea to Kosovo*. Baltimore: The Johns Hopkins University Press, 2002; Lewis, Justin, Rod Brookes, Nick Mosdell, and Terry Threadgold. *Shoot First and Ask Questions Later: Media Coverage of the War in Iraq*. New York: Peter Lang, 2006; MacArthur, John. *The Second Front: Censorship and Propaganda in the Gulf War*. Berkeley: University of California Press, 1992.

Robin Andersen and Justin Lewis

G

GAY, LESBIAN, BISEXUAL, TRANSGENDERED, AND QUEER REPRESENTATIONS ON TV

Representations of varied sexualities on television remain surprisingly controversial, especially on network TV. While representations of gay, lesbian, bisexual, transgendered, and queer (GLBTQ) identities are now quite common across both network and cable television, depictions of same-sex physical intimacy continue to cause concern among TV producers, advertising sponsors, and the viewing public. How have GLBTQ representations of both identities and intimacies changed over the past 50 years?

BACKGROUND

Media representations of sexuality are astonishingly diverse, ranging from homoerotically charged ads in magazines, to the troubling (to some) sexual politics of hip-hop music, to the seemingly sex-obsessed fictional communities on U.S. prime-time television, to the anything-goes world of online pornography. Public debates about how sex could and should be represented in mainstream media reached new heights (or depths) in the late 1990s as we watched newscasters struggle with the President Clinton/Monica Lewinsky affair—how to talk about oral sex and how explicitly? How to display semen-stained clothing? What was so unusual about President Clinton's penis (the infamous "distinguishing marker"), and how to talk about penises at all on the nightly news? Since then, we've debated the pros and cons of anal intercourse thanks to *Sex and the City*, gaped at Janet Jackson's nearly bare breast (sorry, wardrobe malfunction) during the 2004 Super Bowl, danced happily to the Black Eyed Peas' "My Humps," and set our

TiVos to catch *Queer as Folk, The L Word*, and the launch of MTV Networks' Logo, a new cable channel targeting gay, lesbian, bisexual, and transgendered viewers.

Media representations of sexuality have changed dramatically over the past half-century due to two related changes in North American values—first, our growing acceptance of the idea that sex for pleasure (rather than sex for procreation) is a good, healthy activity; and second, our growing acceptance of varied sexual identities and (to a lesser extent) same-sex sexual activities. Obviously, different types of media have different leeway in how they might represent sexual issues. The focus here is on U.S. network television due to its centrality to our entertainment landscape (99 percent of U.S. households have at least one TV set), and the interest is focused on TV representations of sexual minorities—that is, straight, gay, lesbian, bisexual, queer, transsexual, intersexual, and transgendered persons and relationships.

REPRESENTING VARIED SEXUAL IDENTITIES ON TV

Perhaps not surprisingly, the U.S. television industry has a long history of ignoring, stereotyping, and marginalizing varied sexual identities and storylines (see Gross 2001). For example, gay and lesbian issues or characters were almost invisible on television in the 1950s and early 1960s, as networks assumed that the viewing audience was composed wholly of married, monogamous heterosexuals and their children. As the gay rights movement rose to national prominence in the late 1960s and early 1970s, prime-time portrayals of homosexuality increased, though scriptwriters quickly settled on two safe ways to tell gay-themed stories: the coming-out script and the "queer monster" script (Capsuto 2000). While the 1970s ushered in prime-time shows about gay characters, they were typically played by straight actors and marketed to a straight audience, a trend that continues today. In the 1980s, TV depictions of varied sexualities declined dramatically due to the conservatism of the Reagan presidency and growing concerns about HIV/AIDS (and its association with gay male sexuality).

The 1990s told a different story. Increased media activism, the growing number of cable channels (which placed new economic demands on the networks and led to more expansive programming), rising stigma attached to antigay prejudice, and growing recognition of a gay consumer market all contributed to a sharp rise in the number of GLBTQ characters and/or narratives. Indeed, a study by the Parents Television Council published in 2003 found that references to homosexuality grew more rapidly between 1989 and 1999 (a 265-fold increase) than references to any other sexually oriented topic on television, including masturbation, oral sex, and "kinky" sex (LeVay and Valente 2006). Approximately 50 network series had lesbian, gay, or bisexual recurring characters in the 1990s, more than twice the total of all previous decades (Capsuto 2000). Network prime time introduced the first lesbian lead actress/character in 1997 (Ellen Degeneres/Morgan on ABC's *Ellen*) and the first network gay male lead character in 1998 (Eric McCormack on NBC's *Will & Grace*).

In many ways, the 1990s seemed to overcome the long-standing "rules" for how to represent varied sexual identities (especially homosexuality) on television. For most of U.S. television history, producers and writers followed four general rules. First, gay or lesbian characters must be restricted to one-time appearances in TV series or one-shot TV movies. Second, gay and lesbian characters can never just "happen to be" gay—instead, their sexual identity must be presented as a "problem" to be "solved." Third, their problem must be explored in terms of its effect on heterosexuals (that is, the focus is on straight people struggling to understand). And finally, gay and lesbian erotic desire must not be represented on screen (Dow 2001). While there are certainly more GLBTQ representations than ever before on television, they are not necessarily more progressive representations. For example, GLBTQ characters are still more likely to appear in comedies than dramas (where the line between "laughing with" and "laughing at" remains strategically ambiguous), they are still typically played by straight (or not out) actors and marketed to straight audiences (Ellen Degeneres on *Ellen* was a major exception), and depictions of same-sex intimacy remain troublesome for the networks. In the words of Larry Gross, "Same-sex kisses continue to be treated with all the delicacy and attention required for high-risk medical procedures."

What are the barriers to a more expansive representation of varied sexualities on television? One is the Federal Communications Commission (FCC), which enforces the law that governs obscene, indecent, and profane network television and radio programming. FCC guidelines, along with a TV network's Standards and Practices department, encourage the development of generally conservative characters and storylines in an effort to avoid penalties (such as warnings, monetary fines, or license revocation). Another potential barrier is a program's advertising sponsorship. While some cable channels (such as MTV) have sponsors that support progressive or edgy programming, network television in particular has a history of conservative sponsorship that impacts storytelling possibilities (see "Selected Milestones in U.S. Television History" sidebar); this barrier is more applicable to daytime than prime-time network programming. A third potential barrier is the various lobbying groups that monitor TV programming. While there are some high-profile groups advocating for more progressive GLBTQ representations (such as GLAAD, the Gay and Lesbian Alliance Against Defamation), there are many powerful organizations that believe that positive depictions of GLBTQ persons or lifestyles violate standards of moral decency. While network producers struggle to accommodate the often-competing demands of different lobbying groups, the combination of this barrier with the others mentioned above tends to lead to more conservative programming. Finally, genre matters in the types of characters and stories we see on TV.

SELECTED MILESTONES IN U.S. TELEVISION HISTORY

1971—*All in the Family* becomes the first network sitcom to feature a gay character.

1972—*The Corner Bar* is the first prime-time show to feature a recurring or regular gay character.

1983—*All My Children's* Lynn Carson becomes the first gay character on daytime soap operas.

1989—On *thirtysomething*, a recurring gay male couple is shown in bed "the morning after." The episode generated a national debate and lost the network more than $1 million in advertising revenue. The episode was not included in the summer rerun schedule.

1992—*Melrose Place* launches the first of a wave of supporting gay characters throughout network prime-time in the 1990s.

1994—*The Real World* includes gay housemate Pedro Zamora, who is suffering from AIDS both on screen and off.

1997—Ellen DeGeneres comes out as a lesbian, both on *Ellen* and in real life.

1998—*Will & Grace* features the first gay male lead in network broadcast history.

2000—The U.S. version of *Queer as Folk* debuts on cable television, exploring the lives of a group of gay men and women in Pittsburgh and featuring more-graphic-than-network-allows depictions of same-sex sex.

2000—Bianca Montgomery comes out on *All My Children*.

2004—Lesbian and bisexual relationships and lifestyles are the star of *The L Word*.

GENRE MATTERS: SEXUALITY ON DAYTIME SOAP OPERAS

Action-based narratives offer different possibilities (and limitations) than do sitcoms, reality shows, or serialized dramas. For example, it might seem surprising that U.S. daytime soap operas have rendered sexual minorities invisible to a far greater extent than network prime time, given soaps' 70-year history on radio and television for telling educationally oriented narratives. Such stories are not without economic risk, given soaps' more conservative viewing audience and advertising sponsorship as compared with that of prime time, but producers historically resolved this dilemma by choosing "easy" social issues to write about, such as alcoholism, drug abuse, or breast cancer. These issues are considered easy because while the depiction or resolution of the story might be controversial, the issue itself is not (no one, in other words, is "for" alcoholism or cancer [Anger 1999]). With certain topics, however, such as varied sexualities, the inherent risk is greater because the subject matter itself remains controversial.

The first fully fleshed-out gay character was written for NBC's *Another World* in 1974 but the story never aired because network executives got nervous about how viewers would respond. Between 1980 and 2000, daytime soaps featured openly gay or lesbian characters in meaningful roles only five times. The first occurred in 1983, when *All My Children* (ABC) introduced child psychologist (and lesbian) Lynn Carson. Lynn was a marginal character, lasted only two months in Pine Valley (the show's fictional location), and had no on-screen romantic life. In 1988, *As the World Turns* (CBS) introduced gay clothing designer Hank Elliott. Hank appeared regularly on the show but his presence, too, was short-lived and the character departed in 1989 to care for his partner suffering (off-screen) from AIDS.

A much more significant attempt occurred in 1992, when *One Life to Live* (ABC) launched a critically acclaimed storyline featuring Billy Douglas (played by movie-star-to-be Ryan Phillippe), a teen struggling with the coming-out process and the acceptance of his family and friends. While clearly written as a problem-centered narrative, Billy's story was an important TV milestone in that he was depicted as a well-adjusted and functional gay teen. Once the homophobia around which his story centered was resolved, however, Billy faded into the background of the show and eventually exited in 1993. Daytime's fourth gay character, high school teacher Michael Delaney, was introduced on *All My Children* (ABC) in 1995. Linked to one of the show's core kinship networks, Michael's story featured homophobia and the occupational barriers faced by GLBTQ persons in the United States. More significantly, the narrative also revealed at least three other gay residents of Pine Valley, suggesting that a whole gay community/subculture (rather than isolated characters) might actually exist in the world of daytime soaps.

Without question, the biggest GLBTQ milestone in U.S. soap opera history was the revelation in 2000 that *All My Children*'s (ABC) Bianca Montgomery was gay. This story stands out from the others because Bianca was a long-term core character who viewers got to know "before" she was gay, she was the daughter of the single most famous character/actress in daytime history (Erica Kane/Susan Lucci), the revelation of her sexual orientation took place in a lesbian bar, a setting never before depicted on daytime (Jill Sobule's "I Kissed a Girl" was playing in the background), her desire for a sexual partner was made explicit on screen, and over time she was successfully mainstreamed by the writers, transformed from "the lesbian on soaps" to just another character looking for love, sex, and happiness in Pine Valley. While polls in magazines like *Soap Opera Digest* or *Soap Opera Weekly* indicated that viewers were nervous about seeing same-sex intimacy depicted on screen, they accepted Bianca's lesbian identity and her search for a partner.

Part of the difficulty in telling GLBTQ stories on soap operas is that the genre has unique constraints. Soaps are designed to air for decades (ABC's *General Hospital*, for example, debuted in 1963), and their whole reason for being is to celebrate romantic hook-ups, match-ups, break-ups, and make-ups. One or two gay characters cannot survive on a soap opera the way they can on a weekly primetime sitcom or drama. On soaps, gay characters must have a relationship in order to last on the show. In a personal interview, Michael Logan, the resident soap opera critic for *TV Guide*, explained:

> A new hot chick comes on to *The Young and the Restless* and she could be with Victor, she could be with Jack, she could be with Joe and Schmo. There are any number of potential possibilities and that's the way that the writers weave their stories. But you don't have that kind of thing going on with a gay character because there just aren't any other gay characters on that canvas for that character to match up with. [A new gay character would obviously be] for the gay character that we [already] have on the canvas, so the mystery of who so-and-so's going to hook up with...kind of get[s] tossed out.

This means that how a same-sex romance unfolds—and what intimate or sexual details will be depicted on screen—becomes a crucial question. It is crucial for network prime time too (several seasons of *Will & Grace* unfolded before Will had his first romantic kiss), but is much more relevant for daytime since soaps air five days a week and intimate relationships unfold in much greater detail. Indeed, soaps' focus on romance gives the genre the dubious distinction of having more sexual content than any other type of TV programming, according to a Kaiser Family Foundation report, including flirting, open-mouthed passionate kissing, fondling (though not of breasts or genitalia), vaginal intercourse (implied, not depicted), "playful" S & M or bondage scenes, and occasionally what appears to be oral sex (*very* vaguely implied). Totally absent is intimation of other types of sex acts, such as anal sex, group sex, or sex toys. Also absent on daytime soaps, in major contrast to network prime time and cable, are depictions of nudity. Shirtless men are commonly depicted on soaps, but shirtless women are filmed only from the back and both genitalia and backsides are nowhere to be seen. And while soaps have the most sexual content, they are also more likely than sitcoms, dramas, or TV movies to emphasize sexual responsibility and the potentially negative consequences of sexual risk.

Daytime's first same-sex kiss actually occurred on *As the World Turns* (CBS) in June 2001. However, it was between a straight man in drag attempting to harm another man through poisoned lip gloss (it's a long story). Daytime's first *romantic* same-sex kiss was between Bianca and Lena on *All My Children* (ABC), which occurred in 2002 and was widely applauded in the daytime press. The kiss was more than a chaste peck (though no tongues were involved) and did not progress to further on-screen physical intimacy, though an off-screen relationship between Bianca and Lena was implied by the narrative. For the remainder of Bianca's time in Pine Valley (the actress/character exited the show in 2005 though has since returned), however, the writers chose *not* to explore her love/ sex life but instead showcased her rape, subsequent pregnancy, and involvement in a complicated baby-switch storyline. A fully explored same-sex relationship has yet to happen in daytime soap opera.

WHERE ARE WE NOW? THE 2006–2007 TELEVISION SEASON

In August 2006, GLAAD issued a press release analyzing diversity in the 2006–2007 U.S. television season (see http://www.glaad.org/eye/ontv/06-07/ overview.php). Focusing on prime-time comedies and dramas on the broadcast networks, they counted only nine gay or lesbian lead or supporting characters out of 679 television series—1.3 percent of the overall total. While this percentage is about the same as in the 2005–2006 season (then it was 1.4 percent), GLAAD found that the profile of the character roles has been greatly reduced from one year to the next. Not surprisingly, characters and storylines with varied sexualities are more easily found on cable networks and in unscripted reality and competition programming. Interestingly, given our discussion above, for the first time in U.S. television history the three networks that broadcast daytime soap operas (ABC, CBS, and NBC) each had a show with a lesbian or gay character in the 2006–2007 season. In addition, *All My Children* is currently launching only the second storyline in daytime history involving a transgendered/transsexual character (the character is beginning to transition from male to female). While it is true that what viewers will actually be able to "see" on daytime soaps remains constrained by the conservative boundaries of the genre, it is a remarkable transformation in a few short years.

CONCLUSION

Media representations of sexual acts, sexual intimacy, and varied sexual identities will continue to be a controversial issue in the United States for the foreseeable future. Every culture regulates sexual expression to some extent, and our own history reveals a growing acceptance of sex for pleasure along with growing acceptability of same-sex relationships. Given the various barriers to progressive GLTBQ programming that still exist, however, what viewers are able to see on their TV screens will continue to be debated in U.S. households and throughout the industry.

See also Obscenity and Indecency; Media and the Crisis of Values; Pornography; Ratings; Reality Television; Representations of Masculinity; Representations of Race; Representations of Women; Shock Jocks; Sensationalism, Fear Mongering, and Tabloid Media; TiVo.

Further Reading: Anger, Dorothy. *Other Worlds: Society Seen through Soap Opera*. Orchard Park, CA: Broadview, 1999; Arthurs, Jane. *Television and Sexuality: Regulation and the Politics of Taste*. Milton Keynes: Open University Press, 2004; Becker, Ron. *Gay TV and Straight America*. New Brunswick, NJ: Rutgers University Press, 2006; Capsuto, Steven. *Alternate Channels*. New York: Ballantine, 2000; Dow, Bonnie J. "*Ellen*, Television, and the Politics of Gay and Lesbian Visibility." *Critical Studies in Media Communication* 18 (2001): 123–40; Gross, Larry. *Up from Invisibility: Lesbians, Gay Men, and the Media in America*. New York: Columbia University Press, 2001; LeVay, Simon, and Sharon M. Valente. *Human Sexuality*, 2nd ed. Sunderland, MA: Sinauer, 2006; Montgomery, Kathryn. *Target: Prime Time: Advocacy Groups and the Struggle over Entertainment Television*. New York: Oxford University Press, 1989.

C. Lee Harrington

GLOBAL COMMUNITY MEDIA

Community media—small-scale, grassroots, underfunded—have been an important dimension of the global media landscape for a very long time. They have also been a very neglected feature. People have often seen them as temporary, trivial, poorly designed, and thus basically irrelevant to anyone except the handful of obsessive folk who produce them. Yet a brief look at their impact past and present suggests that such dismissiveness is born of a very oversimplified understanding of how these community media have in fact operated. Examples are drawn below from the last three centuries to illustrate the argument, and the importance is underscored of carefully defining our terms.

The headword's three terms need to be made clear straightaway. "Global" and "community" might seem to be opposites, signifying respectively "international" and "cosmopolitan," versus "local" and "real." Here, however, "global" is used to mean worldwide and local simultaneously, and to direct our attention to how, ever faster, the two are coming to be interlinked. "Community" is used here to describe media that are organically part of a social movement, and so for the most part are underfunded, small-scale, and located at the grass roots. "Media" seems by contrast an unproblematic word, used simply to mean broadcasting, cinema, and the press. Here its definition is far wider, and encompasses, as well as those formats, communication activities such as graffiti, buttons, popular song, street theatre, performance art, dance, demonstrations, certain dress choices such as T-shirts, and not least, alternative Internet uses. Some writers also describe these media as "alternative," others as "participatory," "citizens' media," "tactical media," or social movement media.

SOME EARLY EXAMPLES

A major early instance in the United States was the Revolutionary-era press, when many pamphleteers, Tom Paine being the most famous, campaigned to shake off British rule. To some degree it was a war of pamphlets, since loyalists were not slow to publish their own tracts defending the British monarchy. The often uncertain outcome of the Revolutionary War meant that the insurrectionary publications were especially important in helping build momentum against colonial rule.

Only a decade later in France, a similarly energetic flood of publications, ranging from satirical cartoons to angry denunciations of royal abuses to reasoned treatises on monarchical power, was a very significant element in fomenting a republican form of government there too.

THE ABOLITIONIST PRESS

The abolitionist press emerged about three decades later in the United States, though preceded by France and Britain. Some of the earliest U.S. examples were autobiographies by formerly enslaved Africans who had escaped from the Southern states or been freed. At least six of these were written, interestingly enough, by merchant sailors. Because their work, unlike for most of the enslaved, required them to travel by sea and major rivers, they got to see slavery systemically, and also to pick up news of African revolts in New World slaving nations. These early books were soon followed by a stream of publications from some white campaigning writers such as William Lloyd Garrison, and a little later still by the leading African American writer and activist Frederick Douglass, who had himself been born into slavery in eastern Maryland.

THE LABOR PRESS

The labor press, at present almost nonexistent as a social force, was also to be reckoned with throughout the later nineteenth century in Britain, France,

Germany, the United States and other rapidly industrializing nations. It was a central facet of the growth of the labor union movement. In the United States, with its multilingual immigrant workforce of the decades leading from the 1880s through the 1930s, newspapers also came to be printed in a variety of European languages, such as German, Hungarian, Italian, Polish, and Yiddish. In Germany in the later nineteenth century the Socialist press flourished, providing a considerable spectrum from highbrow intellectual journals to newspapers, and from women's publications to pamphlets geared to workers' recreational activity.

THE SUFFRAGIST PRESS

The women's suffrage press, dating from 1848 in the United States, developed its work over the decades that followed, painfully and painstakingly helping build the movement that finally won the right to vote for women citizens after World War I. In New Zealand this right was already conceded in 1893, in France it was not granted until 1945, but in every country the suffragist press was a key element in the ongoing public campaign's eventual success.

It is important to realize that as in the other instances in this period, these publications, were they newspapers, magazines, fliers, posters, or books, mostly did not come out daily, or necessarily regularly. They carried little or no advertising, nor were they glossy. Often they might be just a few pages, and not necessarily designed well. But the demand for them within the suffragist movement, among its women and men members, was nonetheless high.

THREE VITAL CONTRASTS

Before we proceed further, these examples push us to recognize three further important points concerning community media.

First, the media described above had considerable impact in spite of their small size. People sometimes make the mistake of evaluating these media as though they operate in the same way as mainstream media. Yet their objectives are often sharply different, since they are focused on campaigning and mobilizing the public to take on social issues, while big commercial media primarily exist to make a profit by running ads, by entertaining, and sometimes by providing a news service. As a consequence, the mainstream media agenda usually fails to challenge existing social structures based on wealth and political power. By contrast, community media are integral parts of social movements. They enable those movements to have dialogue and fresh perspectives, and are energized in turn by the movements' vitality.

Second, social movement audiences or readers are different from mainstream media users. They are active, aware of their surroundings, committed to social change. When they make use of these media, they are not looking for a break from a tough working day or from a day when the kids have been scratchy-side-out. They are not looking for escape, but for involvement.

Third, the timeframe of these two types of media is completely different. Social movements often take a long time to form; they have peaks and lulls. Slavery

THE DANGERS OF DOCUMENTING COMMUNITY STRUGGLES

In May 2006, 70,000 public school teachers of the state chapter of the National Educational Workers' Union called a strike to protest the declining support for public schools in the state of Oaxaca, Mexico, after the governor refused to meet with educators to discuss the issue. As the civil action grew, the teachers were joined by other unions, groups, and organizations, and the strike became a burgeoning people's movement protesting the accelerating economic hardships brought on by seven years of the North American Free Trade Agreement (NAFTA). On June 14, 2006, Governor Ulises Ruiz sent in state police to dislodge over 600 protestors who had set up an encampment in the town's main square. Sixty civil associations together drafted a letter of support for the protests condemning the police violence and the growing attacks by extra-judicial military forces. The teachers broadcast their messages using a community radio station, and when their station was destroyed, university students helped organizers broadcast over theirs. The protest lasted for months.

By the fall of 2006, working with Indymedia in New York City, American journalist Brad Will went to Mexico to report on the protest for the Independent Media Center. On October 27, 2006, Brad Will was shot and killed while filming and reporting from Oaxaca. Human rights activists continue to call for a full investigation into the death of Brad Will and other Oaxacans who have been killed during the protests. Independent New York–based filmmakers Tami Gold and Gerardo Renique released a videotape titled *Land Rain and Fire: Report from Oaxaca*, distributed by Third World Newsreel (www.twn.org), which offers background, analysis, and documentation of the events leading up to the protest and police brutality against the demonstrators.

---

took many decades to be ended, just as many decades passed before women were allowed to vote, and the labor movement took a long while to win the right to the eight-hour working day, to a paid annual vacation, to health care (all of which are seriously under siege again at the beginning of the twenty-first century). Measuring the true impact of community media requires we grasp this essential contrast in a time frame.

Overall, then, we need to avoid lumping all media clumsily together as though they all operate the same way. Only then can we understand the roles of community media.

COMMUNITY MEDIA IN THE TWENTIETH CENTURY

Examples from the twentieth century have been very numerous indeed. Most have yet to receive a proper description and analysis. Two interlinked developments, according to the German writer Walter Benjamin, have been decisive in this mushroom growth, though his argument is adapted slightly here to bring it up to date.

One is the emergence of cheap and accessible media technologies. In his day he pointed to the still camera and to film, and their production in vast quantities.

Surveying what has happened since then, we would point as well to transistor radios, tiny video cameras, cheap digital editing equipment, cell phones, and the expanding rate of Internet access—all of which give the public the potential to generate their own communications outside their immediate circles, at long distances, today often almost instantaneously.

Benjamin's argument, however, was about much more than hardware (or even software). He interpreted the public's eagerness to take up and use these media technologies when they became available as a signal of the expansion of people's self-assertiveness in the modern era, of a historical decline of political passivity.

He himself linked this shift in attitudes to the Russian revolution and the rise of communism, though he wrote at an earlier epoch when there was much less information than there needed to be of the terrifying developments in Soviet Russia under Stalin, and when the international image of the Soviet Union was for many a beacon of hope in the struggle against Nazism and fascism in 1930s Europe. We need not and absolutely should not, with hindsight, support his endorsement of Soviet-style communism, but given Benjamin's overall values, we should rather link popular media usage with the upsurges in labor demands, women's rights, anticolonial insurgency, civil rights, and global social justice movements.

Of all these media developments, the expansion of easily accessible radio has been by far the most widespread across the planet. As of the time of writing, many parts of the world have no access to television or the Internet, or indeed telephony. Illiteracy rates are very high in many places. As Alfonso Geerts and other writers point out, very cheap radio sets and the ever-growing number of community radio stations are probably the most important community media sector globally. In affluent territories, radio is often forgotten, defined simply as one of a series of delivery mechanisms for music. This assumption is miserably blind to the realities of life in the Southern Hemisphere (though there is nothing wrong with popular music, which is globally important).

TWO OTHER EXAMPLES

Many examples can be found in Atton (2001), Rodríguez (2001), Downing (2001), Couldry and Curran (2003), Opel and Pompper (2004), Rennie (2006), and the further reading they reference. Two cases, however, which deserve a particular mention from the end of the century and the outset of the twenty-first century, are the global Indymedia network, and the emergence of blogging and file sharing.

Indymedia

The Independent Media Center (IMC) network ("Indymedia") emerged in late 1999 in the context of the global social justice movement protests against the World Trade Organization. There are currently about 200 hyperlinked Indymedia centers around the planet, concentrated more in North America and

Western Europe than elsewhere, but in some measure touching much of the globe.

An IMC consists of a connected server and a collective of people who staff it, normally on a volunteer basis. This unit seeks admission to the IMC network, and on satisfying certain basic political and technical standards, is admitted as a member. (Thus, at the extreme, a neo-Nazi, or homophobic, or commercially driven, or religiously evangelistic group, without computer skills, would be excluded on both ideological and technical grounds.)

The content on active IMC sites is often updated daily or at least frequently, with some sites at certain times even placing some 30 postings a day. It is open to people with all views, outside the fundamentally hostile category, to place postings. Its links to all the other sites enable users to check instantly on events from France to Indonesia, from Mexico to South Africa. There is an archive of earlier discussions and postings. Most sites carry photos, audio files, and video files.

The focus is on news concerning global struggles for social justice. The predominant language across the sites is English, but not only are other languages dominant in national sites (Portuguese in Brazil, for instance), there are also translations offered on some sites for some items. Regional languages also play a role on some sites (e.g., Galician in northwest Spain, Quechua in Bolivia).

While there is some control over registration as an IMC in the interests of coherent organization at the most basic level, in many respects the IMC network is a body without a head, and thus a fascinating example not only of very low-cost global/local communication, but also of the potential enabled by a participatory, self-managed operation.

The Blogosphere

The other case can be addressed much more briefly, and it is the growth more or less simultaneously of blogging and file sharing. Extreme exaggeration of their significance was endemic in their early days. There were visions of the imminent collapse of organized news media and of the recording industry, and a complete Pandora's box of cost-free democratic sharing and diffusion.

All that hype aside, both movements, although composed of people with hugely different goals and contributions, signified the appetite and the potential for more significant and unhampered lateral communication, in contradistinction to the vertical media hierarchies that still bestride the globe. The sharp distinction between "mass" communication and "niche media" showed signs of becoming blurred, with the prospect of a richer cultural environment being actually short of utopian.

CONCLUSIONS

So far from being a trivial field for those obsessed by the irrelevant, the study of small-scale "community" media on a global scale shows itself to be a very serious pursuit. In the era of nanotechnologies and the genome project, that should not come as a surprise.

See also Alternative Media in the United States; Blogosphere; Communication Rights in a Global Context; Conglomeration and Media Monopolies; Independent Cinema; Internet and Its Radical Potential; Journalists in Peril; Minority Media Ownership; Parachute Journalism; Pirate Radio; Public Access Television; World Cinema.

Further Reading: Atton, Chris. *Alternative Media*. London: Sage, 2001; Couldry, Nick, and James Curran, eds. *Contesting Media Power: Alternative Media in a Networked World*. Lanham, MD: Rowman and Littlefield, 2003; Downing, John D. H. *Radical Media: Rebellious Communication and Social Movements*. Thousand Oaks, CA: Sage, 2001; Geerts, Alfonso, V. van Oeyen, and C. Villamayor, eds. *La Práctica Inspira: La Radio Popular y Comunitaria Frente al Nuevo Siglo*. Quito: Associación Latinoamericana de Educación Radiofónica, 2004; Opel, Andy, and Donnalynn Pompper, eds. *Representing Resistance: Media, Civil Disobedience, and the Global Justice Movement*. Westport, CT: Praeger, 2004; Rennie, Ellie. *Community Media: A Global Introduction*. Lanham, MD: Rowman and Littlefield, 2006; Rodríguez, Clemencia. *Fissures in the Mediascape*. Cresskill, NJ: Hampton Press, 2001.

John D.H. Downing

GOOGLE BOOK SEARCH

In October 2004, Google announced a partnership with five powerhouse research libraries to scan millions of books into a company database and make them accessible via an online search engine. While the press regarding Google Book Search has been dominated by the discussion over copyright, there are several other questions raised by this massive scan of information. Namely, why did Google and the libraries enter this partnership? How will this partnership affect the future of libraries? And what kind of data can a company gather about what we search for and read?

GOOGLE BOOK SEARCH STATISTICS

5—libraries initial participating in the Google Library Project (Harvard, Stanford, Oxford, the University of Michigan, and the New York Public Library).

32 million—estimated number of published books to be scanned.

7.8 million—volumes in the University of Michigan library. Google has agreed to scan them all.

$150 million to $1 billion—estimated cost of the library scanning project (according to different sources).

$100,000—cost of one book-scanning machine.

$32 billion—estimated annual revenues, U.S. domestic book industry.

$80 billion—estimated annual revenues, worldwide book industry.

3%—percentage of total spending on higher education that is directed to academic and research libraries.

2%—percentage of municipal budgets dedicated to libraries in 1950.

0.5%—percentage of municipal budgets dedicated to libraries in 2005.

THE COPYRIGHT DEBATE

At the time of writing, Google Book Search has deals in place to acquire content from the libraries of Harvard University, Stanford University, Oxford University, the University of Michigan, and the New York Public Library, hence promising one-stop shopping for students, academics, or average folks seeking to gather information on virtually any topic. Though widely heralded in the media as a potential achievement of epic proportions, authors and publishers became concerned that freely available online books would hurt sales of their physical counterparts. In turn, they invoked copyright law to sue Google and stop its scanning program.

Google argues that its program is not designed so that site visitors will "be able to read copyright books through Google Book Search." Instead, "the purpose of this program is to help you discover books. That's a very different thing than saying that this is a substitute for actually buying the books and reading them. In fact, we are looking to direct you, once you've discovered that book, to the place you can find it" ("The Battle over Books: Authors and Publishers Take on the Google Print Library Project," 2005).

The president of the Association of American Publishers (AAP), Patricia Schroeder, notes that, "the bottom line is that under its current plan Google is seeking to make millions of dollars by freeloading on the talent and property of authors and publishers" (Wray and Milmo 2006). Allan Adler of the AAP further argues that if Google is "going to directly promote it[self] through the use of valuable content [and] intellectual property created by others, those others at least should have the right to have permission asked, if not also to share in a bit of the revenue" ("The Battle over Books," 2005).

Under the program's current design, user searches that return works under copyright offer bibliographic data about the book as well as a few sentences of text—or "snippets" as Google deems them. Books no longer under copyright (meaning those over 75 years old) are available in their entirety. Google believes that if anything, they are providing a service that will bring light to millions of "orphaned" books that have been languishing in libraries unseen for years. As Google's lawyer David Drummond states, "We've designed the service to be a fair use one, to be a service that promotes a significant public good that spurs creativity in the society and in the world, and one that does not harm publishers or authors" ("The Battle over Books," 2005).

WHY IS GOOGLE DOING THIS?

Google cofounder Sergey Brin once proclaimed that, "The perfect search engine would be like the mind of God. The mind of God, one might imagine, probably features everything that human beings have ever written, recorded, photographed, videotaped, linked, or designed. Thus, it makes sense that the content of every library would be necessary fodder for 'the perfect search engine'" (Vaidhyanathan 2005, p. B7).

Nevertheless, Google Book Search is by no means a completely charitable endeavor. Google is investing heavily so that it can bolster its reputation as the number-one source for information on the Internet. By partnering with these libraries, not only does Google gain access to troves of content, they also associate themselves with the valuable brand names of Harvard, Stanford, Oxford, the University of Michigan, and the New York Public Library. They can then pitch their program to advertisers as a resource for curious readers who demand access to some of the finest collections in the world. And advertisers are willing to pay heavily to target a person specifically interested in *The Joy of Cooking* or *The Life of Jimi Hendrix*.

However, this project will not come cheaply for Google. The cost of digitizing a library on the scale of the University of Michigan's has been estimated at over a billion dollars. Though Google has hordes of money to pursue these kinds of projects, it is nevertheless taking an enormous financial risk to make the dream of an all-digital library a reality.

WHY ARE LIBRARIES DOING THIS?

Many wonder why a library *wouldn't* want to do this. Google is willing to invest billions in digitizing materials and has agreed not to charge libraries a penny in the process. Each library in the partnership can choose what materials it wants to share and what it wants to keep private (up to this point, only Michigan has agreed to open its complete system to Google). Plus, Google has agreed to defend every library in the partnership for every copyright lawsuit.

One benefit of the digitization partnership stressed by libraries is the importance of preservation. Scanning books could safeguard library collections in times of natural disasters and war; for instance, Hurricane Katrina's destruction of collections within Tulane University's library would have been less devastating if these collections had digital backups.

John Wilkin, the librarian in charge of Michigan's digitization efforts, believes that all materials everywhere should be scanned. In a personal interview in 2006 he stated, "Nothing is too insignificant—it will all have an audience. Every book its reader, every reader its book." Promoting accessibility to a worldwide forum helps a library ensure that it is meeting its mission as a part of a public good and public trust.

Finally, libraries are extremely aware of the dominance of the Internet in today's search for information—and they do not want to appear outdated or left behind. Students overwhelmingly turn to online resources such as Google, Yahoo, and Wikipedia over antiquated card catalogs as their speedy first option for research. The expectation of neatly ranked results and clickable searches holds greater appeal than time spent burrowing through a library's stacks. This demand for speed puts libraries on the defensive, and, as a result, embracing Google as a search mechanism could help a library move from appearing behind the times to appearing as if it is keeping pace with them. Many libraries have therefore decided that they must work with the Internet if they are to remain meaningful and useful for the next generation of researchers and readers.

THE ROYAL LIBRARY OF ALEXANDRIA

The goal of acquiring all knowledge and storing it in one location predates Google Book Search by over two thousand years. The Royal Library of Alexandria, Egypt was rumored to house 500,000 scrolls as well as lecture halls and study areas. Scientists from throughout the ancient world converged there to research mathematics, astronomy, mechanics, medicine, and literature. Modern scholars debate the details of its destruction, as accusations range from Julius Caesar to a series of subsequent invaders. Yet the call for the library's resurrection has been touted by many thinkers ever since, most notably H.G. Wells and his vision of "The World Brain."

THE FUTURE OF LIBRARIES

For large-scale research universities, Google Book Search means that libraries will have to adjust to Google's method of search as the primary means of interface. Overall, libraries will confront more pressure to digitize their collections, and there is a chance that some overlapping materials will be condensed to save time, money, and space. (For example, does the University of California system really need nine copies of every single document the U.S. government publishes?) As many of these big libraries are armed with considerable budgets, there will be more of a shift in resources than outright elimination of services. The University of Texas at Austin, for example, moved almost all the books from its undergraduate library to other libraries on campus so that its main space could be transformed into an "information commons" featuring 1,000 reference books and hundreds of computer terminals.

However, smaller libraries at less wealthy institutions might face dramatic changes. Community colleges can eliminate stacks of books and convert storage space into teaching space, as they will now be able to rely on digital access and interlibrary loans to fill many of their content needs. Librarians at these institutions will shift their focus from developing collections to guiding students in how to navigate the Web, write term papers, and apply for jobs.

If one can imagine the contents of the community college library disappearing, then a potentially similar fate looms for local public libraries. Since libraries often compete for funding with entities such as fire and police departments, it is easy to imagine books being shared online or across county lines. After all, if the average library user can get virtually anything he or she wants on Google, then why would a local city council bother opening new library branches to serve a potentially dwindling public?

DATA, PRIVACY, AND GOVERNMENT SUBPOENAS

In today's economy, technology is used to track almost every transaction. Credit card companies keep histories of every purchase made with the convenience of plastic—from shoes to airline tickets to packs of gum. Cell phone operators have records of every phone call; travel can be traced through the use of Global Positioning Systems; and credit agencies can quickly deliver reports of your payment history to almost anyone.

Information scholar Howard Besser (2001) writes that "today a large number of websites monitor the browsing that goes on at their site, tracking who is looking at what, how often, and for how long. A whole industry has emerged that purchases this kind of personal marketing information from site managers and resells it. In difficult financial times, even licensors who are committed to privacy concerns may find the temptation of payment for this kind of information difficult to resist."

With the development of Google Book Search, the online giant has equipped itself with a superior tool for determining who its customers are—as well as what they are reading. Google earns virtually all of its money from advertisements, and all queries conducted via Google Book Search are recorded in the company's database. For example, when a person signs in to seek George Orwell's *1984*, Google logs the search in the user's profile and tracks what part of the world they are logging in from via an Internet protocol (IP) address. This information is then preserved indefinitely in Google's archives, and is ultimately used to develop targeted demographic profiles to be sold to marketing firms.

While Google's behavior is not atypical for the search industry (virtually all online companies do the same thing), it does conflict with libraries' strong tradition of privacy protection. Libraries dump records on a regular basis—once a checked-out book has been returned, the library destroys any information regarding that transaction. Historically, librarians have even risked going to jail rather than turn over patron information sought via government subpoena. This reflects the belief held by free-speech advocates that libraries represent one of the few public institutions where people can freely pursue open thought and engage in original, controversial research without fear of reprisal.

However, after the terrorist attacks of 2001 this practice was challenged by the Bush administration when it was revealed that hijackers used public library computers to conduct some of their communiqués. In response, the government designed the U.S. Patriot Act to gather information in public places where people do not expect complete privacy.

Google does not hold itself to the same privacy standards as libraries. Thus, the government can gain access to Google's databases by presenting a court-backed warrant seeking information. Plus, under the Patriot Act, "Google may not be able to tell users when it hands over their searches or e-mail messages" (Cohen 2005). Adam Cohen argues in the *New York Times* that "if the federal government announced plans to directly collect the sort of data Google does, there would be an uproar—in fact there was in 2003, when the Pentagon announced its Total Information Awareness program, which was quickly shut down."

LOOKING TOWARD THE FUTURE

If Google becomes the first (and perhaps only) point of reference for an 11-year-old seeking to write a book report, one can imagine the possibilities for it to dominate the future of the search field. Though great potential comes from digitally preserving books and making them accessible online, Google's partnership with prominent libraries raises considerable concern about copyright violations, the future of libraries, the role of publishers in a digital era, and the privacy of user searches. It remains to be seen whether this billion-dollar venture will revolutionize—or compromise—the way we search for information.

See also Advertising and Persuasion; Communication Rights in a Global Context; Internet and its Radical Potential; Net Neutrality; Online Publishing; Piracy and Intellectual Property; Public Sphere; Surveillance and Privacy.

Further Reading: Battelle, John. *The Search: How Google and Its Rivals Rewrote the Rules of Business and Transformed Our Culture.* New York: Penguin, 2005; Besser, Howard. "Commodification of Culture Harms Creators." *Presentation for the American Library Association Wye River Retreat on Information Commons,* October 2001, http://www. gseis.ucla.edu/~howard/Copyright/ala-commons.html; Cohen, Adam. "What Google Should Roll Out Next: A Privacy Upgrade." *New York Times,* November 28, 2005, http:// www.nytimes.com/2005/11/28/opinion/28mon4.html; Cowan, Alison Leigh. "Books for Lending, Data for Taking." *New York Times,* November 20, 2005, http://www.nytimes. com/2005/11/20/weekinreview/20cowan.html; Gandy, Oscar H. *The Panoptic Sort: A Political Economy of Personal Information.* Boulder, CO: Westview, 1993; Leonhardt, David. "The Internet Knows What You'll Do Next." *New York Times,* July 5, 2006, http:// www.nytimes.com/2006/07/05/business/05leonhardt.html; Markoff, John, and Edward Wyatt. "Technology; Google Is Adding Major Libraries to its Database." *New York Times,* December 14, 2004, http://www.nytimes.com/2004/12/14/technology/14google. html; Robins, Kevin, and Frank Webster. *Times of the Technoculture.* New York: Routledge, 1999; Shenk, David. "A Growing Web of Watchers Builds a Surveillance Society." *New York Times,* January 25, 2006, http://www.nytimes.com/2006/01/25/technology/ techspecial2/25essay.html; "The Battle Over Books: Authors and Publishers Take On the Google Print Library Project." *Live at The New York Public Library,* November 17, 2005, http://www.nypl.org/research/calendar/imagesprog/google111705.pdf; Vaidhyanathan, Siva. "A Risky Gamble with Google." *Chronicle of Higher Education* 52, no.15 (December 2, 2005): B7–B10; Wray, Richard, and Dan Milmo. "Publishers Unite against Google." *The Guardian,* July 6, 2006, http://business.guardian.co.uk/story/0,1813439,00.html.

Paul Vinelli

GOVERNMENT CENSORSHIP AND FREEDOM OF SPEECH

Freedom of speech is essential to the proper functioning of a democracy. The right to express ourselves free from government censorship is a fundamental individual liberty, one that Americans hold dear as a defining feature of our nation. However, in a large country with a diverse population, living together in freedom requires of us a great deal of tolerance. A national commitment to freedom of speech means freedom of speech for everyone, even those with whom we disagree, even those whose ideas we feel are dangerous. For this reason, the United States has long had a remarkably ambivalent relationship with freedom of speech, defending it at times, dispensing with it at others.

The founding fathers gave future generations of Americans a great gift in the form of the First Amendment to the U.S. Constitution. Inspired by the writings of seventeenth-century British political theorist John Milton (see "The Bill of Rights" sidebar), they had the foresight to recognize that a government based on the principles of popular sovereignty cannot function effectively without the free flow of information. People who chose their own leaders cannot make informed choices in the voting booth unless they have access to accurate information and a wide range of opinions, to help them formulate their own positions. Leaders chosen by a free people must remain accountable to those voters, with their words and actions open to scrutiny. Only media that are free from government control can effectively serve the "watchdog" function of the "fourth estate." Acting as an unofficial fourth branch of government, a free press can serve as a check against abuses of power by reporting on the activities of the executive, judicial, and legislative branches.

The framers of our Constitution included a prohibition against federal censorship as a reaction to the strict censorship they experienced under the British monarchy. In a democracy, citizens choose their own leaders, who are then, in turn, expected to represent the will of the public. People in power rarely like being challenged, and the urge to silence critics is common among leaders, even those who have been elected. The founding fathers wanted to help our country avoid a situation in which elected officials suppressed dissent. They wanted to insure that people would have a right to complain about the government without fear of imprisonment, and that minority views would have a chance to be heard.

THE CHALLENGE OF LIVING TOGETHER IN FREEDOM

When the First Amendment was adopted in 1791, America was a fairly homogeneous nation. The people who were allowed to vote in the new country were all white males, most of them were of British or French heritage, and the majority were Protestant. When the founding fathers wrote the First Amendment, they could not possibly have imagined how diverse our population would eventually become. As time went on, immigrants from around the world began arriving on our shores, seeking the individual liberties on which our country was founded. Living together in freedom is not that challenging when people

---

THE BILL OF RIGHTS

The First Amendment to the U.S. Constitution is the first of 10 amendments known as the Bill of Rights, all adopted simultaneously by our Congress in 1791. Each of these rights is designed to protect individual liberties. The First Amendment states that: "Congress shall make no law respecting the establishment of religion, or prohibiting the free exercise thereof; or abridging the freedom of speech or of the press; or the right of the people peaceably to assemble, and to petition the Government for a redress of grievances."

---

have a great deal in common. As more people from different ethnic, racial, and religious backgrounds live in greater proximity to one another, the likelihood of disagreement greatly increases. When confronted with words and images that are deeply offensive, or threatening to the people or ideals we cherish, few may be willing to take the position, often attributed to the French philosopher, Voltaire: "I disapprove of what you say, but I will defend to the death your right to say it."[1]

A HISTORY OF AMBIVALENCE

Freedom of expression is often invoked as one of the defining liberties of American democracy. When we take a closer look at our nation's history, though, another story is revealed. We like freedom of speech when it allows us to voice our own views. However, when it comes to those with whom we disagree, or those who are generating words and images that we feel pose a danger to our children, our community, or our nation, Americans have a long history of suspending freedom of expression in exchange for comfort, or security. While it may seem justifiable, at times, to curtail certain extreme forms of expression, many warn that once we begin making exceptions to individual liberty, we are in danger of sacrificing one of the most fundamental principles of our nation. Benjamin Franklin himself cautioned that "those who would give up an essential liberty to purchase a little temporary security deserve neither liberty nor security."[2] Balancing the rights of the individual with the needs of the group is a complex challenge, and the history of our nation reveals that we continue to grapple with finding this balance.

American ambivalence about freedom of speech dates back to our earliest years as a nation. Ironically, less than 10 years after adding the First Amendment to the Constitution, Congress passed the Alien and Sedition Acts of 1798. These laws were designed to curb sedition—criticism of the government—during a period when the United States was engaged in a policy dispute with France. Under this law, anyone who criticized President Adams, or any other aspect of the U.S. government, was subject to steep fines and jail time. Nearly two dozen journalists were arrested and their voices silenced under the Sedition Act. When Thomas Jefferson, a staunch free speech advocate, was elected president several years later, he repealed the law. But the precedent was set. From then on, nearly every time our country has faced domestic or international tensions, efforts have been made to suppress dissent.

PEOPLE IN HISTORY

One of the most important historical figures in the development of freedom of speech is John Milton, the famous seventeenth-century British writer and political philosopher. Writing in opposition to the harsh censorship that he and other writers of the period experienced at the hands of Parliament, he published a powerful essay on the importance of freedom of speech entitled "Areopagitica." In it, he set forth the argument that remains, to this day, the basis for freedom of speech in a democracy, known as "the self-righting principle." According to Milton, though people sometimes make mistakes, if given enough freedom they will eventually find their way to the truth. The danger of censorship, he warned, is that it impedes the quest for truth. Milton believed that in any open encounter, truth would always triumph always falsehood. Thus, in his view, all ideas should be heard, to allow the right answer to emerge. He also argued that the open discussion of ideas is essential for civil liberty. The most famous lines from his essay are these: "And though all the winds of doctrine were let loose to play upon the earth, so Truth be in the field, we do injuriously by licensing and prohibiting to doubt her strength. Let her and Falsehood grapple: who ever knew Truth put to the worse in a free and open encounter?"

DISSENT DURING WARTIME

It is often said that "the first casualty of war is truth."[3] Even in a democracy, the open discussion or debate about domestic and foreign affairs is often seen as a luxury of peacetime. When a country goes to war, support of the war effort becomes a primary national focus. In order to wage a successful military campaign, high group cohesion is required. Many people must work closely together, both at home and abroad, in difficult and dangerous conditions, to achieve victory. Thus, during wartime, it is argued, there is less room for dissent. During times of military conflict, public discourse—from news reports to popular opinion—is generally expected to support the national effort.

This is true in all nations, and despite our Constitutional commitment to freedom of speech, the United States is no exception. When faced with an enemy—actual or perceived—people rally together, and individual liberties are often suspended in the name of security. Those in favor of such limits argue that it is necessary, at times, to sacrifice some liberties to protect the safety of the nation as a whole. Often, dissent during wartime is seen as disloyalty. Others argue that in a democratic society, the free expression of dissent is essential, especially during times of internal discord. Conflict between these two perspectives continues to this day.

During the Civil War, the governments of both the North and the South jailed those who spoke out against those in power. Prior to the outbreak of the war, those advocating succession—or abolition—often found their writings confiscated, their printing presses destroyed, and faced arrest. Once the fighting began, neither side tolerated dissent, and many went to jail in both the North and the South, even ministers who prayed for an end to the conflict. During the First World War, Congress passed the Espionage Act of 1917, which prohibited any speech that challenged the government or the war. Over 2,000 people were prosecuted for dissent. When the constitutionality of that law was challenged, the Supreme Court made its first formal exception to the First Amendment, stating that speech that posed a "clear and present danger" to the nation could be suppressed (*Schenck v. United States*, 249 U.S. 47 (1919)). From then on, with nearly every military conflict, we passed laws or set up policies designed to curtail free speech.

During the Cold War in the 1950s, the McCarthy era was a particularly dark time for free speech in America, when anyone who showed any signs of supporting dissent was branded a "communist." In the 1960s, opponents to the Vietnam War were dismissed as radicals, and people who burned flags or draft cards in protest were sent to jail. In an attempt to suppress growing criticism of our involvement in Vietnam, the Nixon administration tried to stop both the *New York Times* and the *Washington Post* from publishing excerpts from the Pentagon Papers, a military history of the Vietnam conflict (*New York Times v. United States* and *United States v. Washington Post*, 403 U.S. 713 (1971)). In the wake of Vietnam, the government placed strict limits on media access to military activity in the Persian Gulf, in an attempt to limit negative press coverage. Following the events of September 11, 2001, Congress adopted the Patriot Act, which among other things created a broad definition of "terrorist," including dissident groups—allowing for the arrest of Americans exercising their First Amendment rights to peacefully protest government policy. While the government often claims that some sacrifice of free speech must be made during wartime in the interests of national security, critics and constitutional lawyers often argue, in response, that such wartime censorship protects the government from criticism, not external enemies. As our nation grapples with new foreign and domestic military challenges in the early twenty-first century, we continue to struggle with the ongoing question of how to balance individual liberty with national security.

TIMELINE: SOME KEY MOMENTS IN THE HISTORY OF FREEDOM OF SPEECH IN AMERICA

1791—Bill of Rights added to the U.S. Constitution, including the First Amendment.

1798—Alien and Sedition Act: first official exception to the First Amendment.

1842—Congress passes first anti-obscenity statute.

1861–65—U.S. Civil War: freedom of speech suppressed on both sides of the conflict.

1873—Comstock Act adopted, barring the use of the U.S. postal system for the distribution of obscene material.

1915—Supreme Court rules that the medium of cinema is not protected under the First Amendment.

1918—Espionage Act amended to include strict sedition laws. Over 2,000 prosecuted for dissent against American involvement in World War One.

1919—*Schenk v. U.S.*: "Clear and Present Danger" test is born.

1934—Federal Communications Commission (FCC) is established, marking the start of federal regulation of broadcasting.

1940—The Smith Act passed by Congress prior to U.S. entry into World War II. Used as the basis for silencing those accused of communism during the McCarthy era.

1952—*Burstyn v. Wilson*: Supreme Court reverses earlier decision, granting First Amendment protection to film.

1969—*Brandenberg v. Ohio*: The Supreme Court draws a distinction between speech that advocates ideas (protected by the First Amendment) and speech that incites violence (not protected), establishing the "incitement standard."

1971—Pentagon Papers (*New York Times v. U.S.*; *U.S. v. Washington Post*): Federal government tries to stop the publication of Pentagon Papers. The courts rule in favor of the newspapers.

1972—*Gooding v. Wilson*: Establishes the definition of "fighting words," which may be prohibited if likely to create an immediate breach of the peace.

1974—*Miller v. California*, establishing modern definition of obscenity, and excluding it from First Amendment protection.

1978—*FCC v. Pacifica*: Supreme Court upholds the constitutionality of the FCC's decision to punish broadcasters who air language that is "obscene, indecent or profane." Establishes the "safe harbor laws."

2001—Patriot Act adopted by Congress, following the incidents of September 11, 2001, permitting the government to monitor electronic communication, and empowering law enforcement officials to demand records from bookstores and libraries, to identify who is reading "suspect" material. This act was later amended to allow the government to track an individual's Web-surfing habits and search terms.

2004—Congress empowers the FCC to greatly increase fines imposed upon broadcasters for the violation of indecency standards.

HATE SPEECH

One of the most challenging issues facing any country committed to freedom of expression is that of hate speech. In a nation theoretically committed to equality, how do we handle messages that challenge that basic premise? Does freedom of expression extend to those who speak messages of hate? How should we handle extremists who call for the oppression, deportation—or extermination—of specific groups of people? Initially, it might seem like a simple issue: prejudice and hatred are wrong, killing is wrong, so, speech advocating such things is wrong too. However, banning hate speech doesn't eliminate racism or hatred. In fact, the censorship of this form of communication may inadvertently fan the flames of intolerance, because once an idea gains the status of being "taboo" it often becomes more attractive, at least to some.

The issue of hate speech has generated endless debate in our nation. Many fascinating cases have gone before the courts: Does the Klu Klux Klan have the right to march in the streets? Can the Confederate flag be displayed in public buildings? Can universities enforce rules banning hate speech from their campuses? Ultimately, the Supreme Court has ruled that our rights to freely express our views do have limits, particularly if the speech in question can be seen as posing a direct threat to physical safety. The Court created a category of speech called "fighting words," which they defined as "words spoken in a face-to-face confrontation that are likely to create an immediate breach of the peace."

Speech that meets this test may be prohibited by the states (*Gooding v. Wilson*, 405 U.S. 518 (1972)). This is a complex standard to enforce, however, because it is not always clear exactly what kind of speech fits this definition. Not everyone reacts with violence to an insult, and some have learned to simply walk away in response to hate-filled epithets.

The development of the Internet has made the issue of hate speech all the more complex. Web sites preaching racial hatred fall outside the domain of face-to-face speech, and are thus protected by the First Amendment. Civil rights activists worry that this technology has greatly facilitated the spread of the message of intolerance, allowing racist groups to "recruit" new members under the protection of electronic anonymity. With each new communication technology our nation faces new free-speech challenges, and the issue of hate Web sites remains unresolved. While many feel that hate speech is simply too dangerous, and should be denied free-speech protection, others argue that the best answer to the voice of hate is more speech—specifically, messages of tolerance. Since it seems unlikely that banning hate speech will actually eliminate racism, they suggest that the best way for us to combat prejudice is through education, not censorship.

MANY OTHER ISSUES

The topics discussed here are only some of the many examples of American ambivalence about freedom of speech. Other controversies that illustrate our mixed feelings about the First Amendment include debates about flag burning, book banning, freedom of speech in the classroom, cameras in the courtroom, and the right of journalists to withhold the names of anonymous sources. In addition, critics of media deregulation argue that concentration of ownership in the United States has created a dangerous situation in which a handful of media giants control the flow of ideas. Corporate censorship, they warn, has replaced government censorship as the new threat to the proper functioning of our democracy, hampering the press from serving its role as the fourth estate.

It is often said that "with freedom comes responsibility." Exactly what it means to balance freedom of speech with the responsible exercise of that right in a democracy continues to be a matter of debate. Despite the many changes that come with each new communication technology, the deeper issues remain the same. Living together in freedom calls upon Americans of every political persuasion to be ever vigilant. Unless we all guard against our own tendencies towards intolerance and complacency, we risk losing this precious right to let our voices be heard.

See also Al-Jazeera; Alternative Media in the United States; Anonymous Sources, Leaks, and National Security; Blogosphere; Hypercommercialism; Media and Citizenship; Media and Electoral Campaigns; Media Literacy; Minority Media Ownership; Obscenity and Indecency; Presidential Stagecraft and Militainment; Propaganda Model; Public Sphere; Sensationalism, Fear Mongering, and Tabloid Media; Shock Jocks.

NOTES

1. While these words are generally attributed to the French philosopher Francois Voltaire (1694–1778), there is some debate as to the actual source of the quote. Some suggest that the phrase was invented by a later author to summarize Voltaire's views, as expressed in his "Treatise on Toleration."

2. Benjamin Franklin, in a letter from the Pennsylvania assembly, dated November 11, 1755, to the governor of Pennsylvania.

3. This quote is generally attributed to U.S. Senator Hiram Johnson (1866–1945), a staunchly isolationist Republican, who is said to have made this statement as part of a speech before Congress in 1917.

Further Reading: Fish, Stanley. *There's No Such Thing as Free Speech . . . and It's a Good Thing, Too*. New York: Oxford, 1994; Hargraves, Robert. *The First Freedom: A History of Free Speech*. Gloucestershire: Sutton Publishing, 2003; Hentoff, Nat. *Freedom of Speech for Me but Not for Thee: How the American Left and Right Relentlessly Censor Each Other*. New York: HarperCollins, 1992; Levy, Leonard. *Emergence of a Free Press*. New York: Oxford University Press, 1985; McChesney, Robert. *Corporate Media and the Threat to Democracy*. New York: Seven Stories Press, 1997; Mill, John Stuart. *On Liberty*. London: Penguin Classics, 1985; Milton, John. *Areopagitica: A Speech of Mr. John Milton for the Liberty of Unlicensed Printing, to the Parliament of England. London, 1644*. Santa Barbara, CA: Bandanna Books, 1992; Siebert, Fred, Theodore Peterson, and Wilbur Schramm. *Four Theories of the Press*. Urbana: University of Illinois Press, 1956; Tedford, Thomas, and Dale Herbeck. *Freedom of Speech in the United States*. State College, PA: Strata Publishing, 2005; Voltaire, Francois. *Treatise on Toleration*. Cambridge: Cambridge University Press, 2000.

Gwenyth Jackaway

HYPERCOMMERCIALISM

The landscape of popular culture is cluttered with on air commercial messages and many media analysts and public interest groups charge that advertising, promotion, corporate slogans and icons have become inescapable intrusions on everyday life. The trend toward weaving advertising and promotion into the fabric of mainstream media has been termed hypercommercialism and describes the increasing prevalence of sales and marketing in all aspects of media production and structure. Product branding has been recognizable for decades, but now "branded entertainment" embeds advertising into the design of entertainment programs themselves. Along the way, television is transformed into a marketing tool and viewers become consumers of products, not audiences to be entertained. Media managers argue that combining entertainment and sales will satisfy the public, if done with skill and ingenuity. Critics counter that the consequences of hypercommercialism extend to the foundations of American democracy, because such practices affect news programming and press reporting, as well as entertainment genres. The parameters of hypercommercialism are in constant flux, changing with new ownership structures, media technologies, marketing philosophies, symbolic techniques, and production formats, all of which make contemporary commercial culture a dynamic realm, and a battleground issue, from critical and cultural perspectives.

THE COMMERCIAL MEDIA

The economics of TV has had a particular historical trajectory. When commercial interests won the battle over broadcasting in the 1920s, it was decided that television and radio programming was to be paid for by corporate sponsors. But the controversy did result in broadcast regulation that required networks and station owners to broadcast in the "public interest, convenience and necessity." Advertising would pay for TV programming and commercialism came to be the dominant force in American media, the ramifications of which we are only now beginning to fully understand.

In the 1950s, one sponsor paid to produce each program. This practice gave way by the end of the decade to spot advertising, which continues today. Commercials inserted during programming breaks are purchased by multiple advertisers at negotiated prices determined by a combination of ratings, program demographics, time, content, and availability. In recent times, commercial messages have lost some of their persuasive power as ads become shorter, more frequent, and easier to zap (for example, TiVo). In addition, viewers are media literate and wary of such overt persuasions. Celebrity endorsements help, but now celluloid and video stars pitch everything from aspirins to phone companies. Audiences have come to know that every endorsement has its price, making them a little less effective. But when stars use products in movies and TV programs, it still appears to be the discourse of entertainment, not sales. In a strategic game of leapfrog, advertisers step up persuasive technique and media strategy as the old ones lose some of their punch.

Now promotional messages are no longer restricted to spot advertising. In the age of deregulation, when restrictions on the number of commercials allowed in any hour of programming have been removed, contemporary television places products into just about every nook and cranny of airtime. Although spot advertising is not going away, it now coexists with product placement, a practice that embeds the promotion within the program. Both advertising practices continue to evolve, and as they do, critics charge that they exert inordinate influence over TV programs and feature films alike.

INFLUENCING MEDIA CONTENT

Placing brands in films really took off after 1982 when Steven Spielberg's cute alien, ET, ate Reese's Pieces and sales shot up. Then, in 1983, Tom Cruise wore Ray Ban sunglasses in the movie *Risky Business*. Public interest researchers Michael Jacobson and Laurie Mazur noted that in one month Ray Ban reported sales of 18,000, more pairs of that style sold then during the previous 3 years. As plugging in film came to be understood as the industry's golden goose, agencies directed more clients toward the movies, and as advertising interest rose so did its influence on films. Media scholar Mark Crispin Miller first noted that films with product placement contained scenes that slowed the pacing to feature products; had more mythic, less complicated heroes; and ended on a happier note. In essence, the films moved closer to the upbeat, singular attitudes of commercial design. These changes were predictable consequences of embedding products in story lines, and they follow the conventions of industry wisdom. Ads must not stand out from the landscape of media, rather, they must be integral parts of entertainment geography. From the early day of commercials on television, broadcast historian

Eric Barnouw detailed the ways in which advertising professionals learned that commercials that diverged in style and content from programs were ineffective at selling products. Since then, media buyers have long demanded what is called *programming environments*: particular stories and character types that surround the product and its ad campaign with compatible and complimentary messages. In this way viewers and readers are *primed* to be more susceptible to ads and the symbolic culture that sustains them.

The economic success of broadcasters is dependent on programs that please two different constituencies, ad buyers and TV audiences, whose interests sometimes diverge. Many network professionals attempt to create interesting, independent programming, but productions must be attractive to sponsors who pay the bills. Because ad agencies and their clients make "up front" media buys based on the programs they see, producers know well that shows dove-tailed to sponsors' wishes garner the highest rates. In these ways, advertisers come to exert enormous influence on programming design. Nowhere is this more evident than with reality shows, in which entire programs are designed by and for advertisers.

BRANDED ENTERTAINMENT

Product placement on TV has evolved into what the industry now calls *branded entertainment*. Media contracts revolve around *brand integration* deals, a common feature of reality shows. In many of these shows the networks have contracted with *task sponsors*, or companies willing to pay to have entire episodes built around their products. In its third season, *The Apprentice* built programs around, for instance, Dominos Pizza and Staples. Products were designed and pitched to company executives, and through the entire episode, each show featured brand logos in an all-encompassing corporate environment. Another NBC reality show, *The Restaurant*, contracted with Coors, American Express, and Mitsubishi. The three companies paid the entire production costs of the episodes. In the first show, chef/owner Rocco DiSpirito orders beer, then corrects himself, "Make that Coors beer. Kimberly, do not come back without Coors beer for all these people," he says. In addition, dialogue with branded content is being dubbed in after filming (Husted 2003). Such practices alter the programs as advertisers influence the scripts, settings and editing process. As one entertainment writer noted, *The Restaurant* has the feel of an infomercial. Such programs might better be called product placement shows because the advertising content is being scripted, with any pretence to reality being in name only. These shows hark back to television of the 1950s when sponsors controlled programming, and illustrate the current merger of entertainment and promotion.

MAGAZINES

These precepts hold true to magazines as well, where combining advertising and content has been standard practice. Articles written to augment paid adverting by emphasizing promotional themes or featuring products are called *complimentary copy.* When articles are placed on facing pages or used to surround the ad text, they are referred to as *adjacencies.* Much of magazine content is filled with stories generated from advertising departments as complimentary copy, not from the creative inspirations of editors, or the investigative instincts of reporters. Magazines also carry *advertorials* and special advertising supplements formatted to look like feature journalism. They hope the format tricks readers into being less critical and more open to the messages. Indeed, many advertisers reject independent story ideas. In addition, magazine and newspaper editors increasingly rely on public relations professionals who represent corporate clients and celebrities who pitch stories and even write copy.

CREATIVE AND EDITORIAL JUDGMENT

Now magazine copy, much like many film scripts, is submitted to ad agencies offering them the chance to find appropriate insertion points for their products. This merging of media content and product promotion has resulted in increasing demands by manufacturers and their agents that content conform to the messages of the advertising. Chrysler publicly announced such economic *prior restraint* as corporate policy in January 1996. The company's advertising agency sent a letter to magazines carrying its advertising requiring them to submit articles to Chrysler for advanced screening. If the company deemed any editorial content provocative or offensive, it warned, it would pull its advertising.

The American Society of Newspaper Editors prepared a response and on June 30, 1997 sent out an appeal to editors to take a position not to bow to such advertising pressure and to reassert their right to have final authority over the editorial content of their magazines. Milton Glaser, a graphic designer and cofounder of *New York* magazine, hearing of Chrysler's policies wrote, "Censorship of this kind that acts to curtail the exchange of unpopular ideas is unacceptable for all those who care about human freedom and a healthy democratic society" (Glaser 1997). He added that such a practice "violates our sense of fairness and our notion of how a free press work." Chrysler Corporation responded with surprise to the protest, saying it was only making public a policy that many other companies practice covertly.

In film as well, advertisers sometimes try and succeed, in shaping content to their demands. The fight over how to end the popular film *Jerry Maguire* is a case in point. In *Jerry Maguire*, Tom Cruise stars as a struggling sports agent and Cuba Gooding Jr. plays the lovable football player Rod Tidwell, trying to make it big time. Products such as Coke, Visa, and Reebok are plugged, but the film goes further in its support of advertising. Tidwell's very success is measured by his popularity with advertisers. His career goal is to appear in a Reebok commercial, not on the late-night, low-budget, water-bed pitches that are a sure sign of failure. Reebok's placement in the film led to contentions about creative control, ultimately won by the shoe company. The director cut 47 seconds of Tidwell appearing in a Reebok commercial at the end of the movie. Reebok sued, and when the film aired on Showtime, the pitch had been reinserted. At this point advertisers have enormous control over motion picture plot and dialogue, and in this case, endings. By the end of 1998 the talented Gooding was pitching Pepsi on TV spots, still in his Tidwell character.

MEDIA OWNERSHIP: MERGERS, CONSOLIDATION, AND TIGHT DIVERSIFICATION

No discussion of how media culture came to be hypercommercial is complete without mentioning the role of corporate mergers and acquisitions, which took place in two significant waves of consolidation in the 1980s and 1990s. Film industry observer Thomas Schatz, documented the 1989 transformation of the structure of the industry, when a total of 414 media deals worth over $42 billion were struck, the most notable being the $14 billion merger of Time Warner. In 1995 another wave hit, setting a record of 644 mergers totaling $70.8 billion. Along with Disney purchasing Cap Cities/ABC, Viacom's buyout of Blockbuster, and Westinghouse's merger with CBS, the already massive Time Warner bought Turner broadcasting in a $7.3 billion deal. Among other things, CNN, TNT, and TBS gave the new company broadcast distribution for its vast media products of film and TV series, resulting in the largest media library in existence. Changing copyright ownership led to the mining of the past for commercial purposes, and bits and pieces from old movies, characters and cartoons turned up everywhere from ads to merchandise. Time Warner made spectacular profits with vintage Looney Toons, the revenues for syndication and merchandising of Daffy Duck and his friends reached $3.5 billion in 1996.

Media conglomeration has allowed the mega corporations to practice *synergy*, another key piece of the expanding commercial mosaic, in which corporations cross-promote their own stars, programs, and merchandise on their media outlets. When Time Warner wanted to own the production and distribution of its TV shows, it started its own TV network, WB. Because teens comprise the biggest consumer market in the music industry, *Dawson's Creek* was used to sell the songs and artist signed to Warner Bros. record labels. Paula Cole's, *I Don't Wanna Wait*, became a top 10 single after being featured as the show's theme song.

Synergy also provides the economic fuel that propels the trend toward huge media franchises, including summer blockbusters. The primary requirement for synergy is capital, which only huge companies have, first to produce the film that forms the epicenter, then to provide the millions needed to drive the marketing force behind it. These multipurpose entertainment/marketing machines then create film franchises that become lengthy promotions for a vast array of licensed tie-in and brand-name consumer products. One narrative can also lead to movie sequels, TV series, music videos, and sound track albums, video games and theme park rides, graphic novels and comic books. Indeed, the first giant step in this direction was the *Batman* blockbuster. As industry writers like to say, Warner is the Studio that *Batman* built. *Batman* was one of the first films to utilize the whole machine of the company, from the marketing to the tie-ins and the merchandising, all building up the momentum needed for international distribution. Films are no longer singular narratives, rather, they are *iterations* of entertainment supertexts, multimedia forms that can be expanded and resold almost ad infinitum.

RETAIL OUTLETS AND MEDIA BRANDS

Batman—the movie, then the industry—inspired the chain of Warner Bros. retail stores, one of the most significant trends in all of this. These new entertainment/commodity facilities, or retail stores feature branded products. Before the deregulation of the 1980s, merchandise tied to TV shows was not allowed because the program would have been, in essence, an extended commercial. Since then (as in the 1950s), the shows that feature the products that children desire so fervently after seeing them on TV, advertise the product for the length of the program. Tying products to TV programs, films, networks, and the cable services on which they appear give media firms distinct brand identities that create new marketing horizons for massive amounts of commodities. Cable channels and broadcast networks alike now strive to be regarded as brands, especially desirable to specific demographic groups targeted by advertisers, especially children who watch Disney and Nickelodeon. Disney now has over 600 retail stores selling branded products, and Time Warner is in hot pursuit with a couple hundred stores. Viacom has also entered the branded retail-marketing venture. It is this latest aspect of the merger/synergy structure that reduces the cultural differences between movies and advertisements, programming and promotion, entertainment and shopping.

As detailed previously, these economic practices also affect content, which is designed to conform to the atmosphere of what some describe as *commercialtainment*. Disney's animated film *Hercules* illustrates the close connections between corporate synergy and sympathetic media content. In the Disney story, when Hercules becomes a hero he also becomes an action figure. The cultural icons of his success are prestigious tie-in products, from Air-Hercules sandals to soft drinks, all of which are sold, of course, in their own branded, retail outlet depicted in the film. At the time of the movie's release, Disney made up the entrance to its store to look like the store in the film, and the tie-in theme park is also depicted in the text of the movie. The movie's celebration of marketing synergy helps create a cultural attitude in its favor, which helps erase the distinction between cultural narratives, heroes, marketing, and merchandise.

While some critics see supra-narratives that extend and augment across media outlets and formats as constituting a creative realm of media and audience production, other analysts argue that they are indicative of a monolithic media world that crowds out smaller, creative alternatives. Those concerned with the excesses of commercialism argue that such narratives are only successful when they conform to a certain set of requirements, designed to target the highest paying markets. The now standard and highly formulaic action adventure narratives must be hyped with all the advertising that studio money can buy. Because advertising is needed to create the buzz (especially to teen audiences who see movies more than once and buy the tie-in merchandise), spot advertising is now a huge expense for media firms themselves. Such franchises are expensive to make and expensive to advertise, and this is a major rationale for the mega-media corporation, because only they can afford the risk and costs.

Deregulation allowed TV programs to become advertisements. Industry conglomeration created the synergy needed for transforming the rest of entertainment into merchandise. The economics of media content has influenced programming and movie design in its favor, but it has also led to a type of economic censorship of shows and content that advertisers and corporations object to.

CBS AND VIACOM: A CASE OF ECONOMIC CENSORSHIP

As the summer of 2001 drew to a close, in the hot days of August and network reruns, the *New York Times* reported that CBS was shelving several episodes it had planned to rerun of its primetime courtroom drama, *Family Law*. The episodes dealt with the death penalty, abortion, gun control, and interfaith marriage. These are the issues that win or lose presidential elections, they shape public policy, and have enormous impact on personal life. They all represent important controversies, unsettled in the minds of the American public, and the country is in great need of as much public discussion about these matters as possible, whether it is on a fictional drama or nightly news broadcast. The shows were pulled because of advertising pressure from Procter & Gamble; the company deemed the episodes too controversial and threatened to withdraw its commercials. CBS succumbed to the pressure and shelved the episodes.

This incident illustrates the commercial forces at work that often determine which programs are made available to the public, and which are not. The decision to pull the programs was the outcome of these regulatory, economic, and structural changes within the industry. In May 2001, CBS's parent company Viacom signed a $300 million advertising contract with Procter & Gamble (P&G), the largest advertiser on TV. Conditions of the media buy stipulated that P&G would spend about one-third of its total advertising budget on ads for products such as Oil of Olay, Pantene, and Tide detergent, most to be aired on CBS. In securing the huge revenue source for Viacom, CBS agreed to work with the company on projects suited for its needs. It is common industry knowledge that P&G is careful about the programs that surround its products, and it employs a private screening agency to monitor the episodes of TV programs that carry its commercials.

The contract involving such large sums of advertising dollars was made possible because of the 1999 merger between Viacom and CBS, creating at the time the world's second largest media corporation. The $80 billion merger, made possible by the Telecommunications Act of 1996, resulted in a vertically integrated company that was allowed to control two TV networks. For the first time in history, TV networks were allowed to own cable systems. Viacom, primarily a cable firm (with a significant library of television classics), could now control TV networks. In addition, previous regulation limited a single company from owning TV stations that reached over 25 percent of the national audience, but after 1996 the maximum audience percentage was raised to 35. Even with the increase the CBS/Viacom deal was over the limit, yet the FCC allowed the merger to take place.

One of the economic incentives for mega media corporations is the ability to secure the largest portion of national adverting revenue. CBS had learned these strategies with their radio properties soon after the Telecommunications Act. Robert McChesney reported that by September 1997, after quickly purchasing the new legal limit of radio stations (eight in a single market), CBS became one of three companies that controlled more than 80 percent of the ad revenues in about half of the top 50 markets. These station monopolies allow companies to corner national advertising, but result in a less competitive, less diverse market system. Independent stations cannot acquire the high-paying national clients, and smaller advertisers cannot obtain the same rates bought by big-time commercial buyers. Massive ad buys of the kind made by P&G result in fewer alternatives for broadcasters if a major sponsor threatens to pull its commercials. That is exactly what happened at CBS. The summer rerun period is not known for high ratings. The threat made by P&G carried weight because it was to sponsor four commercials for the single episode. Replacing those would not be easy for an August rebroadcast.

But CBS had reason not to pull the hour-long drama. It was the only one in the series nominated that year for an Emmy Award, television's highest honor. Dana Delany, playing a single mother whose son is shot by the gun she owns, was nominated for a guest-actress award. Networks routinely rerun their Emmy-nominated programs in August because voting is still taking place. The willingness to pressure the network might have been more understandable had the program been unbalanced, but the episode presented both sides. While dramatizing the often-tragic outcome of gun ownership, the law firm in the series nevertheless defends the mother's right to own a gun.

This incident became the topic of news because the award-nominated actress herself drew attention to the incident. But in this era of media consolidation, the press has not done an admirable job of reporting on industry conglomeration. When mergers occur, problems are downplayed and there is little public discussion. Tom Brokaw's terse statement about the CBS/Viacom deal is illustrative of the coverage. "What does that mean for the average viewer? Well, probably not very much" (*Action Alert* 1999).

PRESSURES ON THE PRESS

Nonfiction programming, news and information have not been insulated from the consequences of megacorporate ownership and hypercommercialism. Hard-hitting investigations that challenge corporate practices, power, and wealth are rare in this media environment that continually promotes consumption. It has long been understood that even though media organizations are large profit-making organization, information and uninhibited public debate are so essential for democracy that they should be insulated from commercial pressures. This is often referred to as the division between church (the editorial division of a company) and state (the rest of the corporation and its business practices). Media managers and owners have offered congressional testimony confirming this separation. But researchers have documented troubling cases where promotion,

THE SUIT AGAINST NBC

Those concerned with press freedom in the age of corporate media conglomeration point to professional journalists as the ones able to protect the public's right to know. While journalists often resist pressures, their careers and incomes are often on the line, and most are aware that lifestyle stories boost ratings and please managers. Former Gulf-war correspondent Arthur Kent (who became known as the Scud Stud during the war) was hired as *Dateline's* foreign correspondent. Kent was committed to serious news and foreign reporting, and when NBC fired him in 1992, he brought suit against corporate news managers. He said producers were reluctant to air his reports because entertainment division executives believed they had no commercial value. The legal case, including transcripts of testimony, offers rare insights into how corporate executives define news, and how the G.E.-appointed NBC news managers had been told to "bring down the barriers" between news and entertainment. The case demonstrated the loss of editorial autonomy in the news division in pursuit of entertainment fare. Though his case was settled and is considered a victory, Kent concluded that working journalists have less real influence on the daily news agenda then ever before.

entertainment, and other profit-making priorities have crossed the line into news divisions and affected editorial decisions (see "The Suit against NBC" sidebar).

FOX NEWS AND MONSANTO

One case illustrates these concerns. In December 1996 investigative reporters Steve Wilson and Jane Akre were hired by Fox 13 in Tampa Bay to do hard-hitting local reporting. They quickly uncovered a story critical of Monsanto, the largest agrochemical company, the second largest seed company, and the fourth largest pharmaceutical company in the world, and a main advertiser on the Fox Network nationally. Monsanto produces a synthetic bovine growth hormone (BGH) marketed under the name Prosilac. Prosilac is banned in Canada and Europe because of its links to cancers of the colon, breast, and prostate, and the bacterial and antibiotic residues left in milk. Akre found that virtually all milk sold in Florida came from cows injected with Prosilac, and even though labeling is required, consumers were not being informed. After two months of investigation, the reporters produced a news report. But the story was pulled (Wilson 1998). As the incident became well-known among First Amendment scholars and critics, they found that Monsanto was a client of Actmedia, an advertising firm also owned by Rupert Murdoch, who owns NewsCorp, the parent company of Fox News. The case raised concerns about the decreasing number of companies that control the media, and their willingness to protect corporate interest instead of informing the public.

MARKET JOURNALISM

The overall negative effects on journalism are multifaceted and come from a combination of commercial factors. Editor-at-large of the *Columbia Journalism*

Review, Neil Hickey has tracked newsroom developments and he makes the following points: editors pull back coverage of major advertisers to protect ad revenue. They work with marketers, advertisers and promotion experts on story ideas, collapsing church and state, and losing editorial independence. They acquiesce to shrinking news holes that augment the bottom line. Executives cut budgets to satisfy demands for higher profit margins and fail to reinvest in training, support, staff and equipment. Taken together, according to Hickey, these things constitute the "fatal erosion of the ancient bond between journalists and the public" (Hickey 1998).

At the same time, journalists and critics alike have lamented the changes in serious news reporting (Koppel 1997). They point to newsmagazines and other nonfiction fare produced in entertainment divisions and designed to compete for ratings, which use dramatic production techniques, such as intense and mysterious soundtracks to tell theatrical tales and juicy plots of murder and mayhem. Such ratings-boosting fare offers distraction and visceral responses in a world becoming more complicated and less comprehensible.

Most disturbing is the habitual suppression of an entire terrain of information deemed unacceptable to corporate business interests. A conglomerate such as Disney has declined to allow ABC news to cover conditions at its theme parks, and the company is not eager to air stories that detail the conditions under which Teletubbies are made. Few investigative reports show Chinese workers toiling up to 16 hours a day for less than two dollars to make the merchandise sold in Disney's retail outlets. And with the shared directorates between Time Warner and Chevron Corp., it is no wonder that Chevron's role in the destruction of Nigerian wetlands was identified as a censored news story by Peter Philips and Project Censored. From information about faulty and unhealthy products, to the human and environmental consequences of some corporate practices, critical information is harder to find outside the Internet and alternative media outlets. Critics charge that news produced in the age of hypercommercialism increasingly reflects the interests of the wealthy few that own and advertise on the media.

CONCLUSION

The current reliance of commercialtainment of all sorts, and the branding and merchandising of programs and media companies alike, together with programming pressures from advertisers and their agents, are the result of media conglomeration and corporate friendly regulatory decisions. These changes have raised fundamental questions about democracy and the First Amendment. For fictional fare, as creators lose production independence, the singularly positive portrayals of products and corporate sponsors should not be considered programming in the public interest, but uniquely beneficial to commercial interests. At times, corporate interests are at odds with consumer needs and the public's right to be informed. Analysts wonder if this increasingly hypercommercialized landscape can serve the democratic needs of the public. If not, can the course be changed in a direction able to reenvision a more inclusive, less commercial communication system?

See also Advertising and Persuasion; Alternative Media in the United States; Branding the Globe; Conglomeration and Media Monopolies; Government Censorship and Freedom of Speech; Internet and its Radical Potential; Media and the Crisis of Values; Media Reform; Media Watch Groups; Minority Media Ownership; Product Placement; Ratings; Reality Television; Runaway Productions and the Globalization of Hollywood; Sensationalism, Fear Mongering, and Tabloid Media; TiVo; Transmedia Storytelling and Media Franchises; Video News Releases; Women's Magazines.

Further Reading: *Action Alert: Viacom-CBS Merger,* September 10, 1999. http://www.fair.org/index.php?page=13; Andersen, Robin. *Consumer Culture and TV Programming.* Boulder, CO: Westview Press, 1995; Andersen, Robin, and Lance Strate, eds. *Critical Studies in Media Commercialism.* London: Oxford University Press, 2000; Barnouw, Erik, et al. *Tube of Plenty.* New York: Oxford University Press, 1975; Erik Barnouw, Richard M. Cohen, Thomas Frank, Todd Gitlin, David Lieberman, Mark Crispin Miller, Gene Roberts, Thomas Schatz, and Patricia Aufderheide, eds. *Conglomerates and the Media.* New York: The New Press, 1997; Bart, Peter. *The Gross: The Hits, the Flops, the Summer That Ate Hollywood.* New York: St. Martin's Press, 1999; Fuller, Linda. "We Can't Duck the Issue: Imbedded Advertising in the Motion Pictures." In *Undressing the Ad: Reading Culture in Advertising,* ed. K. Frith. New York: Peter Lang, 1997; Gitlin, Todd. *Watching Television.* New York: Pantheon, 1986; Glaser, Milton. "Censorious Advertising." *The Nation,* September 22, 1997, p. 7; Hazen, Don, and Julie Winokur, eds. *We the Media: A Citizen's Guide to Fighting for Media Democracy.* New York: The New Press, 1997; Hickey, Neil. "Money Lust: How Pressure for Profit Is Perverting Journalism." *Columbia Journalism Review* (July/August 1998): 28–36; Husted, Bill. "Coors Tap Flows Freely on TV Show." *The Denver Post,* July 27, 2003; Jacobson, Michael F., and Laurie Ann Mazur. *Marketing Madness: A Survival Guide for a Consumer Society.* Boulder, CO: Westview Press, 1995; Kent, Arthur. *Risk and Redemption: Surviving the Network News Wars.* London: Intersteller, 1997; Koppel, Ted. "Journalism under Fire." *The Nation,* November 24, 1997, pp. 23–24; McAllister, Matthew P. *The Commercialization of American Culture: New Advertising Control and Democracy.* Thousand Oaks, CA: Sage, 1996; McChesney, Robert. *Rich Media, Poor Democracy: Communication Politics in Dubious Times.* Urbana: University of Illinois Press, 1999; Miller, Mark Crispin, ed. *Seeing Through Movies.* New York: Pantheon, 1990; Schatz, Thomas. "The Return of the Hollywood Studio System." In *Conglomerates and the Media,* ed. Eric Barnouw, 73–106. New York: The New Press, 1997; Wasko, Janet. *How Hollywood Works.* London: Sage, 2003; Wilson, Steve. "Fox in the Cow Barn." *The Nation,* June 8, 1998, p. 20.

Robin Andersen

INDEPENDENT CINEMA: THE MYTH AND NECESSITY OF DISTINCTION

In discussing film, production personnel, fans, and critics alike regularly distinguish between "mainstream cinema" and "independent cinema." If judged by economical, ideological, or aesthetic parameters only, though, it does not make sense to have film history, or parts of it, split up between films that are purportedly independent from corporate or government influence, and films that are reputedly fully manufactured and designed through commerce and policy. In every one of the former cases, there are some "big money" strings somewhere; and in every of the latter cases, there is some room for autonomy. Yet the distinction constantly reappears throughout debates on cinema. What, then, is behind this distinction, why is it so persistent, and what *is* independent cinema?

The mainstream–independent distinction is one of cinema's most enduring frames of reference. Precisely because of its power, which is largely rhetorical, it is an instrument of debate used to support arguments about historical and contemporary developments in the economics, ideologies, and aesthetics of cinema. In that sense, the distinction between independent cinema and mainstream cinema is both mythical and necessary. It is mythical, because in the same way myths underscore cultural histories and ideologies as foundational stories, the repeated and continuously updated use of the mainstream–independent cinema distinction underscores beliefs about what cinema is and should be. And it is necessary because such myths not only inform but actually enable the historiography of cinema, its policies, and its practice. As with all belief systems, even if the distinction itself is questionable, the actions in its name are important in creating everyday understandings of film and media practice.

THE BATTLEFIELD METAPHOR

Definitions of mainstream and/or independent cinema often appear futile; every attempt presents an easy target for refutation, leaving us with a battlefield of opinions and discussions, and it is precisely in this battlefield metaphor that the opportunities for a meaningful approach to the distinction mainstream–independent lie.

Mainstream cinema occupies the high ground on the battlefield—its position is unquestioned. While perhaps no one has a surefire definition of what constitutes mainstream cinema, it is safe to say that not too many people seem to care. Debates about *kinds* of mainstream cinema aside (like blockbusters), and debates around certain *kinds* of genres like drama or romance exempted, it appears that mainstream cinema seems pretty well understood in a common sense. It is formulaic, commercial, top-down, and centralized-control driven (especially in terms of budget and planning), and it aims for wide distribution in order to entertain the largest common denominator of audiences. The general ease with which descriptions like this are accepted for mainstream cinema is probably the result of "mainstream" being a "center-position," a position in a debate that is seen as the norm. It is considered evident and self-explanatory, motivated, confident, and secure. In terms of our battlefield metaphor, it is on top of an elevation, in plain sight, overseeing the grounds—static, but in charge.

Independent cinema, on the other hand, occupies the "outsider-position." It is hidden in the bushes, moving like a band of guerillas, sneaky and swift, but also outnumbered, divisive, and internally divided. Practitioners of cinema cannot seem to agree what "independent" means, but they all refer to it as some kind of "counterforce." For James Mangold, "independent" signifies an attitude "against the system, against the grain." Kevin Smith uses a negative definition: "Can this movie ever be made in a studio? If you say no, then that's an independent film." Ted Demme invokes a degree of individuality: "If it's personal to a director, then it's an independent." For Nancy Savoca, it is a mindset: "Independent film is really a way of thinking." And for Alan Rudolph the term is useless: "If you're truly independent, then no one can really categorize you and your film can't be pigeonholed"—hence it cannot be called anything, and certainly not "independent." Academics and critics also appear to struggle with the term. For Emmanuel Levy, independent cinema is characterized by two disguises it can switch between: independent financing, or independent spirit. For Jonathan Rosenbaum, independent means being able to intervene at crucial stages, like having "final cut" over your film. For Geoff King, independent cinema covers a range of practices, hovering in between nonindustrial cinema (like handcrafted avant-garde films) and Hollywood's centralized mode of production. It is not too much of a stretch of the imagination to see all of these attempts to describe a dynamic, constantly moving concept as similar to reconnaissance work: trying to map what's out there, without really capturing it.

As anyone who has ever played chess, Stratego, or Risk knows, battles are about momentum. All the directors, academics, and critics mentioned above can be seen as describing parts, moving fragments of a broader "independent" opposition to the mainstream. This is how we may need to approach the distinction: mainstream cinema is the largest force on the field, and independent cinema gets the attention because of the inventiveness of its movements.

INDEPENDENT CINEMA: A TIMELINE

1909—Formation of the Motion Picture Patents Company (MPCC), founding the industrial organization of standardized film production.

1909—Carl Laemmle starts the Independent Motion Picture (IMP) Company and lures Florence Lawrence and later Mary Pickford to become his stars, "IMP girls."

1912—MPPC patent infringement lawsuit against IMP fails; Hollywood becomes America's main film production center.

1913—D. W. Griffith leaves for Hollywood.

1909–18—Installation of Hollywood's major studios, with strong connections to exhibition and distribution.

1919—*Das Cabinet des Dr. Caligari* (Robert Wiene) and the start of the European avant-garde.

1928—*Un chien andalou* (Luis Buñuel) ignites surrealist cinema.

1930–33—The golden age of exploitation cinema in pre–Hays Code Hollywood.

1934—Installation of the Hays Code of self-censorship in Hollywood.

1945—*Rome, Open City* (Roberto Rossellini), the start of Italian neo-realism.

1946—Launch of the Cannes Film Festival.

1948—The "Paramount" decision, declaring illegal vertical integration of studios.

1949—Start of Cinema 16, New York's prime film society.

1958–59—Introduction of cheap lightweight cameras (Éclair Cameflex, new Arriflex 16).

1959—Independent cinema and the new wave: *A bout de souffle* (Jean-Luc Godard), *Les 400 coups* (François Truffaut), *Les cousins* (Claude Chabrol), and *Hiroshima Mon Amour* (Alain Resnais) set off the French new wave.

1959—High points of independent exploitation cinema: *A Bucket of Blood* (Roger Corman), *Plan Nine from Outer Space* (Ed Wood).

1960—Start of campus film societies throughout the United States.

1963—Breakthrough of the American underground: *Scorpio Rising* (Kenneth Anger), *Flaming Creatures* (Jack Smith), *Blow Job* (Andy Warhol).

1967–69—The influence of Roger Corman: *Wild Angels, The Trip, Bonnie and Clyde* (Arthur Penn), *Easy Rider* (Dennis Hopper and Peter Fonda), *Who's That Knocking at My Door?* (Martin Scorsese), *Targets* (Peter Bogdanovich).

1972—Porn chic: *Deep Throat* (Gerard Damiano), *Emmanuelle* (Just Jaeckin), *Heat* (Paul Morrissey), *Score* (Radley Metzger).

1975–76—High point of the midnight movies circuit: *El Topo* (Alejandro Jodorowsky), Hooper), *The Rocky Horror Picture Show* (Jim Sharman), *Salo* (Pier Paolo Pasolini), *Eraserhead* (David Lynch), *Shivers* (David Cronenberg).

1976—Tax laws in several countries hit independent cinema exhibition.

1989–90—New independent cinema and the proliferation of Miramax: *Sex, Lies, and Videotape* (Steven Soderbergh).

1991—Relaunch of the Sundance Film Festival.

1992–94—New indie sensibilities: *Les nuits fauves* (Cyril Collard), *Claire of the Moon* (Nicole Conn), *Gas Food Lodging* (Allison Anders), *Jungle Fever* (Spike Lee), *Dazed and Confused* (Richard Linklater), *Even Cowgirls Get the Blues* (Gus Van Sant), *Go Fish* (Troch), *Totally F**ed Up* (Greg Araki), *Amateur* (Hal Hartley), *Clerks* (Kevin Smith), and *Reservoir Dogs* (Quentin Tarantino).

1996—Launch of the European Fantastic Film Festivals Federation (Melies).

2000—Indie and mainstream conflation: *American Beauty* (Sam Mendes), *Erin Brockovich*, and *Traffic* (Steven Soderbergh).

THREE MOMENTS OF MOMENTUM

There are, largely, three moments in the history of cinema in which discussions over the distinction mainstream–independent have determined how we understand film and its relationship to culture: (1) the period around World War I, stretching out into the 1920s as far as the advent of sound, when Hollywood installed itself as the center of commercial filmmaking; (2) the late 1950s, stretching out into the 1970s, when the French nouvelle vague set the tone for a new framework in which auteurs (usually directors) became a pivotal mechanism of discussions of cinema; (3) and the late 1980s/early 1990s, stretching out across the 1990s, in which American independent cinema evolved from a single-person endeavor into a close and often comfortable alliance with mainstream Hollywood—encapsulated in that fashionable hybrid term: "Indiewood."

Before we examine each in turn, though, first a qualification: it is a gross generalization to claim that outside these three moments the distinction was not present, or relevant. The moments in film history that fall outside the three key ones remain relevant, as points of inspiration of resistance. For instance, early 1930s exploitation cinema, in and around Hollywood, can safely be regarded as relating as much to the mainstream–independent distinction as any other moment, as the production and reception histories of *Dracula*, *Frankenstein*, *Freaks*, *King Kong*, and less reputable films testify. Another qualification relates to the institutionalization of the term "independent." While the term "mainstream" is equally elusive, it is frequently employed, unproblematically so. But "independent" seems, by its very nature of "outsidership," to be asking for challenge. The three moments explored in more detail here have all consciously employed the label "independent" or "indie" as a trademark term to identify parties during a certain period. In each case, the term originated as a resistance against what was perceived as a monopolistic situation. But in each case it remained active even when the situation had changed dramatically, and "independents" seemed to have become very much like the institution they resisted.

Moment 1: Early Cinema and Hollywood (1909–18)

If we judge, as Tom Gunning does, early cinema to be a "cinema of attractions" in which it is the prime interest of films to attract spectators, then this applies to both mainstream and independent cinema. In the case of mainstream cinema, it means there is space to lay the foundations for formulaic but robust patterns through which audiences can be entertained, shocked, or humored—in other words, there is a space for an industry. According to Georges Sadoul, 1909 marked an important moment in this industrialization, when representatives of the world's major patent holders, distributors, and producers (Pathé, Eastman, Edison, and others) met to discuss conditions for controlling the movie business, and formed the Motion Picture Patents Company (MPPC) trust to regulate it. No sooner than its installation, exhibitors and rogue producers tried to circumvent and resist the MPPC's efforts, and, calling themselves "independents," they moved productions out of reach of the MPPC's areas of control to the geographical fringes of established production areas (such as California, Canada, Belgium, the Balkans, and Latin America).

The appeal of the independents' adventurous use of technology, scenery, and personnel and their "crazy" attitude quickly made them audience favorites, and led to the move to Hollywood and the installation of the star system (Florence Lawrence and Mary Pickford becoming "IMP girls," as one slogan had it—IMP standing for Independent Motion Pictures, later to become Universal). By the end of World War I, the independents had managed to establish wide networks of exhibition and distribution that cornered the market, and led to the classical Hollywood studio system. As one critic said after the birth of United Artists: "The patients are taking over the asylum."

By the mid-1920s, the former independents had become the mainstream, and a new resistance rose, this time against them. It consisted of cine-clubs, political networks (especially in Europe), and avant-garde movements (like surrealism). While this new resistance never declared itself "independent" (it rather saw itself as serving "greater" needs), it did form significant inspiration for a second moment.

Moment 2: Art House, Exploitation, and the New Waves (1959–75)

By the late 1950s, a new opportunity arose for a public debate over the distinction between mainstream and independent cinema—alternatives to mainstream became visible and desirable again. World War II had destroyed much of Europe's commercial cinema (with notable exceptions, like the United Kingdom), and the 1948 "Paramount decision" had declared Hollywood's vertical integration of production, distribution, and exhibition illegal. European art-house films (like Rossellini's *Rome, Open City*), and U.S.-grown exploitation movies, like those from Roger Corman's AIP (American Independent Pictures), profited from the opening, and gradually, in bits and pieces, grew into an alternative for mainstream cinema. The 1959 breakthrough of the French "nouvelle vague," which combined art-house and exploitation elements, gave that development momentum, and publicized it as a new boom of independent production that favored auteur-led enterprises—as Jean-Luc Godard noted, "*Tout est possible.*" Of the many factors facilitating the momentum, the most significant were a vibrant exhibition circuit—comprising festivals, art-house theaters, midnight movies, grindhouses, drive-ins, clubhouses, and campus societies—and an equally vivid film press, encompassing liberal criticism as well as widely available fan magazines and underground publications.

Throughout the 1960s and into the 1970s, it guaranteed visibility and continuity to auteur and independent alternative cinema. It gave Corman the opportunity to offer chances to young talents like Francis Coppola, Martin Scorsese, Brian De Palma, Jack Nicholson, Robert De Niro, Jonathan Demme, Stephanie Rothman, and Peter Fonda; it enabled awards, and success, for the films of Andrei Tarkovsky, Bernardo Bertolucci, Akira Kurosawa, and Rainer-Werner Fassbinder; it created networks of support for revolutionary "Third World Cinema," shaking off cultural colonialism (Cuban cinema, Cinema Novo, even Canadian cinema); it turned obscure underground fare like *Flaming Creatures*, *Scorpio Rising*, *Eraserhead*, *The Rocky Horror Picture Show*, and Andy Warhol's films, into international cult phenomena, and it was lenient and permissive towards films testing the boundaries of taste and decency (like *Plan 9 from Outer Space*, *Sins of the Fleshapoids*, *Emmanuelle*, *Deep Throat*, and *Salo*)—if nothing else, it established independent cinema's "cult appeal" as a prime source of attraction for audiences.

By the late 1970s, though, much of the momentum was lost, interrupted, or destroyed by stringent new tax laws (against exhibitors mainly), a recovery of New Hollywood (fuelled by some of the Corman babes, and quick in recuperating independent genres like horror and science fiction), economic crises, and contra-democratic backlashes curtailing emergent cinemas.

Moment 3: New Indie Cinema (1989–2000)

It is fashionable to claim that the wave of independent cinema called "indie" from the late 1980s throughout the 1990s was incorporated in the mainstream movie business so quickly that it is no more than a blip in the wider scheme of cinema history, a hit-and-run if we stick to our battleground metaphor. But as hit-and-runs come, this one left permanent traces. Gaining momentum since the late 1980s, when, seemingly coincidentally, films without any industry backup to speak of, by young filmmakers unaffiliated with the trench warfare of Hollywood (or similar industries in India, Hong-Kong, or Mexico), or centralized state funding (especially in the European Union, Canada, or Australia) enjoyed success and acclaim. For once, the underlying common thread did not seem to be exhibition or distribution, but a cultural aesthetic: these were films that shared styles and concerns with their audiences. Steven Soderbergh's Cannes prize-winner *Sex, Lies, and Videotape* is usually seen as its symptomatic flag-bearer: small-sized, ironic, immoral, self-reflexive, hip and cool, stylish, hedonistic, noncommitted, challenging (or confusing) gender roles, and filled with doubt and angst.

Before long, the "indies" became associated with the cultural sensitivities of a young and disillusioned post–baby boomer generation, Generation-X: AIDS, paranoia, ennui, rock music, and the impossibility to find true love and meaning in life on a wasted planet. Until 1994, at least, there was no mistaking the momentum of this wave, as evidenced by the films of Hal Hartley, Quentin Tarantino, Richard Linklater, Gus Van Sant, Alyson Anders, Kevin Smith, Todd Haynes, and veterans like Jim Jarmusch, David Lynch, or the Coen Brothers. Nor was it limited to the United States. The films of Atom Egoyan, Patricia Rozema, Pedro Almodovar, Aki Kaurismaaki, Lars Von Trier, the French renaissances of Belgian émigré Chantal Akerman and Polish immigrant Krzysztof Kieslowski, Cyril Collard's *Les nuits fauves*, Eric Rochant's *Un monde sans pitié*, and multiple others all seemed imbued with the same sensibilities. The new "indie" momentum nurtured liberal political efforts, and Anders's, Rozema's, and Akerman's contributions to feminist cinema are a good example of its acute awareness of cultural politics. Next to that, "indies" harbored black, queer, and gay and lesbian cinema of liberation, whose aesthetics of parody, self-awareness, and activist audience role of "reading against the grain" (queering cinema) it encouraged. The films of John Singleton, Spike Lee, Gregg Araki, or Nicole Cohn are integral parts of that effort.

But even as this sort of new liberation rose to prominence, it got tangled up in a sort of middle ground in which its progress was compromised—much faster than any previous independent "wave." Allen J. Scott sees the emergence of a tripartite system of film production, distribution, and consumption as the main cause for this. Up until the 1990s, the realms of independent and mainstream cinema could, at least theoretically, be clearly separated. But since then, synergies, franchising, branching, and multiplatform collaborations had turned the wasteland in between the two (the terrain in between the mainstream's top of the hill, and the independents' bushy lowlands) into a separate area of convergence. Production and distribution companies like Miramax, festivals like Sundance, awards like the Césars, and the Méliès network of genre festivals in Europe all operate in between the two poles, like Bertold Brecht's *Mother Courage* trying to stop the war but ultimately extending it, and increasingly becoming a force in their own right—it even got a name: Indiewood, and it was, again, Steven Soderbergh who was seen as symptomatic of its development. Commentators differ over when exactly Indiewood brought down the "indies," and some argue that its momentum is still alive, surviving the tripartite distinction.

CONCLUSION

With the confusion surrounding the third moment of momentum of "independent" fresh in the public's mind, all debate over whether or not true independent cinema actually exists is conflated and convoluted—impossible to determine amidst the mists on the battlefield. If we try to look to the history of "independent" cinema, it is, however, possible to observe several moments in which, if not the actual existence of "independent" cinema itself, then at least very heated debates *about* and beliefs *in* its existence, can be identified. And that is, after all, what matters: the distinction between independent and mainstream cinema has offered so much food for thought and discussion that its place in the discourse of cinema history and theory is undeniable.

See also Alternative Media in the United States; Bollywood and the Indian Diaspora; Cultural Appropriation; The DVD; Innovation and Imitation in Commercial Media; Online Digital Film and Television; World Cinema.

Further Reading: Bordwell, David, and Kristin Thompson. *Film History; An Introduction,* 2nd ed. New York: McGraw-Hill, 2004; Bowser, Eileen, ed. "The Transformation of Cinema, 1907–1915," vol. 2. In *History of the American Cinema,* 10 vols. New York: Scribners, 1990; Carroll, Noel. *Interpreting the Moving Image.* Cambridge: Cambridge University Press, 1998; Doherty, Thomas. *Pre-Code Hollywood.* New York: Columbia University Press, 1999; Gunning, Tom. "The Cinema of Attractions: Early Film, Its Spectator and the Avant-Garde." In *Early Film,* ed. Thomas Elsaesser and Adam Barker. London: British Film Institute, 1989; King, Geoff. *American Independent Cinema.* London: I. B. Tauris, 2005; Levy, Emmanuel. *Cinema of Outsiders: The Rise of American Independent Film.* New York: New York University Press, 1999; Mathijs, Ernest, and Xavier Mendik, eds. *The Cult Film Reader.* London: Open University Press, 2007; Mathijs, Ernest, and Jamie Sexton. *Cult Cinema, an Introduction.* Oxford: Blackwell, 2008; Mendik, Xavier, and Steve Jay Schneider, eds. *Underground USA: Filmmaking Beyond the Hollywood Canon.* New York: Wallflower, 2000; Pribham, E. Deirdre. *Cinema and Culture; Independent Film in the United States, 1980–2000.* New York: Peter Lang, 2002; Sadoul, Georges. *Histoire du cinéma mondial.* Paris: Flammarion, 1949; Scott, Allen J. "Hollywood and the World: The Geography of Motion-Picture Distribution and Marketing." *Review of International Political Economy* 11, no. 1 (2004): 33–61; Staiger, Janet. *Perverse Spectators: The Practices of Film Reception.* New York: New York University Press, 2000; Staiger, Janet. *Interpreting Films: Studies in the Historical Reception of American Cinema.* Princeton, NJ: Princeton University Press, 1992.

Ernest Mathijs

INNOVATION AND IMITATION IN COMMERCIAL MEDIA

Popular media are often condemned for being repetitive, formulaic, and lacking originality. How accurate are such accusations, or might popular culture be a bit more complex than this generalization? How do innovations emerge from a system of formulas and imitation? And why would so many people find pleasure in media that seem to only offer "more of the same"?

One of the most frequent ways that critics decry a lack of quality and value in popular culture is by accusing mass media of being overly formulaic and repetitive. Such critiques are based on some underlying assumptions: originality is the most valued element of culture, imitation is a sign of creative poverty driven by the industrial nature of popular culture, and true enjoyment can only stem from innovative cultural expressions. While this hierarchy privileging creative originality over formulaic repetition is so widespread to be almost common sense, the actual history of cultural forms suggests that there is a more complex interplay between the processes of innovation and imitation that complicates these basic assumptions.

THE CRITIQUE OF THE CULTURE INDUSTRY

The most profound and influential critique of the imitative nature of popular culture can be attributed to a group of mid-twentieth-century critics typically labeled the Frankfurt School, especially in the work of Theodor Adorno. For Adorno and his colleagues, all of American popular culture—which at the time referred to commercial radio, early Hollywood film, and jazz and popular music as components of a total "culture industry"—was not only perceived as low in aesthetic value, but also contributed to social control and oppression. They believed that popular culture had a numbing, pacifying effect upon its consumers, dulling their critical abilities and potentially enabling the rise of a fascist regime or the continued exploitation of the working class. Adorno offered still-relevant critiques of the standardization of cultural forms, the impact of "pre-digested" media requiring no mental or emotional engagement for consumers, and the "pseudo-individuality" of popular culture that appeared to offer something new. While it is easy to dismiss their broad generalizations as extremely elitist and lacking an understanding of the diversity of popular culture, the Frankfurt School's critical impulse to view popular media as part of a politically dominating culture industry remains powerful and prevalent for media critics decades after their initial writings.

STRATEGIES OF COMMERCIAL CREATIVITY

For many critics of mass culture, there is an inherent conflict between commercial goals and creativity. Within commercial mass media, all decisions are driven, at least in part, by financial and profit motivations. Television networks, film studios, music labels, or other parts of the media industry will rarely invest in creating and distributing a cultural product that they believe will lose money, as such companies must ultimately turn a profit to remain in business. Media industries always consider how a new product fits into established trends, taps into well-known traditions, or offers something familiar to an audience. However, they also realize that merely offering an identical product will not meet consumer demands—people do not want to buy a CD, watch a show, or go see a film that is an exact copy of what they already know. Creating commercially successful mass media involves a delicate balance of offering something familiar along with something new, an alchemy of innovation and imitation.

Cultural industries and the creators working in commercial media rely on many strategies for blending innovation and imitation. *Formula* is a broad and disparaging term, but every medium establishes standards and norms that audiences come to expect. For instance, most media have standard lengths, as pop songs are a few minutes long, television episodes fit 30- and 60-minute timeslots, and feature films run for around two hours. *Genres* are crucial categories that offer assumed structures, themes, styles, imagery, and desired reactions—audiences know what to expect when they watch a sitcom or listen to a country song, and industries try to meet those expectations by adhering to genre conventions. Formulas and genres not only guide the creation of commercial culture, but are used to promote and market new works, reaching out to established audiences looking to find something new but not too different from their established tastes. For critics skeptical of commercial culture, formulas and genres are recipes to limit creativity and innovation, restricting cultural expression to predefined standards and limited possibilities.

Another strategy of commercial culture is to build explicitly upon previous success, such as the widespread proliferation of sequels, prequels, remakes, spin-offs, and clones across media. In the contemporary media landscape, most media production occurs within a few conglomerated corporations that use *synergy* as a strategy to maximize the profits of any successful content across their various media holdings. Thus, a successful comic book like *Batman* will spawn cross-media incarnations across the landscape of the Warner Bros. corporation, spawning feature films, musical soundtracks, animated television adaptations, stories in news magazines, video games, and any other media properties that might tap into the property's established fan base and name recognition. For many critics, such cross-media cloning dominates and crowds out the creative marketplace, eliminating more original works that might not work as well as a video game or action figure.

Other media productions present themselves as original and new works, but use a logic of *recombination*, merging established precedents into new examples—*CSI* combines the detective procedural from *Law & Order* with the scientific investigation from medical dramas, and then spawned a full franchise of spin-off programs mimicking the original formula. And some cultural products do not even hide their lack of originality, as with the proliferation of pop starlets and boy bands who do not deny how they are created by the industry to mimic previous hit makers, with televised programs like *American Idol* and *Making the Band* documenting the imitative process at work. While critics of a more traditionalist perspective see such artificial practices of manufactured celebrity and mass-produced fame as vulgar and distasteful, many viewers and listeners embrace such examples, explicitly embracing the machinery of imitation and the culture industry. Is this a new phenomenon unique to the contemporary media landscape?

THE CYCLE OF IMITATION

Innovations and imitations tend to cycle through commercial media. We can look at the case of reality television in America for an example of a cycle of innovation and imitation at work. Traditionally, prime-time television has offered either fictional scripted programming or public affairs offerings of news and documentaries. In the summer of 2000, CBS aired *Survivor* to surprising ratings success, triggering a wave of reality programs across the prime-time schedule. *Survivor* itself was not a fully original offering, as it was a remake of a Swedish program, and the reality format itself had clear precedents in the game show genre and with earlier programs like *The Real World* and *Cops*. Yet once CBS struck ratings gold through this innovative recombination of previous programming and Americanization of European formats, all networks and cable channels began to imitate *Survivor* under the new label of "reality television." Many subsequent programs emerged by remaking European hits (like *The Mole* and *American Idol*), or by combining *Survivor*'s competitive elimination structure in new scenarios (like *The Amazing Race* or *The Bachelor*). Often such genre cycles emerge quickly in response to an innovative hit, but flame out from oversaturation of imitations that fail to capture the pleasures of the original. Certainly many of these reality television imitations were short-lived, pale comparisons to what appealed to viewers initially about *Survivor*, but many offered new pleasures and potential ways for audiences to engage with a form of programming that felt innovative, even if it was developed through imitation. Thus despite the predictions of critics and many industry executives in 2000, the reality television trend has persisted for years, becoming a new staple of prime-time programming across the world.

A HISTORY OF IMITATION

While many critics decry today's media industries as nothing more than a factory for creating identically shallow cultural products, a more careful look at the relationship between creativity and imitation complicates this simple condemnation. Throughout the history of literature, music, and other art forms, imitation has been a central facet of creative expression. The early landmarks of Western culture, Greek drama and poetry, were nearly all retellings of well-known myths and histories, not original creations emerging from a singular creative genius. Shakespeare based nearly all of his plays on other dramatic works and historical myths, making each masterpiece in some way an "imitation" of a previous work. Classical music is similarly based upon a number of established "formulas" for structuring works, adhering to dance forms or building upon a previous composer's themes and styles. Renaissance art offered "remakes" of the same Biblical and historical scenes, and the model of artistic apprenticeship encouraged artists to learn to imitate and "clone" previous works and styles. In these examples, artistry arises not from sheer originality, but through the ability to express preestablished forms and stories in new ways, offering innovation through combination and alteration, not the singular creation of unique and unprecedented works.

Popular culture similarly thrives on this logic of imitation yielding creativity. Popular music legends like the Beatles and the Who built upon preexisting forms of blues and rock 'n' roll to offer something new in the way they adapted well-established models into their own style, later incorporating external influences like Indian music and operatic structures. Film masterpieces like *The Godfather* series revisited the traditions of gangster films, but inflected them with ideas about American immigration and capitalist business models—just as *The Sopranos* reworked *The Godfather* mythos by incorporating elements of suburban family drama and psychoanalysis. The entire musical genre of hip-hop is based upon a process of building upon previous works through the act of sampling, resulting in creative reworkings of an entire history of music through an aesthetic of remixing, imitation, and commentary. These and many other truly innovative examples of popular culture offer creativity as *synthetic*, building upon established models and traditions, not a romantic myth of originality detached from previous cultural works.

Instead of being directly opposed to innovation, imitation might be seen as a complementary process, present within nearly all modes of creative practice.

In fact, pure innovations that wildly diverge from existing norms and traditions are often difficult for audiences to understand and respond to, as they seem too detached from the cultural expectations that go along with any medium. Such radical innovations rarely emerge in commercial culture, belonging to an avant-garde aesthetic that addresses a narrow and elite niche of media consumers. More influential innovations come from reworking the well-known and common elements of our shared popular culture, whether it is *Fargo*'s playful take on crime film conventions or the thematic mixture of teen drama and horror film in *Buffy the Vampire Slayer*.

THE PLEASURES OF IMITATION

Why might audiences seek out cultural forms that are overtly imitative rather than original forms? One key motivation is to manage expectations, as a viewer wants to anticipate what they'll encounter in something new—we want to know when we see a film whether we are likely to laugh at or be scared by the events on the screen. Likewise, we take comfort in knowing that a television episode will offer a short narrative to be resolved by the end of the hour, guaranteeing storytelling closure following expected conventions. Even beyond genre and structural expectations, there is a distinct pleasure to be had in viewing the familiar and comfortable, knowing that something new will resemble other pleasurable experiences. People become fans of a certain genre or style, coming to appreciate the nuances and subtle differences between similar programs or songs—for a fan of dance music, romance novels, slasher films, or soap operas, there are tremendous distinctions between different examples of what might seem mere clones to a novice audience member. Finally, creators and audiences both enjoy working within the parameters of conventions, exploring how media can simultaneously adhere to established structures and offer something new within the confines of genres and formulas.

Innovation and imitation are thus not mutually exclusive practices, nor can we view one as innately more valuable or pleasurable than the other. However, we can not deny that many imitations in popular media, perhaps even the majority of them, are failures, falling short of their object of mimicry and offering nothing creative beyond the act of cloning. But we cannot attribute such failures to the imitative process itself, as many original innovations fail as well, offering new ideas and forms that cannot deliver on their ambitions or meet audience expectations. Both innovation and imitation have important roles to play both within the creative process and the way that consumers engage with popular culture. As creators, consumers, and critics, we need to think carefully about the balance between these two impulses, and recognize the important roles that both practices offer to our understanding, appreciation, and critical analysis of commercial media, not reducing imitation and innovation to a simplistic hierarchy of value.

See also Cultural Appropriation; Hypercommercialism; Narrative Power and Media Influence; Ratings; Reality Television; Runaway Productions and the

Globalization of Hollywood; Transmedia Storytelling and Media Franchises; World Cinema.

Further Reading: Adorno, Theodor. *The Culture Industry: Selected Essays on Mass Culture.* London: Routledge, 1991; Altman, Rick. *Film/Genre.* London: BFI Publishing, 1999; duGay, Paul, ed. *Production of Culture/Cultures of Production.* London: Sage, 1997; Gitlin, Todd. *Inside Prime Time.* New York: Pantheon Books, 1985; Gray, Jonathan. *Television Entertainment.* New York: Routledge, 2008; Hartley, John, ed. *Creative Industries.* Malden, MA: Blackwell Publishing, 2005; Hesmondhalgh, David. *The Cultural Industries.* Thousand Oaks, CA: Sage, 2002; Mittell, Jason. *Genre and Television: From Cop Shows to Cartoons in American Culture.* New York: Routledge, 2004; Murray, Susan, and Laurie Ouellette, eds. *Reality TV: Remaking of Television Culture.* New York: New York University Press, 2004; Neale, Steve. *Genre and Hollywood.* New York: Routledge, 2000; Negus, Keith. *Music Genres and Corporate Cultures.* London: Routledge, 1999; Steinert, Heinz. *Culture Industry.* Cambridge: Polity, 2003; Wyatt, Justin. *High Concept: Movies and Marketing in Hollywood.* Austin: University of Texas Press, 1994.

Jason Mittell

INTERNET AND ITS RADICAL POTENTIAL

As cyberspace becomes interwoven with the developmental life of individuals, their cultures, and their societies, the Internet increasingly coordinates and structures communications. Social scientists and humanities researchers debate how and whether the Internet reinforces existing power relationships, or frees up sociality from entrenched controls. This article offers a social history of the Internet. In the process, it explores the Internet's "radical potential" for transformative social change.

Networking and electronic messaging lay on the fringes of geek subculture for decades before the Internet introduced cyberspace to American consumer culture. The Internet was once the esoteric domain of information scientists working in the U.S. military industrial complex in the 1960s. Its subsequent exploration and development by visionary technologists with communitarian ideals (the so-called New Communalists) exposed some radical potentials of networking for communications. However, the takeover of the Internet by consolidated media and telecom companies threatens to transform the Internet into another mass media platform.

OPEN NETWORKS BASED IN MILITARY TECHNOLOGIES

The early Internet was developed to be a "dead man's switch" for nuclear retaliation against a first strike by the USSR. Military, industrial, and academic collaborations on early digital networking supported the Internet's development. The stockpiling and preparation of a continual nuclear deterrent was at the center of the U.S. Cold War strategy. After 1953, both the United States and the Soviet Union maintained thermonuclear weapons deliverable via bombers, and later, via intercontinental ballistic missiles. The tenuous balance of the peace hinged upon the deterrent effect of a "mutually assured destruction" (MAD) that would be reliably delivered by the opponent's returned strike. But, owing to false alarms, technical malfunctions, and deficiencies in the AT&T network that made fail-safe communications unworkable, MAD was a giant accident waiting to happen. The command and control system needed strong reliability that could be provided by digital communications networks.

DARPA

The United States created the Advanced Research Projects Agency and the Defense Advanced Research Projects Agency (ARPA and DARPA) in 1958 to develop responses to the Sputnik satellite launch by the USSR. ARPANET was the prototype of today's Internet, and adopted packet switching in 1973 for creating "interlinking packet networks" (Cerf, n.d.). This project developed TCP (Transmission Control Protocol) and IP (Internet Protocol), the system of basic protocols for the Internet, around which new protocols are still developed. The ARPANET and the early electronic data networks bypassed the vulnerabilities of the circuit-switched, analog AT&T telephone system. "Packet switching" broke up continuous messages into standardized chunks, and distributed them through the network in a more efficient way that also provided a more reliable alternative to circuit-switched telecommunications systems available through AT&T. The best feature of the ARPANET was that the system could continue to operate even if a portion of the network was disabled or destroyed. Technically, today's Internet is an elaboration of ARPANET—a software protocol and communications convention for passing standardized packets of data across heterogeneous and interconnected computer networks.

DARPA's mission was, and remains, "to assure that the U.S. maintains a lead in applying state-of-the-art technology for military capabilities and to prevent technological surprise from her adversaries" (DARPA 2003). DARPA cultivates flat organization, flexible roles, "autonomy and freedom from bureaucratic impediments," technical and scientific expertise, and managers who "have always been freewheeling zealots in pursuit of their goals" (DARPA 2006). The ARPANET's development as an information-sharing system, in addition to being a command-and-control system, reflects DARPA's culture of sharing information. J.C.R. Licklider of MIT envisioned a knowledge management project in 1962 that he called the "Galactic Network" that could be enabled through networking: As Barry Leiner and colleagues (2006) explain, "He envisioned a globally interconnected set of computers through which everyone could quickly access data and programs from any site." Licklider and others contributed to the notion of hypertext that was already behind Vannevar Bush's notion of the "memex" machine.

PACKET SWITCHING

Paul Baran, an innovator in packet switching, explains that the ARPANET was not designed merely to survive a first strike by the USSR, nor just to carry the launch orders for a retaliatory second strike against the USSR, but to convince the Soviet military leaders that a reliable and automatic mechanism existed to deliver the retaliation. The creation of redundant paths for packets to reach intended receivers, even if a part of the network is disabled, was the feature of the ARPANET that made it superior to circuit switching on the telephony model. The techniques of open network architectures and signaling were debated publicly by technologists at ARPA and the RAND Corporation (a U.S. defense contractor), in hopes that the Soviets would learn of the U.S. system and also adopt it. In other words, in spite of the paranoia and secrecy surrounding the Cold War military industrial complex, "our whole plan, the concept of packet switching and all the details, was wide open. Not only did Rand publish it, they sent it to all the repository laboratories around the world" (Baran, in Brand 2001).

MOVING BEYOND THE MILITARY INDUSTRIAL COMPLEX

The Internet's growth beyond the military industrial complex was spurred by the U.S. National Science Foundation (NSF), which subsidized connectivity for research universities and other knowledge centers while providing linkages for international networks. The NSFNET "backbone" that was designed to carry bulk Internet traffic was initiated in 1986 and added onto later by NASA and the Department of Energy. International networks such as NORDUNET, BITNET, and EARN connected European academic institutions. BITNET merged with other academic networks into the Corporation for Research and Educational Networking (CREN). Consortia arrangements developed independently of these organizations as new federal and state governments, municipal governments, and corporate members developed "peering" relationships to share growing traffic loads collaboratively.

Despite repeated claims by the United States that democratic and global governance of the Internet is just around the corner, the U.S. Department of Commerce (DOC) still retains formal control over the "root" of the Internet, which is the cluster of servers that maps domain names to unique Internet protocol addresses (such that typing www.prwatch.org takes you to IP address 209.197.113.33). The Internet Corporation for Assigned Names and Numbers (ICANN) manages the creation of top-level domain names and country code domain names and the accreditation of domain name registrars. As there can be only one authoritative root server, the ICANN's proxy management of domain names for the DOC keeps the United States in charge of "ruling the root." The ICANN also settles disputes involving the registration of trademarked names in "cyber-squatting" battles. Other global organizations contribute to Internet governance. The Internet Society is an nongovernmental organization that promotes technology development conducive to open standards, protocols, and administration of the Internet. It has been instrumental in providing training and education while collaborating to establish servers and connectivity in countries around the world.

CONTEMPORARY SOCIAL AND CULTURAL ASPECTS

The discovery of "cyberspace" by the popular press in the early 1990s occurred as an important genre of science fiction, such as the cyberpunk writing of

William Gibson, who was attaining subculture status in North America. While the liminal experience of cyberspace in cyberpunk science fiction was dystopian and difficult to hype, another technoculture that was more amenable to the popular press portrayed cyberspace as an "electronic frontier." John Perry Barlow, Stuart Brand, and other denizens of the WELL electronic bulletin board network joined publishers of *Wired* magazine to cultivate and court the "Digital Generation."

Personal computers with modems and software applications such as the Mosaic Web browser permitted a mass market for Internet-ready machines by 1995. E-mail was a "killer app" that hooked new users. The development of the free and open-source Linux operating system and the Apache Web server software platform enabled low-cost Web presence for Web page publishers; and popular search engines, message boards, and chat rooms provided a sense of direction in cyberspace for new (or "newbie") users. The "Internet Christmas" of 1998 inaugurated a takeoff phase for the diffusion of the Internet, as personal computer makers bundled systems with user accounts for AOL and other Internet service providers (ISPs). Internet Christmas signaled that the unruly potentials of the Internet had been tamed for "e-commerce," and that commercialization would proceed apace without excessive risk of regulatory interference.

TECHNOLOGY AND POLICY

Telecommunications policy and intellectual property law reforms in the United States were implemented to promote private capitalization of the Internet. Federal policy makers exploited the utopian rhetorics of cyberspace to promote the Internet as a commercial mass medium on the U.S. model of private ownership. The Telecommunications Act of 1996 accomplished a large-scale deregulation of information services to promote commercialization, even as it attempted (unsuccessfully) to impose harsh censorship via the "Communications Decency Act." Networking was protected from public interest regulation, which gave upstart hardware and software developers more leeway in competing with established media and telecom companies while providing incentives for established players to develop new business models largely free of regulations.

Policy makers set the commercialization trajectory early in the Clinton administration during the "National Information Infrastructure" (NII) discussions organized by Vice President Albert Gore. This program unlocked markets for carrying traffic and for providing content. The administration expanded the NII principles globally to the "Global Information Infrastructure" (GII) guidelines, as the "content" industries pressed for unprecedented intellectual property protections in what became the Digital Millennium Copyright Act (DMCA) in the United States and the multilateral rules of the World Intellectual Property Organization (WIPO). The DMCA, more than any other legislation, helped effect a "transition from an incentive model of copyright to a control model" that has roiled the Internet's cultures of sharing and gift economies ever since.

AL GORE'S INTERNET?

During the Clinton administration, Vice President Albert Gore organized the "National Information Infrastructure" (NII) discussions that led to the commercialization of the Internet. The accelerated delivery of Internet technology to a mass public created the World Wide Web among other services, and the Internet rose to occupy a major place in the national imagination. When published reports quoted Al Gore as saying, "I invented the Internet," the phrase was considered an outrageous exaggeration, and he was roundly criticized for attempting to take credit for the most important technological development of the century. A few years later, during his bid for the White House in the presidential elections of 2000, he appeared on the David Letterman show and in a comedy routine, presented a Top Ten list of presidential slogans that had been rejected by the Gore/Lieberman ticket. One of the rejected campaign slogans was, "Remember folks, I invented the Internet and I can take it away." Gore received a hearty applause for his self-mocking script, though he did not become the 43rd president of the United States, and the controversy still plagues him.

INCREASING LEGAL BOUNDARIES

The failure of Napster to defend a business model based on peer-to-peer file sharing set an important precedent for digital distribution of media. The *MGM v. Grokster* case decided in 2005 by the U.S. Supreme Court benefited the content industries by exposing technology companies to damages from "secondary liability" for copyright infringement. While it did not go quite so far as to overturn the landmark Sony Betamax ruling, which protected multipurpose information technology designers and also the rights of fair use, the ruling created a new "inducement" doctrine for copyright that introduces new risks to technology innovators whose creations imperil established technology standards and business models. These precedents have eroded the Internet's ability to disrupt the system of intellectual property ownership dominated by a handful of transnational corporations.

A "WALLED GARDEN"?

Once the "content industries" had tamed the Internet to their liking, telecom carriers began to press for the ability to impose price discrimination on packets received from competing services. The operation of Internet service "tiers" for prioritized access and distribution of data departs dramatically from the "network neutrality" principles by which telecom carriers and ISPs have handled traffic traditionally. Cyberlibertarians, media reformers, and consumer groups are alarmed by attempts to erode and bypass these conventions. Federal Communications Commission (FCC) Commissioner Michael Copps is critical of the "access tiering" anticipated as media conglomerates try to extract fees "from anyone who wants to reach their millions of customers.... A handful of broadband barons is poised to destroy what is so precious about the Internet." Such a structure would allow one or two companies to provide the "last mile" of

Internet connection to virtually all American homes." Citizens' access and free speech rights, and equal access to broadband Internet services may be affected by policy-making (or lack of policy-making) at the FCC and in Congress. As the content industries and the telecom giants press for the right to limit competitors' access to their own broadband infrastructures, "netizen" activists are formalizing a federal network neutrality policy.

As access tiering by monopoly or oligopoly ISPs looms as an industry norm, would-be challengers to their market power have been handicapped by the U.S. courts. In a 2005 case that strengthened the hand of the telecom conglomerates, the U.S. Supreme Court removed the ability of Congress or the FCC to require cable broadband networks to interconnect competitive broadband Internet providers. Since the U.S. Supreme Court decided the "Brand X" case, the cable operators offering broadband modems and the telcos offering DSL are legally sanctioned to deny potential competitors access to their customers by network interconnection. As the content industries can now safely enjoy monopolistic rent-seeking privileges online, so too the carriers have become sanctioned gateway monopolists extracting rents through the exercise of immense "network power." Absent effective public interest regulation and network neutrality rules, the next phase of consolidation between media and telecom companies is likely to be massive cross-ownership of broadband content providers and carriers, who will provide "walled gardens" of branded content, with limited or no access to unaffiliated parts of the Web. They will privatize the benefits of an open network, while imposing new social costs, such as closed standards, anticompetitive business practices, greater privacy risks, and continuing erosion of fair use and equitable access to infrastructures.

CONCLUSION

The radical potential of the Internet to overturn long-established power structures has been tempered by deep changes in legal norms, concentrated market power of the major players, and new techniques for harnessing digital culture industries and locking down digital culture. The Cold War history of the Internet demonstrates that, in the end, technocrats privileged the values of openness, interdependence, and decentralization in a survivalist strategy for a different age. These principles, expressed by an open Internet, are eroding, as are peaceful alternatives to nuclear proliferation in an increasingly dangerous world. While cyberspace may not yet completely reflect the values and norms of North American mass society and consumer culture, and still retains alternative and diverse potentials, the rationalization and commercial pressures on the Internet exerted by the economy and the state are broad and deep.

Knowing that corporate colonization of the Internet is, in the end, negotiable, a variety of activist movements are pushing back with proposals for policies on net neutrality, competitive access, community networking, and a reformed copyright and patent framework. Grievances expressed about privacy violations by state and corporate actors are accumulating in court claims coordinated by nonprofits like Electronic Privacy Information Clearinghouse (EPIC) and Electronic

Frontier Foundation (EFF). Cyberliberties activists still use the Internet for bridge-building between students, researchers, artists, programmers, nonprofits, and other beneficiaries of the "free culture" that is enriched and made accessible in cyberspace. Other varieties of resistance to corporate colonization of the Internet include "hacktivism," culture jamming, and academic research of digital copy protections. The conflicts over corporate penetration of cyberspace illustrate how struggles over new-media technologies are connected to larger issues of social and economic equity, peace, human rights, and freedom of expression. The economic and political changes proposed to resolve these Internet issues will reflect the broader social commitment to the values of freedom and openness.

See also Alternative Media in the United States; Blogosphere; Conglomeration and Media Monopolies; Digital Divide; iTunes Effects; Media Reform; Net Neutrality; Obscenity and Indecency; Online Publishing; Piracy and Intellectual Property; Presidential Stagecraft and Militainment; Regulating the Airwaves; Surveillance and Privacy.

Further Reading: Aufderheide, Patricia. "Telecommunications and the Public Interest." In *Conglomerates and the Media,* ed. Erik Barnouw, Richard M. Cohen, Thomas Frank, Todd Gitlin, David Lieberman, Mark Crispin Miller, Gene Roberts, Thomas Schatz, and Patricia Aufderheide. New York: The New Press. 1998; Brand, Stewart. "Founding Father." *Wired* 9, no. 3 (March 2001). http://www.wired.com/wired/archive/9.03/baran. html; Burkart, Patrick, and Tom McCourt. *Digital Music Wars: Ownership and Control of the Celestial Jukebox.* Lanham: Rowman and Littlefield. 2006; Bush, Vannevar. "As We May Think." *The Atlantic Monthly* (July 1945). http://www.theatlantic.com/doc/194507/ bush; Cerf, Vinton G. "A Brief History of the Internet and Related Networks." http:// www.isoc.org/internet/history/cerf.shtml; Copps, Michael. "Media Mergers Are Damaging American Democracy." *The Financial Times*, June 21, 2006, p. 17; DARPA. "Darpa over the Years." October 27, 2003. http://www.darpa.mil/body/overtheyears.html; EFF [Electronic Frontier Foundation]. *MGM v. Grokster.* http://www.eff.org/IP/P2P/MGM_ v_Grokster; Gibson, William. *Neuromancer.* New York: Ace Books, 1986; ICANN [Internet Corporation for Assigned Names and Numbers]. FAQs. October 25, 2006. http://www.icann.org/faq/#udrp; Leiner, Barry M., Vinton G. Cerf, David D. Clark, Robert E. Kahn, Leonard Kleinrock, Daniel C. Lynch, Jon Postel, Larry G. Roberts, and Stephen Wolff. "A Brief History of the Internet, Part I." 1997. http://www.isoc.org/oti/ articles/0597/leiner.html; Lessig, Lawrence. *Free Culture: The Nature and Future of Creativity.* New York: Penguin Books, 2005; Mueller, Milton. *Ruling the Root: Internet Governance and the Taming of Cyberspace.* Cambridge, MA: MIT Press, 2002; Sassen, Saskia. Digital Networks and Power. In *Spaces of Culture,* ed., Mike Featherstone and Scott Lash, 49–63. London: Sage, 1999; Schiller, Dan. *Digital Capitalism.* Cambridge: Harvard University Press, 1999; Smith, Isaac. "Public Policy and the Brand X Decision." Paper, 2006. http://www.freepress.net/news/18803; Taylor, Paul A. "From Hackers to Hacktivists: Speed Bumps on the Global Superhighway?" *New Media and Society* 7, no. 5 (2005): 625–46; Turner, Fred. *From Counterculture to Cyberculture: Stewart Brand, the Whole Earth Network, and the Rise of Digital Utopianism.* Chicago: University of Chicago Press, 2006; von Lohmann, Fred. "Remedying 'Grokster.'" Law.com. 2005. http://www.law. com/jsp/article.jsp?id=1122023112436; Winston, Brian. *Media Technology and Society: A History from the Telegraph to the Internet.* New York: Routledge, 1998.

Patrick Burkart

ISLAM AND THE MEDIA

Particularly in the aftermath of 9/11, the U.S. media's methods of representing Islam, Arabs, and people of Middle Eastern descent have been the subject of much criticism. Critics have argued that the media's representational strategies have deteriorated, going from bad to worse. The dominant pattern of American media representations of Islam has a long history, stretching back beyond recent film, television, and news reports to earlier traveler's tales and colonial endeavors.

HISTORICAL BACKGROUND

Historically, there has been little direct contact between the United States and the region of the world where Islam grew and flourished, that is, the Middle East and North Africa. In the nineteenth century, there were occasional travelers to the region, such as Mark Twain and Herman Melville, and brief military interventions in North Africa. Thus, unlike various European colonial powers, such as Britain and France, the United States did not have a sustained presence or direct involvement with the world of Islam. As a result, knowledge that was produced in the United States of this region, and of Islam, was of an abstract and second hand nature.

Media representations of the Middle East drew heavily from European vocabularies. In early film this meant characterizing the Middle East by a few handy caricatures—vast desert spaces, populated by scimitar-wielding sheiks wearing long white robes, who lived in huge palaces with harems and dancing girls, and were surrounded by snake charmers and flying carpets.

It was only after World War II that the United States turned its attention to the Middle East and became a dominant force in the region. In this context, knowledge had to be produced to help the United States better achieve its foreign policy objectives. Various "area studies" programs were founded after World War II and the Middle East became a subject of inquiry.

ORIENTALIST SCHOLARSHIP AND MODERNIZATION THEORY

Many distinguished scholars from Europe traveled across the Atlantic to take leadership positions at universities in the United States. The end result was the production of at least two ways of understanding the world of Islam: European Orientalist scholarship, and the research conducted from a social scientific approach. The latter championed *modernization theory,* and argued that developing nations could advance by modernizing their economies with the assistance of the United States. By and large, the news media covered the Middle East during this period in ways similar to the rest of the world, they followed the modernization frameworks set by policy makers. Within the context of the Cold War, the U.S. capitalist/modernizing view was held as being superior to the Communist ideology of the Soviet Union. While Islam made an occasional appearance, it was not until the 1970s that it would be a subject of sustained attention.

Orientalist scholars have long viewed the Middle East through the lens of an imaginary construct called "Islam." Edward Said, a prominent critic of Western practices of conceiving and creating ideas about Islam, argues that this image of Islam has little to do with reality and the ways in which Islam is practiced around the world, and more to do with the justifications that were needed by various empires to continue their domination of the region. Islam and the West were counter posed as two separate and distinct entities. In this rhetoric, the West is associated with freedom, democracy, women's rights, liberty, civilization, and Christianity. The world of Islam, its polar opposite, is seen as evil, barbaric, uncivilized, unscientific, and home to a people who hate freedom and are irrational. Thus, it was argued that the superior West should colonize and civilize the backward peoples of the world of Islam.

Said also argued that the common caricature of Islam created a sense of regional identity for Europe and the West, via a process known as *othering,* whereby an individual or group takes all the qualities that they do not wish to be associated with them and attaches these to another individual or group, allowing a seeming contrast to be constructed that flatters the individual or group doing the othering. This false binary was particularly convenient for colonizing forces in drawing attention away from their own systematized acts of barbarism and of suppressing and denying personal freedoms that regularly accompanied the process of colonization and control.

THE 1970s: THE OIL CRISIS AND THE IRANIAN REVOLUTION

The Orientalist view of the Middle East was one among many within the academy and the media. However, since the 1970s it has become the dominant perspective. And since the events of September 11, 2001 it has received a further boost. In the 1970s, two events set the stage for how the Middle East would be understood in the United States. The first was the oil crisis of 1973–74 and the second was the Iranian revolution of 1979. Before the oil embargo instituted by the Oil Producing and Exporting Countries (OPEC), the term Islam barely existed in the culture and in the media. When, all of a sudden, oil prices rose precipitously it was a sharp reminder that oil and energy resources were not "ours" for the taking but rather, according to the rhetoric of the time, were controlled by irrational Muslim men in white robes. Various films, such as *Network*, drew on this theme of rich and powerful sheiks out to control the United States and the world.

Following this event, coverage of the Middle East focused on various crises in the region. The world of Islam, which had largely been marginal to the media, became news worthy in the context of political crises. These included the civil war in Lebanon, the war between Ethiopia and Somalia, the Soviet invasion of Afghanistan, and perhaps most importantly the Arab-Israeli conflict. With the United States squarely in Israel's camp, the Palestinian struggle for national liberation came to be viewed through the rubric of terrorism. The news and entertainment media would largely reflect the view held by political elites.

The most dramatic event, however, that thrust Islam into the spotlight was the 1979 Iranian revolution, which brought the Muslim cleric Ayatollah Khomeini to power. The media presented the revolution as a religiously driven movement that unseated the pro-Western Shah. In reality, it was a popular uprising sparked by many factors including the Shah's rampant corruption and use of intimidation and violence to silence critics. Workers, women, students, and other forces held demonstrations and strikes to demand economic and political justice. Khomeini was able to finally assert control of the movement two years later, and only because he proved most adept at maneuvering between the various forces. Yet, in the United States this popular uprising was seen as a medieval yearning on the part of the Iranian people to found an Islamist state. When students took over the U.S. embassy in Tehran and held U.S. personnel hostage in response to the United States giving sanctuary to the Shah, they were presented as violent, dangerous, and virulently anti-American. Two images that were used frequently by the news media were angry mobs burning U.S. flags, and the stern face of the bearded and turbaned Ayatollah Khomeini.

Images of Islam as violent and dangerous were exacerbated by domestic events, particularly media depictions of the Nation of Islam during their involvement in civil rights protests in the United States. News reports in the late 1950s and 1960s, such as Mike Wallace's report for CBS, *The Hate That Hate Produced*, often constructed The Nation of Islam's message as one of hate, intolerance, and "revenge," and their spokespersons Malcolm X, Elijah Muhammad, and later Louis Farrakhan as dangerous and irrational radicals. Thus, even far from the shores of the Middle East, Islam was viewed with suspicion and depicted as wedded to a philosophy of conflict. Furthermore, since the civil rights era, media reports and retrospectives have often belittled the Nation of Islam's prominent role in the struggle for racial equality, and have marginalized their voice in American politics.

However, not all parties of political Islam were viewed as irrational and dangerous. This is because at various points the United States has supported Islamist groups when they have proved as effective means to weaken leftist and secular groups. For instance, the United States supported the Muslim Brotherhood in Egypt and viewed the group as a bulwark against the secular nationalist President Gamal Abdel Nasser. Similarly, when the Soviet Union invaded Afghanistan in 1979, the United States supported, trained, and funded the Islamist Mujahideen fighters. The film, *Rambo III*, is dedicated to the Mujahideen "freedom fighters."

MUSLIM BAD GUYS

The Islamic "bad guy" has become a stock character in Hollywood television and film. More recently, it is the pervasive image of the Arab terrorist that we see, in films such as *True Lies* and *The Siege* and in television shows such as *24*. But even before the terrorist depiction, there were films such as *Midnight Express* that suggested a cultural disposition and proclivity toward violence, repression, and injustice by stranding the protagonists in a Turkish prison, where torture and chaos reign. Disney's *Aladdin* even begins with a song whose lyrics note of Arabia, "They cut off your ear / If they don't like your face. / It's barbaric, but hey, it's home." The Hollywood association between Muslims and danger has become so solidified a link that even films without Muslim characters can wheel them in to create a sense of danger, as for instance with the brief threat of Arab terrorists that bookends *Back to the Future*, or as in *The Insider*, a film about the American tobacco industry, in which the credentials of Al Pacino's Lowell Bergman as a fearless reporter are established during the opening credits by showing him blindfolded and surrounded by threatening Arabs taking him to interview the leader of a terrorist organization in Lebanon. Meanwhile, on television, Children Now's "Fall Colors: Prime Time Diversity Report" reveals that in the 2003–2004 season, 46 percent of all Arab/Middle Eastern characters on prime time entertainment programs were criminals (compared to 15 percent of Asian/Pacific Islanders, 10 percent of African Americans, and 5 percent of White characters), thereby leaving few other images to contradict the landslide of news and entertainment depictions of the Muslim bad guy (See http://publications. childrennow.org/assets/pdf/cmp/fall-colors-03/fall-colors-03-v5.pdf).

POST 9/11

Since 9/11, the demonization of Islam and of Muslims has only intensified. One of the justifications for the U.S. invasion of Afghanistan was the liberation of Afghan women. This rationale has a long history in Orientalist rhetoric, and asserts that Muslim women need to be rescued from Muslim men by White men who better understand their interests. In reality, the condition for most Afghan women, particularly those in the rural areas, only deteriorated after the U.S. war.

Domestically, thousands of Muslims and Arab Americans have been detained, harassed, and deported since 2001. Such blatant violations of civil liberties are justified by the argument that security threats must be quelled at any cost. Television shows like *24* and *Sleeper Cell* reinforce the idea that there are enemies in our midst who must be vanquished through any means necessary. The news media have failed to expose the injustices faced by Muslims and have, for the most part, accepted the so-called war on terror rhetoric. After 9/11, images of Middle Eastern men were constantly shown on television, identified as Islamic extremists and terrorists. Image and identifier merged and were generalized, helping to codify Islam and terrorism in the eyes of the public, an association that already existed in popular films and media depictions. At its root, this rhetoric casts the world into two camps: the side that represents civilization, democracy, and rationality and the side that is intent on violence, destruction and the creation of an Islamic state—Islam vs. the West. In many ways, the rhetoric in the media has come full circle reflecting some of the key themes developed by early Orientalist scholarship in the nineteenth century, in the process alienating and vilifying Arabs, Arab-Americans, and other people of Middle Eastern descent.

See also Al-Jazeera; Bias and Objectivity; Hypercommercialism; Parachute Journalism; Paparazzi and Photographic Ethics; Propaganda Model; Representations of Race; Sensationalism, Fear Mongering, and Tabloid Media; World Cinema.

Further Reading: Bernstein, Matthew, and Gaylyn Studlar, eds. *Visions of the East: Orientalism in Film*. New Brunswick, NJ: Rutgers University Press, 1997; Esposito, John. *The*

Islamic Threat: Myth or Reality, 3rd ed. New York: Oxford University Press, 1999; Loch-
man, Zachary. *Contending Visions of the Middle East: The History and Politics of Orientalism.* New York: Cambridge University Press, 2004; Media Education Foundation. *Reel
Bad Arabs* (film). Northhampton, MA, 2004; Philo, Greg, Mike Berry, and the Glasgow
Media Group. *Bad News From Israel.* London: Pluto, 2004; Rodinson, Maxime. *Europe
and the Mystique of Islam.* London: I.B. Tauris, 2002; Said, Edward. *Orientalism.* New
York: Vintage, 1978; Said, Edward. *Covering Islam: How the Media and Experts Deter-
mine How We See the Rest of the World.* New York: Vintage, 1997; Shaheen, Jack G. *Reel
Bad Arabs: How Hollywood Villifies a People.* Northhampton, MA: Interlink, 2001; Steet,
Linda. *Veils and Daggers: A Century of National Geographic's Representation of the Arab
World.* Philadelphia: Temple University Press, 2000.

Deepa Kumar

THE iTUNES EFFECT

Apple's iPod digital player and iTunes music service presently dominate the
online music industry. Apple has kept its position by maintaining tight control
over its players and services, but many of its innovations have been adopted by
competitors at lower prices. Will the future see a continuation of Apple's policy
of offering individual downloads, or will alternatives emerge?

With the slogan "Rip, Mix, Burn," Apple introduced its iPod portable music
player in October 2001. The slogan referred to the ability of Apple computers to copy music and create customized CDs. Record company executives
were appalled, arguing that they were losing millions of dollars a year to illegal
downloads. They claimed that the slogan was an invitation to steal copyrighted
material. But the slogan was consistent with Apple's "Think Different" strategy, a
strategy that has paid handsome dividends.

Since it was founded in the late 1970s, Apple has cultivated an image of a
company that is "different." Cofounder Steve Jobs initially suggested that its

---

DIGITAL RIGHTS MANAGEMENT

Digital technologies allow a potentially limitless number of copies to be made that are identical to the original. To thwart this, Apple's iTunes service, as well as all the online services
that provide authorized content from the four major record companies, includes digital
rights management (DRM) in its files. DRM takes two forms: encryption, which allows only
authorized users to play back files by requiring them to purchase an electronic "key"; and
watermarking, an "electronic fingerprinting" technology which restricts copying to a limited
number of players and copies and also enables files to be traced back to their original users.
Both DRM components were given force of law by the Digital Millennium Copyright Act
(DMCA) of 1998. The DMCA made it a crime to bypass DRM, even if we make copies for
personal, noncommercial use after purchasing an original copy of a CD, DVD, or digital file.
A comprehensive DRM system, such as Apple's Fairplay system, covers the entire life cycle of
products, from mastering to manufacturing to distribution to playback.

---

computers be encased in exotic hardwoods, and a famous 1984 Super Bowl ad introducing Macintosh computers implicitly compared Apple's competitors to Big Brother. Apple has aggressively promoted a branded "digital lifestyle" throughout its history. The company's products are noted for innovative hardware and software that is easy to use. Among other things, Apple introduced the mouse, the graphic user interface, color monitors, and laser printers into personal computing.

Despite these innovations, Apple has captured less than 2 percent of the global market for personal computers. Why is this the case? Apple has kept control over its computer operating system, rather than licensing it to other manufacturers (except for a brief, unsuccessful experiment in the mid-1980s). From its inception, Apple rejected the component model followed by its competitors in favor of an end-to-end business model that binds hardware and software into a complete package. The *Wall Street Journal* explained the difference:

> In the component model, many companies make hardware and software that runs on a standard platform, creating inexpensive commodity devices that don't always work perfectly together, but get the job done. In the end-to-end model, one company designs both the hardware and software, which work smoothly together, but the products cost more and limit choice. (Mossberg 2006)

Apple introduced its iPod digital music player in October 2001 for $399, and the dangling white cords of its headphones quickly became a status symbol. By August 2005, an estimated 21 million iPods had been sold, accounting for one-third of Apple's overall revenues. A month later, in September, Apple unveiled a lower-priced version, the iPod Nano. The *New York Times* hailed the Nano as "gorgeous, functional, and elegant…to see one is to want one" (Pogue 2005), while the *Wall Street Journal* stated that the player, the size of five credit cards stacked together, was "gorgeous and sleek…beautiful and incredibly thin…I am smitten" (Mossberg 2005).

Apple's users pay a premium for its elegance and user-friendliness. The company rationalizes its profits on grounds that it devotes massive resources to upgrading existing designs and developing new products. However, its competitors have quickly incorporated Apple's technological innovations into their own products and offered them at lower cost. As a result, Apple has moved further into Web-based services while maintaining its tradition of end-to-end control. The coupling of the iPod music player and iTunes online music service is a case in point. Apple's strategy with iTunes was based on two principles: all downloads were priced at 99 cents each, and these downloads could be played only on iPods.

THE iTUNES "EXPERIENCE"

Apple unveiled its iTunes music store in April 2003. The iTunes service is intended to create an "experience" as much as a store, and "personalization" is a key part of the "experience." Users can post playlists to iTunes and compare their music tastes with others (including recording artists and celebrities). iTunes makes additional recommendations based on a customer's previous selections. As one recording industry executive stated, "Until Apple, it wasn't cool to buy digital music. This was about getting to that pivotal group of people—the people who buy the cool sneakers and wear the right clothes—and showing them that legally downloading music could be cooler than stealing it" (Black 2003).

Within six weeks, Apple had sold 3.5 million songs online. In addition to iTunes's attractive interface and personalized features, a major attraction was its simple pricing. Each download costs 99 cents, and users can "cherry pick" their favorite songs rather than purchase an entire CD. Given that CDs cost an average of $14 and feature an average of twelve songs, the 99-cent rate is slightly less than the cost of a song on CD. It should be noted, however, that iTunes downloads cost ten times more than 45 rpm singles did in the 1950s when adjusted for inflation, even though downloads have no costs for manufacturing, warehousing, and shipping (Harmon 2003).

Some artists, such as the Red Hot Chili Peppers and Metallica, were unwilling to license their recordings to iTunes because they believed that selling individual songs would break up the artistic continuity of their CDs. The Beatles continue to be holdouts, and other groups offer only a smattering of their recorded output on iTunes. The "unbundling" of CDs also met with resistance from the recording industry, which is concerned that downloads will cannibalize CD sales. The four major record companies (Universal, Sony/BMG, Warner, and EMI, who collectively sell 85 percent of recordings around the globe) would prefer a variable pricing model for downloads rather than a flat 99-cent fee. New singles or hits in demand could sell for $1.49, while "oldies" or less popular cuts could sell for less than 99 cents. Apple does allow variable pricing for downloads of entire CDs, yet the company expressed concern that higher prices for individual downloads would send potential customers in search of songs fleeing to unauthorized peer-to-peer networks.

By October 2006, Apple's iPod accounted for 76 percent of digital music players, and iTunes music store was responsible for 88 percent of digital music sales (Mossberg and Boehret 2006). However, Apple sees little money from the sales of iTunes downloads. Out of each 99-cent download, the record company receives approximately 30 cents, the artist receives twelve cents, middlemen receive ten cents, and song publishers receive eight cents. Of the remaining 40 cents, up to 23 cents go to credit card processing fees. That leaves 17 cents to pay for bandwidth charges and costs related to maintaining the iTunes Web site, as well as customer service. Essentially, Apple is using the iTunes store (which is relatively unprofitable) to bolster sales of its iPod players (which are highly profitable). Given the iPod's success, Apple appears to be transitioning from computers into consumer electronics, using services like iTunes to spur demand for its products. In a move that signaled their intention to move into video hardware and software, Apple unveiled a Video iPod in October 2005, which featured a 2.5-inch screen and sold for $299 or $399, depending on storage capacity. The iTunes service also offers downloads of TV shows, short films, and music videos for $1.99 each.

NAPSTER

Apple's iTunes and other services supported by the major record companies are intended to replace unauthorized services such as Napster and subsequent peer-to-peer file trading services. Napster was released on the Internet in August 1999 and functioned as a music search engine. Napster featured an online database of song titles and performers searchable by keyword, and linked participants to a huge and constantly updated library of music files (all files provided by users, without authorization by record companies). Napster also relied on MP3 files, which contained no protection against copying. Between February and August 2000, the number of Napster users rose from 1 million to nearly 7 million, making it the fastest-growing software application ever recorded. The major record companies filed suit against Napster, claiming it was a music piracy service, and the service was shut down in July 2001. However, CD sales in the U.S. rose 4 percent in 2000, when Napster was at its height, indicating that users often sampled music on Napster before purchase.

Apple continues to maintain tight control over the creation, manufacturing, and distribution of its products, leading critics to charge that the company is more concerned with maintaining the market dominance of their costly and highly profitable players than with allowing an open market for digital music. The company has refused to make iTunes software compatible with music players from other manufacturers. MP3 files may be converted to Apple's proprietary AAC format, but songs purchased from other services, such as Napster, will not play on iPods. If a user wants to shift from an Apple player to a rival brand, he or she must replace all the music they downloaded from the iTunes store. As *The Economist* put it, "It is as though a person's entire record collection worked on only one brand of gramophone" ("Apples Are Not the Only Fruit," 2006).

In addition to tethering Apple users to its proprietary formats, the rights of users can be altered at any time at Apple's discretion. The Apple system initially allowed downloads to be burned onto 10 consecutive CDs; after that, their order must be rearranged to prevent widespread copying. In May 2004, Apple reduced the number of CD copies from 10 to 7, while raising the number of playback devices from 3 to 5. The system also detects and blocks similar playlists, and does not allow songs to be edited, excerpted, or sampled except exclusively on Apple's terms.

MUSIC AS A SERVICE, RATHER THAN A PRODUCT

To date, three primary approaches to authorized music delivery have developed:

- The à la carte model used by Apple, in which customers buy individual tracks. After downloading, the songs can be copied (with restrictions) onto portable players and burned onto CDs.
- The subscription model used by Emusic, in which customers pay a monthly fee and download a specified number of songs per month. Subscribers to

Emusic, which features artists that aren't signed to major record companies, pay $9.99 per month to download 40 songs or $14.99 to download 64 songs.

- The streaming model, such as RealNetworks' Rhapsody, in which users pay a monthly fee to listen to songs online. Customers then pay an extra fee (usually less than a dollar per track) to download songs for CD burning or to add them to portable players.

To date, the iPod has reaped spectacular profits for Apple, and iTunes dominates the online music market, but the future of both is far from certain. Despite the growing capacity of digital music players, a study in September 2005 found that half of iPod owners had less than 100 songs stored on their players, with the average loaded with just 375 songs (Austin 2005). A 60-gigabyte iPod will hold 15,000 songs; consumers are unlikely to spend $15,000 to fill it up. Cell phones or similar "all in one" devices ultimately could absorb the functions of portable music players such as the iPod; similarly, the streaming model, which provides flows of music on demand, may be the most likely model for the long term. Such services will also have important "community" features, such as sharing playlists, and members may suggest songs by directly offering clips to each other (Rhapsody already features such capabilities). As music becomes a service instead of a product, people will be less and less concerned with owning music; instead, instant access will be more important.

Musical recordings have a relatively short history, and their physical forms shape the ways we interact with them and how we perceive their value. The "album" originated in the early twentieth century with bulky collections of 78-rpm discs. These discs were limited to three or four minutes per side, which shaped the contours of the modern pop song. Each subsequent format, from LPs to CDs, has been more compact while allowing more storage and greater possibilities for programming by users; an iPod can store up to 15,000 songs in a box smaller than a deck of cards. Each format also has reduced our physical interaction with music, such as changing LPs or loading CD players. An iPod can be programmed to play until its battery expires. With LPs and CDs, the work as a whole must initially be engaged on the creator's terms. With an iPod, the user has complete control over the flow of music.

A BRIEF TIMELINE

October 2001—Apple introduces the 5GB iPod.

April 2003—iTunes launches online, charging 99 cents per song.

September 2005—Apple introduces the iPod Nano.

October 2005—Video iPod unveiled; video purchases made available on iTunes.

September 2006—Feature film purchases made available on iTunes; 80GB iPods released; Apple announces that 70 percent of car models in the U.S. for the next model year will offer the ability to connect an iPod.

Unlike earlier forms of recording, digital files have no physical presence unless they are burned into CDs. Since they have no physical form, we view digital files as inherently less valuable than LPs or CDs. This lack of physicality undermines the notion of intellectual property, which in part accounts for the widespread copying of software and public support of file sharing. At the same time, digital files enable us to sample, collect, and trade music in new ways. While these files lack physical presence, possessing them in many ways is more intense and intimate than older "hard goods" such as LPs and CDs. For example, digital files enable us to contain huge amounts of data in small devices. We also can sort and regroup these files effortlessly, which transforms the listening experience. A collection of digital files in a hard drive becomes what one writer termed "an ocean of possibility [in which] daily life gets a different kind of soundtrack, endlessly mutable and instantly reconfigurable" (Moon 2004).

Older forms of copying recordings required substantial time and attention, while digital files allow for easy copying and customization. We simply "grab" cuts and "drag and drop" them into personalized collections. The popularity of digital files, as well as music in the form of telephone ring tones, indicate that access and convenience are increasingly important to listeners. Music becomes "less about an artist's self-expression than a customer's desire for self-reflection" (Goldberg 2000). In cyberspace, people collect lists rather than objects. As the physicality of recordings fades away, the playlists posted by customers of iTunes and other services may replace the mix CDs currently traded among friends. These playlists may be geared to a theme, an event, an experience, or a relationship. They also serve as a sort of "branding" for the creator.

The disappearance of hard goods, in the form of physical recordings, heightens the transition from a world of cultural goods to a world of cultural services. The result is that "value" is not an inherent character of the product, but the manner in which it reaches the consumer. The popularity of song files and playlists indicates that digital value is created through process, rather than products. In cyberspace, the old market-based economy of buyers and sellers is replaced by a new network-based economy of servers and clients. Rifkin claims that "in markets, the parties exchange property. In networks, the parties share access to services and experiences...based on network relationships, 24/7 contractual arrangements and access rights." As music loses its physicality, value must be created through networks and "experiences" like iTunes, which tether listeners to companies through proprietary hardware and restrictions on use. Ultimately, digital formats may cause music to return to an intangible essence altogether, in which it "would stop being something to collect and revert to its age-old transience: something that transforms a moment and then disappears like a troubadour leaving town" (Pareles 1998). We no longer will "own" recordings; instead, we will access them in fleeting ways on corporate terms.

See also Digital Divide; Internet and Its Radical Potential; Mobile Media; Online Digital Film and Television; Piracy and Intellectual Property.

Further Reading: "Apples Are Not the Only Fruit." *The Economist* (July 8, 2006): 75; Austin, Ian. "Objects in Ears Are Not as Full as They May Appear." *New York Times,*

September 12, 2005, C8; Black, Jane. "Where 'Think Different' Is Taking Apple." *Business Week Online,* August 5, 2003. http://www.businessweek.com/print/technology/content/aug2003/tc2003085_3215_tc112.htm; Goldberg, Michelle. "Mood Radio: Do On-line Make-Your-Own Radio Stations Turn Music Into Muzak?" *San Francisco Bay Guardian,* November 6, 2000. http://sfbg.com/noise/05/mood.html; Harmon, Amy. "What Price Music? How Your Favorite Song Went On 99-Cent Special." *New York Times,* October 12, 2003, Sec. 2, 1; Moon, Tom. "Mix Master iPod Opens Up a World of Sound." *Chicago Tribune,* January 16, 2004, Sec. 2, 3; Mossberg. Walter. "iPod's Latest Siblings." *The Wall Street Journal,* September 8, 2005, B1; Mossberg, Walter. "In Our Post-PC Era, Apple's Device Model Beats the PC Way." *The Wall Street Journal,* May 11, 2006, B1; Mossberg, Walter, and Katherine Boehret. "The New iPod: Ready for Battle." *The Wall Street Journal,* October 4, 2006, D1; Pareles, Jon. "With a Click, a New Era of Music Dawns." *New York Times,* November 15, 1998, 22; Pogue, David. "Defying Odds, One Sleek Ipod At a Time." *New York Times,* September 15, 2005, B1; Rifkin, Jeremy. "Where Napster Has Gone, Others Will Follow." *Los Angeles Times,* August 21, 2000. http://www.latimes.com/news/comment/2000821/t000078663.html.

Tom McCourt

JOURNALISTS IN PERIL

Journalism can be a dangerous job. Each year dozens of journalists are killed in incidents all over the world. Some of the reporters die accidentally in the course of their work. Many others are murdered for reasons relating to their reporting. Why has journalism become one of the most dangerous professions on earth?

The amount of risk in the work of a journalist depends on the kind of reporting a particular journalist undertakes. Investigative reporters and correspondents who cover armed conflicts face the greatest dangers, but many journalists make enemies in the course of doing their work. Others find themselves in dangerous places while covering breaking news. As a result, journalism can be considered one of the world's most dangerous occupations.

The wars in Iraq and Afghanistan and the recent upsurge in terrorist activity—and the response to it—have proven to be deadly stories to cover. "Journalists hoping for a career overseas face perils that did not exist when I began my foreign coverage in Southeast Asia in the 1950s," says Peter Arnett, an award-winning reporter who covered the war in Vietnam as well as the 1991 war in Iraq. "We ... rarely faced an issue more dangerous than expulsion," he explains. Journalists have traditionally been considered objective observers instead of participants in a conflict or story, which kept them for the most part from being targeted for violent actions. But over the past three decades and especially since the September 11 attacks in 2001, the profession has seen the continual erosion of its independent status. "Being a journalist used to be a badge of neutrality, which hopefully would get you safe passage from both sides. Now it's just the opposite," says Susan Bennett of the Freedom Forum, a free press foundation. Many people now see reporters, like soldiers, as fair game for attack.

AMERICANS FACE DANGERS ALL OVER THE WORLD

Paul Klebnikov was an American of Russian descent who worked as editor of the Russian-language edition of *Forbes* magazine. Klebnikov was a fluent Russian speaker who was proud of his Russian roots and was determined to improve the quality of journalism in Russia.

After a typical day at work—on July 9, 2004—Klebnikov left his office at 9 PM and started walking towards the nearest subway station. As he walked, a car pulled up and pumped nine bullets into his chest. Though he died within half an hour, Klebnikov was able to describe his assailants to colleagues, but he did not know what could have brought on such a savage attack. He was 41 years old.

Russian police later arrested two men for the killing, but they were found not guilty by a jury, perhaps because of outright intimidation by friends of the defendants. A judge later ordered a retrial, but the accused disappeared before they could be retried. Even though police still maintain that they found the "shooters," they did not know who ordered the "hit" on Klebnikov, or why. One theory was that Klebnikov was punished for writing an unflattering book about a Chechen businessman. Another was that he was killed for writing a book critical of a Russian oligarch. Before his death Klebnikov told his family he had been given some incriminating and dangerous information. Yet the world may never know why Paul Klebnikov was killed, or who was behind his murder.

Media organizations like the International Press Institute (IPI) and the Committee to Protect Journalists (CPJ) painstakingly document attacks on journalists. CPJ found that 580 journalists were killed between 1992, when it started keeping records, and 2006. That is an average of three journalists killed per month—a shockingly high statistic. In 2006, IPI statistics show that 100 journalists were killed around the world. This is the largest number of reporter deaths in one year in recent history, and is due mostly to the increasingly dangerous situation in Iraq.

CPJ says that most of the journalists killed in recent years were specifically targeted because of their work. "If popular imagination suggests journalists are typically killed by an errant bullet or a mortar bomb in battlefields, CPJ's data show that the majority—seven out of every 10—are targeted in retaliation for their reporting and hunted down to be murdered," wrote CPJ's Matthew Hansen. "Even in war zones, CPJ's analysis shows, murder is the leading cause of death." Worse, most of those who took retribution killed with impunity. CJP found that 85 percent of the killers faced neither investigation nor prosecution for their crimes.

A QUESTION OF REVENGE

In the United States, our Bill of Rights—the first 10 amendments to the Constitution—specifically spells out freedom of speech and freedom of the press as basic rights to which all citizens are entitled. The American founders understood that a free and vibrant press was essential, and that the press should serve as a watchdog over the government keeping elected officials accountable to the public. Yet even in America, journalists are sometimes attacked and even killed for what they have written. In many other countries, where freedom of the press is not as entrenched as it is in the United States, revenge killings of journalists are commonplace.

The point of the revenge killing is to punish a journalist for what he or she has written, and to scare other journalists from pursuing similar subjects. "A journalist is the voice of his or her community," says Pedro Díaz Romero, former human rights prosecutor for Colombia's attorney general's office. "To take the life of a journalist is to shut down a channel of information for the community. And after one journalist is killed, you may not need to kill another, as a threat or act of physical intimidation may be enough to send the message to the community at large." Some of the most common places for revenge killings are countries that have been racked by war—including Iraq, Algeria, and Bosnia. But the killing of journalists is also widespread in some nations that are relatively stable but fairly lawless, like Russia and the Philippines.

REAL PEOPLE, TRUE CRIMES

In the Philippines, where more than 80 percent of the public gets its news from radio, broadcast commentators constitute the majority of victims of revenge killings. One of them was Apolinario "Polly" Pobeda, the popular host of an AM radio show in Lucena City. In May 2002 two men stopped Pobeda as he was riding his motorcycle to work and shot him repeatedly. Pobeda suffered seven gunshot wounds, including one to his head. On the radio program that he hosted, "Nosi Balasi" ("Who Are They?"), Pobeda had often criticized corrupt local officials—particularly Lucena's mayor, whom the journalist had accused of being involved in the local drug trade. "My husband was killed because he exposed the wrongdoing of the government," Rowena Morales says. According to his wife, Pobeda had received repeated anonymous death threats, including one about a month before his murder—but he had kept on working.

In Russia, the spread of capitalism has fueled corrupt business deals worth billions of dollars, with government officials often benefiting from the same industries they are supposed to be regulating. After the Soviet Union fell apart in 1991, a new breed of journalist was born who after years of Soviet control was anxious to do real independent reporting. But some of those investigations had deadly consequences.

One of the most courageous journalists to work in Russia in its post-Soviet years was Anna Politkovskaya, a reporter for the Moscow-based newspaper *Novaya Gazeta*. Politkovskaya came to fame for her fearless coverage of two separate wars in the breakaway Russian region of Chechnya. Politkovskaya investigated such dangerous topics as the disappearances of young Chechen men, often without a trace, by Russian soldiers, and of torture of Chechens by Russian officers. Politkovskaya's reporting won her awards around the world, but it also made her enemies. Politkovskaya had been threatened and attacked numerous times in retaliation for her work. In February 2001, CPJ research shows, security agents detained her in Chechnya. She was kept in a pit for three days without

VERONICA GUERIN: IRELAND'S CRUSADING JOURNALIST

Veronica Guerin's murder in 1996 caused headlines around the world. She was Ireland's best known and most fearless crime reporter. The IPI lists her as one of its "50 Heroes of Press Freedom."

In 1994, Guerin started to write about crime for Ireland's *Sunday Telegraph*. She took on criminal bosses and drug lords in her fearless reports. Guerin used nicknames for underworld characters to avoid libel laws, but she still made her point—and plenty of enemies. In 1994 and 1995, Guerin was shot at and physically attacked in response to her work. She was offered protection by her paper, but complained that it got in the way of her reporting. "I vow that the eyes of justice, the eyes of this journalist will not be shut again," she said after one of the attacks. "No hand can deter me from my battle for the truth."

On June 26, 1996, Guerin was sitting in her car outside of Dublin, at a stop light, when two men on a motorcycle drove up to her car and shot her dead. Her death, the first ever of an Irish journalist, shocked the nation. Irish Prime Minister John Bruton called it "an attack on democracy." The following criminal investigation led to over 150 arrests and a hunt against Irish organized criminal gangs. Several men were later jailed for Guerin's murder.

Guerin's life has been immortalized in two movies and several songs. The IPI writes, "Veronica Guerin devoted her career and life to exposing the drug barons and leading figures in Dublin's underworld. 'I am simply doing my job,' she said. 'I am letting the public know how this society operates.' She paid the ultimate price for her pursuit of truth."

---

food or water while a Russian officer threatened to shoot her. Later that year, she had to flee to Austria after receiving death threats from a military officer accused of crimes against civilians. She returned to Russia and continued to work but those she exposed kept her in their sights. One afternoon in October 2006, Politkovskaya was shot and killed as she carried groceries into her apartment building. It was clearly a professional contract killing and those who worked with her understood it was linked to her work.

COVERING WARS

War is always a dangerous place for journalists to work. Reporters have been killed covering wars as long as there has been modern journalism. But the dangers are increasing. In World War I, for example, only 2 reporters were killed, according to statistics from the Freedom Forum. The battlefields of Europe became more dangerous during World War II, and from 1941 to 1945, 69 war correspondents lost their lives covering the conflict. One of the most dangerous assignments was flying with Allied troops on bombing raids over Nazi-held territory when planes were regularly shot down. The most famous reporter to travel with foot soldiers was Ernie Pyle of the Scripps Howard newspaper chain. Even though Pyle made it through the whole war in Europe unhurt, he was hit in the head and killed by a Japanese sniper while on a routine patrol near Okinawa in

1945. Covering the Vietnam War was also dangerous; the Freedom Forum lists 63 journalists who lost their lives there.

Modern insurgent movements create a particularly dangerous atmosphere for the journalists who try to cover the countries in which they operate. Consider the case of American Daniel Pearl, a reporter for the *Wall Street Journal*. Starting in October 2000, Pearl served as the South Asia bureau chief for the paper, based in Bombay, India. After the September 11th attacks, he frequently traveled to Pakistan on reporting trips. On one of those trips, Pearl asked his contacts to arrange a meeting with a leader of an insurgent group. Instead, on January 23, 2002, Pearl was kidnapped. Pearl's religion—Jewish—was one of the factors in his kidnapping and murder. Although the kidnappers sent a list of demands, which included the release of all Pakistani prisoners from U.S. custody, there were no negotiations. Pearl was beheaded by his kidnappers, four of whom were later caught and brought to justice. A major Hollywood movie made about Pearl's murder has brought worldwide attention to his case—and to the perils faced by reporters trying to cover modern terrorism.

The single most dangerous place for journalists to work since 2003 has been Iraq. The American-led war that overthrew Iraqi leader Saddam Hussein led to an upsurge in ethnic violence. More journalists have now died in Iraq since 2003 than died covering World War II or the Vietnam conflict.

Foreign reporters, included several Americans, have been killed in Iraq. This loss of life in Iraq began during the invasion itself, in March 2003. The award-winning writer Michael Kelly, editor of the *Atlantic Monthly* and a columnist for the *Washington Post*, was the first American journalist to die during the Iraq war. While embedded with U.S. troops, Kelly was killed when the Hummer in which he was riding went off the road into a canal to try to avoid enemy fire. In one of the most controversial incidents, one Ukrainian and one Spanish television cameraman were killed on April 8, 2003, when a U.S. tank fired directly into Baghdad's Palestine Hotel, where most of the foreign press corps was living during the invasion. The U.S. military was roundly criticized after that incident because it had been informed that journalists were staying in that particular hotel. Reporters also refuted U.S. claims that troops were being fired upon when they attacked the hotel. Later a tank commander said the camera lenses had been mistaken for binoculars used to spot targets.

That same day, Tareq Ayoub, a correspondent for the Arabic news channel Al-Jazeera was killed when U.S. forces fired a missile into the station's Baghdad office. Al-Jazeera, based in Qatar, had been highly critical of the Bush administration—and said that it had specifically alerted the Pentagon to the location of its Baghdad office so that its journalists would not be attacked. The U.S. military never said whether the missile attack on Al-Jazeera was intentional or accidental—but the incident, like the Palestine Hotel attack, was decried all over the world. In a letter to Defense Secretary Donald Rumsfeld, the Committee to Protect Journalists wrote that, given the protection journalists receive under the laws of war, "these attacks violate the Geneva Conventions." Other international journalists and press freedom organizations also condemned the

U.S. attacks. Reporters Without Borders declared, "We can only conclude that the U.S. Army deliberately and without warning targeted journalists."

The vast majority of the journalists who have died in Iraq have been Iraqis. About a third of them have been killed in bomb or mortar attacks, simply due to being in the wrong place at the wrong time, according to CPJ. The organization estimates that about two-thirds of those who have died have been the victims of revenge killings, in incidents tied specifically to their work. A wide range of Iraqi media outlets, and of foreign media with Iraqi employees, have been affected. Among the worst hit have been state-owned media like the television station Al-Iraqiya and the newspaper *Al-Sabah*, because of their ties to the U.S.-supported Iraqi government. Those two media outlets have been particularly hard hit by insurgents: on a regular basis their reporters have been murdered and their offices have been attacked.

A typical case of an Iraqi journalist targeted for his work is So'oud Muzahim al-Shoumari, a correspondent for the satellite channel Al-Baghdadia. Al-Shoumai, who did on-camera reporting and anchored a news program, was found shot in Baghdad on April 4, 2006. Al-Shoumari had regularly confronted Iraqi police about suspicions that they were committing extrajudicial killings. He regularly interviewed authorities about human rights violations and the daily suffering of the Iraqi people. These kinds of revenge attacks are sometimes related to the reporters' ethnicity, either the majority Shiite or minority Sunni branches of Islam. In the case of al-Shoumari, who was a Sunni, his colleagues suspect it was members of a Shiite militia who killed him.

THE PLUSES AND MINUSES OF EMBEDS

The streets of Iraq, and to some degree Afghanistan, are now so dangerous that foreign journalists can barely travel and find it difficult to work. "It's hard to imagine anywhere more difficult," says Alastair Macdonald, Baghdad bureau chief for the Reuters news agency. "I don't wake up every morning sweating about the risks I'm taking, but I do know that if I walk 100 yards to the edge of our secure area and out on the streets I'd be taking a major, almost suicidal, risk."

In order to get out of their hotels and to cover the work of troops first-hand, reporters can be "embedded" with the American military, or with other coalition forces. During an "embed," journalists are assigned to a military unit and go out into the field along with it. The good thing about these "embeds" is that they give reporters the chance to get onto the front lines with the troops and to see things they would not see otherwise. The bad thing is that journalists increase their already high level of risk by being embeds, because the soldiers and their convoys are constantly coming under attack.

Although the vast majority of victims of violence in Iraq were not embedded when they died, several of the Westerners killed or seriously injured in Iraq sustained their injuries while they were embedded. On May 29, 2006, CBS cameraman Paul Douglas and soundman James Brolin were killed when, on an embed, they got out of their car to inspect a checkpoint. On January 29, 2006, ABC anchorman Bob Woodruff was seriously injured when an improvised bomb went off near the tank where he was traveling as an embed. Woodruff, who was standing in the hatch of the tank with most of his body exposed, sustained serious head injuries. Although he was in a coma for weeks and underwent several surgeries, he survived and made a miraculous recovery.

LESSENING THE DANGERS?

Journalists pick their profession despite the dangers. Some of them choose ways to lessen the amount of risk they face. For example, journalists may turn down assignments to war zones or stay away from investigative reporting. Yet other journalists face the risks with quiet stoicism because they understand that the regular people they cover often have it even worse than the journalists. "There is a constant concern for safety," explains ABC News correspondent Jake Tapper, who has spent a great deal of time in Iraq. "It takes a real toll on you, but it makes you appreciate how difficult, in a far deeper way, it is for the troops there and the Iraqi people."

Yet many journalists are willing to face great risks because they believe that they are telling stories that need to be told. "Journalism is a high calling and sometimes a mortal one. Journalists risk their lives to bring the story of war home," said Tom Rosenstiel of the Project for Excellence in Journalism. "They are as courageous as aid workers, doctors, nurses, even soldiers. People who give their lives so that the public can understand the world should be perceived as patriots and heroes." Whether reporters are perceived as heroes or not, the reality is that the profession of journalism is now, and will always be, laden with risks.

See also Al-Jazeera; Anonymous Sources, Leaks, and National Security; Bias and Objectivity; Embedding Journalists; Government Censorship and Freedom of Speech; Paparazzi and Photographic Ethics; Parachute Journalism; Presidential Stagecraft and Militainment.

Further Reading: Collings, Anthony. *Words of Fire: Independent Journalists Who Challenge Dictators, Druglords, and Other Enemies of a Free Press.* New York: New York University Press, 2001; Committee to Protect Journalists. www.cpj.org; Daniel Pearl Foundation. www.DanielPearl.org; Foerstel, Herbert N. *Killing the Messenger.* Westport, CT: Praeger, 2006; International Press Institute. www.freemedia.at; Klebnikov Foundation. www.paulklebnikovfund.org; Reporters Without Borders. www.rsf.org; Sullivan, George. *Journalists at Risk: Reporting America's Wars.* Minneapolis: 21st Century, 2004.

Beth Knobel

MEDIA AND CITIZENSHIP

In today's large-scale societies, most communication about politics takes place through mass media. This places unique responsibilities in the hands of media organizations and journalists. The successes and failures of media in making citizenship possible have been and continue to be hotly debated. In particular, since the 1960s, there has been a decrease in political engagement and participation, and the media coverage of politics is often blamed for causing cynicism. Though today we have an unprecedented access to political information and participation, there is only limited evidence that the rise in new technologies and new forms of participation has truly transformed citizenship.

In historical terms, the idea of citizenship is a relatively new arrival. Though the ancient Greeks famously whiled their hours away talking about politics and making political decisions in the Assembly, their political arrangement—democracy through direct participation—was an anomaly that was viewed with equal measures of contempt and ridicule by their contemporaries. The idea of citizenship has only really gained strength since the mid-1700s, even if the roots of democratic thought have been around for much longer.

Many observers tie the rise in notions of democracy and citizenship to the emergence of the printing press—the first true mass medium. Benedict Anderson argued that newspapers contributed to the formation of the nation-state through the creation of "imagined communities" of readers within geographical and linguistic boundaries. To Anderson, "The members of even the smallest nation will never know most of their fellow-members, meet them, or even hear of them, yet in the minds of each lives the image of their communion" (1983, p. 6).

Alongside the rise of the democratic nation-state, of course, came the idea of citizenship as a form of belonging to the nation. The German sociologist Jürgen Habermas saw print media as providing unprecedented opportunities for citizens within particular nations to hold governments accountable for their actions, and for enabling debate about important issues. The rise of democratic nation-states, starting in the late eighteenth century, brought with it a newly complex set of relationships between governments, citizens, and media. In democratic societies, governments cannot simply rule with the absolute power of emperors and kings. Instead, democratic governments depend upon public approval for their legitimacy. And while ancient Greek city-states were small enough to be governed through face-to-face discussion, our large and complex societies require mass media to facilitate the process of communicating government decisions and expressing public opinion. Under such circumstances, the media have a complex set of responsibilities. As Jefferson famously quipped, "If I had to choose between government without newspapers, and newspapers without government, I wouldn't hesitate to choose the latter." Democratic thinkers often describe the media as a "fourth estate," or as a crucial check on the power of government. By scrutinizing the actions of government and other concentrations of power in society, media ensure the accountability of these organizations. Further, the media are responsible for undertaking surveillance of the environment and informing citizens of what is happening around them, providing them with the knowledge to understand the meaning and significance of ongoing events. Finally, the media are expected to provide a platform for public political discourse, serving as a channel for the advocacy of diverse political viewpoints and thereby facilitating the formation of public opinion.

For their part, citizens are expected to take an active part in democracy. At a minimum, they must stay informed about ongoing events in society, and about how their governments are reacting to them, in order to be able to make rational decisions in elections (see "Why Citizens Need the News" sidebar). Some scholars, however, believe that such a level of participation is inadequate. The idea that citizens need to be more intimately involved in politics is not new; the eighteenth-century philosopher Jean-Jacques Rousseau argued that "the English people believes itself to be free; it is gravely mistaken; it is free only during the election of Members of Parliament; as soon as the Members are elected, the people is enslaved; it is nothing." Today, a growing chorus of scholarly, political, and journalistic voices expresses concern about the limits to citizen participation within the framework of representative democracy, suggesting that citizens ought to be actively engaged in making the decisions that shape the futures of their countries by participating in direct discussion of political matters through the mass media.

WHY CITIZENS NEED THE NEWS

Providing information to citizens is seen as one of the most important roles of the media. The reason why this role is so central is that in today's mass societies, where political decisions often are made in locations and contexts distant from the citizens affected by them, most of us have little chance of finding out about these decisions without drawing in some way on the mass media. In order to make informed and rational decisions in elections, and, more broadly, to understand events that affect their lives, citizens are therefore expected to seek out information from media. We need to understand the policies and characters of those who represent us in government, but also how global events like tsunamis and terrorist attacks as well as local events like school closings and festivals impinge upon us. While newspapers were once the dominant political medium, television has been the most significant source of information for most people since the 1970s. Today, the average American spends 4.5 hours a day watching TV, though most of their television consumption is entertainment-oriented rather than political. By contrast, the Internet is emerging as a key source of political information—according to a study by the Pew Internet & American Life Project, 26 million Americans used the Internet every day in August 2006 to gather information about the upcoming midterm elections.

CONTEMPORARY CHALLENGES: A CRISIS OF PUBLIC COMMUNICATIONS?

It is certainly the case that alongside the rise of increasingly sophisticated forms of communication between politicians and citizens, there has also been a corresponding decline of participation in politics. At least since the 1960s, observers have noticed that in Western democracies, particularly the United States and the United Kingdom, fewer people are voting in elections. This period has also seen a decline in other forms of political engagement, such as newspaper readership, membership in voluntary associations, and trust in politicians. As a result, there is a "crisis of public communications" (Blumler and Gurevitch 1997). Because of the limited opportunities for participation, people may be turning away from conventional institutions, including parties and elections, and engaging in other forms of political action. Certainly, during the same period, there has been an increase in "single-issue politics," where people mobilize around a particular cause—including environmental politics, antidevelopment activism, antiwar protests, and the global justice movement. Some blame the crisis of public communications on the media, suggesting, among other things, that the negative tone of campaign reporting turns off citizens because it makes them view politics as a dirty game for insiders, where citizens can only be passive spectators or couch potatoes.

In recent years, scholars have invested hopes in new media technologies and genres as a way of enhancing citizenship and boosting political participation. First, some suggest that new television genres, such as talk shows and comedy, can engage groups who are otherwise disenchanted with politics. A study conducted by the Pew Center for People and the Press after the 2004 presidential elections showed that young people (anyone under the age of 30) increasingly rely on shows like *The Daily Show with Jon Stewart* for their political information—21 percent cited these as their main source of knowledge about the elections.

Secondly, ever since the invention of the Internet, its interactive potential has been much heralded by observers (see also "Television Talk Shows, Politicians, and Democracy" sidebar). Research shows that although governments and political parties have invested heavily in interactive Web sites and online information provision, new technologies do not necessarily challenge the top-down orientation of conventional politics. As James Janack found in his study of discussion on Howard Dean's campaign blog, supporters of Dean controlled debate to focus it on issues of strategy and style over substance. Contributors who wanted to actually discuss *politics* were silenced by other posters who felt that such discussion was inappropriate.

Nevertheless, new technologies have made possible media forms that are more participatory and democratic. They have led to the rise of citizen journalism, and user-created content, which is now an increasingly important part of the content produced by mainstream news organizations. In addition, there are today at least 60 million active blogs—a number that is rapidly increasing.

At the same time, we are faced with new questions about how media should handle the realities of an increasingly globalized world where the nation-states to which citizens belong are undermined by transnational and global developments and interests. Some observers suggest that the global nature of life in contemporary societies is shifting our allegiances in all areas of life. We engage with global corporations like Nike and Coca-Cola, social movements like Greenpeace, and many of us are part of or affected by the unprecedented movement of individuals and groups across previously fixed national borders. The question on the minds of many scholars today, then, is whether mass media can contribute to the formation of citizenship that goes beyond the nation-state.

TELEVISION TALK SHOWS, POLITICIANS, AND DEMOCRACY

Since the 1970s, television has been the most important source of political information for citizens. Television's emphasis on visually appealing, short-and-snappy personalized storytelling has, according to some observers, fundamentally transformed the nature of political discourse. In particular, new television genres, such as talk shows, are seen by politicians as a crucial way of reaching women, ethnic minorities, and other groups in society that are less tuned in to conventional politics. As a result, presidential candidates have increasingly subjected themselves to the talk-show treatment. Bill Clinton was one of the first to do this when he played the saxophone on the *Arsenio Hall Show*. In the 2000 Gore–Bush contest, both candidates appeared on Oprah Winfrey within a few weeks of each other. George Bush talked about his struggle with alcoholism, revealed that his favorite sandwich is peanut butter and jelly on white bread, and his favorite gift is kissing his wife. Gore, on the same show, said that his favorite breakfast cereal is Wheaties and that his favorite musical group is the Beatles. Critics allege that such appearances blur the boundaries between politics and popular culture. They fail to test the policies of politicians, but merely highlight their personalities. As such, they might risk trivializing politics and alienating voters. Supporters of talk-show politics, on the other hand, contend that by bringing politics and popular culture closer, we can engage people who are otherwise turned off from politics.

If anything, the growing availability of mass media technologies, and their increasing complexity, raises more questions than ever about the relationship between media and citizenship.

See also Bias and Objectivity; Blogosphere; Bollywood and the Indian Diaspora; Digital Divide; Global Community Media; Media and Electoral Campaigns; Nationalism and the Media; News Satire; Political Entertainment; Propaganda Model; Public Opinion; Public Sphere; User-Created Content and Audience Participation.

Further Reading: Anderson, Benedict. *Imagined Communities: Reflections on the Origin and Spread of Nationalism.* London: Verso, 1983; Blumler, Jay, and Michael Gurevitch. *The Crisis of Public Communication.* London: Routledge, 1997; Habermas, Jürgen. *The Structural Transformation of the Public Sphere.* Cambridge, MA: MIT Press, 1962/1989; Janack, James. "Mediated Citizenship and Digital Discipline: A Rhetoric of Control in a Campaign Blog." *Social Semiotics 16,* no. 2 (2006): 283–301; Lewis, Justin, Sanna Inthorn, and Karin Wahl-Jorgensen. *Citizens or Consumers? What the Media Tell Us About Political Participation.* Buckingham: Open University Press, 2005; McNair, Brian. *Introduction to Political Communication.* London, Routledge. 1995; Street, John. *Mass Media, Politics and Democracy.* London: Palgrave, 2001; Zoonen, Liesbet van. *Entertaining the Citizen: When Politics and Popular Culture Converge.* Lanham, MD: Rowman & Littlefield, 2005.

Karin Wahl-Jorgensen

MEDIA AND THE CRISIS OF VALUES

The conflict between the need for free expression and the importance of social responsibility has always accompanied the study of literature, the fine arts, and various forms of information transmission since at least the time of Aristotle's *The Rhetoric* and *Poetics.* However, concern for such values surged when printing technology made newspapers, magazines, and books available on a much wider scale and as literacy became more widespread. The advent of new technologies in the twentieth century—film, radio, sound recording, television, the Internet—has provoked even more discussion, pitting defenders of freedom of expression against guardians of public morality and responsibility. Groups such as the Parents Television Council, whose stated mission is "to ensure that children are not constantly assaulted by sex, violence, and profanity on television and in other media," represent one side of the issue. Other groups, such as media-watch group Fairness and Accuracy in Reporting (FAIR), which attempts to offer "a well-documented criticism of media-based censorship" and advocates "greater diversity in the press," champion the ideal of freedom of the press. Can a balance be struck between these two camps so that human values can guide the production and usage of the media today?

The discussion of values in the media divides itself into considerations of: (a) the role of the media in society as either a major influence on public attitudes and behavior, or merely a reflection or reinforcement of a given society's values; (b) the specific mechanism of media influence on the values of readers,

AGENDA SETTING: ALL MONICA ALL THE TIME

In late January 1998, all the major media in the United States and many other countries were focused on the upcoming visit of Pope John Paul II to Cuba. Of the pontiff's many trips, this was considered one of the most historic, since he would be meeting with Fidel Castro, an avowed Marxist dictator who had officially banned the practice of the Catholic religion in his country. The event was featured on the cover of several major news magazines and the anchors of the major network nightly news were heading to Havana for live coverage of the visit. On Friday, January 23, Tom Brokaw of the *NBC Nightly News* announced that every edition of the following week's news would include features about the contemporary situation in Cuba.

The next day, Monica Lewinsky, a former White House intern, revealed that she had been conducting a sexual affair with President Bill Clinton. Within hours, all coverage of the Pope's visit to Cuba ended, and virtually every television channel, every newspaper, every magazine, and every Internet blog was devoted almost exclusively to the sexual scandal. The historical visit of the Pope to Cuba, with its ramifications for the relationships of the United States, the Catholic Church, and Communism, was forgotten.

What put the Lewinsky story at the top of the media agenda? What made this story such a significant matter? The people's right to know? The well-known power of sexual scandal to sell newspapers and raise ratings? A "vast right-wing conspiracy" against a popular liberal President? This and many other examples of the media's ability to set the agenda of public discourse and the motives that drive the agenda-setting process fascinate media critics across the political, moral, and ideological spectrum.

viewers, or listeners; (c) the rights and duties of government to control media activity; (d) the rights and obligations of those who own or control the means of media production; and, finally, (e) the aesthetic values of the media as art forms.

MEDIA CONTENT

A great deal of the popular discussion of values in the media revolves around the question of content. Studies of media effects keep revolving around the presentation of sexuality, violence, gender, race, and politics and their influence on media consumers. It has often been pointed out that the concern about such influence over the centuries has usually emerged from the elite members of a culture and their perception of the lower classes as helpless in the face of the media onslaught. The thinking that developed in the 1920s and 1930s, for example, used the model of the media as a "magic bullet" or a hypodermic needle, transmitting messages to the mass of poorly educated, passive, and easily influenced media consumers, whose opinions and behaviors were bound to be heavily influenced by the media's overwhelming messages, such as Hitler's (and some would say Roosevelt's) political propaganda, the sexual allure of Hollywood movie stars such as Rudolph Valentino or Mae West, or the glorification of violence in gangster movies and pulp fiction. This theory, however, was not based on actual sociological data and, in its simple form, has been largely discredited by subsequent empirical research.

After World War II, however, more scientific studies of the media in Europe and America, using controlled experiments, interviews, and other sociological methods, found that people were much more selective in their media usage than previously thought, tending to pay attention to and remember the media messages that were more consistent with the personal values and attitudes they already held. Conservative or liberal citizens would read magazines and newspapers and listen to radio messages that reinforced their political viewpoints. Media theorists concluded that most media messages, rather than forming or changing public values and attitudes, tended to reinforce those already in place. It also became clear, on the basis of the sociological research, that the mass media represented only one of many influences on an individual's opinions, attitudes, and behavior. The media's messages are always competing with the influence of family, friends, coworkers, religious leaders, and educators, as well as many popular role models and opinion leaders. Meanwhile, according to these "limited-effects" theorists, the general consensus of public opinion in American society exerts a centripetal pull towards a common set of values—ideals of financial success, family solidarity, respect for the law, and other "respectable" attitudes and behaviors—to which both mainstream and marginalized members of society pay allegiance. The mass media, in their search for as large an audience as possible, strive to reflect that consensus.

The cultural revolution of the 1960s, however, challenged both this view of a naturally developed "American consensus" and the role of the media as a mere reflection of the values of the culture. Many experts began to ask whether, rather than reflecting social values, the media actively shape public attitudes and opinions and create cultural meaning. They also claimed that the values thus created by the media tended to benefit the socially, financially, and politically powerful while marginalizing and disempowering the poor and powerless members of society. They pointed, for example, to the massive amounts of advertising and media depiction of such addictive and health-threatening products as tobacco and liquor (while other substances, such as marijuana, were represented as dangerous and socially disapproved) as well as fast food, airline travel, and other products and services that are harmful to the environment and personal health.

They pointed to the coincidence of the campaigns on behalf of gas-guzzling automobiles in post–World War II America with the major legislation for interstate highway construction, the decline of support for public transportation in most urban areas, and the growth of the energy industry. They demonstrated many similar connections between the media promotion of certain messages and the financial interests of large corporations and their political allies.

This depiction of the media as actively creating and promoting social attitudes was reinforced by the findings of other researchers, who studied the long-term reinforcement of certain values and attitudes through a steady, consistent presentation of a message in a specific direction. The portrayal of minorities in subservient and demeaning roles in Hollywood films, for example, or the depiction of foreigners as dangerous in television series, or the presentation of impossible standards of beauty in advertising, all serve to reinforce the hegemony of certain social groups and to marginalize and disempower others.

SPECIAL MODELS OF MEDIA INFLUENCE

Whatever theory is followed, much research is still being conducted to determine whether the consumption of media messages serve as: (a) a stimulus to certain behavior and a reinforcement of values and attitudes (the predominance of white males as financial or political power figures in the news); (b) the modeling of behavior (the 1950s television family life on *Father Knows Best* or the glamour of drug consumption by the Beatles and other popular musicians of the 1960s); (c) a catharsis of socially unacceptable behavior (pornographic material or violent video games as cathartic release, political satire as an escape valve for the discontent citizenry); or (d) desensitization, whereby previously objectionable attitudes or behavior no longer shock or offend as, for example, society becomes accustomed to more permissive sexual mores, more levels of aggression or frankness in language and behavior, or various alternative lifestyles that move into the mainstream.

Definite conclusions are hard to reach. George Gerbner's Mean World Index, for example, has demonstrated a strong correlation between the heavy viewing of television and the formation of a view of the world as dangerous. But even this study could not establish a cause-and-effect relationship between media and social behavior. Despite many controlled laboratory experiments and years of qualitative research, opinions still vary on the effect of the mass media on consumer opinion and behavior and whether they tend to merely reflect or actively mold social values.

Whatever theory holds sway, there always remain several constant questions about bias in the presentation of news stories or portrayals in entertainment; the appeal to sensationalism or shock value to promote television ratings, sell newspapers, or pack the movie theaters; the agenda-setting that decides what merits front-page coverage or more television or radio time; the bottom-line quest for revenue from subscriptions or advertising income; and other matters, which all affect the content of the media.

GOVERNMENT CENSORSHIP AND REGULATION

Does the government have a right—and even a responsibility—to regulate the activity of the mass media in order to safeguard society against any harm? The role of the mass media in the United States is largely shaped by the First Amendment, which states that "Congress shall make no law…abridging the freedom of speech or of the press." Over the more than 200 years since the U.S. Constitution was written, various legal rulings, including Supreme Court opinions, have extended the protection of the freedom of the press to advertising, film, entertainment content in magazines and newspapers, and to television and radio. Such decisions go hand in hand with the general legal attitude that forbids "prior restraint," the attempt of the government to prevent the publication or broadcast of expression. Even this principle, however, has been abandoned in a few cases of national security or other situations where media information might present a "clear and present danger" to society. There are also legal restrictions against and punishment for libel, obscenity, and indecency. Pornography, however, is protected as a case of freedom of expression. The distinction among these items and the application of each term to a specific case is, of course, quite complex. In most cases, consistent with the "prior restraint" principle, the Federal Communications Commission (FCC) or the courts are reactive rather than proactive, waiting until after the questionable media message has been published or transmitted and complaints are received.

The government has considerably more control over radio and television content and production because of the ownership situation of these media. Broadcast media, unlike books, newspapers, magazines, film, and sound recording, make use of a portion of the electromagnetic spectrum that is seen as a limited natural resource, like land and water, and therefore requiring distribution by the government.

Meanwhile, the FCC, with its five commissioners appointed by the White House, is often criticized in terms of the balance it should be maintaining between the interests of the industry owners and those of the consumers, as well as its relationships with lobbyists, media corporations, and politicians. Like many members of federal regulatory commissions, the FCC members are recruited from and often return to the executive offices of the very industries they are supposed to be regulating during their time in public office, raising the question of conflicts of interests.

RIGHTS AND OBLIGATIONS OF MEDIA OWNERS

Media ownership in the United States is corporate and profit-driven, as opposed to the paternalistic system in the United Kingdom and Canada, for example, or the state control of the media in China or Cuba. This has led to a general understanding of media ventures not as public services but as opportunities to achieve gigantic profit. The Hollywood studios, the national radio and television networks, and the newspaper giants have become some of the country's most profitable industries. This has led to the creation of a business oligopoly, in which the smaller media operations cannot compete with the media giants. In recent years, even this elite group of media owners has merged and concentrated media ownership into the hands of a very few media conglomerates, creating a situation where a megacorporation's reach extends to every area of media activity. (See "Conglomeration and Media Monopolies" for examples of the rise of the major media corporations and their relationship to the FCC.)

The principles that govern corporate efforts to achieve maximum profitability cannot automatically be applied to media corporations. Whereas McDonald's sells food products and General Motors sells automobiles, the product of media corporations is: (a) information, which ideally should be helping to develop the well-informed citizenry on whom a legitimate democracy depends, and (b) entertainment, whose social impact should not be underestimated. Media conglomeration has led to the replacement of independent bookstores by the giant bookstore chains, the presence of only one major newspaper in most metropolitan areas, the automation of local radio stations, and the prominence of blockbuster movies over smaller studio or independent films. While this might be seen as simply another case of survival of the fittest in the corporate media jungles, other critics point to the elimination of the competitive incentive and other benefits inherent in capitalist business practices and the homogenization of media consumers.

Meanwhile, the phenomenon of globalization provokes new questions of human values. The worldwide dominance of the Hollywood film industry and the American music industry, for example, raises the specter of corporate and cultural imperialism. The convergence of media messages, the partnership of political and corporate elites, and the "echo effect" of the same corporate-driven messages being delivered worldwide threaten to drown out or marginalize alternative voices. (See "Cultural Imperialism and Hybridity" for specific examples of such "media imperialism.")

AESTHETIC VALUES

The media are rightfully evaluated in terms of the quality of their artistic elements. Critical reviews are issued and awards are given for almost every genre of mass communication. Pulitzer Prizes are bestowed annually on newspaper writers and photographers as well as theatrical presentations; National Book Awards are given to works of both fiction and nonfiction. Academy Awards are given to films, Emmy Awards to television productions, Peabody Awards to radio and television programming, and Grammy Awards to achievements in an ever-expanding list of sound-recording categories. All such awards represent critical judgment of artistic achievement in various mass media. Some would maintain that, in considering a work of art, aesthetic qualities such as verbal eloquence, visual composition, or dramatic or musical skill must be considered as paramount in this area even if, in some cases, the judgment that is rendered may conflict with other values. Is nudity in a film (*American Beauty*) or in a live performance (*Hair*), obscene language in a novel (James Joyce's *Ulysses* or Toni Morrison's *Beloved*), or violence on a television show (*The Sopranos*) essential to the artistic integrity of the material in question? Can a musical performance that is considered by many to encourage antisocial behavior or encourage stereotypes (such as rap music) still be acknowledged as artistically valid and even praiseworthy for aesthetic reasons? Should the sexual display or the religious imagery of Madonna's performances be defended as exercises in artistic license, or can there be legitimate concern that such artistic expression is a degradation of moral standards or a mockery of religion? May ethnic slurs or demeaning images of racial groups be allowed as free expression, or should they be treated as hate speech and therefore liable to judgments beyond the boundaries of aesthetic norms?

SUMMARY

In the areas of media content, social influence, government control, business interests, and artistic merit, the ongoing tension between individual expression and initiative versus the interests of society at large will continue to pose important questions about human values.

See also Bias and Objectivity; Children and Effects; Conglomeration and Media Monopolies; Cultural Imperialism and Hybridity; Global Community Media; Government Censorship and Freedom of Speech; Hypercommercialism; Media Literacy; Obscenity and Indecency; Pornography; Ratings; Regulating the Airwaves; Runaway Productions and the Globalization of Hollywood; Sensationalism, Fear Mongering, and Tabloid Media; Violence and Media.

Further Reading: Bagdikian, Ben H. *The Media Monopoly,* 3rd ed. Boston: Beacon Press, 1990; Bandura, A. *Psychological Modeling: Conflicting Theories.* Chicago: Aldine Atherton, 1971; Bittner, J. R. *Law and the Regulation of Electronic Media.* Englewood Cliffs, NJ: Prentice-Hall, 1994; Carey, James W. *Communication as Culture: Essays on Media and Society.* Boston: Unwin Hyman, 1990; Curran, James, and Michael Gurevitch, eds. *Mass Media and Society,* 2nd ed. New York: St. Martin's Press, 1996; Day, L. A. *Ethics in Media Communications: Cases and Controversies.* Belmont, CA: Wadsworth, 1997; Fallows, James. *Breaking the News: How the Media Undermine American Democracy.* New York: Pantheon, 1996; Foerstel, N. H. *Free Expression and Censorship in America.* Englewood Cliffs, NJ: Prentice-Hall, 1997; Halberstam, David. *The Powers That Be.* Urbana: University of Illinois Press, 2000; Jamieson, Kathleen Hall. *Dirty Politics: Deception, Distraction, and Democracy.* New York: Oxford University Press, 1992; Klapper, J. T. *The Effects of Mass Communication.* New York: The Free Press, 1960; Lazarsfeld, Paul F., B. Berelson, and H. Gaudet. *The People's Choice.* New York: Columbia University Press, 1944; Lee, Martin A., and Norman Solomon. *Unreliable Sources: A Guide to Detecting Bias in News Media.* New York: Carol Publishing Group, 1992; McChesney, Robert W. *Corporate Media and the Threat to Democracy.* New York: Seven Stories Press, 1997; Medved, Michael. *Hollywood vs. America.* New York: HarperCollins, 1992; Newcomb, Howard, ed. *Television: The Critical View.* New York: Oxford University Press, 1994; Signorielli, N., and M. Morgan, eds. *Cultivation Analysis: New Directions in Media Effects Research.* Newbury Park, CA: Sage Publications, 1990; Tuchman, G. *Making the News: A Study in the Construction of Reality.* New York: Free Press, 1978; Watkins, J. J. *The Mass Media and the Law.* Englewood Cliffs, NJ: Prentice-Hall, 1990.

Michael V. Tueth, S. J.

MEDIA AND ELECTORAL CAMPAIGNS

The development of mass media in the twentieth century transformed the way political candidates run for public office, and in doing so changed forever the American electoral process. Political campaigns use media to reach vast numbers of voters, and candidates hire cadres of media professionals to produce slick advertisements and formulate compelling sound bites at costs that escalate with every presidential campaign. As American democracy continues to adapt to ever more sophisticated media marketing strategies, visual and rhetorical

THE CHECKERS SPEECH

In 1952, vice presidential candidate Richard Nixon made television history in a half-hour address to the nation that became known as the Checkers speech. The Republican ticket included Dwight D. Eisenhower as the presidential candidate, and the campaign was designed around a classic political strategy that denounced incumbent mismanagement and corruption and called for a political turnover with a fresh start. It was therefore disastrous when allegations of campaign finance corruption were made against the vice-presidential candidate. When Republicans called on Nixon to drop out of the campaign, he appealed to his party to let him explain himself on television. Nixon made an emotional appeal, telling the story of how someone gave his family a little cocker spaniel dog that his daughters named Checkers. He then stated forcefully that he would not give the dog back. The issue of corruption was all but ignored, but at this historic moment, Nixon successfully used the new medium of television to speak directly to the public, and he remained on the ticket. Nixon went on to become president in 1968, and was later impeached because of the Watergate scandal.

devices have drawn fire from critics who worry that in an age of mass media, it may be getting harder, not easier, for the public to decide who can best represent their interests, values, and vision for the future.

During elections, audiences come to know and recognize political candidates primarily through the mass media imagery, interviews, and events that depict them. Debates, conventions, campaign stops, and political advertisements reach millions of viewers, and candidates have access to the public in ways unthinkable before mass media. Television has been an especially important player since the 1950s, heralding the most significant changes in the way elections are carried out. As the broadcast medium brought sights and sounds into the homes of the American electorate, pictures of candidates and advertisements provided voters with new ways to choose their leaders. The successful 1952 campaign of Dwight D. Eisenhower played to television audiences with skillfully stylized, fast-moving ads. Democratic opponent Adelaide Stephenson understood less about television formatting, and because of his lengthy speeches became known as an "egghead." Political strategists have learned over the years to carefully hone their candidate's speech and image, turning the media into a battleground for electoral victory, while often losing sight of the issues. Elections now include targeted, negative advertisements, zinger sound bites in televised debates, and lavish convention spectacles, all part of stage-managed campaigns. Many complain that contemporary electoral campaigns in this media age often seem to obscure more than they illuminate about politics and the candidates they promote.

THE PARTY CONVENTIONS

Historically, conventions were contentious gatherings where party platforms were debated and hammered out, and politicians vied for their party's nomination. Now, both political parties pick their candidate before they ever hit the convention floor. In recent years, editors, journalists, and TV hosts have complained that the national party conventions have become little more than carefully choreographed infomercials, selling candidates and parties in nationally televised feel-good events where balloons drop amid sparkling atmospheres, red, white and blue banners, and sounds of patriotic pop songs. Throughout convention week, media time is filled with highly produced docuvideos, carefully crafted rhetoric, and image-enhanced candidates. With so few delegates willing to enter into on-camera debate in the name of party unity, members of the news media have begun to ask what is left to cover. Some networks now say they will no longer carry national presidential conventions during prime time.

VISUAL LANGUAGE

Election campaigns, ideally, should inform voters about the candidate's past political actions and current policy formulations in order to understand their divergent visions of democracy and how their leadership will affect the country. Yet viewers are often expected to judge candidates' personal attributes, and even qualities of character, such as integrity and trustworthiness, through pictures. Television images of some candidates fail to convey those qualities. For example, negative opinions of Michael Dukakis were evoked by images that seemed to make his head appear too large, and his shoulders too small. He was labeled "a wimp" during the presidential race against George H. W. Bush in 1988, a negative attribute based solely on appearance, not substance. Many credited much of the success of Ronald Reagan and Bill Clinton to their ability to appear sincere and humane on camera.

RACIALLY CODED VISUAL MESSAGES IN THE 1988 PRESIDENTIAL CAMPAIGN

Negative advertisements are able to create powerful impressions of candidates and their positions, often using questionable visual strategies that evoke anxiety and fear. The most historically significant example of such a campaign is the racially charged presidential campaign of 1988 in which George H. W. Bush defeated Michael Dukakis.

The 1988 Bush campaign, headed by Lee Atwater, exploited white fears of black criminals by featuring Willie Horton in advertisements. After the Democratic convention early in the race, Dukakis enjoyed high poll numbers, but the Bush campaign conducted focus groups and found that the Horton incident would be a damaging issue for Dukakis. Horton, in jail for murder, had raped a white woman and assaulted her fiancé while on furlough from a Massachusetts prison. Three other white inmates had also escaped the furlough program, one a police officer who committed murder while on leave. But the Republican campaign focused on Horton. One ad designed by Bush supporters featured a criminal mug shot of Horton, and the official campaign spot made it seem like many dangerous murderers had escaped while on furlough. Though untrue, the grainy black and white images of dark criminals walking though prison gates raised fears about the program, and misrepresented the facts. Viewers were not told the program was actually started by a previous Republican governor. After the election, critics pointed out that the metaphor of a white woman being raped by a black man has long been associated with white fear toward African Americans, and the coded visual language of the attack ads excited those fears.

Negative attack ads have become features of most media campaigns, and while some say they contain useful information for the electorate, others argue that the visual manipulation of pictures and graphic imagery create implied meanings hard for candidates to address in issues debates. Voters now regularly assert that they do not like it when candidates "go negative," and would like to hear more about issues, but polling data shows ironically that negative advertisements are often effective tools in winning elections.

CANDIDATES AND POPULAR MEDIA

During the 1990s, political candidates broke out of the confines of serious news programming and began to visit shows across the media spectrum. From Bill Clinton playing the saxophone on Arsenio Hall, to George W. Bush talking to Regis and Kathy Lee, presidential candidates now make appearances on *Saturday Night Live* and other late-night venues as well. Viewers want to see the candidates in casual, unscripted settings where they can be themselves, and such appearances bring the democratic process into the daily lives of millions of diverse potential voters. Oftentimes, however, the potential for serious discussion is overshadowed by more trivial fare that has come to be known as "politics lite." Many serious topics could be discussed and debated on talk shows, but hosts such as Oprah mostly ask candidates questions about what they ate for breakfast and which is their favorite color. Such personal trivial pursuits of the candidates led one MTV viewer to ask Bill Clinton if he wore "boxers or briefs?"

When George W. Bush appeared with Regis Philbin during the 2000 election, he opened his jacket for viewers to see what he was wearing. Governor Bush was dressed like the celebrity host, wearing the dark matching signature tie and shirt, the Regis line of clothes. By doing so, the candidate was using celebrity association, a marketing strategy that seeks to transfer the popularity of the host onto the politician. In this way, candidates now sell an image of themselves to media audiences and associate themselves with the popularity already enjoyed by celebrities, hoping to turn that recognition into votes without having to elaborate their political views. In contemporary media-driven campaigns, voters are often entertained as audiences and addressed as consumers, not informed as citizens or provided with political positions.

News figures have criticized the candidates for doing what they call feel-good interviews on talk shows like Regis, Oprah, and Rosie O'Donnell, allowing them to avoid the serious press with their tough questions. But the "serious" press has also been criticized for not asking issue-oriented questions during campaigns.

DAN QUAYLE AND MURPHY BROWN

In another historic first for television, during the 1992 race for the White House, Vice President Dan Quayle illustrated the party's platform and the issue of family values by referring to a fictional television character, Murphy Brown, who had made the decision to have a child out of wedlock. The boundary between fiction and politics blurred even further when producers of the program worked actual footage of Quayle's speech into an episode of *Murphy Brown*. On the show, Murphy and her friend Frank are shown with the baby, listening to the speech on television as the vice president criticizes her choice. The incident certainly drew attention to the issue, but the Republicans did not win a second term in office. Dan Quayle went on to become the first vice president to appear on a television commercial after leaving office. He was shown enjoying Wavy Lays during the next Super Bowl.

ELECTIONS AS HORSE RACES

The news media have a tendency to report elections as if they were horse races, frequently citing poll numbers and using visuals that turn states either red or blue as they tally up the electoral college votes. These stories come with greater regularity as Election Day grows near. With a seemingly endless supply of sports metaphors, news stories make the race more exciting by talking about how the candidate must "step up to the plate," deliver a "knock-out punch," or do well in the "final stretch." In this way, news commentary focuses more on strategy details and numbers and less on political platforms and visions. In the excitement, a critical approach to what are often persuasive forms of campaign strategies is lost. Journalists often report admiringly on a candidate's ability to garner higher numbers, and many times inadvertently, they legitimate the superficial, image-based, marketing strategies employed to win votes.

TELEVISED DEBATES

Richard Nixon and John F. Kennedy went on television in the first debate to be broadcast live in 1960. It came to be called the Great Debate, because it demonstrated the power of the image. Those who watched the debate on television judged Kennedy to be the winner, and more of those who listened on the radio believed Nixon had won. Over the years, after many such televised events, the visual image of the candidates, their clothes, expressions, and nonverbal cues, continues to create enduring impressions, making some argue that in the age of the image, substance and political content are lost.

But documentaries, and many other uses of film and video that educate and inform, show that information and understanding do not necessarily have to be lost in a visual age. Candidates explaining their preference for policies and their stands on issues in a debate format should elucidate much, even on television. Increasingly, it is the way the medium is used as a marketing tool, not its inherent failure, that creates problems for democracy. Though debates are billed as spontaneous, unscripted interactions, candidates are highly coached by political consultants adept at shaping messages that have been carefully tested. Candidates memorize many of the same sound bites that appear in their campaign advertising, repeating single, unexplained phrases over and over. In his first debate against George W. Bush, Al Gore repeated 10 times that he would put social security in a "lock box." After the debate, much of what the public learns depends on how the news media report and interpret it. News commentators and campaign strategists themselves provide political "spin" after each debate. Their job is to assure viewers that their candidate won, and that image and appearance should be taken as the legitimate measure of a candidate's worth: the color of their tie really does mean something. Critics charge that there remain few dedicated political analysts in the media who are willing to keep public officials accountable for what they say by checking the facts or comparing their current statements with previous positions. Instead, the media personalities and marketing consultants act as theater critics, evaluating the candidates' performance, image, and delivery. After half a century of image politics on television, the image itself has become the topic of legitimate news.

CYNICISM AND SATIRE

To those citizens who wish to be taken out of the confines of simple self-interest and contemplate a better world on a bigger scale, the simple slogans that pass the test of focus groups rarely challenge existing economic or social disparities and other social problems that trouble American democracy. Seeking solutions to serious problems and creating a better world is the stuff of political vision, but such visions usually take more than sound bites to express. Marketed messages are not a language that can question why so many young black men are in jail, or why one out of five children in this country go to bed hungry. Politicians are left with vague generalities that do not offend swing voters, or narrowly defined issues dictated by political consultants. Some media critics argue that hour-long dramatic series such as *Law and Order* and *West Wing* present more clearly articulated issue debates than most of what is on TV during election campaigns.

As superficial language and marketing persuasions permeate campaigns, the formats begin to look predigested and carefully crafted, and they have become the brunt of jokes on late-night comedy satire. The popularity of those programs has shot up, especially among the young. In 2000, a poll done by the Pew Center for People and the Press showed almost half of people in their twenties were getting their election news from late-night talk show hosts such as Jon Stewart, Bill Maher, David Letterman, Jay Leno, and Conan O'Brien. The popularity of TV's political comedy is an indication to some that young people are becoming more cynical, dropping out of politics and refusing to vote. To others it indicates the sophistication of viewers who reject the way politicians "stay on message" with prepackaged rhetoric. Recent concerts to "rock the vote" have attempted to reinvigorate a youthful electorate and bring them back into the election process.

FOLLOW THE MONEY

Most importantly, media campaigns are expensive, with the combined costs now reaching the trillion-dollar figure. As the costs of political advertising on television and other media outlets continue to rise, only those who are already wealthy or well funded can afford to run for political office. In 1997, President Clinton made a speech asking broadcasters to offer free time to political candidates, but with billions of dollars at stake media corporations lobbied heavily on Capitol Hill to defeat the proposal.

Such huge sums of money in the political process have serious consequences for democracy. Both Republicans and Democrats throw lavish parties at their national conventions, paid for with money from wealthy contributors and large corporations. When parties and candidates must continually raise money to cover the costs of pricey media campaigns, they become dependent upon and beholden to the corporate dollars that fund them. The Center for Public Integrity and other public interest groups have worked hard on this issue, looking for the most effective ways to achieve campaign finance reform.

THE FUTURE AND NEW TECHNOLOGY

Initiatives to make television more open to unscripted candidates with less money are in the works, but much of the continuing debate about the electoral process and democracy is taking place around new media technology. Many have looked to the Internet as part of the solution to the problems of influences and entrenched media practices. Online discussion and commentary is seen as a place where average citizens can have a greater voice in politics, but that will be restricted to a small group with access and resources who can use the familiar language of politics. With the development of the Internet, the American democratic process continues to adapt to new media technologies.

See also Advertising and Persuasion; Anonymous Sources, Leaks, and National Security; Bias and Objectivity; Blogosphere; Internet and Its Radical Potential; Media and Citizenship; Media Literacy; Media Reform; Narrative Power and Media Influence; Nationalism and the Media; News Satire; Political Entertainment; Political Documentary; Public Opinion; Representations of Race.

Further Reading: Diamond, Edwin, and Stephen Bates. *The Spot: The Rise of Political Advertising on Television.* Cambridge, MA: MIT Press, 1992; Frank, Thomas. *What's the Matter with Kansas? How Conservatives Won the Heart of America.* New York: Metropolitan Books, Henry Holt and Company, 2004; Jamieson, Kathleen Hall. *Dirty Politics: Deception, Distraction, and Democracy.* New York: Oxford University Press, 1992; Lewis, Charles, and the Center for Public Integrity. *The Buying of the President 2004: Who's Really Bankrolling Bush and His Democratic Challengers, and What They Expect in Return.* New York: HarperCollins, 2004; Lewis, Justin. *Constructing Public Opinion: How Political Elites Do What They Like and Why We Seem to Go Along with It.* New York: Routledge, 2001; Mayer, Jeremy D. *Running on Race: Racial Politics in Presidential Campaigns, 1960–2000.* New York: Random House, 2002.

Robin Andersen

MEDIA LITERACY: CREATING BETTER CITIZENS OR BETTER CONSUMERS?

Since the 1930s there has been a small but growing movement of educators who stress the importance of media literacy. Media literacy has been broadly defined as the ability to access, analyze, evaluate, and produce messages in many forms of media. While it is the most media-saturated society, the United States lags behind other industrialized nations in media education. Media education is still not a regular feature of the U.S. educational system and there are many differing perspectives over precisely what constitutes media literacy. At the heart of these debates is the question of whether media literacy should be about teaching people the skills and knowledge they need to be more sophisticated consumers of media or the skills and knowledge they need to be more engaged and critical citizens.

Advocates of media education argue that we must all learn how to make sense of electronic and visual media just as we have to learn traditional literacy skills such as comprehension, interpretation, and evaluation of written texts. Educators take it for granted that students must be taught how to interpret and produce texts such as poems, stories, and essays. From a media literacy perspective, we should also be students of the media and learn how to critically engage with advertisements, television programs, films, and new media forms as well. Although most of the 50 states now include some mention of media literacy in their educational standards, media education has yet to become a full part of the curriculum in most schools. Only a small percentage of students in the United States participate in any focused media education. The move away from educational practices that encourage critical inquiry and the increased emphasis on standardized testing that emerged at the beginning of the twenty-first century has stalled attempts to advance media literacy in the nation's schools. However, a growing media literacy movement composed of educators, activists, independent media practitioners, and concerned citizens is fighting to establish the importance of media education in a world that is saturated with media images and stories.

MEDIA SATURATION AND THE NEED FOR MEDIA LITERACY

For the citizens of industrialized nations media are inescapable. In the United States, for example, virtually every home includes at least one television, and two-thirds of households have three or more. In these homes, the television is on for almost seven hours a day and the average American watches over four hours of television daily. Television is, of course, only one of many media technologies that compete for our time. Use of the Internet and other new media, such as video games, is rising every year. As new forms of media are introduced, however, television viewing is actually increasing rather than declining. People are simply adding to their overall electronic media exposure every year. Because we live in media-saturated environments it is essential that we engage in critical reflection on the media that are so much a part of our daily routines. This will not happen automatically, however. Media are ubiquitous. In other words, there is so much media in our lives, and media images surround us to such a great extent, that they have become almost invisible. As the media scholar Marshall McLuhan is quoted as saying, "We don't know who discovered water, but we're pretty sure it wasn't a fish." The notion that educational interventions are necessary for individuals to achieve an elevated understanding of the media is at the heart of the U.S. media literacy movement that has been developing in various forms since the 1930s.

THE DEVELOPMENT OF THE MEDIA LITERACY MOVEMENT

In the 1930s a number of English teachers in Madison, Wisconsin, became concerned about the social impact of commercial radio and formed a small group dedicated to studying radio programming. This group added television to their mission in 1953 and became the American Council for Better Broadcasting. Thirty years later they changed their name to the National Telemedia Council (NTC) and they continue to operate under this title. The avowed mission of the group is not to critique the media industries but to encourage appreciation of quality programming. As stated on their Web site: "From the beginning, we have taken a positive, non-judgmental attitude and embraced a philosophy that values reflective judgment and cooperation rather than confrontation with the media industry."

This cooperative approach marked the first three decades of media education until the rise of the critical viewing movement in the late 1960s. Concerns about the effects of television violence helped spur public and private investment in media education efforts, which peaked during the 1970s. This critical viewing approach was aimed at critiquing media messages and pointing out the possible negative effects of media consumption.

Despite the spread of media education in the 1970s, the 1980s saw a conservative turn in education that emphasized a focus on traditional reading, writing, and computation skills. Few new media education programs or innovations were introduced during this decade and media literacy fell by the wayside throughout most of the United States. This was not true in other parts of the industrial world however, as media education continued to develop and expand. Small pockets of media educators continued to communicate with one another, and toward the end of the decade two important groups were founded in California: Strategies for Media Literacy, in San Francisco, and the Center for Media and Values (later to be called the Center for Media Literacy) in Los Angeles.

During the 1990s a growing number of conferences and publications indicated that the media literacy movement was again on the rise in the United States. In 1992, the Aspen Institute sponsored a conference with the goal of creating a recognizable identity and clear mission for an increasingly disparate movement. It was at this conference that the standard definition of media literacy was first developed: "A media literate person can access, analyze, evaluate, and produce both print and electronic media."

Another key development occurred in 1997 when the Partnership for Media Education (PME) was formed to, among other things, organize annual national conferences for media practitioners and educators. This small group became the Alliance for a Media Literate America (AMLA) in 2000. According to their Web site they are "the first national membership organization dedicated to media literacy." Like the NTC, AMLA is concerned with not being confrontational with the media industries. In their own words: "While media literacy does raise critical questions about the impact of media and technology, it is not an anti-media movement. Rather, it represents a coalition of concerned individuals and organizations, including educators, faith-based groups, health care-providers, and citizen and consumer groups, who seek a more enlightened way of understanding our media environment."

Despite AMLA's mission of creating a broad coalition, the organization's approach is not without controversy. AMLA accepts funding from media corporations such as Time-Warner, which has led some in the media literacy community to question whether this compromises their ability to promote critical thinking about media. In 1999 Channel One was one of the sponsors of the National Media Education Conference put on by AMLA's predecessor, PME. Channel One is a private for-profit enterprise that provides television equipment to schools at no financial cost. They also produce a daily news program that includes 10 minutes of editorial content and two minutes of advertising. Teachers in Channel One schools are required to show the program each day and students are required to sit through it. Critics of Channel One say that the news programming is devoid of any substantive content and the real point of the programming is to expose a captive audience to commercials. A 2006 study supported this criticism when it revealed that students remembered the ads but not the news stories covered in a given program. Because of Channel One's involvement in the 1999 conference, some media educators boycotted the event.

In response to these concerns over AMLA's focus on cooperation with corporate media, in 2002 a number of educators, media practitioners, and activists founded the Action Coalition for Media Education (ACME). Believing that sponsorship always affects outcomes, ACME is committed to complete independence from the media industries and accepts no corporate funding. ACME advocates for a three-pronged approach to media literacy that includes media education, independent media production, and media reform activism. At the core of the ACME philosophy is the notion that both media content and the social context in which content is produced are important. ACME thus supports a type of media education that concerns itself not only with analyzing media messages but also with understanding media industries and their practices and motivations. In regard to the major difference between the two organizations, it is stated on the ACME Web site: "AMLA seeks to be a 'big tent' media literacy organization and specifically rejects 'media bashing' which we view as a limitation on criticism and reform." The split between AMLA and ACME is evocative of the disparity in media literacy advocates' views on the philosophies, goals, and strategies of media education. In fact, ACME advocates the use of the term media education as distinct from media literacy, where media literacy is focused on messages while media education deals with both messages and structures.

THE MEDIA LITERACY DEBATES

There is quite a bit of disagreement among media literacy advocates about key issues related to media education. For example, AMLA describes the functions of media literacy in this way:

> Media literacy empowers people to be both critical thinkers and creative producers of an increasingly wide range of messages using image, language, and sound. It is the skillful application of literacy skills to media and technology messages. (AMLA http://www.amlainfo.org)

While this commonly accepted approach to media literacy is focused on messages, or the content of media, others have argued that content must be understood contextually. A contextual approach focuses on issues such as ownership of the media, structural factors behind what sorts of messages are produced and by whom, what is missing from media content, the consequences of growing up in an environment saturated with commercial values, and the role of the media in promoting or inhibiting democracy. The message-based approach, however, advocates for a version of media literacy that focuses on teaching students to be more adept consumers of media messages, rather than both critical readers *and* active participants in, and even challengers of, the media system itself. This difference in philosophy is indicative of just one of a number of unresolved issues in the media literacy community.

Renee Hobbs, one of the founders of AMLA, has framed these differences in approach and philosophy among media literacy advocates as the "Seven Great Debates." The questions addressed in these debates can be recognized as falling into two broad and overlapping categories: questions about media education strategies and questions about media education goals.

MEDIA EDUCATION STRATEGIES

One of the key strategic debates revolves around the teaching of media production skills as a central aspect of media literacy education. Advocates of a focus on production argue that it allows students to directly experience the media literacy insight that all media messages are constructions rather than reflections of the real world (see "Core Concepts of Media Literacy" sidebar). They also suggest that students can be empowered by learning how to use media technologies to create artistic and creative media of their own. Skeptics, however, argue that too often media production education simply teaches students to imitate familiar commercial media forms and conventions, without any critical reflection on the power of those conventions to shape our values and beliefs.

Another issue of contention related to educational strategies is whether media literacy should be focused on popular culture. Educators and administrators often discount the importance of popular culture, dismissing it as something that is trivial and has no place in the academic environment. Most media literacy advocates, however, recognize the central role that popular culture plays in our lives. In fact, many media educators would agree that the so-called popular culture created by commercial industries has now become *the* culture in which we all grow up, rather than something that stands outside, or on the margins, of culture itself.

A third strategic debate in the media literacy movement is about whether media education can best operate within traditional school settings. While schools do represent the most organized and widespread method of formal education in industrialized nations, critics argue that the central mission of schools is to reproduce the status quo and reinforce existing social hierarchies. Scholars like Henry Giroux point out that learning does not take place only in schools but that the media themselves offer powerful stories, information, arguments, and images that teach us about the world and our place in it. Furthermore, since media affect us all, media literacy should not be considered an educational project that is only meaningful to children. Those who suggest that media literacy is needed for adults as well as children therefore argue that it must be developed both inside and outside of traditional educational settings.

Finally, media literacy proponents also differ on whether media literacy is most effective when it is taught as a stand-alone, self-contained subject area or whether it should be integrated throughout the curriculum. Some educators suggest that media are so pervasive, and have such a powerful impact on our understanding of the world, that the topic must be addressed in fields such as history, civics, science, literature, and so on. Others, however, suggest that media deserve focused critical attention all on their own. These educators worry that a purely integrative approach runs the risk of avoiding important questions about the media themselves while marginalizing key issues related to media and the role they play in shaping our identities and our societies.

MEDIA EDUCATION GOALS

The first of the debates about media education goals revolves around the question of whether media literacy should adopt a so-called protectionist stance. In other words, should it be about protecting people, primarily children, from the negative influence of mass media in promoting violence, irresponsible sexual behavior, unhealthy eating habits, sexist and racist stereotypes, and the like? Or does this sort of approach run the risk of alienating students who do take real pleasure in the media that they use on a daily basis?

Another central question about the goals of media literacy is whether media education should have an explicit political agenda. Some in the media literacy movement claim that it is possible, indeed desirable, for media education to be nonideological—focused on developing autonomous critical thinking among students without embracing a particular point of view. Others, however, argue that there is simply no such thing as purely autonomous thinking and that all of our understandings of the world are embedded within unstated ideological assumptions. These educators believe it is impossible to address the role of the media in society without acknowledging social inequality and hierarchies of power.

A third debate, which at its core is about the goals of media education, is about the role of corporate funding of media literacy projects and curricula.

AMLA, for example, does accept corporate funding, based on the rationale that commercial media must take responsibility for educating consumers about the material they produce and distribute. They also point out that media literacy education in the United States is still underdeveloped and the visibility and financial resources of big media organizations is necessary in order to get the message out to as many people as possible. ACME, on the other hand, believes that funding from corporate media inherently limits the critical possibilities of media education and hinders the potential for connecting media literacy to issues of media reform and activism. For example, Channel One's "Media Mastery" media literacy curricula, which has been made available to thousands of schools, does not include any mention of the corporate role in shaping media content.

CORE CONCEPTS OF MEDIA LITERACY

Despite many differences in their approaches to media literacy, many educators and advocates agree on a number of core concepts, such as the following:

1. All media are constructed and media construct our sense of reality. Media images do not just appear from nowhere. They are made by people and organizations in order to convey particular ideas. Media therefore are not just reflections of reality. Most of what we think we know about people, places, and events that we have not experienced comes to us directly from media. Even when we experience something ourselves our understandings of what we have experienced may be shaped by media images and stories.

2. Different members of the audience will interpret media in different ways. Not everyone will respond to media messages in the ways that the producers intend. Our backgrounds play an important part in how we read a given message. However, media messages will often be read similarly by large numbers of people and often we do accept the producers' vision.

3. Most media is created by profit-oriented businesses and has commercial implications. In the United States only a small number of large corporations own and control the vast majority of the media people read, see, and hear. The primary purpose of this media is to generate profits for the shareholders of the corporations. Information and entertainment are secondary considerations. In television, for example, the point of the programs is to get viewers in front of the set so that they may be exposed to the "real" programming—the commercials.

4. Media contain value messages and have social implications. All messages reflect the biases of their producers. Even media that appear to be just for entertainment tell us stories about the world that suggest how we should think about it. Movies, for example, show us images of men and women interacting and suggest to us what it means to be a real man or a real woman and what are acceptable sorts of gender relations.

5. Each medium has a unique aesthetic form that influences its content. A news story in a primarily visual medium such as television will convey its messages differently

and affect us differently than if it appeared in a primarily print medium such as a newspaper. Media are art forms as well as forms of communication and can be appreciated for how they use the unique qualities of each medium to connect with their audience.

PUTTING THE DEBATES IN CONTEXT: CONSUMERISM VS. CITIZENSHIP

The standpoints that various media educators adopt on the questions noted above are a function of their overall perspectives on the purpose of media literacy. Underneath these various debates about strategies and goals, the essential question that really divides the media literacy community is this: *Is media literacy aimed at creating more sophisticated consumers of media or is it about nurturing engaged citizens?* It is one thing to teach children how to decode an advertisement for fast food, for example, so that they may see how the image of a hamburger is artificially constructed, and doesn't resemble the actual product that you purchase at the counter. It is another thing entirely to encourage an understanding of fast food as a megabillion-dollar global industry that is spreading particular industrial practices and ways of thinking about food, labor, the environment, and the like throughout the world. The consequences of these varying approaches are very different. The student who learns the tricks behind fast-food advertising, but stops there, may feel that this wisdom is sufficient and that they are now free to enjoy their burger and fries from a more informed perspective. The student who learns about the fast food industry's unfair labor practices, cruel treatment of animals, negative impact on the environment, and contributions to obesity and rising health care costs may choose to have a completely different relationship with these companies in the future. This student may simply decide to stop patronizing fast food establishments or they might get involved in working for reform of the industry or educating others about its harmful practices.

Each of the seven questions noted in the debates listed above may be understood in terms of this crucial difference in understanding the central purpose of media literacy.

MEDIA EDUCATION STRATEGIES AND THE CONSUMER/CITIZEN QUESTION

For example, the perspective of media literacy advocates on the teaching of production skills as part of a media literacy curriculum is informed by their position on whether media literacy is about creating sophisticated consumers or engaged citizens. While most educators would agree that teaching production skills can be an important part of media education, they differ on the context in which those skills are taught. Simply teaching the technology, without considering larger questions of how the technology is a crucial part of a hierarchical system where dominant ways of seeing are defined by those in positions of power in society, can lead to students simply trying to emulate what they are so used to viewing every day on their television screens and computer monitors. Advocates of media education for citizens rather than consumers believe that students should also be asked to consider how technology may be used to either resist or, more commonly, reinforce systems of social control. These students would be asked to produce their own media that comment on or go against the grain of the commercial media forms that they are so used to seeing.

Media educators' positions on popular culture in the classroom likewise can be understood as an expression of their overall stance on the central underlying issue of consumerism versus citizenship. Critics argue that we should acknowledge the pleasure that we derive from popular culture. But, they say, we cannot ignore the ways in which so much of popular culture encourages a consumerist relationship to the world, and discourages critical thinking about social issues, while simultaneously reinforcing politics of divide and conquer that turn citizens against one another based on differences of race, class, gender, and sexuality. Rejecting popular culture outright, however, as vulgar and trivial, ignores the crucial role that it plays in shaping our perceptions of ourselves, others, and the world we all inhabit. Media educators who are concerned with fostering citizens who are capable of thinking critically about key issues facing our society (war, the environment, poverty, inequality, racism, sexism, homophobia, etc.) believe that they must engage with the popular culture that shapes our deepest understandings of these issues.

Educators' perspectives on whether media literacy is primarily about creating better consumers or better citizens also play out in the debate over whether media literacy is best promoted in traditional school settings. While the purpose of schools in democratic nations is purportedly to prepare students to assume an active role as participants in their societies, critical education scholars have argued that this is primarily a myth. From a critical perspective the real mission of the U.S. education system is to teach students to willingly accept their preassigned social roles based on the socioeconomic, racial, and gender groupings to which they belong. Those who advocate for a critical sort of media literacy aimed at developing citizens who can challenge established power relations are thus more prone to advocate that media education should take place on a large field encompassing many sites in addition to and outside of traditional school settings. They also contend that in the current media-saturated environment a well-developed sort of media literacy is needed not just for schoolchildren but for adults as well. Community groups, alternative media organizations, religious institutions, libraries, and other public spaces all represent potential alternatives for media education.

However, because schools will invariably play a central role in the development of media literacy efforts, advocates from both perspectives also debate on how best to implement media education in schools. The question of whether media education should be focused in courses specifically about the media or integrated throughout the curriculum may also be understood within the framework of consumerist versus citizenship approaches to media literacy. Those who advocate for a sort of media literacy that is concerned with the relationship between media and democracy would seem to be naturally in favor of courses in history and social studies, for example, dealing with the role the media play in shaping our understandings of the world and public opinion about important social issues. However, from this perspective it is also crucial to have courses specifically devoted to media education in order to avoid losing focus on the centrality of media to the promotion of democracy.

MEDIA EDUCATION GOALS AND THE CONSUMER/CITIZEN QUESTION

In regard to the question of whether media literacy should assume a protectionist stance, those who argue against protectionism point out that people actually receive a lot of pleasure from the media they use and that attempting to protect them from something they have freely chosen is, at best, heavy-handed and insensitive, and at worst, an attempt to justify censorship. However, for those who emphasize the cultivation of engaged citizens rather than sophisticated consumers, a critical stance on the media does not assume that people must be protected from "bad" media and it does not ignore the pleasure that media provide. These critics do argue, however, that the stranglehold of commercial media on our culture is detrimental to democratic ideals. They suggest that, contrary to supporting censorship, they want an opening-up of the media system to more diverse voices and ideas. While recognizing that media do offer audiences all sorts of pleasures, they also ask how commercial industries have come to define what pleasure is and why there is such a narrow range of acceptable pleasurable images on display in the mass media—extremely limited notions of femininity, masculinity, and proper gender relationships, for example.

Educators' perspectives on whether media literacy should be explicitly political or ideological are also clearly related to their sense of its purpose. Those who believe that media literacy should be about cultivating citizenship unavoidably must deal with what might be considered political issues—issues of power, control, access to resources, and the ability to create and implement public policy. Critics of this sort of approach to media education argue that teachers should not impose their own ideological perspectives on students and that a political approach runs the risk of alienating students, parents, administrators, and school boards. Responding to this criticism, others suggest that the *avoidance* of issues such as media ownership and control, corporate concentration and conglomeration, and hypercommercialism and profiteering in the mass media is tacit acceptance of the status quo and therefore just as political as focusing in on these trends and raising critical questions about their impact on democracy. They also argue that asking students to recognize and think critically about power in the media and in the real world, and how it impacts on their lives, is not the same as pushing a particular political ideology on students.

Finally, the different positions that media literacy advocates hold on the role of corporate sponsorship of media education are also quite clearly a function of whether they believe that media literacy is a matter a learning how to read messages in a more sophisticated manner in order to be better consumers of media, or whether media literacy must go beyond messages in order to ask citizens to confront the power of the media industries themselves. Clearly, from the latter perspective, corporate sponsorship of media literacy projects and curricula means that the potential to confront corporate power will be severely diminished. Advocates of citizen-oriented media education argue that lessons in media literacy created by the Time Warner corporation, for example, will never address questions about the monopolization of the media environment by a small handful of profit-oriented firms and whether or not this is good for democracy.

See also Advertising and Persuasion; Children and Effects; Hypercommercialism; Media and Citizenship; Media and the Crisis of Values; Media Reform; Media Watch Groups; Public Access Television; Television in Schools; Violence and Media.

Further Reading: Auferheide, P. *The Daily Planet: A Critic on the Capitalist Culture Beat.* Minneapolis: University of Minnesota Press, 2000; Giroux, H. A. *Living Dangerously: Multiculturalism and the Politics of Difference.* New York: Peter Lang, 1996; Jhally, S. *The Spectacle of Accumulation: Essays in Culture, Media, and Politics.* New York: Peter Lang, 2006; Kubey, R., ed. *Media Literacy around the World.* Piscataway, NJ: Transaction Publishers, 2001; Macedo, D. P., and S. R. Steinberg, eds. *International Handbook of Media Literacy.* New York: Peter Lang, 2007; Potter, J. W. *Media Literacy,* 3rd ed. Thousand Oaks, CA: Sage, 2005; Silverblatt, A. *Media Literacy: Keys to Interpreting Media Messages,* 2nd ed. Westport, CT: Greenwood Publishing Group, 2001.

Bill Yousman

MEDIA REFORM

"Media reform" refers to a broad-based social movement that aims to improve existing telecommunications laws, regulations, and policy in order to bring about a more democratic media system. Issues that media reformers are concerned with include media ownership; the regulation of the television, cable, and radio industries; the quality of journalism; intellectual property; the future of the Internet; and the ideological dominance of commercialism over civic values of community, democracy, and communication rights.

The media reform movement is concerned with a broad range of issue areas and is comprises a network of diverse local, regional, and national organizations committed to a wide array of strategies and tactics. Since the advent of radio technology, citizens and corporations have made organized efforts to influence media laws, regulations, and policies. In general, the media reform movement addresses the effects of a for-profit media system that increasingly fails to fulfill the communications needs of a democratic society. According to the media reformers, media systems should supply the critical information that citizens need to make decisions in a system of self-governance and representative government, and they should provide a forum for civil debate. The failure to meet these requirements is sometimes referred to as the "democratic deficit" by media critics and reformers. Media reform is also concerned with the increasing concentration of media ownership; in the last 20 years, the number of major corporations who own the vast majority of media companies has decreased

---

DID YOU KNOW?

The media industry is changing rapidly. Concentration of ownership in all forms of media is increasing.

Television

According to the Stop Big Media Coalition, between 1995 and 2003, 10 of the largest TV-station owners went from owning 104 stations with $5.9 billion in revenue to owning 299 stations with $11.8 billion in revenue.

Newspapers

Stop Big Media also reports that two-thirds of independent newspaper owners have disappeared since 1975. At time of printing, less than 275 of the nation's 1,500 daily newspapers remain independently owned, and more than half of all U.S. markets (cities and regions) are dominated by one paper.

Radio

Since the Telecommunications Act of 1996, radio has become the most concentrated medium—at one point Clear Channel Communications owned more than 1,300 radio stations, in addition to 42 television stations in 28 different broadcast markets.

Source: Who Owns the Media? http://www.stopbigmedia.com/chart.php (accessed April 30, 2007).

---

from 50 to 10 large conglomerates, according to industry analyst Benjamin Bagdikian. As fewer corporations control more and more channels of information, there is less access to a diversity of viewpoints. Media reformers note that the main motivation for the media companies is profit rather than their role as information providers in the public sphere. Another area that media reform works on is the hypercommercialization and privatization of public spaces and forums.

EARLY CHALLENGES TO COMMERCIALIZING THE BROADCAST SYSTEM

Media reform scholar and activist Robert McChesney notes that the history of citizen resistance to the commercial radio system is often ignored and marginalized. In general, traditional broadcast histories generally agree that the public was not opposed to the trend of private enterprise regulation of the broadcast media system. McChesney argues that this historical consensus naturalizes the system of corporate ownership of the broadcasting infrastructure by marginalizing or ignoring resistance and diverse perspectives about the early direction of broadcast regulation, especially by educators who understood the powerful potential of the mass media. Scholars and public interest historians

KEY MOMENTS IN MEDIA POLICY AND MEDIA REFORM

1927—Radio Act of 1927.

1934—Telecommunications Act of 1934.

1967—Public Broadcasting Act (creates Public Broadcasting System [PBS]).

1969—*Red Lion Broadcasting Co. v. Federal Communications Commission (FCC),* which upheld the constitutionality of the Fairness Doctrine, regulated by the FCC to require broadcasters to present controversial issues of social significance in a fair, equal, and balanced manner.

1971—WLBT in Jackson, Mississippi loses broadcasting license due to a civil rights movement legal battle.

1976—After continued efforts by media activists, the FCC requires cable television operators to provide PEG (Public, Educational and Government) channels and production facilitates; creation of Public Access Television system.

1987—Fairness Doctrine ended as a result of deregulation of media regulation laws.

1996—Telecommunications Act of 1996: sweeping deregulation of telecommunications policies, including radio ownership restrictions.

1998—Pirate radio protest in Washington, DC, at National Association of Broadcasters (NAB). Activists replace NAB flag with a pirate flag.

1999—Independent Media Center (www.indymedia.org) global network of independent media producers and activists begins.

2000—FCC authorizes low-power FM radio stations.

2002—Angels of Public Interest demonstration against new FCC chairman, Michael Powell.

2003—National campaign to keep ownership regulations for newspapers and television; FCC receives over 2 million comments. The FCC, despite nationwide outcry, passes regulation changes. Free Press hosts the first National Conference on Media Reform.

2004—Ownership regulation changes restricted due to lawsuit by media reform organization, Prometheus Project. Media reform is the second most important issue Americans polled care about, after the Iraq War.

2006—FCC announces new review of ownership laws; Network Neutrality campaign begins. Media reform organizations form the Stop Big Media Coalition.

have demonstrated that there has always been citizen resistance to the trends of corporate media. When uncovered, these marginalized historical moments offer lessons to today's reformers.

CIVIL RIGHTS, CITIZEN INVOLVEMENT, AND MEDIA REFORM

An example of a marginalized historical moment of media reform is the WLBT television licensing case. During the late 1950s, civil rights activists in Jackson, Mississippi, were actively working to get better coverage on their local television station, WLBT. Despite filing continuous Fairness Doctrine complaints to the Federal Communications Commission (FCC) regarding racist coverage at WLBT, the station remained completely biased in their support of segregation. The Fairness Doctrine was regulated by the FCC and required broadcasters to present controversial issues of social significance in a fair, equal, and balanced manner. Some complaints about the station included, but were not limited to: no coverage of the civil rights movement in Mississippi or nationally, outright support for segregation and racist policies through opinion and news pieces, and interrupted broadcasts from national news networks, especially during the airing of the announcement of the Supreme Court decision that desegregated the school system (*Brown vs. Board of Education*). In addition, Jackson had a 40 percent African American population, while the television station had an entirely white staff. Local organizers in Jackson gained the attention and the support of the leadership of United Church of Christ and other allied religious denominations. The United Church of Christ had recently created the Office of Communications, Inc. (OC, Inc.), headed by Everett Parker. Working with local civil rights organizers in Jackson, Everett Parker and OC, Inc. challenged the broadcasting license of WLBT, which was up for renewal in 1964.

The license challenge launched a 16-year legal battle over the Jackson station. This challenge was the first time a broadcast license had been challenged over unfair/unbalanced coverage. There was no process for citizens to get a hearing with the FCC. The only people who could participate in the regulatory process were economic stakeholders or people who had electrical interference issues with the station. The FCC denied the license challenge. OC, Inc. appealed the decision a number of times until the license was eventually revoked. Afterwards, a lengthy period of transition occurred, during which WLBT become more diverse, produced better coverage of civil rights issues, and improved the reporting and portrayal of the African American community of Jackson. It became the first majority black-owned television station in the South. The "WLBT case," as it came to be known, created a legacy of citizen involvement with media. Additionally, as a result of the WLBT case, OC, Inc. challenged the FCC to incorporate an Equal Employment Opportunity rule. This rule took effect in the 1970s under continuous pressure from OC, Inc and led to affirmation action programs in the broadcasting industry.

MEDIA OWNERSHIP

Media ownership is at the center of many policy debates and media reform campaigns. In the last two decades, the number of corporations that own major media outlets, like television stations, radio stations, cable, book publishing companies, and music labels has gone from 50 to a concentration of 10 major corporations. Media ownership rules have been increasingly relaxed. In this round of deregulation, laws that formerly regulated the industry to correct market failures such as monopolies and price-rigging were removed or changed, usually to the benefit of corporate interests. The 1996 Telecommunications Act is a classic example of a deregulation law that encouraged media companies to concentrate their ownership of radio stations. In 1995, one owner could own no more than 65 radio stations nationwide; after the act, one owner could own an unlimited number of radio stations. By the year 2002, the corporation Clear Channel owned 1,300 stations across the United States. In 2003, another phase of deregulation began, because the 1996 Telecommunications Act required the FCC to review ownership laws every two years.

In late 2002, the FCC proposed that similar deregulation policies take effect in the television and newspaper industries. Unlike 1996, when there was minimal citizen awareness of media ownership issues, in 2003 a broad-based coalition of bipartisan organizations, citizen groups, academics, media workers, artists, and consumers organized and inundated the FCC and the U.S. Congress with over 2 million comments stating that the change in ownership laws was unnecessary and bad for democracy. Despite this unprecedented outcry, the FCC approved the ownership changes. However, a lawsuit brought by the low power FM activist group, Prometheus Project, and the public interest law firm, the Media Access Project, successfully got a stay on the enactment of the law. The appellate court decided that the FCC had failed to adequately research the impact of concentrated ownership on diversity and localism.

THE INTERNET AND BROADBAND

Despite the seeming ubiquity of the Internet, many Americans are still without access to the Internet. Media reform is concerned with a variety of aspects related to the Internet and broadband connectivity (high-speed Internet access). Media and information technologies are increasingly converging, or coming together to be accessed on the same "pipe" or connection. Telecommunications policies are being designed currently, yet there is limited debate about the direction of these policies that will dramatically affect the future of the Internet. Media reformers work to bring awareness of the potential impact of these policies.

In 2006, Congress took up a major overhaul of the Telecommunications Act called the Communications Opportunity, Promotion and Enhancement Act of 2006, or COPE Act. This act attempted to encourage increased deregulation of the telecommunications industry. Included in this act was a stipulation that would have ended network neutrality, commonly known as "net neutrality." Despite over $175 million spent on lobbying by larger corporations, the COPE Act was successfully resisted by media reform organizations. Net neutrality is one of the key design principles of the Internet that ensures that the network does not discriminate between types of information or the types of parties involved and that information transmitted through the Internet can be equally accessed by all Internet service providers and users.

While the 2006 COPE Act was defeated, corporations are still lobbying for a rewrite of the Telecommunications Act that would have significant implications for the future of the Internet. Media reformers are seeking to write net neutrality into the law.

STOP BIG MEDIA COALITION

In response to a new round of FCC-proposed ownership law changes, media reformers created the Stop Big Media Coalition in 2006. The coalition is actively working to educate the general public about the impact of the ownership rule changes, similar to the campaign of 2003. This round of rule changes includes removal of ownership restrictions on newspapers and television stations. Media reform experts predict that if the rules are enacted, one company could own the major daily newspaper, eight radio stations, and three television stations in the same town; thus consolidating the flow of local political and cultural information through one corporation. The FCC and major media corporations state that consolidation will not hurt the diversity of viewpoints available because people can access information via the Internet. Additionally, the U.S. television spectrum, through which television is broadcast, is transitioning to a digital system, which allows television stations to broadcast on multiple channels in just one analog (nondigital) station. However, the ownership rule changes will also permit one owner to broadcast on 12 to 18 digital channels. In the fall of 2006, media reform research revealed that despite work to increase diversity in ownership of television stations over the last 20 years, women, who comprise 51 percent of the U.S. population, own less than 5 percent of all commercial television stations; and minorities, who comprise 33 percent of the U.S. population, own less than 4 percent of all commercial television stations.

In addition to organizing in response to the proposed ownership rule changes as well as Internet regulation policies, media reformers are actively working to ensure that public broadcasting systems like PBS and National Public Radio are adequately funded by the U.S. government. Media reformers are also working to expand the number of community media outlets, like low power FM radio stations, which broadcast at very low wattage. Finally, media reformers continue to strengthen networks and collaborative strategies in order to expand public interest and concern over the future of democratic media systems.

See also Alternative Media in the United States; Communication Rights in a Global Context; Conglomeration and Media Monopolies; Digital Divide; Hypercommercialism; Media and the Crisis of Values; Media Literacy; Media Watch Groups; National Public Radio; Net Neutrality; Public Access Television; Public Broadcasting Service; Piracy and Intellectual Property; Pirate Radio; Regulating the Airwaves; Surveillance and Privacy; Video News Releases.

Further Reading: Andersen, Robin, and Lance Strate, eds. *Critical Studies in Media Commercialism.* London: Oxford University Press, 2000; Bagdikian, Ben H. *The New Media Monopoly.* Boston: Beacon Press, 2004; Byerly, Carolyn M., and Karen Ross. *Women and Media: A Critical Introduction.* Malden, MA: Blackwell, 2006; Cohen, Elliot D., ed. *News Incorporated: Corporate Media Ownership and Its Threat to Democracy.* Amherst, NY: Prometheus Books, 2005; Goodman, Amy. *Static: Government Liars, Media Cheerleaders, and the People Who Fight Back.* New York: Hyperion, 2006; Halleck, DeeDee. *Hand-Held Visions: The Impossible Possibilities of Community Media.* New York: Fordham University Press, 2002; Herman, Edward S., and Noam Chomsky. *Manufacturing Consent: The Political Economy of the Mass Media,* 2nd ed. New York: Pantheon Books, 2002;

Klinenberg, Eric. *Fighting for Air: The Battle to Control America's Media.* New York: Metropolitan Books, 2007; McChesney, Robert, W. *Telecommunications, Mass Media and Democracy: The Battle for the Control of U.S. Broadcasting, 1928–1935.* New York: Oxford University Press, 1994; McChesney, Robert, Russell Newman, and Ben Scott, eds. *The Future of Media: Resistance and Reform in the 21st Century.* New York: Seven Stories Press, 2005; Mills, Kay. *Changing Channels: The Civil Rights Case That Transformed Television.* Jackson, MI: University Press of Mississippi, 2004; *Outfoxed: Rupert Murdock's War on Journalism.* DVD. Produced and directed by Robert Greenwald. New York, NY: The Disinformation Company, 2004.

Brenna Wolf

MEDIA WATCH GROUPS

Embedded in the First Amendment's protection of freedom of the press is the notion that any democratic society requires an active and empowered media serving as "watchdog." But when the media become many citizens' only or key source of much information, watching the watchdog has often proved as complicated and involved a task as watching others in power, leading to the foundation of numerous media watch groups of various political stripes. What role do such groups play in policing and/or affecting media coverage?

Media watch groups have proliferated to a point where any complete assessment of the field is impossible. Some have ceased operations, but just as new media provide unlimited growth possibilities for fresh publications and broadcasts, the business of watching media for bias, inaccuracy, and obscurantism continues to involve steadily greater numbers of participants. Whether the audience for media watch reporting is growing in proportion to the supply of material is unknown, but the fecundity of the field guarantees a continuing presence of checks and balances against poor journalism practice—and against flawed media criticism. Yet somehow, plenty of both persist. The fragmentation of media watch activity and its relatively low profile among most readers and viewers suggests that even amid greater scrutiny than ever before, media outlets can put forth lazy, biased, and inaccurate reporting with only limited exposure to broadly publicized censure and concomitant possible abandonment by audiences. Media watch organizations find themselves targeted in turn, often by each other, sometimes for their methodology, more often still for their perceived ideological bias.

Increasingly widespread distrust of media may be considered at least partially an effect of media watch activity, as could declining audience share for the most powerful and established media producers. The work of media watch groups, whose reporting and analysis may be carried onward to larger audiences through other channels, including well-funded partisan operations reaching targeted recipients as well as broader constituencies made aware of selected controversies by media coverage. As mainstream media have begun to pay attention to the myriad alternative perspectives circulating on the Internet, the chance of a media watch group's reporting finding larger audiences and achieving an impact grows.

Consider the example of the much-covered downfall of radio personality Don Imus following his racist slur about the Rutgers University women's basketball team after their advance to the 2007 national championship game: Imus, who for an extended period managed to balance a serious persona ratified by prestigious political and media guests with a crude jokester persona that brought him a large audience, was suddenly brought low not only because of his own clumsy response and a cultural tipping point involving the identity of his victims, the political climate of the moment, and evolving standards for public discourse, but because his words were propelled into the court of public opinion by a media watch organization. The impact of the work of a diligent young researcher for Media Matters for America was not immediate, for the antennae of the public are not generally attuned to such frequencies, but it began there, and its growth was sustained by the ready provision of contextual material. Another media watch group, Fairness and Accuracy in Reporting (FAIR), sent detailed quotes from Imus's long track record of such offenses to online subscribers. That and other documentation reverberated over the Internet and was amplified in the blogosphere, making it impossible for mainstream media to continue to accept the phrase as a harmless joke. The reexamination of not only Imus's oeuvre but of his guests' association with him, the networks of influence that keep alive voices of intolerance, and the evolution of standards for mediated discourse was also led by media watch organizations from across the spectrum, as conservatives reacted to perceived censorship by liberals decrying racism and sexism. Imus was ultimately dislodged from his radio and cable television shows by the market consideration of lost advertisers rather than any sudden media watch group–inspired development of corporate morality, but the imbroglio demonstrated that a market for the products of such critics clearly exists in the realm of public opinion.

PROMINENT MEDIA WATCH GROUPS

That represents a change from the long-time status quo, which had largely allowed mainstream media to ignore external critiques. The student-staffed Project Censored, founded by Sonoma State University professor Carl Jensen in 1976, has regularly identified important news under-covered by the mainstream press, but its annual reports are seldom recognized in the media they criticize. Even as the organization has grown under Jensen's successor Peter Phillips into an operation that wins awards, publishes a yearly book, and achieves widespread recognition in alternative newspapers and on the Internet, it remains as unknown to most Americans as the stories ignored by major media. Other media watch organizations generally suffer the same fate. Most remain barely known, if at all, by the public, but like Media Matters's Imus report, their work can percolate through layers of media cross-reporting, sometimes surfacing to embarrass friends and foes alike.

For example, FAIR, known for its criticism of proconservative bias in media, attracted attention for its study critiquing the selection of experts appearing on the PBS show *NewsHour*, debunking some conservatives' notion of a "liberal" bias on the program by pointing out that white males constituted a grossly disproportionate majority of guest experts, even on stories focused on minority concerns. By extending its focus from facts to sources, FAIR, which since 1986 has emphasized "media practices that slight public interest, peace and minority viewpoints," has demonstrated recognition that opinion and analysis require every bit as much attention as news reporting. Like Project Censored, FAIR advocates for more diversity of coverage rather than the curtailing of expression contrary to its aims. From supporting more coverage of the popular nuclear freeze movement during the Reagan administration to its advocacy on behalf of small publishers threatened by proposed postal rules favoring large entities, FAIR has sought to encourage greater attention to populist causes affected by disproportionately scant coverage.

Less inclined to point to lacunae in the news landscape and more focused upon negating ideological enemies is the Media Research Center (MRC), founded in 1985. The MRC claims the mantle of "America's Media Watchdog," calling itself at the top of its home page "The Leader in Documenting, Exposing, and Neutralizing Liberal Media Bias." Its emphasis on the liberal political leanings of what it claims is a substantial majority of journalists, and the notion that such beliefs regularly affect coverage, is a leitmotif of media criticism from the right. Claiming the support of public opinion, which also registers a higher degree of belief in liberal bias than conservative bias (among those detecting any bias), MRC further personalizes its approach through the prominent featuring of the opinions of its founder and president, L. Brent Bozell III. The organization boasts a $6 million annual budget, which supports both news- and entertainment-oriented analysis, as well as its own news service and free-market institute.

THE JOURNALISM REVIEWS

Established watchdogs such as the *Columbia Journalism Review* (*CJR*) and the *American Journalism Review* (*AJR*) retain a voice as media watch organizations even as their editorial energies are channeled more toward reporting on media issues rather than systematically monitoring bias. *CJR*'s famed "Darts and Laurels" feature approaches the criticism function in highly truncated form, but the pithy summaries of good and bad journalistic practice likely receive more attention than all of the more lengthily analyzed correctives of competitors combined, at least among journalists.

DIY MEDIA WATCHDOGS

Established leaders in the media watch field, already experiencing the flux created by the growth of the Internet, may face new competition from not only new sources, but alternate modes of discourse. Fresh on the heels of the success of *The Daily Show with Jon Stewart*, YouTube and other Web sites have arrived to offer a gigantic new community of users the opportunity to practice their own forms of media vigilance. Social networking sites such as MySpace and Facebook invite their users to rank and rate news according to their own preferences. With democratization often comes dilution of critical sensibility, but the invitation to participate in shaping or reshaping media's messages portends new horizons for media-watching cohorts joined together in new ways. When MoveOn.org sought to energize its members in 2004, one of its gambits was to coordinate house parties featuring Robert Greenwald's documentary detailing the nefarious methods of Rupert Murdoch's Fox News, "Outfoxed." Citizens' acquisition of the lexicon and outlook of media watch professionals is likely to continue apace. With ever-increasing numbers of news consumers obtaining their information from the Internet, ready access to media beyond the nation's borders can serve as a reality check against nationalist and establishmentarian blinders, though guidance may still be needed for the majority who would not yet think to explore abroad, even at the keyboard. A Babel of voices may diffuse some of the critical clarity required to upgrade journalistic standards, and even invite more vague and misleading reportage geared toward the lowest common denominator. But the wisdom of crowds will be tested as engagement with the ethos of critical media consumption is given the opportunity to grow.

SCHOLAR WATCHDOGS

While *CJR* and *AJR* are affiliated with educational institutions, their perspectives more closely mirror the backgrounds of the professional journalists who guide them than those of media studies and journalism scholars. The scholarly practice of media criticism has enjoyed an extended boom, however, and many media watch groups cite scholars from diverse disciplines on framing, agenda-setting, and priming, to name a few of the more prominent theoretical constructs. Other media critics straddle academe and journalism, attracting multiple and mixed constituencies in the process. The media-focused work of foundations such as Annenberg and Pew attracts substantial attention, while media watch communities of a sort could also be said to revolve around specific columnists, such as *The Nation*'s press critic Eric Alterman, Professor of English at Brooklyn College of the City University of New York, who is also senior fellow and "Altercation" Weblogger for Media Matters for America, having been dropped as a blogger by MSNBC.com. Scholarly credentials might boost a writer's status as an avatar of media criticism, but the lack of same could hardly be said to stand in the way of participation through readership and subscriber status, letters to the editor, and informal opinion leader activities. Readers of *The Nation*, like those of publications such as *CounterPunch, The Progressive, Mother Jones*, or the *American Prospect*, could be classed generally as media watch groups in their own right, highly attuned to the procorporate bias of mainstream media and not shy about trumpeting it.

Numerous academic scholars have over the years also developed media critiques for educational and documentary videotapes produced by a variety of independent media organizations. One of the first such productions featured Professor Herbert I. Schiller in a humorous critique of the *New York Times*, produced by the Paper Tiger Television collective, which began as a public access channel in New York City in the early 1980s.

Some scholars have emerged as leaders of different kinds of media watch organizations. A notable example is Robert McChesney, a media historian who is founder, president, and board chairman of *Free Press*, a policy-oriented organization emphasizing democratization of U.S. media systems. Active in media literacy circles vigilant against increasing corporate control of the national communication sphere, McChesney and his allies in and beyond academia have foregrounded political economy, where the template for journalism is constantly being transformed. Ben Bagdikian, former dean of the graduate journalism school at the University of California, Berkeley, laid out the rationale for emphasizing media ownership and control in his classic *Media Monopoly*, which through successive new editions chronicled the ever-shrinking number of major corporations controlling the vast majority of U.S. media. Much of the media activism of politically active groups such as MoveOn.org and *Free Press* concentrates on policy issues, watching media less for what it says than for who controls what gets said, and through what avenues.

"FOLLOW THE MONEY!"

The famed Watergate source Deep Throat's instructions to reporter Bob Woodward in *All the President's Men*—"Follow the money!"—applies to the criticism not only of media but of media watch groups. Accuracy in Media (AIM), a conservative voice founded in 1969 by Reed Irvine and now chaired by his son, Donald Irvine, makes the case that Media Matters, for example, is beholden to the Democratic Party and especially to Hillary Clinton, and that its partial funding by billionaire George Soros through the Democracy Alliance contributes to a liberal bias in its reporting. Diverting attention from the precipitating phraseology in the aforementioned Imus case to how it was reported, AIM suggested that "something is fishy" in the Imus affair, blaming ideological bias born of Media Matters's funding source for its approach to reporting Imus's comments. AIM, which claims to have started with a budget of $200, does not disclose the sources of its own reported annual budget of more than $1 million on its Web site, where it invites "strapped" donors to give the organization their cars if they lack cash to donate. Mediatransparency.org documents a steady stream of funding—millions of dollars over the years—for AIM from various iterations of the Scaife Foundation, perhaps the single most significant funder of rightist political causes in the United States with more than $340 million invested so far in ventures that include the Arkansas Project, which unsuccessfully sought to destroy President Bill Clinton with reports that included unsubstantiated murder allegations. Just ahead of the 2000 presidential election, Pittsburgh *Tribune-Review* publisher Richard Mellon Scaife demanded that all photos of and prominent references to Democratic candidate Al Gore be removed from the paper's front page, leaving Republican George W. Bush to dominate that key space. Searching AIM's Web site reveals no reference to that affair.

Funding remains a key determinant of any media watch group's sustainability. AIM and MRC are the major media watch groups on the right, with MRC claiming a budget five times the size of its older peer. Project Censored's use of students to perform much of its work has kept it going strong despite limited funds. FAIR, an early pacesetter, has in some respects, such as its $800,000 annual budget, been eclipsed in the increasingly crowded field on the left by Media Matters's deepened pockets ($6 million annual budget) and the rise of Free Press from a project of the Media Education Foundation to an independent and influential organization with a $5 million annual budget, raised mostly from foundations. Other foundation-supported media watch groups include the Institute for Public Accuracy, led by Norman Solomon, and the Media Alliance, which supports political action and other activities beyond critique. The Center for Media and Democracy, which sponsors PR Watch, Sourcewatch, and Congresspedia, spends about a half-million dollars a year, most of it from a long list of foundations, and gets a good deal of bang for its buck by dominating criticism of the influential public relations industry. Also dominating its media watch sector is the Adbusters Media Foundation, which publishes the 120,000-circulation "culture-jamming" *Adbusters* magazine, operates a Web site, and runs PowerShift, an advocacy advertising agency. Diversified approaches to economic survival can be found in the model of Media Channel, produced by Globalvision New Media, a project of the Global Center. Fledgling media organizations can use the Global Center Foundation as a fiscal sponsor by paying it an administrative fee, keeping open a door for still more media watch and activism organizations to join the field.

Locally focused media watch efforts in the United States appear to have a more difficult time staying afloat. Grade the News (GTN), an award-winning media watch site focused on the San Francisco Bay Area, had to curtail its activities with the lapse of a Knight Foundation grant, just as the region's journalistic quality absorbed a major blow with the takeover of almost all of its newspapers by the budget- and staff-cutting Medianews Group. GTN's methods, utilizing metrics such as column inches; numbers of seconds devoted to broadcast stories; source diversity; and story impact estimates, generate grades for newscasts and newspapers. As incubators of novel media watching praxis, locally based enterprises offer many interesting models that may take root if they survive their beta stages. Retro Poll, also based in the Bay Area, uses students and volunteers to survey randomly generated national samples, measuring responses to opinion questions against answers to factual questions about news, to show that people relying on certain news sources have an inferior grasp of documented facts, correlating with distinct opinion responses at odds with what has in some quarters been referred to as "the reality-based community." News Trust, which allows its readers to rate stories, and applies measures to rate and weight the value of the raters and the ratings, offers a model for media watching that invites scalable applications with potential value for prospective news consumers and producers alike. As Web 2.0 generates new interactive methods of surveillance of and feedback to news producers, the world of media watching is likely to evolve in diverse and unpredictable directions, but the struggle for funding will continue to mute the effects of most such enterprises.

Hope springs eternal for the prospects of a media watcher breaking through to broader consciousness through the viral characteristics of the Internet, but there is little hope for the sector as a newsstand financial proposition. In print, *CJR* and *AJR* survive on reputation and a mix of funding, and trade publications such as *Editor & Publisher* continue to perform media watch functions, mostly for industry audiences. The high-profile bust of *Brill's Content*, a glossy media criticism magazine that briefly achieved a circulation of more than 325,000 but never made money and folded not long after reducing its frequency from 10 annual issues to 4, provides a cautionary tale for anyone hoping for an expanded audience for journalism critique. *Brill's Content*, which attracted advertising befitting an anticipated high-end readership, did bid to engage a broader segment of the public in holding media to account, but its financial failure demonstrated that media watch entrepreneurship has its limits, and that the consumer market alone will likely not sustain such a scale of activity. The issue of advertising revenue to support critical journals also poses a particularly difficult problem in an age when commercial ad buyers have demonstrated their willingness to exert significant influence over media content, making challenging independent analysis all that more difficult to disseminate to a broad public.

THE FUTURE OF MEDIA WATCHING

One of the simplest and most direct models of media criticism to emerge has come from another old media format: television. When Jon Stewart plays back the self-contradicting statements of politicians and juxtaposes official absurdities against common sense, using visual evidence, along with the obligatory look of exaggerated befuddlement, he and the producers of *The Daily Show* on Comedy Central advance media criticism to a stage many consider long overdue. Fans of *The Daily Show* and loyal members of *The Colbert Report*'s "Colbert Nation" in effect become part of a media watch community that not only calls to account those in power as mainstream media seldom have, but ignites in a difficult-to-reach demographic an actual interest in the news, even as trends show declining newspaper readership and news awareness among young people.

Meanwhile, much media critique will, of course, remain trenchant and continue to be a main feature of alternative media and publications, even as it finds its way into more mainstream venues such as Comedy Central. The growth of Internet bloggers able to disseminate almost instantaneous comments about news stories, reporters, errors, exaggerations, and outrages in a media environment ripe with such fare guarantees the continuation and growth of media watching.

See also Alternative Media in the United States; Bias and Objectivity; Blogosphere; Conglomeration and Media Monopolies; Global Community Media; Hypercommercialism; Media Literacy; Media Reform; News Satire; Public Access Television; Public Broadcasting Service; Sensationalism, Fear Mongering and Tabloid Media; User-Created Content and Audience Participation.

Further Reading: Alterman, Eric. *What Liberal Media? The Truth About Bias and the News.* New York: Basic Books, 2003; Bagdikian, Ben. *The New Media Monopoly.* Boston: Beacon Press, 2004; Bennett, W. Lance. *News: The Politics of Illusion.* New York: Longman, 2004;

Entman, Robert M. *Projections of Power: Framing News, Public Opinion, and U.S. Foreign Policy.* Chicago: University of Chicago Press, 2003; Goldstein, Tom. *Killing the Messenger: 100 Years of Media Criticism.* New York: Columbia University Press, 2007; Hall Jamieson, Kathleen, and Paul Waldman. *The Press Effect: Politicians, Journalists, and the Stories that Shape the Political World.* New York: Oxford University Press, 2003; McChesney, Robert. *The Problem of the Media: U.S. Communication Politics in the Twenty-First Century.* New York: Monthly Review Press, 2004; Phillips, Peter, and Project Censored. *Censored 2007: The Top 25 Censored Stories.* New York: Seven Stories Press, 2006; Schudson, Michael. *The Sociology of News.* New York: W. W. Norton and Company, 2002; Solomon, Norman. *The Habits of Highly Deceptive Media: Decoding Spin and Lies in Mainstream News.* Monroe, ME: Common Courage Press, 1999; Zelizer, Barbie. *Taking Journalism Seriously: News and the Academy.* Thousand Oaks, CA: Sage, 2004.

Christopher A. Vaughan

MINORITY MEDIA OWNERSHIP

For many years, minority-owned media have provided audiences with content they could not find in the mainstream media. Now, as the buying power of minorities grows, media giants are targeting minority audiences they long ignored. Should government play an active role in helping minority-owned media remain competitive?

In the United States, minorities owned mass media outlets as early as 1780. Though now "minority" tends to be synonymous with people of color, minority-owned media included non-English-speaking European ethnic groups for nearly 200 years. (The French language *La Gazette Francaise* was launched in 1780 in Newport, Rhode Island.) Wherever immigrants, exiles, foreign businesspersons, or colonizers gathered in large numbers, news publications emerged to serve the new communities.

Now, however, minority-owned media typically refers to outlets owned by and targeting African Americans, Latinos, Asian Americans, Native Indians, and Arab Americans. The owners are either immigrants or native born as are their audiences. They trace their tradition back to the Spanish-language *El Misispi*, launched in 1801; the African American *Freedom's Journal* founded in 1827; the Cherokee language the *Cherokee Phoenix*, first published in 1828; and the Chinese-language the *Golden Hills News*, established in 1854, to name a few. In the twenty-first century, such media outlets include newspapers, magazines, broadcasting outlets, and Web sites.

TIMELINE

1801—Spanish-language *El Misispi.*

1827—African American *Freedom's Journal.*

1828—Cherokee-language the *Cherokee Phoenix.*

1854—Chinese-language the *Golden Hills News.*

1949—WERD-AM in Atlanta, the first black-owned station, goes on the air.

1966—The ruling in *United Church of Christ v. Federal Communications Commission (FCC)*, 359 F.2d 994 (1966), opens broadcast licensing hearings to aggrieved members of the public.

1973—*TV 9, Inc. v. FCC*, 495 F.2d 929, 937 (D.C. Cir. 1973), directs the FCC to give favorable consideration to an applicant who proposed to include ethnic minorities among its owners and managers.

1978—FCC issues the Statement of Policy on Minority Ownership of Broadcast Facilities, 68 F.C.C.2d 979 (1978), adopting a policy of promoting minority broadcast ownership.

1990—U.S. Supreme Court ruling in *Metro Broadcasting, Inc. v. FCC*, 497 U.S. 547 (1990) that the government's purpose in promoting diversity in programming by its distress sale policy and consideration of minority ownership in comparative licensing hearings is constitutionally valid.

1995—U.S. Supreme Court ruling in *Adarand Constructors, Inc. v. Pena*, 515 U.S. 200 (1995) makes affirmative action minority ownership programs highly suspect and overturns *Metro Broadcasting*'s use of the intermediate scrutiny test.

1996—Telecommunications Act of 1996 spurs consolidation of ownership in the radio industry.

1999—FCC adopts Failed Station Television Rule. Television Rule Review, 14 F.C.C.R. 12,903, PP 13–14, 74, created to foster minority television ownership by requiring public notice of a sale of a TV station.

2001—General Electric Company–owned National Broadcasting Co. (NBC) acquires Spanish-language Telemundo Communications Group for $1.98 billion.

2001—Viacom acquires the Black Entertainment Television network (BET) for $3 billion.

2001—The National Telecommunications and Information Administration (NTIA), reports that minorities own 449 of the 11,865 full-power commercial radio and television stations in the United States, a mere 3.8 percent.

2003—The FCC repeals the Failed Station Solicitation Rule (FSSR) 1999 Television Rule Review,14 F.C.C.R. 12,903, PP 13–14, 74, created to foster minority television ownership

2003—The FCC votes to relax its media ownership rules.

2003—The FCC approves the merger of Univision, America's dominant Spanish-language TV network, and Hispanic Broadcasting Corporation, the largest Spanish-language radio network.

2004—In Philadelphia, in *Prometheus Radio Project v. FCC*, 373 F.3d 372 (2004), U.S. Court of Appeals for the Third Circuit in Philadelphia rules that the FCC made irrational and inconsistent assumptions in reaching its justifications for easing ownership rules. The court also orders the FCC to consider proposals to promote minority ownership.

2004—*La Opinión* and *El Diario/La Prensa*, the largest and oldest Spanish-language newspapers in the United States, merge to form ImpreMedia LLC.

2005—Comcast acquires substantial interest in the new TV One, targeting African Americans.

2005—Time Warner acquires previously black-owned *Essence* magazine.

2006—The FCC starts public hearings on its proposal to revise media ownership rules.

2007—Federal regulators approved the sale of Univision to Broadcasting Media Partners Inc.

WHAT DOES "MINORITY OWNED" MEAN?

"Minority owned" doesn't quite mean what it used to. In the past, minority ownership typically meant full financial ownership of a media company. During the latter part of the twentieth century, however, minority ownership required only 51 percent of a company's voting stock be held by one or more minority members under federal law. In the twenty-first century, however, federal lawmakers and regulators are considering whether federally regulated broadcast outlets may be merely minority controlled. That would mean minorities who run but own less than 51 percent of stock in a radio or television station would still qualify for government tax breaks and other incentives, even though whites own the majority of stock in the company.

WHY GIVE INCENTIVES TO ENCOURAGE MINORITIES TO OWN RADIO AND TELEVISION STATIONS?

First, the Federal Communication Commission (FCC) regulates and awards licenses to broadcasters. By law, the commission must regulate in the public interest. The public interest is served in part by "the widest possible dissemination of information from diverse and antagonistic sources," the FCC has said, and media targeting minorities has long played a major role in bringing diverse views to the public. The FCC, however, had operated for nearly 40 years before it first took race into consideration when awarding licenses to own and operate broadcasting stations in 1973.

Under the First Amendment, print outlets cannot be regulated. Consequently, a revision of the meaning of ownership would have no legal or regulatory authority over newspaper, magazine, and book owners. Nevertheless, some are troubled by the emergence of newspapers and magazines aimed at minorities but not fully owned by them. Historically, a minority media outlet's audience was its owner's community. For the most part, owner and audience shared the same cultural values, the same collective identity. And while profit was important to minority media owners, the message was always as important, sometimes more, particularly with African American and Latino media owners. The content they produced had political and cultural significance for their audiences and challenged the white establishment.

Critics of minority-controlled media fear that the traditional political and cultural message will be diluted under white ownership that sees its audience mostly as a commodity to sell to advertisers. In 2001, for example, the

National Latino Media Council, a coalition of Latino civil rights and media organizations, unsuccessfully petitioned the FCC to deny approval of the then pending NBC-Telemundo merger. Among the concerns the council raised was that after the buyout, "programming aimed at Latino audiences [would be] in the hands of non-Latinos, and we cannot dismiss the importance of Latino ownership."

DOES CONSOLIDATION HURT OR HELP?

The survival of minority media ownership became a hot-button issue in 2001. That October, General Electric Company–owned National Broadcasting Co. (NBC) acquired Telemundo Communications Group for $1.98 billion. The following month, global media colossus Viacom acquired the Black Entertainment Television network (BET) for $3 billion. Even before BET and Telemundo changed hands, Time Warner had acquired ownership of African.com and New blackvoices.com in 2000. According to a 2001 report by the National Telecommunications and Information Administration (NTIA), minorities owned 449 of the 11,865 full-power commercial radio and television stations in the United States, or a mere 3.8 percent. Of that small percentage, 426 were commercial radio stations, or 4 percent of total commercial radio ownership. The remaining 23 were commercial television stations, or a paltry 1.9 percent of the country's 1,288 commercial television licenses. Meanwhile, minorities of color represent about 30 percent of the U.S. population.

The merger and buyout trend continued. By 2005, the media conglomerate Comcast, the largest U.S. cable TV operator, owned a substantial interest in the new TV One, targeting African Americans. Time, Inc., a division of the media colossus Time Warner, bought full ownership of the black-owned Essence Communications, the publisher of the successful *Essence* magazine targeting black women.

Consolidation—or concentration of ownership by a small number of companies in one industry—of course transcends the minority media market; it is a worldwide business phenomenon in the twenty-first century. Many argue that when big companies become bigger, small and local ones have difficulty competing for advertisers and investment capital. Minority broadcasters, mostly single-station owners, say recent industry trends have made it nearly impossible for them to grow or stay in business. Should government play an aggressive role to help minority-owned media remain competitive?

SOCIAL RESPONSIBILITY OR FREE MARKETS?

One camp—minority broadcasters, media reform advocates, civil rights activists, and liberal legislators and regulators (mostly Democrats)—say Congress and the FCC must do more to enable minorities to own broadcast stations. Generally, this camp believes that the government has a social responsibility to ensure that the publicly owned television and radio airwaves provide diverse views. Without ownership by minorities (and women), issues that interest minorities are less likely to be aired. They point to a number of studies that have found links between minority ownership and increased public affairs programming and news relevant to minority audiences. They contend that government should actively promote more minority ownership by, for instance, reviving a 1978 program to allow a capital gains tax break to anyone selling an outlet to a minority buyer stemming from the Statement of Policy on Minority Ownership of Broadcast Facilities and the Failing Station Solicitation Rule of 1999 to make it easy for minority bidders to buy stations through an auction process.

The leading advocates for increased government regulations to promote minority media ownership include the Media Access Project, Minority Media and Telecommunications Council, National Telecommunications and Information Administration, Office of Communication of the United Church of Christ, and the Media Access Project.

Generally, media executives, free-market advocates, legislators, and regulators (mostly Republicans) muster in the opposing camp. They gather under the big tent of deregulation. They believe that government should do as little as possible to compel broadcast owners to meet their public interest obligations. Allow companies to compete for customers, they contend, and the public interest will be served because companies will be forced to give the public what it wants or go out of business. They don't believe that minority ownership necessarily provides programming diversity. Based on this view, BET, now owned by Viacom, still has to give its African American audience meaningful content or it will lose money. So even if small black-owned outlets go out of business, black consumers will still be able to get black-centric content from BET, the deregulation camp contends.

List-leading proponents of free-market solutions to achieve diversity include former FCC commissioner chairman Michael Powell, Adam D. Thierer of the Progress and Freedom Foundation, and Mara Einstein of Queens College in New York City.

The primary theater for this battle was the six public meetings that the FCC scheduled in 2006 and 2007 for discussion of its media ownership rules. The FCC's six media ownership rules in question limit the number and types of media outlets a company can own. The FCC, dominated by deregulation-minded commissioners, revised the rules in 2003, generally allowing any one entity to own more and different types of media. But the U.S. Court of Appeals for the Third Circuit in Philadelphia (*Prometheus Radio Project v. FCC*, 373 F.3d 372 [2004]) ruled that the FCC made irrational and inconsistent assumptions in reaching its justifications for easing ownership rules. The court also ordered the FCC to consider proposals to promote minority ownership.

How further deregulation of media ownership limits might affect ownership by minorities and women was an important question for debate at those public hearings. Media reformists argued that without ownership limits, media conglomerates are likely to buy more broadcast stations, newspapers, magazines, and Web sites that target minorities and dilute their distinctive ethnic-centered content and coverage of issues important to people of color.

THE QUESTION OF CONSOLIDATION

Is consolidation among minority media owners a winning counteroffensive to prevent white-owned corporate media giants from owning minority media? Maybe.

In early 2004, Lozano Communications Inc., the owner of Los Angeles–based *La Opinión*, merged with CPK Media, the owner of New York–based *El Diario/La Prensa*, to form ImpreMedia LLC. *La Opinión* was established in 1926. *El Diario/La Prensa* was founded in 1913. "The opportunities this new company presents for *La Opinión* and its readers allow us to become competitive on a national level," said Monica Lozano, CEO of the newspaper and senior vice president of ImpreMedia.

By 2007, ImpreMedia had become a Latino-owned news publishing giant; it owned and managed the largest distribution of Spanish-language print media in the United States. In addition to two original newspapers, the company owned *El Mensajero* in San Francisco, *La Raza* in Chicago, and *Vista* magazine, among its 10 print publications and 8 online properties by 2007. The New York–based company's outlets reached a combined 10 million adult Latinos each month that year.

In 2003, the Hispanic Broadcasting Corporation, once the largest Spanish-language radio network in the United States, merged with Univision. As a result, Univision became the largest Spanish-language television and radio broadcaster operating in the United States. The Department of Justice and the FCC approved the merger that year. But by 2007 it was no longer minority owned. In March of that year, federal regulators approved the sale of Univision to Broadcasting Media Partners Inc., an investor group that includes Madison Dearborn Partners, Providence Equity Partners, TPG, Thomas H. Lee Partners, and Saban Capital Group.

COMMUNICATION POLICY AS A CIVIL RIGHTS ISSUE

Congress's Communication Act of 1934 created the FCC to regulate the electromagnetic airwaves in the public interest. Though the meaning of public interest has changed over the years, the belief that licensees should serve minority interests stems from the FCC's "Blue Book," developed in 1946 to measure radio broadcasters' performance. Those concerns were iterated in the FCC's "1960 Program Policy Statement," which dealt with television programming. The FCC, however, did little to ensure that minority interests were served. In the 1950s, for example, while the black press flourished, only one minority-owned and operated station, WCHB in Inkster, Michigan, existed, founded in 1956. (Black-controlled Radio One currently owns WCHB.) WERD-AM in Atlanta, the first black-owned station, went on the air in 1949.

That started to change when civil rights activist Everett C. Parker, director of the Office of Communication of the United Church of Christ, filed a "petition to deny renewal" with the FCC against WLBT-TV in Jackson, Mississippi, on grounds that the station discriminated against African Americans. In *United Church of Christ v. FCC*, 359 F. 2d 994 (D.C. Cir. 1966), the federal D.C. Circuit Court of Appeals ruled that the members of the public who could show that a licensing decision would harm them could participate in the licensing process.

Specifically, the court told the FCC that African Americans in Jackson, Mississippi, had the right to challenge the renewal of a license to a radio station owner accused of racial discrimination. WLBT lost its license.

That ruling created a process that greatly increased a minority's chances of owning a station. That process was a comparative renewal hearing. In such hearings, the FCC compared the merits of an incumbent station licensee with a new applicant and granted a license to the one who could best serve the public interest. (Under the Telecommunications Act of 1996, comparative renewal hearings were eliminated, allowing the FCC to grant a broadcaster's renewal application if the FCC believed statutory requirements were met.)

In 1973, a federal court ruling, *TV 9, Inc. v. FCC*, 495 F.2d 929, 937 (D.C. Cir. 1973), directed the FCC to give favorable consideration to an applicant who proposed to include ethnic minorities among its owners and managers. That ruling prompted the FCC's landmark Statement of Policy on Minority Ownership of Broadcast Facilities, 68 F.C.C. 2d 979 (1978), in which it adopted a policy of promoting minority broadcast ownership. The FCC said minority broadcast ownership tended to create more diverse programming.

In the 1980s, the FCC and the courts affirmed the desirability of media ownership diversity. But in the 1990s, the forces behind the anti–affirmative action movement dampened that commitment. The 1978 program allowed a capital gains tax break to anyone selling an outlet to a minority buyer. As a result, 200 minority-owned stations were launched within less than 20 years. But the incentive was killed in April 1995 because of allegations of fraud. Mark Lloyd, director of the Civil Rights Forum on Communications Policy, said, "The Republican Congress teamed up with President Clinton to kill the most effective method for increasing minority ownership, the tax certificate. With minority-owned broadcast licenses stuck at around 3 percent, loss of the tax certificate makes any progress beyond that invisible ceiling impossible."

In *Adarand Constructors, Inc. v. Pena*, 515 U.S. 200 (1995), the U.S. Supreme Court ruled that so-called minority preference policies could only be justified by a compelling government interest, narrowly tailored to achieve the goal, and the least restrictive means for achieving it, or "strict scrutiny." This ruling made affirmative action minority ownership programs highly suspect and overturned *Metro Broadcasting, Inc. v. FCC*, 497 U.S. 547 (1990) use of the intermediate scrutiny test. After the Adarand Constructors ruling, the FCC abandoned a proposal for credits to help minorities and women bidding in the auction of FM licenses in 1995.

In 2003, the FCC repealed the Failed Station Solicitation Rule (FSSR) 1999 Television Rule Review, 14 F.C.C.R. 12,903, PP 13–14, 74, created to foster minority television ownership by requiring public notice of a sale of a TV station. The following year, the court in *Prometheus Radio Project v. FCC* said the repeal was unjustified because the FCC had not considered the impact the repeal might have on declining minority station ownership. The court also noted that the FCC had not yet considered the Minority Media and Telecommunications Council's proposal for prohibiting race and gender discrimination in the buying and selling of broadcast outlets.

BEYOND BROADCAST

Beyond the FCC deliberations in 2007, the battle of media ownership deregulation and its impact on minority media ownership were certain to continue at other public meetings, in news periodicals, on Web sites, in federal courts, in Congress, and in the court of public opinion. For example, African Americans have been the most vocal in voicing their concerns about the consolidation of media outlets targeting minorities in the hands of white ownership. In a story about Time Warner's purchase of *Essence* in 2005, the black-owned *Chicago Defender* likened the reaction in some black circles to Robert L. Johnson's sale of BET to Viacom in 2001 as a "firestorm." In that news report, Linda Jefferson, senior vice president and director of media services for black-owned Burrell Communications, said she was troubled by the sale of *Essence* because "a growing issue is the lack of African Americans 'controlling our own stories.'" Earl Graves, the founder and owner of *Black Enterprise* magazine, lamented that "there wasn't an open bidding process in which black entrepreneurs could have made an offer for the company and possibly preserve *Essence* as a black-owned business and institution."

But Ed Lewis, the founder of Essence Communications, and the African American who sold *Essence* to Time Warner, reasoned that even under white ownership *Essence* would remain a black women–centric publication: "[Time Warner] has no desire to change what has been a rock solid mega-brand, which we have done for over 35 years. And from the standpoint of the editorial tone of the magazine, it's always going to be the same because that's what's most important with regard to how we disseminate the kind of information that African American women want."

See also Alternative Media in the United States; Conglomeration and Media Monopolies; Digital Divide; Global Community Media; Hypercommercialism; Media and Electoral Campaigns; Media Reform; Media Watch Groups; Regulating the Airwaves; Representations of Race; Shock Jocks.

Further Reading: Bendixen and Associates. "Ethnic Media in America: The Giant Hidden in Plain Sight." http://news.newamericamedia.org/news/view_article.html?article_id=0443821787ac0210cbecebe8b1f576a3; Consumers Union. "Media Ownership: Minority Ownership." http://www.hearusnow.org/mediaownership/20/; Dines, Gail, and Jean M., Humez, eds. *Gender, Race, and Class in Media.* Thousand Oaks, CA: Sage Publications, 2003; Einstein, Mara. *Media Diversity: Economics, Ownership, and the FCC.* Mahwah, NJ: Lawrence Erlbaum Associates, 2004; Honig, David. "How the FCC Helped Exclude Minorities from Ownership of the Airwaves." http://www.fordham.edu/images/undergraduate/communications/dh%20mcgannon%20lecture%20100506.pdf; Honig, David. "History of FCC Diversity Initiatives." Minority Media and Telecommunications Council. http://ww.awrt.org/advocacy/Diversity/History_FCC-Diversity_Initiatives.pdf; Meiss, Guy, and Alice Tait, eds. *Ethnic Media in America: Building a System of Their Own.* Dubuque, IA: Kendall/Hunt Publishing, 2006; Miller, Sally M. *The Ethnic Press in the United States: A Historical Analysis and Handbook.* Westport, CT: Greenwood Press, 1987; Napoli, Philip M., ed. *Media Diversity and Localism: Meaning and Metrics,* Mahwah, NJ: Lawrence Erlbaum Associates, 2007; Rodriguez,

America, and Kofi Asiedu Ofori. *Reinventing Minority Media for the 21st Century: A Report of the Aspen Institute Forum on Diversity and the Media*. http://www.aspeninsti tute.org/atf/cf/%7BDEB6F227–659B-4EC8–8F84–8DF23CA704F5%7D/DIVERSITY. PDF; Wilson, Clint C., Felix Gutierrez, and Lena M. Chao, eds. *Racism, Sexism, and the Media: The Rise of Class Communication in Multicultural America*. Thousand Oaks, CA: Sage Publications, 2003.

Arthur S. Hayes

MOBILE MEDIA

Mobile media have been with humanity since we began walking and talking simultaneously. Today's technologies give us the capacity to reach anyone at any time, regardless of where we or they might be. But this means we also are on call, literally, whether we want to be or not. Mobile communication begins in every human being. We walk and we talk. The act of being human is an act of mobile communication.

A BRIEF HISTORY OF MOBILE MEDIA

Technologies entered the process of mobile communication with the invention of portable writing systems. Carvings on a wall are not mobile. Scribblings on papyrus, parchment, and paper are—because they can be carried along with us. Writing implements ranging from brushes to quills and pens of various shapes and constructions allow us to become producers as well as consumers of mobile written media.

The end of the nineteenth century brought a burst in both traditional portable written media and new media that extended the range and content of communications. Laptops in Victorian times were fold-up, portable desks, not computers, and the Kodak camera, introduced by George Eastman in 1888, was a camera that anyone could take anywhere.

Mobility in media progressed only slightly in the first part of the twentieth century. Radios by Transitone placed in automobiles in 1929 were the rare step forward. But the transistor, invented in 1948, revolutionized communications, and embodied Buckminster Fuller's "dymaxion principle" (*Nine Chains to the Moon*, 1939) of technologies getting smaller and smaller and doing more and more. It did not take long for radios to move from behemoths in the living room to devices you could hold in your hand and take with you on a walk in the park.

The ancestors of the cell phone soon followed, but it would be decades before cell phones would become widespread. In the meantime, portable communication devices had a vibrant life in fiction, ranging from Dick Tracy's talking wrist watch, to car phones in movies such as in the 1951 version of the movie *Sabrina*, to *Star Trek*'s communicators—which many cell phones have come to resemble in the twenty-first century.

A TIMELINE OF MOBILE MEDIA

3000 B.C.—Reed pens and papyrus in use in Egypt.

300 B.C.—Paper in China.

100 B.C.—Parchment in Pergamom.

1450 A.D.—Gutenberg introduces printing press in Europe.

1850s—First modern fountain pens in Europe.

1870s—Victorian portable laptop desks in widespread use.

1880s—Waterman mass-produced fountain pens.

1888—Kodak camera by George Eastman.

1929—Transitone radios in automobiles.

1946—Motorola and Bell operate first commercial mobile phone system.

1948—Transistors invented independently in the United States and in Europe.

1973—Martin Cooper of Motorola makes first call on handheld mobile phone.

1981—First laptop computers.

1992—PDAs (personal digital assistants).

1998—Bluetooth standards established.

2001—iPod launched by Apple.

2002—First widespread cameras in cell phones in the United States.

2006—80 percent of world's population has cell phone coverage; 2+ billion in use.

2007—iPhone launched by Apple.

2007—More than 100 million iPods in use.

THE MODERN ERA

Microchip technology replaced the transistor in the 1980s and facilitated the rise of laptop computers. RadioShack's M100 was an early successful model, and by the end of the decade IBM-compatible laptops weighing a few pounds or less were commonplace.

The cell phone became ubiquitous in many parts of the world in the 1990s and the early twenty-first century. Eighty percent of the world's land mass had mobile phone service in 2006. Japan, Israel, and Hong Kong, among other nations, have more than 100 percent cell phone saturation (meaning there are more cell phones than people in those countries). As of 2007, Africa had the sharpest growth rate in cell phones. Historians of technology call this kind of growth "leapfrogging"—it occurs when a culture with few technological assets catapults to the most advanced stages.

Advances in wireless technology such as Bluetooth have made cell phones not only wireless but "handless." At the same time, integration of cell phones with laptop Internet functions resulted in all-purpose, small, mobile communication devices, with which users could not only talk, but send text messages, watch television programs downloaded from the Web, listen to radio via live-streaming, and in fact receive on this one device the dozens of services that only a decade earlier had been dispersed over discrete, nonintegrating media such as television, radio, and the Internet.

MOBILE USES AND CONCERNS

As a device for receipt of content formerly available only via mass media, the new all-purpose mobile communication device stirred little controversy until the corporate giant Verizon attempted to restrict text messages from a pro-choice group to consumers who had signed up to receive them. Immediate and overwhelmingly negative responses to the announcement caused Verizon to rescind the policy (Liptak 2007). The specter of corporate censorship was then added to other controversial issues raised by the use of cell phones. As a device for conversation—as in talking on the phone in public or driving one's car while talking on the phone—the cell phone has been the object of a variety of social concerns.

These concerns include the appropriateness of talking on the cell phone in certain public places, ranging from restaurants to movie theaters to funeral homes. Such battles over proper social cell phone etiquette have resulted in their being banned in certain places in the United States—such as the "quiet" cars on Amtrak trains. Talking and driving presents the use of two powerful technologies, a combination that many believe pushes human multitasking abilities to the edge. Highway safety agencies tie cell phone use to car accidents and numerous states levy hefty fines on those who find it hard to separate driving from talking on their cell phones. Another set of concerns pertains to the "right" of people not to answer their cell phones when called—to be offline or unavailable, without insulting the caller.

Cell phones have also been at the center of debates over surveillance and privacy. Many parents in particular have enjoyed the access to their children that phones give them, allowing them to "check up" on children at all hours. The devices also convince many parents that their children are safer, since they are able to call home or emergency services in a matter of seconds. But teens may be less enthusiastic about their parents' abilities to keep a cellular leash on them. Surveillance issues are also writ large with the advent of better mobile tracking that allows authorities to locate a cell user: when our every call can be recorded and geolocated, many worry about the potential for abuse of such information, especially when phones are being used by political dissidents. Some in the medical profession, such Dr. George Carlo have attempted to raise issues of harmful medical side effects of cell phone use. Such concerns are usually not taken seriously, and debates over health issues remain underreported by the mainstream media.

Whatever the resolution of such social issues, mobile media continue to increase in popularity, and indeed have become extensions of the self for many people. What the device looks like when in use, when held close to one's ear, has become as significant a criterion in the decision to purchase as what the device can do and how it can perform. Meanwhile, the photos, songs, and icons one chooses to carry in one's phone are used to announce and perform various individual and group identities.

In recent years, too, the camera function of cell phones has allowed various forms of citizen journalism, or at least a contribution to the journalistic process, with newsrooms soliciting and often using photos sent in real time to them by everyday citizens. The most notable cases of cell phone journalism was the stealth recoding of the assassination of Saddam Hussein, which caused international embarrassment to the United States because of its sensitive political nature and the perceived brutality of the recorded scene. Certainly, if concerns over surveillance surround cell phones, the devices' camera function also allows a different form of surveillance, as users have employed cell phones to record everything from unethical behavior by teachers, to police treatment of protesters, to breaking news events. With YouTube and other social networking sites allowing instantaneous and mass circulation, we may be entering an era of do-it-yourself reality television and journalism, in which the cameras are always potentially rolling.

THE FUTURE OF MOBILE TECHNOLOGY

iPods, introduced in 2001, are a distinctly twenty-first-century portable medium and have none of the controversy surrounding cell phones. This is because the iPod is fundamentally a one-way medium, the equivalent of the transistor radio from half a century earlier, in which users listen to music obtained from the Internet at times of their choosing. But iPods, handheld computers, cell phones and now iPhones are becoming increasingly integrated in single devices that do all the tasks of these previously distinct mobile media.

This enormous growth of mobile technology has taken a toll on older media, ranging from public phone booths—disappearing rapidly from public places—to paper telephone directories, neither of which is necessary when everyone has a cell phone in his or her pocket. As advertisers seek space on every emerging medium, shifting revenues to new media devices, critics worry about the intrusion of commercial messages into yet another personal space.

We can expect even more of this in the future, as older technologies continue to merge into and be co-opted by new all-purpose mobile media—which may, at some point, come to be implanted in our bodies, as the ultimate convenience or intrusion, depending upon one's point of view.

See also Blogosphere; Hypercommercialism; The iTunes Effect; Media Reform; Online Digital Film and Television; Online Publishing; Paparazzi and Photographic Ethics; Surveillance and Privacy; User-Created Content and Audience Participation.

Further Reading: Agar, John. *Constant Touch: A Global History of the Mobile Phone.* London: Icon, 2005; Brin, David. *The Transparent Society.* Boston: Addison-Wesley, 1998; Carlo, George, and Martin Schram. *Cell Phones: Invisible Hazards in the Wireless Age.* New York: Carroll and Graf Publishers, Inc., 2001; Castells, Manuel, Mireia Fernandez-Ardevol, Jack Linchuan Qiu, and Araba Sey. *Mobile Communication and Society: A Global Perspective.* Cambridge, MA: MIT Press, 2007; Glotz, Peter, and Stefan Bertsch, eds. *Thumb Culture: The Meaning of Mobile Phones for Society.* New Brunswick,

NJ: Transaction, 2005; Ito, Mizuko, Daisuke Okabe, and Misa Matsuda, eds. *Personal, Portable, Pedestrian: Mobile Phones in Japanese Life.* Cambridge, MA: MIT Press, 2005; Katz, James. *Magic in the Air: Mobile Communication and the Transformation of Social Life.* New Brunswick, NJ: Transaction, 2006; Kavoori, Anandam, and Noah Arceneaux, eds. *The Cell Phone Reader.* New York: Peter Lang, 2006; Levinson, Paul. *Cellphone: The Story of the World's Most Mobile Medium, and How It Has Transformed Everything!* New York: Palgrave/Macmillan, 2004; Ling, Rich. *The Mobile Connection: The Cell Phone's Impact on Society.* San Francisco: Morgan Kaufmann, 2004; Liptak, Adam. "Verizon Reverses Itself on Abortion Messages," *New York Times*, September 28, 2007. http://www.nytimes.com/2007/09/28/business/28verizon.html?_r=1&oref=slogin; Messaris, Paul, and Lee Humphreys, eds. *Digital Media: Transformations in Human Communication.* New York: Peter Lang, 2006; Steinbock, Dan. *The Mobile Revolution: The Making of Mobile Services Worldwide.* Philadelphia: Kogan, 2007; Wakefield, Tony, Dave McNally, David Bowler, and Alan Mayne. *Introduction to Mobile Communications: Technology, Services, Markets.* Boca Raton, FL: Auerbach, 2007.

Paul Levinson

NARRATIVE POWER AND MEDIA INFLUENCE

Pluralistic democracy depends on a contest of competing public narratives. Media present a variety of different and sometimes conflicting stories within a multiculture and, thereby, mirror the distribution of political power in society. Narrative analysis can provide a critical lens for understanding media power and influence.

Narrative communication is as old as bards and as contemporary as bloggers. Whether stories are told by word of mouth or transmitted by satellite, they help to shape community and to define culture. Narrative communication is an interactive collaboration between speaker and listener, writer and reader, or producer and viewer, situated in a particular social context. The *tellers* of tales ascribe meaning to behavior, foundation to belief, and root to ritual. They wield great power even when committed to neutrality or objectivity.

A narrative is composed of two elements: story and storyteller. These are so tightly interconnected as to seem inextricable ("Who can know the dancer from the dance?"). Yet, when one hears the caution to "consider the source," analytical distinctions have already emerged. Story consists of four components—character, event, place, and time. No story can exist without at least one *character*, although that character needn't be human or even familiar to human experience. (Think of the fabled Chicken Little or Ray Bradbury's Martian.) Further, any story must include at least one *event*: something happens. Not every action needs be visible, as in a person's thinking process that leads to a difficult decision. Characters and events are necessarily located some *place*— real or imagined, internal or external, recognizable or alien. Finally, the characters, events, and locale of a story are situated in *time*, whether measured by

DEFINITIONS

"Narrative" is used to describe so many different communication acts that its definition can become slippery. Here are some meanings for the word, each legitimate in other analytical contexts, but *not* included in this discussion:

- Narrative as a literary genre distinguished from poems, plays, and essays
- Narrative as a rhetorical mode distinguished from the lyric and dramatic
- Narrative as a compositional technique distinguished from the expository

"Narrative," used here, is *a rhetorical construct* that emerges collaboratively between teller and listener (or writer and reader, producer and viewer).

---

history, season, day, or clock. To grasp any story, regardless of the technology of its transmission, depends on seeing the meaningful connections among character, event, place, and time.

Story*telling*, the second element of narrative communication, is comprised of (1) a narrator, (2) an audience, and (3) the sequencing of information. Stories do not exist apart from their telling. Some narrators are clearly visible in their own stories, standing center stage. Others are virtually invisible, hidden behind the scenes. Likewise, some narrators are reliable, and others prove untrustworthy. A teller and an audience cocreate meaning. When they fail in that effort, a frustrated teller might say, "I guess you just had to be there," acknowledging both the importance of context to a story and the difficulty of narrative collaboration with an audience. Inasmuch as storytelling occurs in time, a narrator must *sequence* events, one before the other, each new word or image supplanting its predecessor. Temporality makes narrative more akin to dance or music than to painting or architecture. A story, when it is being told, is never there all at once. Even when two events occur simultaneously in the story (e.g., the gangland execution of rivals at the same moment that the murderer stands up at a family baptism in *The Godfather*), the *telling* of those events cannot be simultaneous. A narrator must decide how and why to sequence information for an audience, choosing what details to include or exclude, what characters to empower or marginalize, what events to promote or demote. In other words, *how* a story is told is telling in itself.

AN EXAMPLE: THE U.S. PRESIDENT AS NARRATOR

Consider the narrative role of a U.S. president. "Commander-in-Chief," "Chief Executive," and "Party Leader" are among the more familiar titles accorded any president. However, "national narrator," an unacknowledged role, trumps the others in potency. Every four years, citizens of voting age have the opportunity to elect the narrator of their collective story. *Who* tells the nation's story makes a substantial difference to the story itself, as well as to its audiences. Which characters will be cast in major roles? Who will be marginalized as minor characters? Who will become hero, and who villain? Who might be silenced altogether?

NARRATIVE STUDIES

Narrative studies is an interdiscipline drawing intellectual perspectives from the arts, humanities, social and behavioral sciences (especially cognitive psychology), and natural sciences (especially neuroscience applied to memory). Narrative studies seeks to address four questions:

1. How do human beings *acquire* knowledge through stories and storytelling?
2. How do human beings *store* and *retrieve* knowledge through stories and storytelling?
3. How do human beings *disseminate* knowledge through stories and storytelling?
4. How do human beings *validate* or *invalidate* knowledge through stories and storytelling?

The concurrent study of media is implicated in each of these questions.

Which events will take prominence in the national plotline, and which will be subordinated or denied? What locales will be privileged? What themes will emerge?

When pulling the curtain on a voting booth, a citizen considers which presidential candidate is more likely to tell the nation's story in a way that values his or her own viewpoints, priorities, and communities. The meaning of the story to multiple audiences, both domestic and international, resides in the sensibility of its teller. Think how different the American story sounded when told by John F. Kennedy versus Richard Nixon, or consider the differences between Bill Clinton and George W. Bush as national narrators.

For most of U.S. his*tory,* women have been relegated to the status of minor characters. Until emancipation, African Americans were not considered characters at all. Hundreds of years passed before women and persons of color moved from the margins of America's story toward its center. The same could be said of the *events*, *places*, and *times* featuring those characters. The power of a teller to construct narrative reality is so great, and the attendant privilege so seductive, that most tellers are reluctant to relinquish their role. (Witness the 22nd Amendment to the U.S. Constitution legislating presidential term limits.) America's story is likely *really* to change when the demographic profile of the storyteller changes. Electing a woman or person of color as national narrator will represent a fundamental power shift; both possibilities have encountered considerable cultural resistance.

THE NARRATIVE ROLE OF MEDIA

It might seem that representatives of the media—professional print and electronic journalists, as well as citizen journalists in digital formats—would fit into a narrative model as *meta*-narrators, secondhand reporters of other people's stories and storytelling. The word "reporter" itself reinforces presumptions of impartiality and distance, as in *court reporter*. However, the narrative role of media is much more significant than the reporter model suggests. Media representatives—whether writers, broadcasters, documentarians, or bloggers—reveal their points of view with every word choice, photo selection, and edit. They define character, underscore event, privilege place, and announce time. They roll out a story incrementally, one moment at a time, in order to prompt specific interaction with an audience. It would be much healthier for the democratic contest of narratives to acknowledge this power of media rather than to ignore or deny it.

In 2007, in the wake of multiple campus shootings at Virginia Tech University and the media coverage that followed, one student spoke her frustration to a TV broadcaster: "You've got your story." She made her point with the second pronoun: "You've got *your* story." Apparently, this student, a first-person participant, felt co-opted into "your" [the broadcaster's] story. Bill Moyers, legendary independent journalist, looks to the Internet to democratize media monopolies, empowering more first-person storytellers: "Freedom begins the moment you realize someone else has been writing your story and it's time you took the pen from his hand and started writing it for yourself."

In acknowledgment of media influence, consider five guidelines of narrative ethics:

1. To ensure fairness to all "characters," determine whose story is being told, and the possible consequences of giving voice to another.
2. To ensure fairness to all "audiences," determine what selection and sequencing of information will best assist comprehension and responsiveness.
3. To ensure fairness to "events," determine all relevant contexts, including "place" and "time," required for understanding.
4. To ensure fairness to other media sources, any secondary or tertiary representation should specify prior transformations from medium to medium (e.g., a TV broadcast, edited into a clip for YouTube, then incorporated into a blog).

To ensure fairness to oneself as "narrator," interrogate all human sources for the accuracy and completeness of their statements.

See also Audience Power to Resist; Bias and Objectivity; Blogosphere; Media and Electoral Campaigns; Minority Media Ownership; Presidential Stagecraft and Militainment; Propaganda Model; Public Access Television; Representations of Class; Representations of Race; Representations of Women; Transmedia Storytelling and Media Franchises; User-Created Content and Audience Participation.

Further Reading: Andersen, Robin. *A Century of Media, A Century of War*. New York: Peter Lang, 2006; Coles, Robert. *The Call of Stories: Teaching and the Moral Imagination*. Boston: Houghton Mifflin, 1989; Iser, Wolfgang. *The Implied Reader: Patterns of Communication in Prose Fiction from Bunyan to Beckett*. Baltimore: Johns Hopkins University Press, 1974; Lakoff, George. *Thinking Points: Communication our American Values and Vision*. New York: Farrar, Straus, and Giroux, 2006; Lakoff, George, and Mark Johnson. *Metaphors We Live By*. Chicago: University of Chicago Press, 1980; Mumby, D. K. "The Political Function of Narrative in Organizations." *Communication Monographs* 54

(1987): 113–27; Rich, Frank. *The Greatest Story Ever Sold: The Decline and Fall of Truth From 9/11 to Katrina.* New York: Penguin, 2006.

James VanOosting

NATIONAL PUBLIC RADIO

The news and public affairs programs of National Public Radio (NPR) have been showered with awards. Its affiliated stations provide the sole outlet for non-commercial radio programming in many communities. To the majority of the American public, National Public Radio *is* public radio. Yet the system has faced many internal and external challenges throughout its history, and it is arguable as to how "public" NPR remains today.

Public radio in the United States was formally inaugurated in 1970 with the creation of NPR (replacing National Educational Radio) and the earmarking of federal funds for the production of programming. NPR's founders hoped that renaming the system "public" would have greater appeal than the often dry and amateurish "educational" system it replaced. However, the name change raised several implications that were ignored at the time of NPR's founding and continue to nettle it to the present. First, a "public" broadcasting system implies ownership by the public. Yet National Public Radio and its television counterpart, the Public Broadcasting Service (PBS), as well as many public radio and television stations, are privately owned and operated on a nonprofit basis, which raises significant barriers to public participation. A second problem concerns its contradictory mission. Public broadcasting was designed to promote national identity through broad appeal; at the same time, it was intended to represent public diversity by giving a voice to those who are overlooked or ignored by commercial broadcasters. Finally, public broadcasting differentiates itself from commercial broadcasting on grounds of "quality." Yet "quality" cannot be defined objectively, involving as it does both innovation and a canonical approach to culture, and sophisticated production values versus rough-hewn "authenticity." Given its often-contradictory mission, public broadcasting in the United States operates in a highly uncertain environment. It is a fractious coalition of diverging interests, ranging from government funding entities (the Corporation for Public Broadcasting), national organizations (NPR and PBS), stations, and independent producers, each of whom seek leverage over the others.

Public radio has attempted to cope with these uncertainties in several ways. First, it has increasingly sought to develop a "brand" by standardizing programming in a manner similar to that of commercial broadcasters. Public radio stations seek "core" audiences that will provide them with funding; therefore, these stations devote more and more of their airtime to programs produced by NPR and other services in order to build a consistent audience base. These programs attract upscale audiences who will contribute financially to stations, yet they squeeze out local innovation, public involvement, and service to minorities— all of which are central tenets of public broadcasting's mission. Second, public radio on the local and national levels has adopted audience research methodologies developed by commercial broadcasters. Consultants and focus groups are used for decisions on programming, audiences are "managed" and packaged for advertisers, and more and more stations have replaced volunteers with employees. Third, public radio increasingly defines audiences through ratings, which are also used by the commercial broadcast industry. Public broadcasters can't quantify "service" as commercial broadcasters can quantify profits, yet ratings provide them with a numerical basis for decision making. In theory, ratings indicate popular preferences; in practice, they provide proof of demographics to potential sponsors. As a result, public radio increasingly resembles its commercial counterparts. As NPR and its affiliate stations increase efficiency in an uncertain environment, these measures undermine the very reason for their existence.

PUBLIC RADIO INTERNATIONAL

Although many people view NPR as the primary organization for public radio in the United States, Public Radio International (PRI) actually distributes more programming to stations. PRI was founded in 1982 as American Public Radio (APR), a consortium of stations located in large markets—Minnesota Public Radio, New York's WNYC, Cincinnati's WGUC, San Francisco's KQED, and KUSC in Los Angeles. These stations, which produced much of their own programming, chafed under NPR's control of programming distribution. APR's first program was Minnesota Public Radio's *A Prairie Home Companion*, which initially was rejected by NPR. The program subsequently became one of public radio's major successes.

Rather than providing a complete schedule of programming, as did NPR, APR offered individual programs to public radio stations on an exclusive market-by-market basis. As NPR focused on news following its near-demise in the early 1980s, APR became the largest supplier of cultural programs in public radio. In response to a threatened antitrust suit from APR, NPR began "unbundling" its programs, offering them as groups, in 1987. However, APR offered producers more money, and many popular NPR programs, such as *Mountain Stage* and *Whad'ya Know*, jumped to APR distribution. Costs for the most popular programs rose dramatically for stations at a time when many of these stations were hard hit by declines in federal and state funding.

In 1994, reflecting its broader goals and growing collaboration with the BBC, APR changed its name to Public Radio International and began producing as well as distributing programming. PRI continued to draw listeners through programs such as *Marketplace*, which attracted corporate funders and reflected public radio's increasingly close ties to business. PRI has distributed many of public radio's most notable programs, yet these programs come at a high cost. By offering individual programs to stations, PRI introduced marketplace economics into the public radio system. While this move may have led to greater competition and, arguably, more diversity, critics have noted that PRI has devoted most of its efforts to reaching upscale audiences through classical music and business-oriented news and public affairs programming, relegating the less popular "conscience" items to NPR and other sources.

HISTORY

National Public Radio can trace its lineage to the University of Wisconsin, where experimental station 9XM (now WHA) was established in 1914. Before World War I, many land-grant colleges in the Midwest were broadcasting educational programs as well as news and weather. By 1925, 171 educational organizations had stations on the air, accounting for almost one-third of the radio stations in the United States. However, by 1936 only 38 educational radio stations remained due to Depression-era funding cuts as well as federal regulations (most notably, the Communications Act of 1934) that favored commercial broadcasters. The Ford Foundation, which throughout the 1950s and early 1960s nearly single-handedly set the agenda of what would become public broadcasting, virtually ignored radio; it was added to the Public Broadcasting Act of 1967 only at the last minute. While the number of noncommercial radio stations had grown throughout the 1950s, most were low-powered student laboratories with very limited budgets. A 1969 study recommended that federal funding be directed to the most well-established noncommercial radio stations as a form of triage, and that a national programming service be created to provide consistent programming to these stations. The resulting service, NPR, was formally incorporated on March 3, 1970.

A former executive recalled that "in part, NPR was a missionary enterprise whose role was to broadcast programs which would *not* be commercially viable" (Looker 1995, p. 113). NPR's first production was a tape of 20 concerts by the Los Angeles Philharmonic, and it began live programming with coverage of the Senate Foreign Relations Committee hearings on Vietnam in April 1971. NPR's flagship program, *All Things Considered*, was modeled on the Canadian Broadcasting Corporation's (CBC) *This Country in the Morning*, whose "long-form" reports of narratives interspersed with "actualities" (taped interviews and ambient sound) marked a significant departure from the 60-second news spots that were standard fare on commercial network radio. *All Things Considered*'s first broadcast, on May 3, 1971, was carried by 104 stations and included nearly half an hour of excerpts from May Day protests by Vietnam veterans, a 16-minute story about a heroin-addicted nurse, a CBC piece about war, and a contribution from WOI in Ames, Iowa, about waning business at a barbershop. It concluded with a conversation between poet Allen Ginsberg and his father.

All Things Considered won its first Peabody Award for excellence in radio journalism in 1973, yet the program's success heightened tensions between NPR and its affiliated stations. Local station submissions to NPR were intended to account for one-third of *All Things Considered*, yet many were rejected on grounds of poor quality or lack of national interest. In addition, NPR reporters would at times suddenly "appear" to cover an event in a local affiliate's coverage area without giving the station prior notice, and the varying length of the program's segments offered few opportunities for local stations to address listeners. The biggest complaint, however, was that much of *All Things Considered*'s "populist" programming was at odds with the high-culture agenda of the university stations that formed the backbone of the public radio system. While these stations may have welcomed the raised profile and prestige afforded by national programming, many chafed at carrying programs that did not "fit" their affluent audiences or clashed with classical music programming.

Such conflicts are inevitable whenever new structures are overlaid on older organizational forms, and station representation has been an ongoing source of conflict within the public radio system. Public radio has been subject to fluctuations in federal and state funding, which contributes to the system's instability. NPR continued to turn in a "hard news" direction with the implementation of *Morning Edition* in November 1979. Reflecting the growing clout of consultants with backgrounds in commercial radio, *Morning Edition* was designed on a "clock hour" format, with set time segments for stories and frequent cutaways to local stations. To some critics, *Morning Edition* represented a milestone in NPR's history: the transformation from a *program*, or series of contiguous programs, to a *service*, or as Looker notes, "something that listeners would not listen to from beginning to finish" (1995, p. 123).

THE REAGAN YEARS

The election of Ronald Reagan to the presidency in 1980 plunged public broadcasting into crisis. The new administration initially proposed to end all funding for public broadcasting; the final budget included drastic funding cuts. NPR then embarked on a series of self-sustaining venture capital projects that would replace government funding by 1987. The projects were ill-conceived and haphazardly implemented, however, and NPR came within 24 hours of filing for bankruptcy in June 1983. The network was rescued by a last-minute loan from the Corporation for Public Broadcasting, but the bailout would have a cost. NPR would have to open its satellite system to competitors such as American Public Radio, and nearly all federal funding would go to stations, who then would purchase programming from NPR and its competitors (NPR presently receives only 2 percent of its funding directly from the federal government). NPR would stake its reputation on news and public affairs programming, and cultural and performance programming would continue largely as afterthoughts.

NPR showed a profit by 1985, but the days of significant innovation at the network were over. National programming decisions were now driven by stations, which increasingly relied on commercially derived audience research methodologies to determine their schedules. As federal and state funding continued to shrink, listener donations became the fastest-growing sector of support for public radio stations. These stations sought shows that would retain audiences in midday and during evenings (after the "tent poles" of *Morning Edition* and *All Things Considered*), as well as shows that could be "stripped," or programmed at the same time every day. Programming that didn't fit into this mold was axed; one public radio consultant quipped that the best time to schedule radio drama was "1938" (Stavitsky 1995).

AMERICAN PUBLIC MEDIA

One of the most notable recent trends in public radio has been the development of "super-stations" whose signals, relayed by repeater antennas and satellites, may cover statewide areas or reach across the United States. The first, and leading, public radio superstation is Minnesota Public Radio (MPR), which extends into seven states and Canada. MPR originated with KSJR, a classical music station located northwest of Minneapolis, in January 1967. Under the leadership of William Kling, the station developed a regional news service and formed MPR in 1974. Within a year, MPR operated six stations around Minnesota. MPR greatly benefited from its association with *A Prairie Home Companion*, establishing a marketing operation in 1981 to sell merchandise related to the program, and was a principal partner in the formation of American Public Radio in 1983. By the end of the 1980s, MPR controlled 17 stations, including operations in North Dakota and Idaho.

MPR spent much of the following decade expanding and consolidating its operations. In a controversial move, it took over KPCC in Pasadena, California, in 1999. In 2004, MPR broke off from PRI and formed American Public Media to distribute its leading programs to stations, including *A Prairie Home Companion* and *Marketplace*. American Public Media also offers a syndicated classical music service to public radio stations. Its defenders laud MPR's expansion and professionalism, while its detractors fault it for focusing on entrepreneurial activities and edging out smaller, localized stations. Its success has ensured that MPR has, in many ways, set the agenda for public radio in the United States.

THE 1990s AND 2000s

NPR had come of age by the mid-1990s. *Newsweek* hailed NPR as "the *New Yorker* of the airwaves," and President Bill Clinton told an assemblage of NPR executives and funders, "I'm just an NPR kind of president." NPR's coverage of the first Gulf War raised its listenership by 30 percent, and more of its news and public affairs programming focused on Beltway politics, establishing NPR as a player on the Washington scene. By 1997, *Morning Edition* and *All Things Considered* alone consumed 40 percent of NPR's budget. As it targeted opinion leaders and wealthy audiences on the local and national levels, underwriting announcements became integrated into public radio programming. The system became increasingly reliant on companies engaged in controversial policies and activities, such as Monsanto, Archer Daniels Midland, and Wal-Mart, who see public radio sponsorship as an inexpensive and effective form of "damage control" for their corporate images. Public radio increasingly promoted programs like *Car Talk*, which, in addition to showcasing corporate funders, created opportunities for merchandising spin-offs. Consultants framed "audience service" in terms of listener dollars raised per program; by this logic, *Car Talk* was the most important "service" offered by public radio.

NPR's occasionally tenuous finances were stabilized when it received a $236 million windfall from the widow of McDonald's founder Ray Kroc in 2003. Yet NPR has hesitated to share its fortunes with stations. Instead, the network has been pouring more and more money into its news operations, and news continues to dominate cultural programming at the local level. Daytime classical music and evening jazz, which historically comprised the bulk of station broadcasts, have fallen by the wayside as stations (particularly those in large markets) switch to all-news programming, relying heavily on NPR satellite feeds and augmenting them with syndicated news and talk programs. In addition, larger stations have aggressively expanded their operations by acquiring additional stations. Iowa, Colorado, and Minnesota public radio now operate as umbrella organizations that feed programs to local affiliates. NPR currently operates two channels on Sirius satellite radio, but the "tent poles" of *Morning Edition* and *All Things Considered* remain firmly staked to terrestrial broadcasting. Stations, which purchase programming from NPR and other suppliers, would never allow their two chief moneymakers to bypass them.

NPR also has entered the webcasting fray by offering streams of programming to stations for rebroadcast on their Web sites, and the results have confounded consultants who claim that public radio listeners approach radio passively, listening to stations rather than discrete programs. A director at Boston's WGBH found that *Morning Edition* was downloaded approximately 14,000 times a week in December 2005 despite no promotion whatsoever. In contrast, the program's RealAudio stream drew less than 50 listeners a week (Janssen 2005). Yet the existence of a digital divide ensures that substantial portions of the U.S. population will lack access to broadband technology in the foreseeable future (although NPR historically has had little interest in less-than-affluent audiences). Most importantly, the local stations that form the core of the public radio system largely vend the programs—they don't create them. Instead, many public radio stations have become little more than jukeboxes for syndicated programming.

A 2005 Harris Poll found that NPR was the most trusted news source in the United States. NPR has cultivated an affluent, graying audience of approximately 20 million listeners per week, yet it has had little success in attracting young or minority listeners, which bodes ill for its long-term future. More ominously, nearly half of all public radio stations in the United States operated in the red in 2003. The *New York Times* noted that "To remain viable, many managers say that their local stations must gain more leverage vis à vis NPR by producing and promoting more of the kind of distinctive, localized programs and segments that help shape public radio's eclectic character" (Clemetson 2004). Radio is uniquely suited to fill the role of a public medium. Its low cost and mobility afford a sense of immediacy and flexibility that make it ideal for reflecting a community's history and constructing a community's possibilities. As it is buffeted by technological change and internal politics, public radio may have to rediscover the concepts of localism and diversity if it is to remain viable in the twenty-first century.

See also Conglomeration and Media Monopolies; Media and Citizenship; Nationalism and the Media; Pirate Radio; Public Access Television; Public

Broadcasting Service; Public Opinion; Public Sphere; Regulating the Airwaves; Sensationalism, Fear Mongering, and Tabloid Media; Shock Jocks.

Further Reading: Clemetson, Lynette. "All Things Considered, NPR's Growing Clout Alarms Member Stations." *New York Times,* August 30, 2004, E1; Collins, Mary. *National Public Radio: The Cast of Characters.* Washington, DC: Seven Locks Press, 1993; Engelman, Ralph. *Public Radio and Television in America: A Political History.* Thousand Oaks, CA: Sage, 1996; Janssen, Mike. "Jacking Into Podcasts." *Current,* January 31, 2005, 1; Ledbetter, James. *Made Possible By . . . The Death of Public Broadcasting in the United States.* New York: Verso, 1997; Looker, Thomas. *The Sound and the Story: NPR and the Art of Radio.* New York: Houghton Mifflin, 1995; McCauley, Michael. *NPR: The Trials and Triumph of National Public Radio.* New York: Columbia University Press, 2005; McCourt, Tom. *Conflicting Communication Interests in America: The Case of National Public Radio.* Westport, CT: Praeger, 1999; Stavitsky, Alan. "'Guys in Suits with Charts': Audience Research in U.S. Public Radio." *Journal of Broadcasting and Electronic Media* 39, no. 2 (Spring 1995): 177–89; Witherspoon, John, Roselle Kovitz, Robert Avery, and Alan Stavitsky. *A History of Public Broadcasting.* Washington, DC: Current, 2000.

Tom McCourt

NATIONALISM AND THE MEDIA

Throughout the last century, the mass media often played a key and defining role in projects of nationalism: Hitler's use of radio and film helped fashion Nazi Germany, Roosevelt's "fireside chats" on national radio aimed to unite America in tumultuous times, Mao's "little red book" gave a bible of communism to China, and, more recently, extremist Hutus used the radio in Rwanda to provoke a genocidal campaign against the country's Tutsi population. The media can espouse and transmit a national ideology, it offers us access to moments of shared national glory or failure, it tells the national history, and it creates images of our fellow citizens. To what degree, then, is the media responsible for nationalism, for the construction of national identity, or indeed for the very idea of the nation?

As Benedict Anderson argues, the nation is an "imagined community"—we can never see all of our fellow citizens or commune with them; rather, we create constructs and images of what the nation is, what it means to belong to the nation, who belongs and who does not, and what the purpose and character of the nation are. To a certain degree, each one of us may operate with slightly different notions of what the nation is, since some of these acts of national construction will occur at a personal level. However, all nations also engage in communal and shared acts of construction. With few other institutions that address an entire country's population, the media frequently becomes our national "construction site." Not only does the media circulate images of the nation for nearly all to see, hear, and read, but it also mediates our access to most other countrywide institutions, such as our national leaders, government, holidays, and public figures.

Thus, for instance, terms such as "American way of life," "all-American boy or girl," or "American values" are frequently defined in and by the media.

BATTLESHIP POTEMKIN (1925)

Whereas American films often sing love songs to democracy and capitalism, other nations have offered their own filmic narratives of national ideology. Director and early innovator of film Sergei Eisenstein's famous *Battleship Potemkin*, for instance, acted as powerful propaganda for Soviet communism. The film tells the story of a peasant massacre by Cossack troops at Odessa in 1905, and of the mutiny on a Tsarist navy battleship that led to the crew coming to the peasants' assistance. The film casts dispersion on individuals who act as individuals, instead focusing on the peasants and the crew as a unified force. In this way, the villainous ship captain and doctor, who try to serve rancid meat to the crew, are contrasted with the revolutionary power of the sailors as a mass. Thus, Eisenstein depicted an incident from Russian history in a way intended to evoke pride in and admiration of the power of the group. Just as, for instance, the lone hero figures of American Westerns romanticize American capitalist and libertarian individualism, *Battleship Potemkin* romanticizes the proletarian unity and camaraderie of Soviet communism.

Blockbusters with megalomaniacal villains and plots often pose a threat to the "American way of life," and hence define what that way of life entails. Stars such as Julia Roberts, Reese Witherspoon, Tom Hanks, and Will Smith are marketed as and become national illustrations of the "all-American," from the way they look and dress to their mannerisms and character. And "American values" are embodied particularly in the nostalgic dream-worlds of *Leave It to Beaver*, *The Waltons*, and other earlier family sitcoms and dramas.

Meanwhile, the news constantly draws lines around the nation, telling us where and what to care about as "our own," whether this be through coverage of disasters and tragedies that focus most attention on dead Americans and their stories, or whether this be as simple and mundane an act as reporting on "American" weather, business, or sports news. More prominently, in times of war or crisis, much news coverage eschews the rest of the world's news to offer more in-depth coverage of the ongoing conflict. Behind newsroom editors' and producers' decisions here is the belief that we care more (or only) about those of our own nationality than about others—but their decisions perpetuate such patterns of caring, by imploring us to care about such issues more than about others. In other words, on a daily basis, the news reinforces the borders between the "us" of our nation, and the "them" of the rest.

MAKING THE NATION

Far from just demarcating the borders of the nation, though, the media plays a key role in filling it with meaning. As literature and history instructors have long complained of, many people are introduced to national literature and history though the media, whether this be filmic adaptations of American novels, or blockbuster recreations of history, as with, for example, *Pearl Harbor*, *Titanic*, and *Saving Private Ryan*. Many young people now "know" the 1950s, 1960s, or

AMERICAN IDOL

Though based on the British *Pop Idol, American Idol* (FOX, 2002–) has been thoroughly Americanized. The reality competition program's promise to take a "nobody" on a ride from obscurity to fame and fortune attempts to enact and perform the American dream, whereby "anyone can make it." In the early stages, auditions are held in various cities, leading producers and host Ryan Seacrest to suggest that the show includes "America's best," and that it represents the nation. Then, when viewers' votes are tabulated, Seacrest announces grandiosely that, "America has voted." Seacrest is particularly fond of this phrase when countering the audience's vote to the bluntly honest evaluations of judge Simon Cowell, who as a Briton is made iconic of a dictatorial elite snobbery that is then contrasted to the supposed democratic openness and supportiveness of American voters, the live studio audience, and the two American judges. While the show launches a young performer's career as a pop musician, then, it also fashions a powerful myth of the American dream, American democracy and stated love of diversity, and foreign elitism.

1970s through media such as *I Love Lucy*, Jimi Hendrix albums, or *Saturday Night Fever*, respectively. Similarly, our political system and America's allegiance to democracy and capitalism become embedded in certain media narratives, whether overtly or subtly. All the while, the fires of national supremacy and superiority are quite often stoked by romanticized retellings of moments in history—as in *U571*, a film that rewrites the capture of the German enigma machine in World War II as an American, not British, accomplishment—and by replaying moments of legitimate triumph, as in national sporting events. For better or worse, few things are as capable of waving the flag as are the media.

As a result, numerous leaders have discovered ways to manipulate the media directly, or via falsified information, in order to fashion the nation in their preferred image. From fear mongering to censorship, savvy and powerful leaders can frame the agenda for media discussion, especially in journalism. Particularly if the press is weak or acquiescent, political leaders can literally edit recent history for their own purposes, with the media becoming either a knowing or unwitting accomplice. Indeed, in times of war or national crisis, leaders have often called upon the media to do their "national duty" by putting the requirements of nationalism and patriotism "before" journalistic ethics, as if a commitment to journalistic ethics was not itself a patriotic act. Hence, for instance, following the terrorist attacks of September 11, 2001, journalists were encouraged and/or shamed into reporting favorably on the administration and its policies, lest they appear "anti-American." At times like this, one wonders if the media regards its duties as those of journalistic vigilance, or of flag-waving.

EXCLUSION AND INCLUSION

The media also holds considerable power to determine who belongs in the nation and who does not. Identity often works through "alterity," meaning that we all tend to identify ourselves by who and what we are *not*. Thus, as an instrument of national identity construction, the media offers us images that include and exclude. In particular, film and television narratives have notoriously depicted citizens of other countries and races in demeaning and inferior ways, allowing us to feel nobler by comparison. Films such as *Black Hawk Down*, for example, perpetuate centuries-old racist depictions of Africans as savages; whereas depictions of Britons in film and television frequently posit them as uptight, humorless, class-obsessed snobs. In general, one often finds foreign women depicted in wholly sexual terms, as if the world existed for American male sexual conquest; while foreign males are either comically inept and effeminate fops, or overly aggressive and predatory. Such types allow the American characters in a film to retain the role of sympathetic hero, and allow the audience to feel assured in the righteousness of their national identity, but in the process they create wholly erroneous and offensive depictions of foreigners.

Many such images and types then spill over from the realms of fiction into journalistic reporting, which can tend to rely upon age-old racist and nationally chauvinist depictions in telling the supposed truth of the world's events. We see foreign nations most often in the news when they are struck by war, famine, or disease. Similarly, such types are rife in the tourist industry, as nations and national identities are branded for marketing purposes, creating, for instance, the "spiritual" East Asian, or notions of "wild" Africa. With today's globalized media system, American images of foreigners are traveling overseas with ease, and thus risk threatening international relations when foreigners are faced with demeaning images of themselves in media as diverse as blockbusters, magazine ads, and cable news.

Furthermore, however, such images create considerable problems for national identity back home in America too. With each demeaning image of a foreigner, immigrants or those of the same racial background as the imagined foreigner are then faced with the task of overcoming the image. When many media texts so gleefully depict Arabs as insane, wife-beating terrorists, for instance, Arab Americans face considerable prejudice that effectively excludes them from feeling welcomed into the American national identity. Thus, while media images

EARLY LANDMARKS IN NATIONALISTIC MEDIA

1925—Sergei Eisenstein directs the Soviet revolutionary film, *Battleship Potemkin*.

1933—President Franklin Delano Roosevelt begins delivering his radio "fireside chats."

1935—Leni Riefenstahl directs a Nazi propaganda film of the 1934 Nuremberg rallies, *Triumph of the Will*.

1940—Winston Churchill addresses England with his famous, "We shall fight them on the beaches" speech.

1953—The British Broadcasting Corporation (BBC) offers extensive coverage of the coronation of Queen Elizabeth II.

1964—*Quotations from Chairman Mao Zedong*, or the "Little Red Book," is released in the People's Republic of China. Over 900 million copies are believed to have been published and circulated.

of American and not-American may at times be helpful tools for creating ideal notions of Americanness that call upon all Americans to live up to and earn the label of "American," they can also place obstacles in the way for those of certain national, racial, religious, and ideological backgrounds.

MEDIA BATTLEGROUNDS

However, to see the media as a purveyor of racist and exclusionary images alone would be a considerable mistake. After all, precisely because the media is often a key site of national identity construction, it is also a key battleground, in which national identity can be debated and challenged. Bold and innovative journalism, films, songs, television, and other media can challenge a nation's ideas of itself, can call for reflection upon and revision of past constructions, and can pose new images. No national identity is written in stone. The past century has shown how thoroughly a nation can redefine itself: Russia went from monarchy to communism to attempts at capitalist democracy; many of the world's countries have gone from being colonial vassals to independent nations; and numerous countries have divided into several smaller nations. Therefore, the media can always play a role in scrambling former identities and reevaluating them for the future.

Nevertheless, as much *potential* as the media have, we must always inquire into the interests of those who own the media if we are to determine which messages and images of nationality will be welcomed and which will be actively excluded. Hence, in America, with most media outlets running as commercial ventures owned by a few large corporations, we might expect anticapitalist messages to struggle reaching the light of day. Or, in countries where dictators strictly police the media, democratic messages will be rare. In this way, those who control the media have significant influence over defining the nation. If the media is a battleground for determining national identity, many Americans have no access whatsoever to media production, and thus have no access to the battleground; as a result, although it is often said that there are "two Americas"—one Republican and one Democrat—a third America exists of a vast population who are continually under- or misrepresented by a media system over which they have no control.

At the same time, though, independent media sources have always existed in even the most brutal dictatorships, allowing underground poetry, film, literature, or news to implore citizens to rethink official, mainstream scripts of national identity. Blogs, for instance, have been used to considerable success in numerous countries, and political protest music has thrived since the advent of recorded music. Such independent voices may lack the volume and reach of their mainstream equivalents, but they still ensure that national identity never truly atrophies in one position.

TRANSNATIONALISM AND BEYOND

As much as the media creates national borders, increasingly it is also moving beyond these borders, too. Thus, just as the media can create national identity, a growing number of films, programs, Web sites, and so forth are creating transnational identities. Sizeable immigrant communities often establish media that speak to their consumers not just as Americans, or as citizens of another nation, but as *both*. Many of America's larger cities have foreign-language radio stations and television programs addressing such individuals and communities, while cheaper international phone charges, the Internet and e-mail, and large networks of piracy and legitimate media trade allow people to live in one country but feel connected to more than one. Home, in other words, is becoming ever more a mindset, and one that requires no set physical location.

American media are particularly pervasive around the world, leading some to worry about the prospects of American national identity seeping into especially the younger, media-hungry generations of non-Americans. By contrast, non-American media does not often travel as easily around the world, and thus we must not overstate the possibilities for a mediated transnational identity. Nevertheless, when, for instance, one can check a foreign newspaper daily online, watch imported videos, listen to imported music, and subscribe to foreign satellite stations, one may be able to be American *and* another nationality.

Meanwhile, the explosion of global media also increases the possibility that some of us will fashion cosmopolitan, global identities, leaving the notion of the singular national identity behind us. Or, if not truly international identities, at least the media might fashion regional identities, as, for instance, the European Union funds trans-European media initiatives, or as Al-Jazeera and other satellite services address transnational viewerships predominantly in a set range of countries.

Ultimately, then, the media have been the very tools that made national identity and nationalism arguably the most important unit of identity for twentieth-century world politics, and it continues to do so; however, the media is now also offering alternatives and ways beyond the nation for some, and ways to challenge and attack mainstream myths of nationality for others.

See also Al-Jazeera; Alternative Media in the United States; Bollywood and the Indian Diaspora; Cultural Imperialism and Hybridity; Government Censorship and Freedom of Speech; Islam and the Media; Media and Citizenship; National Public Radio; Political Documentary; Presidential Stagecraft and Militainment; Propaganda Model; Public Opinion; Representations of Race; Runaway Productions and the Globalization of Hollywood; Sensationalism, Fear Mongering, and Tabloid Media; Tourism and the Selling of Cultures; World Cinema.

Further Reading: Anderson, Benedict. *Imagined Communities: Reflections on the Origin and Spread of Nationalism.* London: Verso, 1991; Downing, John D. H. *Radical Media: Rebellious Communication and Social Movements.* Thousand Oaks, CA: Sage, 2000; Gellner, Ernest. *Nations and Nationalism.* Ithaca, NY: Cornell University Press, 1983; Hutnyk, John. *The Rumour of Calcutta: Tourism, Charity and the Poverty of Representation.* New York: Zed, 1996; Lull, James, ed. *Culture in the Communication Age.* New York: Routledge, 2000; McCrisken, Trevor, and Andrew Pepper. *American History and Contemporary Hollywood Film.* New Brunswick, NJ: Rutgers University Press, 2005; Miller, Toby, Nitin Govil, John McMurria, and Rick Maxwell. *Global*

Hollywood 2. London: BFI, 2005; Morley, David. *Home Territories: Media, Mobility and Identity*. New York: Routledge, 2000; Morley, David, and Kevin Robins. *Spaces of Identity: Global Media, Electronic Landscapes and Cultural Boundaries*. New York: Routledge, 1995; Naficy, Hamid, ed. *Home, Exile, Homeland: Film, Media, and the Politics of Place*. New York: Routledge, 1999; O'Barr, William M. *Culture and the Ad: Exploring Otherness in the World of Advertising*. Boulder, CO: Westview, 1994; Rajagopal, Arvind. *Politics after Television: Hindu Nationalism and the Reshaping of the Public in India*. New York: Cambridge University Press, 2001; Ross, Steven J., ed. *Movies and American Society*. Malden, MA: Blackwell, 2002; Said, Edward. *Orientalism*. New York: Vintage, 1979; Zelizer, Barbie, and Stuart Allan, eds. *Journalism After September 11*. New York: Routledge, 2002.

Jonathan Gray

NET NEUTRALITY

Network Neutrality—or "Net Neutrality" for short—is the guiding rule that preserves the free and open Internet. Net Neutrality mandates that Internet service providers not discriminate including speeding up or slowing down Web content, based on its source, ownership, or destination. Net Neutrality protects consumers' right to direct our online activities based on our own personal motivations. With Net Neutrality, the network's job is to move data in a nondiscriminatory manner.

Nondiscrimination provisions like Net Neutrality have governed the U.S. communications networks since the 1930s. On June 27, 2005, in a 6 to 3 decision (*National Cable & Telecommunications Association vs. Brand X Internet Services*), the United States Supreme Court ruled that cable companies like Comcast and Verizon are not required to share their cables with other Internet service providers (ISPs). This controversial decision put Net Neutrality provisions in jeopardy.

This ruling in part followed the FCC's decision in 2002, which stipulated that cable companies do not offer telecommunication services according to the meaning of the 1996 Telecommunication Act. The FCC ruled that cable services are information services, which manipulate and transform data instead of merely transmitting them. "Since the Act only requires companies offering telecommunication services to share their lines with other ISPs (the so-called 'common carriage' requirement), the FCC concluded that cable companies are exempt from this requirement" (see http://www.buzzflash.com/contributors/05/07/con05238.html).

The requirement of "common carriage" basically enforced net neutrality. Being deemed a common carrier meant that a transportation is considered a public service and must be upheld universally without discrimination. After telecommunications companies became exempt from the rules of common carriage, many public interest groups pushed for some kind of neutrality rules, so that ISPs could not discriminate against Web sites. Cable and phone company lobbyists pushed to block legislation that would reinstate Net Neutrality.

FLASHPOINTS IN NETWORK NEUTRALITY

1. In 1860, a U.S. federal law subsidizing a coast-to-coast telegraph line stated that "messages received from any individual, company, or corporation, or from any telegraph lines connecting with this line at either of its termini, shall be impartially transmitted in the order of their reception."

2. In 1937, the SEC. 202. [47 U.S.C. 202] Discrimination and Preferences stated that; "(a) It shall be unlawful for any common carrier to make any unjust or unreasonable discrimination in charges, practices, classifications, regulations, facilities, or services for or in connection with like communication service, directly or indirectly, by any means or device, or to make or give any undue or unreasonable preference or advantage to any particular person, class of persons, or locality, or to subject any particular person, class of persons, or locality to any undue or unreasonable prejudice or disadvantage."

3. As early as 1957, business users and corporations began to lobby for a policy allowing them to build wholly proprietary systems.

4. In 1968, at a proceeding known as the Computer Inquiries, the FCC decided that the companies providing communications services would not be allowed to interfere with or discriminate against information services.

5. In 1980, at the Second Computer Inquiry, the FCC decided that even regulated telecommunications companies, which were the foundation of the U.S. telecommunication infrastructure, would be allowed to establish subsidiaries that could bypass existing regulation.

6. In 1982, when a federal court broke up Ma Bell, it required the Baby Bells to "provide nondiscriminatory interconnection and access to their networks."

7. The early infrastructure of the Internet was created by DARPA with ongoing support from government officials as a U.S. publicly funded research network governed by an Acceptable Use Policy (AUP) that prohibited commercial activity. In the early 1990s, the existing Internet infrastructure was privatized and the AUP prohibiting commercial activity was lifted.

8. In 1992, the advancement of The National Information Infrastructure(NII) initiative sought to "Promote private sector investment, through appropriate tax and regulatory policies."

9. In 1996 there was an amendment to the Common Carrier provision in the 1934 Communications Act (44), asserting that the term *telecommunications carrier* means any provider of telecommunications services, except that such term does not include aggregators of telecommunications services. The ruling further stipulated that "a telecommunications carrier shall be treated as a common carrier under this Act only to the extent that it is engaged in providing telecommunications services" This amendment amounted to removing the existing Common Carrier requirements from Internet Service Providers.

10. In 2002 the FCC issued a Declaratory Ruling for cable modem service, classifying it as an "information service." This classification change meant that cable companies

would not be required to offer broadband Internet on the same nondiscriminatory basis that has been the foundation of the Internet.

11. On June 27, 2005, the U.S. Supreme Court ruled that cable companies are not required to share their cables with other ISPs.

THE NET NEUTRALITY DEBATE HEATS UP

The Net Neutrality debate began to heat up in early 2006 as a House Energy and Commerce Committee bill was tabled that included the provisions essentially mandating Net Neutrality. On one side ISPs like AT&T, Verizon, and Comcast lobbied hard to remove Net Neutrality provisions from the bill, while civil society groups like Free Press and the Center for Digital Democracy began rallying public support for Net Neutrality.

On April 24, 2006, a band of consumer and public interest groups calling itself The SavetheInternet.com Coalition, launched a campaign claiming to "defend the free and open Internet." Charter members of the SavetheInternet.com Coalition include: Professors Larry Lessig of Stanford University and Tim Wu of Columbia University, Free Press, Gun Owners of America, right-of-center Instapundit blogger Glenn Reynolds, MoveOn.org Civic Action, Consumers Union, Consumer Federation of America, Public Knowledge, Common Cause, the American Library Association and U.S. PIRG. Later the coalition swelled to "more than a million everyday people who have banded together with thousands of non-profit organizations, businesses and bloggers" (see http://www.savetheinternet.com/=coalition).

Around the same time the SavetheInternet.com Coalition formed, an anti–Net Neutrality coalition dominated by corporations with a financial stake in an unregulated Internet, called HandsOffTheInternet, began advocating against Net Neutrality rules.

On June 8, 2006, the House Energy and Commerce Committee passed the Communications Opportunity, Promotion, and Enhancement (COPE) Act (HR 5252) with a 321–101 vote, without the accompanying Network Neutrality Act (HR 5273). The Net Neutrality Act would have essentially made Net Neutrality an enforceable law.

After the COPE Act passed, the house the bill moved to Senate, with advocates on either sides engaging in a fierce battle to sway this critical vote. Supporters of the COPE Act claimed the bill would support innovation and freedom of choice. Net Neutrality advocates said that its passage would make ISPs gatekeepers of the Internet.

The June 28, 2006, Senate vote on a Net Neutrality friendly amendment offered by senators Olympia Snowe (R-Maine) and Byron Dorgan (D-N.D.), fell to a 11–11 tie. Shortly after, U.S. Senator Ron Wyden (D-Ore.) placed a "hold" on the COPE Act legislation essentially stalling the bill until changes were made.

HandsOffTheInternet claimed that this sticks consumers with a high bill and lets big new media corporation off the hook. They also claimed that they have not and will not discriminate against Web sites. They claimed that Net Neutrality is a new regulation that "fundamentally changes the Internet."

However, those fighting for Net Neutrality pointed to statements made by William L. Smith, chief technology officer for Atlanta-based BellSouth Corp., saying that "an Internet service provider such as his firm should be able, for example, to charge Yahoo Inc. for the opportunity to have its search site load faster than that of Google Inc." (see http://www.washingtonpost.com/wp-dyn/content/article/2005/11/30/AR2005113002109_pf.html). The SavetheInternet.com Coalition also pointed to existing cases of discrimination such as the 2004 case where North Carolina ISP Madison River blocked their DSL customers from using any rival Web-based phone service (see http://www.freepress.net/news/13604).

Not long before the Senate voted on the COPE Act, Alaska Republican Ted Stevens, head of the Senate Commerce Committee, made the fateful remark: "The internet is not something that you just dump something on. It's not a big truck. It's a series of tubes." The statement was humorously conveyed on *The Daily Show with Jon Stewart*, and even remixed into a techno song, which was widely distributed online. Shortly after the Ted Stevens debacle, the SavetheInternet.com Coalition received a further boost when Internet pioneer Sir Tim Berners-Lee forcefully argued in favor of Net Neutrality in a *New York Times* interview (see http://www.nytimes.com/2006/09/27/technology/circuits/27neut.html?ref=circuits).

Over the summer, hundreds of Internet users concerned about Net Neutrality inundated the Internet with videos and blog entries encouraging fellow citizens to get involved in the issue. As the Senate's August recess drew to a close, citizens supporting Net Neutrality rallied in 25 cities nationwide, delivering SavetheInternet petitions to their senators and urging them to oppose the phone and cable companies' attempts to gut Net Neutrality. The citizen-led movement would later be described by *Salon* as "a ragtag army of grass-roots Internet groups, armed with low-budget videos, music parodies and petitions" (see http://www.salon.com/tech/feature/2006/10/02/slayers). The telecoms employed Mike McCurry, Bill Clinton's former press secretary, to lead their lobbying effort with the industry-funded group HandsOfftheInternet. The group produced its own online videos poking fun at the SavetheInternet.com Coalition and relaying their view of Net Neutrality.

Throughout 2006, the nation's largest phone and cable companies spent more than $100 million on D.C. lobbyists, think tanks, ads, and campaign contributions to defeat Net Neutrality. During this same time, the SavetheInternet.com Coalition grew to include 850 groups, some previously mentioned, making it a formidable grass-roots organization. The coalition also includes thousands of bloggers and hundreds of small companies that do business online. This diverse coalition resulted in more than 1.5 million Americans contacting their representatives urging them to support Net Neutrality. The HR 5252 bill died with the end of 109th Congress, and the situation looked positive for Net Neutrality proponents with the new Democrat controlled House and Congress.

On December 28, 2006, AT&T officials agreed to adhere to Net Neutrality provisions if allowed to complete an $85 billion merger with BellSouth. The SavetheInternet.com Coalition called this "a victory we can hang our hats on."

A VICTORY WITH HISTORIC PROPORTIONS

Regardless of the side one is on concerning this issue, one thing is for sure: the outcome is bound to shape our communications system well into the future. Shortly before AT&T agreed to abide by Net Neutrality provisions, remarks made by Geov Parrish of WorkingforChange.com, indicated the serious and contentious nature of the struggle: "Name the last time a lobby with that much power and money was stymied in its top legislative priority by a citizen movement...Offhand, I can't think of any examples at all. And this during the most corrupt, lobbyist-pliant Congress in recent American history" (see http://www.workingforchange.com/article.cfm?ItemID=21498).

In keeping with past success, SavetheInternet.com launched the latest manifestation of the campaign with an online video called "Save The Internet: Independence Day." The video outlines how everyday Internet users and grass-roots organizations can save Internet freedom. "Save The Internet: Independence Day" quickly made its way around the net through users sharing the video with friends and family. Also crucial to the circulation of this video are independent media outlets and bloggers, who are also threatened by a non-neutral Internet.

MAKING NET NEUTRALITY LAW AND MORE

In 2007, the SavetheInternet.com coalition began pushing Congress to make Net Neutrality law. Using their (now award winning) "Independence Day" video, the coalition began campaigning for a faster, more open, and accessible Internet. On January 8, senators Byron L. Dorgan (D-S.D.) and Olympia J. Snowe (R-Maine) sponsored the Internet Freedom Preservation Act of 2007, which would protect Net Neutrality.

On June 11, 2007, at the SavetheInternet "Party for the Future" celebration of Net Neutrality victories, the SavetheInternet.com Coalition unveiled the "Internet Freedom Declaration of 2007." The Declaration sets forth a plan not just for winning Net Neutrality in Congress, but establishing faster, universal, and affordable broadband for everyone. The declaration calls for "World Class Quality through Competition," "An Open and Neutral Network," and "Universal Affordable Access." The declaration is a big step in media reform, changing the terms of debate from defending against further media deregulation, to demanding a truly public media infrastructure.

In March 2007, SavetheInternet.com supporters rallied for "in-district" meetings with members of Congress and their staff. The rallies resulted in several members pledging to support Net Neutrality legislation when it came to a vote in Congress.

On March 15, 2007, all five FCC Commissioners were brought before the House Subcommittee on Telecommunications and the Internet to testify about their decisions regarding Net Neutrality. Members of the House pressed FCC chairman Kevin Martin to take a stronger position in support of Net Neutrality. The hearing was the first time in three years that commissioners had appeared before the subcommittee.

In May 2007, an "Ad Hoc Public Interest Spectrum Coalition" made a proposal to the FCC on how the auction of the valuable 700 MHz spectrum should be conducted. The 700 MHz spectrum can be used to offer wireless Internet and the proposal asserted the auction should provide "new entrants (to) have the opportunity to enter the market in competition with incumbent providers" (see http://www.publicknowledge.org/node/962). The coalition includes the Consumer Federation of America, Consumers Union, EDUCAUSE, Free Press, Media Access Project, New America Foundation, and U.S. Public Interest Research Group. As of June 4, a quarter-million people have contacted the FCC urging the agency to use the 700 MHz spectrum to offer a more open and competitive Internet service ecology.

On March 22, 2007, the FCC unanimously voted to seek public comment on the possibility of adding a Network Neutrality principle to its 2005 Internet Policy Statement. The comment period ended on June 15, 2007, and tens of thousands of submissions were made.

In 2007, Democratic candidates Hillary Clinton, John Edwards, Barack Obama, and Bill Richardson, among others, all stated their strong support for legal protections for Net Neutrality. Supporters were joined by GOP candidate Mike Huckabee (R-Arkansas), who told a collection of bloggers that Net Neutrality must be preserved.

See also Alternative Media in the United States; Blogosphere; Communication Rights in a Global Context; Conglomeration and Media Monopolies; Digital Divide; Internet and Its Radical Potential; Media Reform; Piracy and Intellectual Property; Public Access Television; Regulating the Airwaves; Surveillance and Privacy; Video News Releases.

Further Reading: Cohen, Elliot D. *Web of Deceit: How Internet Freedom Got the Federal Ax, and Why Corporate News Censored the Story* (July 2005) at http://www.buzzflash. com/contributors/05/07/con05238.html; Community Internet: Broadband as a Public Service. *FreePress May 2005* at http://www.freepress.net/docs/comminternetbro churefinal.pdf; *Communications Act of 1934* at http://www.fcc.gov/Reports/1934new. pdf; Net Neutrality: Fact vs. Fiction. *FreePress* (May 2006) at http://www.freepress.net/ docs/nn_fact_v_fiction_final.pdf; *The National Information Infrastructure: Agenda For Action* at http://www.eff.org/Infrastructure/Govt_docs/nii_agenda_govt.paper; *Net Neutrality, History.* Wikipedia at http://en.wikipedia.org/wiki/Net_neutrality#History; *Pacific Telegraph Act of 1860: Chapter 137, U.S. Statutes 36th Congress, 1st Session* (June 16, 1860) at http://www.cprr.org/Museum/Pacific_Telegraph_Act_1860.html; Schiller, Dan. *Digital Capitalism: Networking the Global Market System.* Cambridge, MA: MIT Press, 1999; Shooting the Massager. *FreePress* (July 2007) at http://www. freepress.net/docs/shooting_the_messenger.pdf; *Telecommunications Act of 1996,* FCC at http://www.fcc.gov/Reports/tcom1996.pdf; U.S. Supreme Court to Hear "Brand X" Case on March 29, 2005. *Center For Digital Democracy* at http://www. democraticmedia.org/news/washingtonwatch/BrandXPR030705.pdf; Wu, Tim. *Network*

Neutrality, Broadband Discrimination (April 2005) at http://www.freepress.net/docs/timwu.pdf.

Steve Anderson

NEWS SATIRE: COMEDY CENTRAL AND BEYOND

Can we connect the rise in popularity of news satire programs like *The Daily Show with Jon Stewart* and *The Colbert Report* to reported lows in news consumption from traditional news programs among American youth, and if so, how? Critics of news satires contend that they engender cynicism and withdrawal from meaningful politics, offering a poor substitute for the news, while supporters see them as accessible supplements, offering contextualization of the news, critical media literacy skills, and hence a helpful addition to our daily news consumption.

At day's end, as millions of Americans ponder their choices for an evening's entertainment and/or for receiving the nightly news, in recent years an unlikely pair of competitors have been added to the mix: Comedy Central's *The Daily Show with Jon Stewart* (1999–) and *The Colbert Report* (2005–). Both shows deal with current news, but in a satiric-parodic manner, poking fun at newscasters, analyzing and commenting on sound bites and newsclips, subjecting newsmakers to lampooning and silly interviews, and yet also frequently offering a substantive critique both of news delivery and of the topics under discussion. Jon Stewart and Stephen Colbert have staged something of a coup in the realm of

---

JON STEWART ON *CROSSFIRE*

A lightning rod event that threw Stewart and his love-hate relationship with traditional news into the very center of the spotlight was his appearance on CNN's now-defunct *Crossfire* (1982–2005) in 2004. Three years later, the clip of this appearance remained one of the most requested and watched television moments on Internet sites ifilm.com and YouTube.com, with nearly 4 million views at ifilm alone. Hosts Paul Begala and Tucker Carlson invited him onto their one-a-Democrat/one-a-Republican show, no doubt expecting Stewart the funnyman to appear; rather, Stewart opened by imploring them, as representatives of mainstream news media coverage, to "stop hurting America." Stewart objected to the divisiveness, and spurious desire to reduce any and all matters to an argument, promoted by *Crossfire* and other programs of its ilk. Calling such a format "theater" and "hackery," Stewart received significant applause and support from the in-studio audience. His appearance also inspired intense discussion on blogs and at watercoolers across the country about the appropriateness of his comments, but more so, about the appropriateness of debate shows such as *Crossfire* and *Hannity and Colmes* (Fox News Channel, 1996–). It marked a rare moment in which a guest of a news show openly and without restraint challenged the very format of a news show, and thus, given the experimental format of *The Daily Show* itself, Stewart's appearance had many talking about what news shows should look like.

---

news consumption, leading to accolades as various as *The Daily Show*'s Television Critics Association Award in 2004 for Outstanding Achievement in News and Information, and Stewart's nomination as *Entertainment Weekly*'s Entertainer of the Year in 2004; and leading to criticism that both make a mockery of the news and of politics.

THE DAILY SHOW WITH JON STEWART

The Daily Show premiered quietly with then-host Craig Kilborn in 1996, offering a playful look at the day's news. After three years with the show, Kilborn stepped down and was replaced by Jon Stewart. Rapidly, the nature of its news and political satire developed, and with especially strong coverage of the 2000 and 2004 election campaigns (the former presciently named "Indecision 2000"), *The Daily Show with Jon Stewart*'s star was in the ascendancy. Audiences are treated to 15 minutes of play with and satiric commentary on the news before Stewart welcomes a guest, who can range from a media figure, to a writer of a political bestseller, to a politician. Stewart's comic style is quite unique, mixing funny faces and "shtick" with often astoundingly incisive and even unforgiving interviews, in unpredictably uneven amounts. By 2004, Stewart and his show were in the media spotlight, as people tried to work out whether this was a hard-nosed journalist with a comedian inside him, or vice versa.

For instance, *The Daily Show*'s Indecision 2004 election coverage included, amongst hours worth of other segments, an item on the Democratic primaries that reported on a debate as if it was a rap "battle" or contest, a piece that mocked special interest group attack ads on the candidates, and the parsing of and commentary on each of the presidential debates. The rap battle played with the alienating language and countenance of many politicians, pointing to their inapproachability to youth, and to politics' existence on a very upper-middle-class Ivy League plateau. The satiric attack ads encouraged viewers to distance

---

STEPHEN COLBERT ADDRESSES THE PRESS

Colbert's own *Crossfire* moment came in 2006, when invited to speak to the White House Correspondents Association awards dinner, a yearly gathering of White House press, politicians, and the president. Colbert stayed in character, delivering, through backhanded satire, a damning critique of the Bush White House and of the press's own lack of effectiveness in reporting on national and international matters. Another clip in heavy demand on YouTube.com, before C-SPAN lay legal claim to it and themselves circulated it to thousands of viewers, the speech was met with a cool reception by the press corps, and they did not even discuss it publicly until a few days later when Internet buzz demanded it. As did Stewart's *Crossfire* appearance, or Stewart's follow-up interview on PBS's *Charlie Rose Show*, Colbert's act of exporting his news and political satire outside of the comfortable borders of his show into another venue underlined the degree to which the new news satire of Stewart and Colbert is often as much political as it is entertainment

themselves from the larger-than-life assertions and allegations that such ads tend to peddle. And the debate coverage interrupted candidates' carefully rehearsed platitudes with irreverent response and objection. The various skits and interviews offered pure slapstick and transgressive humor, but also devious satire.

CREATING CYNICAL "STONED SLACKERS"?

Behind some commentators' concern regarding the show was the supposition that *Daily Show* viewers might be using the show as an outright substitute to watching or reading the news. Since the rise of David Letterman, Jay Leno, and Conan O'Brien in the 1990s, with their own fondness for little quips and even preproduced segments regarding the day's news, and given the overall popularity of late-night talk shows with young viewers, some had correlated this with disturbingly low voter turnout rates and political apathy amongst the young, worrying that such shows might be creating a nation of ill-informed citizens gaining all their news from jokes. This background murmur increased in volume in 2004, when Stewart's coverage of the presidential election and campaigning frequently threw him into the public eye, and when news sources as various as Ted Koppel, the *Boston Globe*, and Bill O'Reilly suggested that *The Daily Show*'s viewers were learning all their news from the show. As Stewart himself has often been quick to point out, the show's prime commitment is to entertainment, and so segments and jokes are constructed with comedy more than informational vigor in mind.

O'Reilly also charged *Daily Show* viewers with being little more than "stoned slackers" who mindlessly accept Stewart's own politics as their own. Moreover,

---

TIMELINE

1993—*Politically Incorrect* with Bill Maher debuts on Comedy Central.

1996—*The Daily Show* debuts on Comedy Central with host Craig Kilborn.

1997—*PI* moves to ABC, becoming the first and only of the new wave of political satires to exist on network television.

1999—Kilborn leaves *The Daily Show* and is replaced by Jon Stewart.

2000—*The Daily Show* reports at length on the presidential election, "Indecision 2000."

2001—*The Daily Show* wins its first Peabody Award for its election coverage.

2002—*PI* cancelled by ABC, following advertiser boycott.

2003—*Real Time with Bill Maher* begins on HBO; *Countdown with Keith Olbermann* debuts on MSNBC.

2004—Stewart appears on and attacks *Crossfire*; *Dennis Miller* begins on CNBC.

2005—Stewart hosts the Oscars; *The Daily Show* wins its second Peabody Award for its election coverage.

2005—Stephen Colbert leaves *The Daily Show* to start *The Colbert Report*.

2006—Colbert delivers an infamous address to President G. W. Bush and the White House Correspondents Association.

---

some have expressed concern that *Daily Show* viewers will come to see all politics as a joke, replacing caring with cynicism, action with laughing. Critics contend that, rather than seek to change the system, the show and its resulting audience subject the system to nothing more than a few jokes. Or, as Michael Kalin wrote in the *Boston Globe*, "Stewart's daily dose of political parody...leads to a 'holier than art thou' attitude toward our national leaders. People who possess the wit, intelligence, and self-awareness of viewers of *The Daily Show* would never choose to enter the political fray full of 'buffoons and idiots'. Content to remain perched atop their Olympian ivory towers, these bright leaders head straight for the private sector" (Kalin 2006).

CREATING CRITICAL NEWS CONSUMERS?

However, critics of *The Daily Show* have often overlooked the degree to which many of its jokes require a fair knowledge of the news to understand and appreciate what is being said in the first place. Behind Stewart's tomfoolery is often a sophisticated analysis or discussion of the news that assumes foreknowledge of the players and issues involved. Indeed, charting empirically what before was only casual intuition, in 2004, a National Annenberg Election Survey concluded that late-night comedy viewers were more likely to know issue positions and backgrounds of presidential candidates than were nonviewers, and that *Daily Show* viewers were particularly well informed, possessing "higher campaign knowledge than national news viewers and newspaper readers—even when education, party identification, following politics, watching cable news, receiving campaign information online, age, and gender are taken into consideration" (National Annenberg Election Survey 2004). The study asked six questions about candidate's platforms and policies to 19,013 adults, and whereas those who had watched no late-night comedy programs in the previous week averaged 2.62 correct answers, and whereas Letterman and Leno viewers averaged 2.91 and 2.95 respectively, *Daily Show* viewers averaged 3.59. The Annenberg study was careful not to suggest causation—it remained unclear whether *The Daily Show* created or simply attracted better-informed viewers—but it adds empirical weight to the notion that *The Daily Show* appears more likely to be cultivating knowledge, and inspiring news discussion, rather than silencing it. Certainly, in premier universities across America, one can often hear students and professors alike discussing items from last night's *Daily Show*, or wondering aloud how Stewart will respond to today's news.

News satire's potentially positive effects on its audience include: (1) offering news-processing time, (2) making news accessible, and (3) teaching critical media literacy. News often flies by us at a remarkable speed, usually dictated in a firm, all-knowing manner. As such, it constantly risks passing us by as confusing and decontextualized. By poking fun at the news, though, news satire can encourage viewers to examine daily events more closely and to think about them more deeply. Thus, news satire can allow us the time to think about issues embedded in the news that a newscaster's 30-second article overlooked.

Moreover, whereas the realm of news and politics have often proven alienating and distant to the common person, and youth in particular, comedy can empower an audience member by positing them as a knowing insider. This presumption of knowingness will be highly problematic and worrying if it is not accompanied by *actual* information, but when information is present, comedy can sometimes offer a greater sense of personal involvement. Comedy even allows a degree of honesty and frankness that the news' stated obsession with objectivity can sometimes obscure; indeed, as Jeffrey Jones argues of news satire, "there seemingly is an underlying recognition that [it] expresses a measure of truth, honesty, or realness that is missing from more formulaic political coverage" (Jones 2004, p. 6). The "inside the Washington beltway" mentality behind much news coverage misses multiple perspectives and opinions, and even when presented gutturally and in incomplete form, some of these perspectives are welcomed and given voice in news satire, as perhaps the preeminent form of political entertainment. Hence, whereas critics like Kalin see *The Daily Show* as disconnecting viewers with politics, the show might instead (or, in addition) connect and welcome some to politics.

Curiously, meanwhile, for all the powers that many attribute to the media (believing that they cause violence, eating disorders, rampant consumerism, short attention spans, and so forth), media literacy programs and courses are still all too rare. However, in concentrating not only on the news, but on how it is told, *The Daily Show* and other news satires may play a small role in shoring up this gap, and in teaching critical media literacy. In particular, the news' memory is often tragically short, as best illustrated when *The Daily Show* contrasts political speeches of today with directly contradictory remarks by the same speaker a year ago, when the nightly news has already forgotten the earlier speech. Similarly, when Stewart, as a comedian, can ask more incisive and probing questions of his political guests than do his millionaire newscaster counterparts, one is forced to demand more of traditional news.

THE COLBERT REPORT AND REAL TIME WITH BILL MAHER

For its part, *The Colbert Report* took aim at a specific format, and even a specific show: Bill O'Reilly's *The O'Reilly Factor* (Fox News Channel, 1996–). Colbert made a name for himself on *The Daily Show* as a field reporter and "analyst," frequently adopting an abrasive, unapologetically defensive character that segued easily into his mock role on *The Colbert Report* as an unabashedly Republican, O'Reilly-worshiping journalist. Colbert's show involves numerous self-laudatory homages, includes frequent irate monologues delivered to the camera, and specializes in inflammatory rhetoric, as does its satiric target. More directly *parodic* than *The Daily Show, The Colbert Report* thus directs its audience's attention to news format and news personalities alike.

Bill Maher has also proven to be an unflinching new news satirist of note, in some senses Stewart and Colbert's forebearer. With *Politically Incorrect* (Comedy Central, 1993–97; ABC, 1997–2002) and then *Real Time with Bill Maher* (HBO, 2003–), Maher mixed news satire and "straight talk" with a news talk show format, often to considerable success—and controversy. As do Stewart and Colbert, Maher adheres to the belief that the news and the world of politics are so heavily steeped in spin, deceit, and ignorance that the common person's laughing attention is the first tonic needed in a lengthy recovery period, and he seeks to deliver and direct this attention weekly. More openly opinionated than either Stewart or Colbert, Maher has adopted a more angry style that is warmly appreciated by his fans, but that also keeps away many detractors. Indeed, Maher illustrates the fine line between levity and seriousness that news satire must walk, for Maher's clearly stated libertarian-meets-liberal politics and his off-the-cuff remarks have angered some viewers, even leading to an advertiser boycott and the eventual cancellation of *Politically Incorrect* in 2002, following post-9/11 comments that some found to be offensive.

BEYOND COMEDY CENTRAL

Maher, Stewart, and Colbert could all be accused of preaching to the converted, in that they tend to attract like-minded audiences, and thus one might regard skeptically the notion that their political humor or media literacy primers have lasting importance. However, as in religion, perhaps "preaching to the converted" is the most common form of preaching, concentrating on renewing and reinvigorating the "faith" and conviction of the converted. Countless polls reveal low levels of trust in journalists and in politicians, and yet many of us revert to blind trust of them in many instances; the power of news satire, even when reiterating the already known, then, may lie in its ability to offer reminders of the severe problems with news and political rhetoric, and therefore of the continuing need for vigilance and attention.

The popularity of news satire has clearly created a stir in the news community. Stewart in particular was a frequent guest or topic of many traditional news programs in 2004 especially, but beyond Stewart, several news channels have experimented with adding humor and satiric commentary. Thus, for instance, CNBC hired comedian Dennis Miller to mix news talk and comedy in his ill-fated *Dennis Miller* (2004–05), while more successful has been MSNBC's *Countdown with Keith Olbermann* (2003–), whose host regularly mixes reporting with impressions of popular culture figures, amusing graphics, and a generally sardonic wit applied to most items. Therefore, albeit slowly and gingerly, news satire is expanding into the news itself, no doubt setting the stage for another round of debates regarding the future of news and the appropriateness of news satire within that future.

See also Media and Citizenship; Media and Electoral Campaigns; Media Literacy; Political Documentary; Political Entertainment; Presidential Stagecraft and Militainment; Public Opinion; Public Sphere; Ratings; Sensationalism, Fear Mongering, and Tabloid Media.

Further Reading: Bakalar, Nikolas, and Stephen Kock, eds. *American Satire: An Anthology of Writings from Colonial Times to Present.* New York: Plume, 1997; Buckingham, David. *The Making of Politics: Young People, News and Politics.* New York: Routledge, 2000; Glynn, Kevin. *Tabloid Culture: Trash Taste, Popular Power, and the Transformation of American Television.* Durham, NC: Duke University Press, 2000; Gray, Jonathan. *Watching with The Simpsons: Television, Parody, and Intertextuality.* New York: Routledge,

2006; Griffin, Dustin. *Satire: A Critical Reintroduction.* Lexington: University Press of Kentucky, 1995; Jones, Jeffrey P. *Entertaining Politics: New Political Television and Civic Culture.* New York: Rowman and Littlefield, 2004; Kalin, Michael. "Why Jon Stewart Isn't Funny," *The Boston Globe,* March 3, 2006. http://www.boston.com/ae/movies/oscars/articles/2006/03/03/why_jon_stewart_isnt_funny/; National Annenberg Election Survey. "Daily Show Viewers Knowledgeable About Presidential Campaign, National Annenberg Election Survey Shows." Press Release. September 21, 2004. http://www.annenbergpublicpolicycenter.org/naes/2004_03_late-night-knowledge-2_9–21_pr.pdf; Stewart, Jon, and The Writers of *The Daily Show. The Daily Show with Jon Stewart Presents: America (The Book).* New York: Warner, 2004.

Jonathan Gray